CONTEMPORARY TOURISM

Diversity and Change

TOURISM SOCIAL SCIENCE SERIES

Series Editor: Jafar Jafari

Department of Hospitality and Tourism, University of Wisconsin-Stout, Menomonie WI 54751, USA.
Tel: (715) 232-2339; Fax: (715) 232-3200; E-mail: jafari@uwstout.edu

The books in this Tourism Social Science Series (TSSSeries) are intended to systematically and cumulatively contribute to the formation, embodiment, and advancement of knowledge in the field of tourism.

The TSSSeries' multidisciplinary framework and treatment of tourism includes application of theoretical, methodological, and substantive contributions from such fields as anthropology, business administration, ecology, economics,
geography, history, hospitality, leisure, planning, political science, psychology, recreation, religion, sociology, transportation, etc., but it significantly favors state-of-the-art presentations, works featuring new directions, and especially
the cross-fertilization of perspectives beyond each of these singular fields. While the development and production
of this book series is fashioned after the successful model of Annals of Tourism Research, the TSSSeries further
aspires to assure each theme a comprehensiveness possible only in book-length academic treatment. Each volume in
the series is intended to deal with a particular aspect of this increasingly important subject, thus to play a definitive
role in the enlarging and strengthening of the foundation of knowledge in the field of tourism, and consequently to
expand its frontiers into the new research and scholarship horizons ahead.

Published and forthcoming TSSSeries titles include:

JÓZSEF BÖRÖCZ (Rutgers University, USA)
Leisure Migration: A Sociological Study on Tourism

MICHAEL CLANCY (University of Hartford, USA)
Exporting Paradise: Tourism and Development in Mexico

DENNISON NASH (University of Connecticut, USA)
Anthropology of Tourism

PHILIP L. PEARCE, GIANNA MOSCARDO & GLENN F. ROSS (James Cook University of North Queensland,
Australia)
Tourism Community Relationships

TREVOR SOFIELD (University of Tasmania, Australia)
Empowerment of Sustainable Tourism Development

BORIS VUKONIĆ (University of Zagreb, Croatia)
Tourism and Religion

NING WANG (Zhongshan University, China)
Tourism and Modernity: A Sociological Analysis

Related Elsevier journals

Annals of Tourism Research
International Journal of Hospitality Management
International Journal of Intercultural Relations
Tourism Management
World Development

CONTEMPORARY TOURISM
DIVERSITY AND CHANGE

ERIK COHEN

The Hebrew University of Jerusalem, Israel

2004

ELSEVIER

Amsterdam – Boston – Heidelberg – London – New York – Oxford
Paris – San Diego – San Francisco – Singapore – Sydney – Tokyo

ELSEVIER B.V.	ELSEVIER Inc.	**ELSEVIER Ltd**	ELSEVIER Ltd
Sara Burgerhartstraat 25	525 B Street, Suite 1900	**The Boulevard, Langford**	84 Theobalds Road
P.O. Box 211	San Diego	**Lane, Kidlington**	London
1000 AE Amsterdam	CA 92101-4495	**Oxford OX5 1GB**	WC1X 8RR
The Netherlands	USA	**UK**	UK

First edition 2004

Library of Congress Cataloging in Publication Data
A catalog record is available from the Library of Congress.

British Library Cataloguing in Publication Data
A catalogue record is available from the British Library.

ISBN: 0-08-044244-7

⊗ The paper used in this publication meets the requirements of ANSI/NISO Z39.48-1992 (Permanence of Paper). Printed in The Netherlands.

Contents

List of Figures

Acknowledgments

Chapter 2: Originally published in *Sociological Review*, 22, 1974, pp. 527–555; reprinted by permission of Blackwell Publisher Ltd.

Chapter 3: Originally published in *Social Research*, 39, 1972, pp. 164–182; reprinted by permission of *Social Research Quarterly.*

Chapter 4: Originally published in *International Journal of Comparative Sociology*, 14, 1973, pp. 89–103; reprinted by permission of Brill Academic Publishers.

Chapter 5: Originally published in *Sociology*, 13, 1979, pp. 179–201; reprinted by permission of Sage Publications Ltd. © BSA Publications LTD.

Chapter 6: Originally published in *Religion*, 15, 1985, pp. 291–304; reprinted by permission.

Chapter 7: Originally published in *Annals of Tourism Research*, 15, 1988, pp. 371–386; reprinted by permission.

Chapter 8: Originally published in *Annals of Tourism Research*, 15, 1988, pp. 29–46; reprinted by permission.

Chapter 9: Originally published in Butler, R. and Pearce, D. (eds.), *Change in Tourism*, London, Routledge, 1995, pp. 12–29; reprinted by permission of Thomson Publishing Services.

Chapter 10: Originally published in *Pacific Tourism Review*, 2, 1998, pp. 1–10; reprinted by permission of Cognizant Communication Corporation.

Chapter 11: Originally published in *Annals of Tourism Research*, 10, 1985, pp. 5–29; reprinted by permission.

Chapter 12: Originally published in *Leisure Studies*, 6, 1987, pp. 181–198.

Chapter 13:   Originally published in *Visions in Leisure and Business* 16, 1997, pp. 4–14.

Chapter 14:   Originally published in *Annals of Tourism Research*, 13, 1986, pp. 533–563; reprinted by permission.

Chapter 15:   Originally published in *International Journal of Comparative Sociology*, 12, 1971, pp. 217–233; reprinted by permission of Brill Academic Publishers.

Chapter 16:   Originally published in *Cahiers du Tourism*, Ser. B, No. 27, 1982, pp. 1–34; reprinted by permission.

Chapter 17:   Originally published in Butler, R. and Hinch, Th. (eds.), *Tourism and Indigenous People*, International Thompson Business Press, 1996, pp. 227–254.

Chapter 18:   Originally published in P. Teo *et al.* (eds.), *Interconnected Worlds*, Pergamon, 2001, pp. 157–175; reprinted by permission.

Chapter 1

Introduction

The Permutations of the Sociology of Tourism

Tourism became a rapidly growing social phenomenon and an increasingly important global industry in the first decades following the Second World War. It soon climbed to the second, and eventually the first spot in international trade. However, sociologists and anthropologists have been slow in recognizing its social and cultural — as against economic — significance. It was only by the mid-1960s that a few social scientists began to show a cursory interest in tourism, usually in the course of study of other issues (Boissevain 1977:524); at the time, only a few publications related expressly to the topic (e.g. Forster 1964; Nuñez 1963). The first systematic works in English appeared in the 1970s and only in the 1980s has the field of tourism research begun to achieve academic recognition — even though it was still accorded low academic prestige. I myself heard at the time some denigrating remarks on this emergent field from one of the editors of a prestigious sociological annual, even though he had invited me to prepare a review article on the topic.

The academic infrastructure of tourism studies was also slow to develop: the first session devoted to tourism at an important international conference took place only in 1974 (Smith ed. 1977; Smith and Brent co-eds. 2001:XV). The first English-language journal devoted to the social sciences of tourism, *Annals of Tourism Research*, appeared a year earlier, in 1973 (Swain *et al.* 1998). A few departments of sociology or anthropology began offering courses on tourism from the mid-1970s onwards (Graburn 1980; Murphy 1981). And only by 1986 was an international academic forum devoted to the field, the *International Academy for the Study of Tourism*, founded.

It is hard to pinpoint the reasons for this belated awareness of the academic community of such a widespread, massive and enormously complex phenomenon as tourism. In my view, the deeper roots for the relative neglect of tourism, at least in sociology, are to be found in the primacy of intellectual attention of the main proponents of the discipline from its very inception to the domains of work, power and class. The iconic work at the foundations of the discipline is doubtlessly Max Weber's *Protestant Ethic and the Spirit of Capitalism* (1958 [1904]); the major problem which dominated early sociology and engendered the principal directions of its development, was that of the emergence of modern capitalism or more broadly of Western rationality. Under the circumstances, sociologists focused on "serious" human endeavors; true enough, they were aware of "leisure" as a modern phenomenon, but they saw it primarily as a security valve, helping to restore the modern individual from the tensions and fatigue of work, so that he could continue to engage in it. Leisure was considered as an auxiliary mechanism, rather than a topic of intrinsic interest.

Tourism, in particular has been commonly regarded as a frivolous, superficial activity, whose lack of seriousness was contrasted by social critics with the efforts, devotion and hardships suffered by the genuine travelers of earlier times (Boorstin 1964). Tourism thus fell between the chairs: it was neither a serious productive — or creative — activity, nor did it involve — as do, for example, sports — a serious effort, which would endow it with the halo surrounding "work." Only when the focus of sociological concern gradually shifted, in the late 1980s and the 1990s, towards the study of consumption and of popular culture — as crucial constituents of late modern society — did tourism come into its own. As it became a reputable field of study, articles, books and journals devoted to tourism proliferated, and sub-fields soon emerged.

In the course of its becoming a legitimate subject of sociological and anthropological concern, the approach to tourism on part of the researchers underwent gradual changes (cf. Jafari 2001). Boorstin's (1964) spirited critique of the tourist denigrated tourism, while exalting earlier traveling. MacCannell's (1973) crucial insight that such an attitude reflects a common-sense view of tourism and should hence itself be subjected to sociological analysis, rather than serve as its premise, was a fundamental step which constituted "tourism" as an autonomous field of study. MacCannell offered a view of the tourist which was virtually the opposite of Boorstin's: that of the alienated modern as secular pilgrim in quest of authenticity, which — since it is absent from his own world — he hopes to encounter in other places or other times (MacCannell 1973, 1976). The tourist's quest, however, according to MacCannell, is hampered by the locals — or the tourist establishment — at the destination, who create a "front" of "staged authenticity," which in touristically developed spaces appears unpenetrable; the effort of the tourist to experience the "real" life of the locals in their authentic "back" region is thus thwarted. Unlike the religious pilgrim (Turner 1973), the tourist is precluded from reaching his goal "out there." The more popular tourism becomes as a substitute for religion, the lesser the chance that it will lead to secular "salvation" — the tourist's vicarious participation in the authentic life of others. Accepting the premises of MacCannell's argument, one can only conclude that most tourists are indeed deluded by the "staged authenticity" of tourist settings, and suffer from a "false touristic consciousness."

Whatever the theoretical merit or empirical support for MacCannell's basic argument, its principal importance lies in the fact that it has established the crucial link between the study of tourism and that of modernity, thereby initiating a process by which tourism as a subject of sociological interest gradually moved from the margins of the discipline closer to its center. Its centrality was further enhanced with the recent turn in sociology to a concern with post-modernity.

MacCannell provided a basic paradigm for the study of tourism, which largely dominated the sociological discourse on the topic during the last quarter of the twentieth century. However, much of the discourse consisted of critical appraisals of the paradigm on a theoretical level. The application of MacCannell's ideas to systematic research was rather modest; moreover, empirical studies tended more frequently to disprove, rather than support, MacCannell's argument as originally formulated (e.g. Selänniemi 2001). The mass of tourists turned out to be neither alienated, nor in practice pursuing authenticity (whatever their rhetoric regarding their desire for authenticity may have been).

The theoretical critique and the limited empirical support for MacCannell's paradigm led to its qualification and gradual reformulation. The main stages of this process have been recently outlined by Ning Wang in his *Tourism and Modernity* (2000). Wang focuses on the changing interpretation of the concept of "authenticity" in theoretical discourse: his point of departure is MacCannell's "objective" authenticity, which stresses the issue of the "genuine" as against the "staged" character of the sites, sights, events and objects experienced by the tourist; the concept is defined by the researcher and used by him as a tool of analysis. The discourse moved from such an "etic" view of the concept to a more "emic" one, namely "constructed" authenticity — which stresses the tourists' own perception of "authenticity" — the features of a site, sight, event or object which, in their eyes, qualify it as being "authentic"; thereby the status of the concept changed from a tool of analysis to its empirical object. Eventually, the discourse moved to a completely subjectivized view of the concept, which Wang calls "existential" authenticity: the fullness and exaltation of "real living" experienced by tourists in unfettered, liminal situations; it becomes irrelevant whether the external circumstances are perceived as "authentic" or not.

The concept of "existential" authenticity brings the discourse of authenticity into the purview of another theoretical approach to tourism, emanating from the work of the anthropologist Victor Turner. Though, like MacCannell, Turner also saw tourism as a modern version of the pilgrimage, his approach led to an emphasis on its experiential quality: the tourist's sense of freedom from structure and his abandonment to playful, "ludic" behavior, may — despite their lack of "serious-ness" — engender profound subjective experiences which are, in an existential sense, "authentic" (cf. Gottlieb 1982; Moore 1980; Wagner 1977).

Wang's exposition can be reformulated so that it, on the one hand, becomes more germane to MacCannell's original semiotic approach, and, on the other, to the study of changes in the nature of tourism, accompanying the post-modern tendencies in Western society. Departing from the well-known semiotic distinction between the sign and its referent, it emerges that the stages in the process of reinterpretation of the concept of authenticity reflect a progressive destabilization of the sign-referent link. In "objective" authenticity the link is stable: the concept (sign) "authenticity" can be in principle unequivocally applied (by the researcher) to the sites, sights, events and objects (referents), which tourists encounter on their trip — and, by implication, it can be "objectively" determined whether or not they are foiled by "staged authenticity." In "constructed" authenticity the link is loosened up: rather than assuming that "authenticity" is independently verifiable, it becomes a matter of the subjective judgments of the tourists themselves. Hence, owing to the diversity of their criteria of judgment, the referents of "authenticity" vary from one person to another: what may be judged as authentic by one tourist, may be seen as inauthentic by another.[1] Finally, in "existential" authenticity, the link between the sign and referent is broken: "authenticity" becomes self-referential, since the authenticity of the external circumstances is irrelevant for the tourist's existential experience of authenticity.

While the permutations which the concept of "authenticity" underwent largely resulted from the internal dynamics of the theoretical discourse of the topic, this discourse was not unrelated to the changes occurring in contemporary society, and especially to its post-modern trends: the gradual switch in consumption practices from concern with material goods to emphasis on "experiences" in Western soci-eties; the equalization of experiences derived from different "finite provinces of meaning" (Schuetz 1973: Vol. 1:230) under conditions of the alleged vanishment of "originals" (and hence of "real" authenticity) and of the ascent of simulacra in our world (Baudrillard 1988); and the process of globalization which, while radically curtailing distances, also destabilized the "traditional" overlap between ethnicity, language, culture and territory, thus confounding the prevalent modern image of the world as consisting of neatly bounded geographical and socio-cultural entities, which tend to become increasingly stranger to the individual the further away he travels from his home.

These developments had a significant impact on Western tourism, leading to the alleged emergence of the "post-tourist" (Ritzer and Liska 1997). His appear-ance portends the demise of the MacCannellian paradigm of authenticity, as well as an acute shift in the discourse of tourism. For in "post-tourism" the quest for authenticity in MacCannell's sense ceases to be the principal cultural theme legitimizing one's engagement in tourism, as it had allegedly been for modern tourists (whatever the extent to which they actually sought to realize it in their travel). The craving for enjoyment and fun, pure and simple, becomes a culturally sufficient justification.

Abandoning himself to the enjoyment of surfaces, the post-modern tourist ceases to inquire into the genuineness or authenticity of the objects of his experience. Indeed, if the claim of some post-modernists (e.g. Baudrillard 1988) that the contemporary world is devoid of "originals" were true, the tourist's quest for "objective" authenticity on his trip would become a pointless and frustrating project.

The desire for enjoyment and fun is congruent with the post-modern nivellation of all "finite provinces of meaning" — it can be equally derived from staged and contrived attractions as from unadulterated ones. The post-modern tourist thus resembles in some respects Boorstin's depiction of the tourist — but with the important difference that he is not naïve or fooled, but reflective and resigned: owing to the pervasive inauthenticity of the post-modern world he abandons himself to the enjoyment of surfaces of attractions, rather than examining them in depth for their genuineness. Tourism tends to become a playful "as if" experience, the enjoyment and fun derived — like in the theater and other forms of art and leisure — from imagining that the experienced contrivances are "real." Disneylands and other theme parks are the most representative, but by no means the only, such fun-provoking, ludic contrivances. However, the engagement in fun and play may reach different degrees of intensity — at the extreme, like in ecstatic abandonment to fun or in "deep play" (Geertz 1973), they may attain the level of an existential experience, approximating Wang's concept of "existential authenticity."

But since the experience of "existential authenticity" is, as I pointed out above, devoid of a definite external referent, it is not necessarily dependent on the distinguishing "placeness" of a particular destination — as does the experience of objective authenticity by the modern tourist.

"Existential" authenticity can, in principle, by realized anywhere, if the right mood of liminality and absence of ordinary constraints is created. Post-modern tourism, motivated by a quest for fun and enjoyment, even if it may lead to experiences of "existential" authenticity, consequently tends to become an ever less distinctive "extra-ordinary" (Graburn 1977) pursuit, resembling increasingly a familiar leisure activity. Like the rest of the contemporary world, tourism, too, becomes "disenchanted"; while the study of tourism appears to be destined to merge seamlessly with the study of leisure.

This raises the question of the "future of tourism" — not so much as an institutionally organized enterprise, but rather as a culturally distinct type of activity. I shall return to this question in the concluding chapter of this book (Chapter 19).

A Strand in the Web: The Course of my Involvement in the Study of Tourism

The preceding brief review of what I consider to be the principal sequence of permutations in the sociological study of tourism forms the context within which my own involvement with the field can be situated.

Though an eager traveler, my own attitude to tourism, like that of many intellectuals (MacCannell 1973), was initially rather negative. I believed as did many others at the time, that tourism brings about the "destruction of everything that is beautiful" (Turner and Ash 1975:15). Indeed, while in the course of three decades of engagement in the field my views became more discerning and sophisticated, my attitude to tourism remains up to the present basically critical, though not necessarily negative. My prolonged engagement with tourism was, in fact, to a significant extent due to this critical attitude. However, I never made a conscious decision to devote myself to the study of tourism as a life-long project. In fact, my growing involvement with tourism was, especially in the early stages, a reaction to fortuitous circumstances. As was the case with other social scientists who embarked on the study of tourism at the time, I initially stumbled on the topic as a serendipitous consequence of quite another endeavor: an anthropological study of Jewish-Arab relations in a mixed town in Israel, conducted in 1966. In the course of the analysis of my data I realized the unexpected significance which the encounter of young Arab males with female foreign youth travelers had for the former (Cohen, forthcoming-b).

The resulting article (Chapter 15) was only indirectly a study in the anthropology of tourism, dealing mainly with the role the female tourists played in the life of the young Arab males; but, while writing the article, I became aware of tourism as an unexplored field. I was surprised at the scarcity of sociological literature on tourism, and the absence of a conceptual framework within which I could place the young travelers whom the Arab youths encountered in the town. My conceptualization of a typology of tourists, within which those travelers could be placed marks my turn to tourism as an autonomous sociological concern. This typology (Chapter 3) was based on the extent to which exposure to the strangeness of the host environment, as against ensconcement in the familiarity of an "environmental bubble" of the home environment, is found in any particular tourist role; the young travelers in the town, could now be classified as "drifters" and occupy the pole of the typology opposite that of the "organized mass tourists": the latter being marked by maximum ensconcement in the familiarity of the bubble, the former by maximum exposure to strangeness.

Though triggered by a particular concern arising from the analysis of my field material, the quest for a typology was also motivated by a broader interest, namely my critical attitude to "ordinary" tourism: if this kind of tourism appeared destructive, is there another kind of tourism which is more wholesome to its physical and social environment? At the time I believed to have found it in the "drifter," whom I conceived of as engaged on a temporarily and spatially "open-ended" trip, conducted virtually entirely in strange surroundings, without resort to the services of the tourism establishment. Soon enough, however, I found it necessary to qualify the concept (Chapter 4), as I realized that the emergence of a mass-drifter movement, leading up to the contemporary "backpacking" phenomenon, engendered a secondary tourist system of its own, which catered to the drifters' particular tastes, needs and budgets; I perceived that system as separate, but paralleling the tourist establishment of "ordinary" mass tourism.

By the late 1970s I started my first empirical research project expressly devoted to the study of what at the time I conceived as drifter tourism: the penetration of tourism into the hill tribe area of northern Thailand and the islands of the south of the country (Cohen 1996a). This empirical work expanded and ramified in various directions over the last twenty-five years, often constituting the background for the development of more abstract theoretical ideas.[2]

Though my tourist typology was based on a general socio-psychological variable, familiarity vs. strangeness — which, according to Schuetz (1944:507), "are general categories of our interpretation of the world" — I made no attempt to relate tourism to any of the principal theoretical issues which preoccupied sociologists at the time, such as the nature and the tensions of modernity (though I claimed (Chapter 3) that tourism is an eminently modern phenomenon, involving a generalized interest in the environment). It was only after the publication of MacCannell's (1973, 1976) work, that I became engaged in some deeper sociological concerns relating to tourism. Reorienting my typological approach from tourist roles to tourist experiences, I sought to qualify MacCannell's conception of the tourist as a secular pilgrim in quest of authenticity, by developing a "phenomenology of tourist experiences" (Chapter 5).

The gist of my argument was that, though recognizing the centrality of "authenticity" as a cultural theme in modernity, I questioned whether all tourists pursue authenticity to the same extent or in the same mode. Taking up MacCannell's claim that the alienation of moderns induces them to seek authentic life elsewhere, I argued that the intensity and depth of their quest for authenticity will depend on the extent of their alienation. This approach yielded a five-fold typology of "modes of tourist experiences," the more extreme types going beyond MacCannell's paradigmatic conception of the modern tourist as mainly seeking a vicarious experience of the authenticity of others; I claimed that some tourists are alienated enough to experiment with alternative lifeways encountered on their trip as potential "elective Centers," or even to embrace such a center and thus spiritually abandon modernity.

The "phenomenology" article sought to reconcile Boorstin's and MacCannell's views of the tourist, by claiming that the less alienated tourists would primarily seek "recreation" on their trip, while the more alienated ones will be in quest of authenticity. However, I noted that beneath the apparently superficial desire for recreation, there may lurk a deeper, perhaps unconscious, cultural theme, hinted at in the morphology of the word itself, "re-creation"; implicit in the term is, thus, an eminently religious motif, of a person being re-created or reborn (particularly at a pilgrimage center). I sought to explore further the affinity between touristic recreation and religion, under the influence of Victor Turner's processual approach in anthropology, in an article on "Tourism as Play" (Chapter 6).

In my early theoretical articles exploring the implications of MacCannell's concept of authenticity, I still accepted that concept uncritically, in the sense implicit in his writings: as "objective" authenticity, in Wang's terminology. I undertook a critique of the concept only in "Authenticity and Commoditization" (Chapter 7), an article influenced by my empirical work on commercialized tourist crafts (Cohen 2000). My basic argument was that authenticity is not an objectively given trait of a site, sight, event or object, but is socially constructed; hence it should not be used as an analytical concept of the researcher, but rather be itself submitted to empirical analysis: researchers should investigate which traits of a site, sight, event or object induce tourists to judge it as "authentic." Hence, for example, commercialized tourist crafts, judged "unauthentic" by experts, may still be perceived as "authentic" by tourists, insofar as they feature those diacritical traits by which the tourists judge "authenticity."

By the early 1990s I started to realize that some important changes are taking place in contemporary tourism, which could not be adequately dealt with within the ongoing discourse of authenticity, however sophisticated it may have become. In the last theoretical article in this book (Chapter 9) I attempted to grasp these ongoing changes in terms of a transition from the serious quest for authenticity as the principal legitimizing cultural theme, to a ludic desire for fun, which is unconcerned with the authenticity of the sites, sights, events or objects which satisfy this desire. I argued along the same lines which later led Ning Wang (2000) to propose the concept of "existential" authenticity, a state of being which — as I pointed out above — is unrelated to the authenticity of the surroundings in which it occurs.

My principal concern in that article was with the changes in the nature of the attractions in the course of the process of transformation of contemporary tourism. I argued that this process is accompanied by a rising significance of "contrived" attractions, and a concomitant decline of "natural" ones. This leads to a "deplacement" of destinations, the loss of local distinctiveness and the gradual dissolution of the boundary between tourism and "ordinary" leisure.[3]

These trends raise the spectre of the disappearance of tourism — a question recently raised explicitly by MacCannell (2001). In the concluding chapter of this book (Chapter 19), I shall attempt to outline an approach to this question.

The Structure of the Book

The selection of articles to be included in this book was influenced by several considerations. The principal one was my intention to reprint only those articles which I consider to have made an original theoretical or empirical contribution to the field of tourism studies. This led to the exclusion of several major literature reviews such as "The Sociology of Tourism" (1984b) and the more theory-oriented "Sociology and Tourism," co-authored with Graham Dann (Dann and Cohen 1991). A lengthy review of the more narrow sub-field of "Tourist Arts" (1992) was also excluded.

A second consideration was to present a wide spectrum of my work, though the emphasis would be on the theoretical rather than empirical contributions. Most of the articles in this book therefore deal with general theoretical issues (Part One) or with the interface of the field of tourism with other fields (Part Two). In Part Three, I have included a few empirical studies which are representative of my work on tourism in different parts of the world, and have not been reprinted in other collections of my articles.

The third consideration was to present the course of the development of my theoretical work on tourism, as outlined in the foregoing section. This led me to include some early articles, particularly in Part One, which may appear partially superseded by later work, but have been of some significance in the past. The weaknesses of these articles, from the perspective of my present position, will be pointed out in the comments which follow.

Part One starts with an attempt to define "the tourist" Chapter (2), originally published in 1974. It offers a cumulative definition, which, departing from the everyday, common-sense connotation of the term, seeks to expose its principal, sociologically significant analytical dimensions. The main implication of that exercise is that along each dimension the concept has fuzzy boundaries, so that a variety of other traveling roles besides that of the fully-fledged "tourist," possess a touristic component.

It should be noted that, from a contemporary perspective, the article is flawed in that it "essentializes" the tourist — seeking to uncover that essential trait which on *a priori* grounds distinguishes the tourist from other kinds of travellers; the article claims that this consists of a quest for "novelty and change." Though this is a fairly encompassing motive, it may still exclude some individuals who should be regarded as tourists, even if differently motivated — like Western post-tourists in quest of the familiar (Ritzer and Liska 1997) or travelers from non-Western societies, who, according to some critics, have been excluded from the prevailing West-centered definitions of "tourists" (Alneng 2002).

Chapter (3), published in 1972, proposes what to the best of my knowledge was the first analytically construed typology of tourist roles. The article emphasizes the great variety of tourists, against the tendency, common at the time, to conceive of "the tourist" in monolithic, often stereotypical, terms. However, as already pointed out, the article missed the opportunity to relate the analysis of tourism to any of the dominant discourses in the sociology at the time, a step taken shortly after its publication by MacCannell (1973).

Chapter (4), published in 1973, presents the first detailed description of the "drifter"; the article has been written in order to qualify the over-idealized conception of this type of tourist in the preceding chapter. While based on very limited empirical information, the article prefigured many of the traits of the contemporary "backpacker," which were in the last few years much more thoroughly documented by a new generation of researchers (e.g. Murphy 2001; Riley 1988; Scheyvens 2002; Sørensen 2003; Uriely *et al.* 2002).

Chapter (5), published in 1979, departs from MacCannell's paradigmatic view of the tourist as an alienated modern in quest of authenticity; it seeks to reconcile Boorstin's and MacCannell's diametrically opposed views of the tourist, by proposing a typology of modes of tourist experiences, based on the proposition that the tourist's intensity of the quest for authenticity will depend on the degree of his alienation from his own society. The article, as Selwyn (1996:6) has pointed out, makes primarily *a priori* claims, whereas it is weak on ethnographic evidence. Its strength thus hinges on the correctness of MacCannell's original argument, which remains a contested matter to this day (e.g. Selänniemi 2001; Uriely *et al.* 2002).

The article, transposing MacCannell's claim into terms of Shils' idea of a sociocultural Center, assumes that people will either be attached to the Center of their own society, or, alienated from it, seek an "elective Center" elsewhere. But it misses the theoretical significance of "multi-centeredness" (though it mentions it): the increasing propensity of "post-modern" individuals to identify with more than a single Center, a point which was recently highlighted by other researchers (Uriely *et al.* 2002).

Chapter (6), published in 1985, claims to discern in the apparently superficial playfulness of recreational tourists a deep-lying religious motif. This is my most speculative attempt at an exegesis of the "theological" dimension of tourism — specifically, by pointing to the analogy between tourism as play at a (vanished) Reality and religious "play theology" in a radically secularized world, which "plays theology" though "God is dead." Touristic recreation is here interpreted as a ludic (playful) activity, an "as if" game of make-belief, which culminates in a playful re-capture of a transcendent Reality, in the existence of which the participants do not seriously believe any more. An interesting, but little explored question, is whether such a ludic attitude also marks the visits of post-modern tourists to the sites of New Age religions.

Chapter (7), published in 1988, offers a reinterpretation of the concept of authenticity, claiming that it is a socially constructed concept and hence should not be used as an analytical tool, but rather itself become a subject of empirical investigation; the article explores the relationship between authenticity and commercialization, claiming that commercialization does not necessarily impair the perceived authenticity of sites, sights, objects or events.

Chapter (8), also published in 1988, seeks to explicate the research programs inherent in what I considered at the time to be the three principal traditions in tourism research, emanating from the respective works of Boorstin, MacCannell and Turner. The article explores the dynamics of the relationship between these traditions — but misses an ironic turn in the contemporary view of the post-modern tourist: an implicit rehabilitation of Boorstin's initial position, so fiercely criticized by MacCannell, albeit with an important qualification — the post-tourist is reflectively and playfully (and not naively) enjoying the surfaces of contrived or staged attractions, since he is resigned to the alleged disappearance of originals and of authenticity from the post-modern world.

Chapter (9), published in 1995, deals with the process of transformation in contemporary tourism, dwelling on the dual trends of decline of the centrality of "natural" attractions and of the quest for authenticity, and the rise of "contrived" attractions, which satisfy the contemporary tourist's desire for playful enjoyment and fun. These trends endanger the continued sense of "placeness" of destinations and threaten to erase the boundary between tourism and ordinary leisure.

In view of recent studies of "cultural tourism" (e.g. Lacy and Douglass 2002), the dichotomy made in the article between "natural" and "contrived" attractions appears too simplistic: new cultural attractions, established particularly in major Western urban centers are neither "natural," in that they are part of the local environment or culture, nor necessarily "contrived," established merely to attract tourists for commercial reasons. Rather, they are edifices of a global culture, and though their creation may be based on economic motives, they also help to endow the locality with a new image and a new source of local pride. A novel approach to the classification and dynamics of attractions, taking account of the contemporary interpenetration of the global and the local, and of the blunting of the boundaries between them, therefore appears necessary.

Part Two of the book diverts the direction of the analysis from major theoretical issues to the elucidation of the relationship between tourism and other disciplinary domains. Most articles included in this part are thus inter-disciplinary, and one (Chapter 14) was written in co-operation with a linguist.

Chapter (10), published in 1998, proposes a comparative perspective on the interface of tourism and religion. It purposely ignores the principal link between the two domains, already much emphasized in the literature — the alleged emanation of tourism from pilgrimage and the claim that tourists are secular pilgrims — paying attention to other, more neglected aspects of the relationship: in particular, it examines the implications of the theological precepts of various religions for their believers' engagement in tourism, for their choice of destinations and for their conduct on the trip, as well as the complexities resulting from religious sites, rituals and festivals becoming popular tourist attractions.

Chapter (11), published in 1985, as the introduction to a collection of articles on tourist guides (Cohen ed. 1985), applies the conceptual framework of leadership theory to the analysis of the structure and dynamics of the guide's role. The article highlights the stresses inherent in the guide's role and the consequent differentiation of sub-roles, focusing on various specific tasks involved in guiding tourists.

Chapter (12), published in 1987, seeks to employ the typology of tourist roles (Chapter 3) to the analysis of the differential approach of law enforcing agencies to various kinds of tourists. The principal assumption is that these agencies tend to victimize non-institutionalized tourists, especially drifters, while extending protection to the institutionalized mass tourists. This was, to the best of my knowledge, the first attempt to apply the perspective of the sociology of tourism to a criminological issue.

The article was written at a time when drifters, often called "hippies," were still met with animosity by the authorities of many countries; such attitudes have mellowed over time — contemporary backpackers appear to be much less subject to victimization on the part of the authorities.

While stressing the victimization of drifters, the article fails to take sufficient account of the growing attractiveness of wealthy mass tourists to corrupt police in some countries: such police may cooperate with criminals in the victimization of wealthy tourists rather than defend them — a point which I discussed in a later article dealing with the gem scam in Thailand (Cohen 1996b).

Chapter (13), published in 1997, proposes a theoretical model for the study of the interface of tourism and crime, by applying some general insights of several leading theories in criminology to the distinguishing features of tourist-oriented crime. The article highlights the greater vulnerability of tourists in comparison to locals, and dwells upon the emergence of forms of "guardianship" specifically intended to protect tourists from the threat of victimization.

Chapter (14), published in 1984 and co-authored with Robert Cooper, seeks to apply some general approaches of contemporary linguistics to the specificities of linguistic situations in tourism. The article proposes the concept of "tourist talk," the language of the foreign tourists spoken by locals, as a parallel to "foreigner talk," the local language spoken by newcomers, such as migrant laborers, in their host environment. The typology of tourists (Chapter 3) is again used to explore the linguistic differences between various touristic situations.

Part Three of the book includes samples of my empirical work in different parts of the world — Israel, the Pacific Islands and Thailand, which either raised or empirically explored some of the issues dealt with in my theoretical work.

Chapter (15), published in 1971, my first publication related to tourism, emerged from a study of Jewish-Arab relations in a mixed town in Israel. Adopting a functionalist approach, I sought to highlight the unexpected role which the foreign tourist girls came to play in the life of the local Arab youths, suffering from the constraints and lack of hope due to their marginalization in Israeli society. The article is also an early case-study of the consequences of the "process of globalization" — an analysis of the manner in which local fates come to be entwined, through tourism, with remote people and places.

Chapter (16), published in 1982, is the only part of a wider study of Pacific tourism, conducted in the course of two sojourns at the University of the South Pacific in Suva, Fiji, in 1974 and 1975, which reached completion. Departing from the Western concept of the "Earthly Paradise," the article shows how paradisiac qualities came to be ascribed to the Pacific islands — and, how, eventually, the image of the Pacific island paradise became the model for the establishment of contrived touristic paradises by the tourist industry. The disenchantment of paradise as it is turned into a consumer product, exemplifies the broader process of substitution of contrived for natural attractions, discussed in Chapter (9).

Chapter (17), first published in 1996, takes up a similar theme in a different context: excursions to the last remnants of "hunter-gatherer" groups in Thailand — the tourist quest for the ultimate "Other." But the "original," "authentic" lifeways of these "primitive" people have already been so thoroughly transformed, and even destroyed, by the wider social forces, that the encounter between the tourists and the "hunter-gatherers" has to be mostly overtly staged to create the illusion of a primitiveness which does not exist anymore — a point which Dean MacCannell made in his "Cannibal Tours" (MacCannell 1992).

Chapter (18), finally, first published in 2001, applies a general idea proposed in an earlier article (Chapter 9) to contemporary Thailand. It claims that Thailand is undergoing a process of "touristic transition," involving a gradual decline of "natural" attractions due to general processes of development as well as the growth of the tourist industry, and the concomitant rise in the number, size and importance of "contrived" attractions. However, the gradual detachment of the "contrived" attractions from the ambience of their geographical and cultural surroundings leads to the loss of "placeness" of Thai destinations, with Thailand becoming the gate of tourism to new destinations in the touristically less developed neighboring countries of continental Southeast Asia.

The criticism of the dichotomy of "natural" and "contrived" attractions, in the above discussion of Chapter (9), appears also to apply to this chapter: contemporary Bangkok, the hub of the nation, is gradually becoming a world metropolis and is developing attractions, such as musical events, film festivals and fairs, of a global, rather than a local character, which could not be described as "contrived."

The themes, theoretical foci, methodologies and empirical backgrounds of the articles in this collection are highly diverse. It would therefore be futile to attempt some "integration" in the concluding chapter of the book (Chapter 19). Rather, I have preferred to devote it to "a look ahead," the complex issue of the future of tourism, which both projects, as well as qualifies, some of the major themes raised in the body of this book.

Part One

Theory

Chapter 2

Who is a Tourist? A Conceptual Clarification

Introduction

Who does not know a tourist? Tourism is so widespread and ubiquitous in our day that there are scarcely people left in the world who would not recognize a tourist immediately.

Indeed, the stereotype of the tourist, as the slightly funny, quaintly dressed, camera-toting foreigner, ignorant, passive, shallow and gullible,[4] is so deep-seated that it tends to dominate not only the popular imagery but also some serious writing on the subject.[5] The tourist in our day has become a cultural type with apparently clearly recognizable traits; few sociologists who deal with the subject have hence bothered to define the tourist role carefully.[6]

But the unreflective acceptance of the common-sensible view of the tourist harbours some inherent dangers. The principal manifestations of contemporary tourism are indeed well-known and easily recognizable; but they do not comprise the whole range of touristic phenomena. Indeed, one of the more interesting features accompanying the contemporary tourist boom is the extraordinary proliferation of diverse forms of tourism, ranging from short excursions to round-the-world trips, from sea-side vacations to veritable expeditions into almost unknown parts of the world, such as Antarctica or Greenland, from organized and routinized mass-travel to leisurely, individualized exploration or drifting off-the-beaten-track.

In addition to fully-fledged tourism, there exist many traveller roles which possess a "touristic component" of varying strength; prominent examples are the Italian or Irish immigrant who pays a visit to the "old country," the young professional engaging in "touristry," who is in a search for jobs which will give him an opportunity to see the world while working (Pape 1965), the pilgrim who combines devotion with some "religious tourism" (Chapter 10) or the person who "takes the waters" at a spa, ostensibly to improve his health but actually to enjoy himself (Lowenthal 1962). Such a "touristic component" is also present even in a short pleasure trip (Wall 1972), an outing or a picnic. Instead of a clearly bounded phenomenon, tourism upon closer inspection turns out to be a vaguely delimited sphere and to merge imperceptibly with other types of travel. There exists no strong gradient between travellers who are tourists and those who are not.

As logicians have shown, most empirical concepts have vague boundaries.[7] I do not propose to engage here in a lexicographical exercise to clarify the meaning of tourism. Rather, I want to point out that, under conditions of conceptual vagueness, we tend to preoccupy ourselves primarily with those phenomena most obviously covered by our concept (e.g. the fully-fledged tourist), while disregarding the peripheral ones (e.g. partial tourist roles). Where this periphery is extensive, as in the case of tourism, this procedure obviously leads to distorted generalizations. The aim of this chapter is to provide an analytical definition of tourism which will isolate the "touristic component" from a variety of travellers' roles and thus overcome the problem of vagueness of boundaries of tourism. Three aims will be served by this procedure: first, it will provide a more adequate basis for sociological generalizations on touristic phenomena than that used hitherto; secondly, it will draw attention to a variety of interesting but neglected forms of partial tourism; and thirdly, it will serve to integrate the sociological analysis of tourism within the broader but as yet underdeveloped field of a sociology of travel and travellers, which in turn should be viewed as a sub-field of the sociology of migration and migrants.[8]

Mathematicians have developed a most useful tool to deal with vague concepts such as tourism — the idea of "fuzzy sets."[9] In modern set theory, "fuzziness" is contrasted with "crispness" and defined as ". . . a type of imprecision which is associated with fuzzy sets, that is, classes in which there is no sharp transition from membership to non-membership" (Bellman and Zadeh 1970:B–141). Fuzzy sets include in addition to full members (members enjoying grade 1 membership in the set) with partial membership grades (between 0 and 1) (ibid.:B–143). A person engaged in "touristry," or a pilgrim-tourist, exemplifies such partial membership grades in the set "tourists." This conceptual tool enables us to formulate sharp definitions of vague phenomena: ". . . our basic assumption is that a fuzzy set A — despite the unsharpness of its boundaries — can be defined precisely by associating with each object x a number between 0 and 1 which represents its grade of membership in A" (ibid.:B–143). We shall see in the following that the idea of fuzzy sets can be most fruitfully applied to the concept of tourism.

An Analytical Definition of Tourism

A review of the historical and contemporary definitions of the term "tourist" offered by dictionaries, though not excessively informative, will provide us with some starting points for a more analytical definition. Obviously, the term is derived from "tour," meaning "... a journey at which one returns to the starting point; a circular trip usually for business, pleasure or education during which various places are visited and for which an itinerary is usually planned" Webster (1961:2417).[10] Accordingly, The Oxford English Dictionary defines the tourist as "one who makes a tour or tours; especially one who does this for recreation; one who travels for pleasure or culture, visiting a number of places for their objects of interest, scenery or the like" (*Oxford* 1933:XI, 190). Other major dictionaries tend uniformly to reiterate the contention that a tourist is one who travels for pleasure.

The term is of relatively recent origin and has its roots apparently in the beginning of the nineteenth century (Ogilvie 1934:661). The *Oxford English Dictionary* quotes Pegge as stating in 1814 that "A Traveller is now-a-days called a Tourist" (*Oxford* 1933:XI, 190). Dumazedier claims that "... Stendhal invented the very word 'tourist' ..." (Dumazedier 1967:123), probably at about the same time as it first appeared in England.

Social scientific definitions of the term "tourist," going beyond its general, common-sense meaning, are rare in the English literature. One of the more interesting ones, offered by Ogilvie, the author of one of the first comprehensive treatises on the subject, states that the term tourist "... is now used in the social sciences ... to describe any person whose movements fulfil two conditions: first, that absence from home is relatively short, and second, that money spent during absence is money derived from home and not earned in the places visited" (Ogilvie 1934:661). Ogilvie thus ingeniously translates the contention found in other definitions, namely that a tourist is a traveller for recreation or pleasure, into economic terms: the tourist is, economically speaking, a consumer and not a producer.

With the proliferation of international travel in recent years, it has become necessary to operationalize the term "tourist" for statistical purposes, so that tourist statistics can be collected on a comparative basis. The U.N. Conference on International Travel and Tourism at its meeting in Rome in 1963, therefore proposed the following operational definition for international tourists:

> temporary visitors staying at least 24 hours in the country visited and the purpose of whose journey can be classified under one of the following headings:

(i) Leisure (recreation, holiday, health, study, religion, sport);
(ii) business, family, mission, meeting (Cosgrove and Jackson 1972:45).

"Excursionists," in contrast to tourists, were defined as "... temporary visitors staying less than 24 hours in the country visited (including travellers on cruises)."

This definition of (international) tourism is the most specific, but also the most inclusive of the various definitions quoted. It probably embraces all kinds of (international) travellers, with the exception of migrants and migratory workers, and hence comes close to the meaning of the German term *Fremdenverkehr*. Whatever its merits for international travel statistics, it is too broad for sociological purposes, since it tends to obliterate the differences in the roles of various travellers who do not travel in pursuit of work (e.g. the traveller for pleasure the conventioneer and the pilgrim).

In our attempt to provide an analytical definition of the tourist role we shall glean some elements from the various definitions quoted and add some of our own. Our aim will be to specify clearly the various significant dimensions of the tourist role and to indicate the manner in which the tourist role differs, along each dimension, from other types of traveller roles.[11]

Generally, the tourist role is by most definitions classified within the *genus proximus*, the wider category, of roles of "travellers." However, one definition quoted above (that of the U.N. conference), defines him as a visitor rather than as a traveller. This variant approach helps to draw our attention to the two main sociological aspects, or components, of the traveller's role: first, the aspect of movement, of "travel" in the narrow sense of the term of making a journey, usually of some length. For lack of a more adequate term, we shall call this aspect the "traveller" component. And secondly, the aspect of sojourn, of staying at a place which is not one's own, of visiting countries, people, or institutions for some, usually relatively short, periods of time. We shall call this the "visitor" component.[12] This component is usually included in the broader meaning of the term traveller; but the traveller component is not necessarily included in the term visitor.

The emphasis upon this or that component of the role in the literature seems to depend on the perspective taken: the traveller component is emphasized by those who look at the process from the point of view of the travelling individual; while the visitor component is chiefly emphasized by those who look at the process from the point of view of interaction between the traveller and the society or locality visited by him. As we shall see further on, the two components of the traveller role are also differentially emphasized in the two varieties of the tourist role, namely, the "sightseer" vs. the "vacationer."

Travelling is such a ubiquitous, complex and variegated phenomenon, that it is astonishing that social scientists, though much concerned with "geographical mobility," pay but scant attention to travelling as a form of human activity: its varieties, norms, motives, the role-sets which it embraces, or its social significance. Indeed, in a systematic survey of the literature I was unable to find a single attempt by a sociologist — or anyother social scientist — to deal systematically with the phenomenon of travelling, though there exist excellent studies of some of the more colourful types of travellers.[13] The fact, then, that tourists can be classified into the broader category of travellers, does not help us much towards achieving a base point for our definition of the tourist role.

In order to capture the *difflerentia specifica*, the peculiar traits which characterize the tourist within the general realm of traveller roles, I have isolated six dimensions of the tourist role; these dimensions are partly based on the definitions presented above, and partly implied in them:

(1) The tourist is a *temporary* traveller, possessing a fixed place of abode, which is his permanent address even during his trip; this circumstance differentiates him from the nomad, wanderer, hobo and other types of permanent travellers. Whereas for the tourist travelling is an exceptional, and often also an unaccustomed state, a role which he takes up only occasionally or even rarely, for the wanderer it is a complete way of life. How long — or how short — such a temporary state of travelling has to be for the traveller to become a tourist is difficult to specify precisely; this is one of several elements of "fuzziness" in the concept of the tourist to be dealt with below.

(2) The tourist is a *voluntary* traveller, who goes on a trip of his own free will, is able to terminate his trip whenever it pleases him and is free to return to his permanent place of abode. This circumstance differentiates him from involuntary or forced travellers, such as the exile, the refugee, the prisoner of war, etc.

(3) The tourist is a traveller on a tour, a *round-trip*, so that his point of departure is also his final destination. This circumstance differentiates him from the emigrant, who moves on a one-way-trip, from one permanent abode to another. As Williams and Zelinsky (1970:506) have put it: "...tourism can be considered as a simple or many-destinational impermanent (italics mine) migration." Though the difference between a round-trip and a one-way-trip appears to be fairly clear, here too an element of fuzziness is involved, having to do mainly with the different degrees of permanence with which persons move from their fixed place of abode to other destinations.

(4) The tourist is on a relatively *long* journey, and not merely on a short trip or excursion. This circumstance differentiates the tourist from the day-tripper or mere excursionist. But how long precisely a trip has to be to become a journey or a tour cannot be determined in general terms; this depends on a variety of circumstances, such as cultural and other characteristics of the traveller and of his destinations.

(5) The tourist is on a *non-recurrent* trip, or at least on one which he undertakes rarely, rather than on a trip which he embarks on regularly and to which he is well accustomed. This circumstance differentiates the tourist from the commuter or week-endhouse owner; recurrency, however, is a continuous

variable and hence the boundaries between what is recurrent and what is not are not sharply definable.

(6) The tourist is a traveller, the purpose of whose trip is *non-instrumental*; that is, his trip is not a means to another goal (like a business trip) but an end in itself. This definition would exclude from the category of tourist, businessmen, travelling salesmen, international representatives, missionaries and other travellers whose trip serves primarily economic, political or religious purposes.

The most common non-instrumental purposes of tourist travel mentioned in the literature are pleasure, recreation and culture. But should every type of non-instrumentally motivated travel be seen as tourism? Here we touch upon what to my mind is the basic differentiating characteristic of tourism, which is of sufficient theoretical significance to merit some discussion: tourism connotes a change from routine, something different, strange, unusual or novel, an experience not commonly present in the daily life of the traveller. However much tourist itineraries may be routinized, as far as the tourist establishment is concerned, they offer an attraction, even to the mass tourist, precisely because they promise at least some subjective element of novelty and change. I therefore view the expectation of pleasure derived from novelty or change as the central non-instrumental purpose of the tourist trip and the major differentiating element between this and other traveller roles.[14] An important corollary of this is that it is not so much the objective characteristics of a trip — for example, its length, the places visited, etc. — which will help us to decide whether a traveller should be considered a tourist, but primarily the specific expectation of novelty and change promised by the trip. This statement clarifies somewhat the uncertainties of classification en countered in the discussion of the other dimensions of the tourist role, though it does not do away completely with the element of fuzziness in the concept of tourism. As a general rule one can say that, in so far as even a lengthy trip becomes routine for the world traveller, its touristic component will be reduced; conversely, even a short trip from home could possess an appreciable touristic component for an otherwise highly stationary person. Still, we can expect empirically that, other things being equal, the further the trip, the greater will be generally the element of novelty and change expected by the tourist. It would, indeed, be irrational and inefficient for a tourist to seek out a far away point if he could enjoy an equal amount of novelty and change at a nearer destination. This consideration is alluded to in a different way by Williams and Zelinsky (1970:75) in their discussion of "intervening opportunities"; ". . . a tourist proceeding from his home to a distant country will pause along the route at attractive intermediate stops — or . . . might even forego the more distant point for the closer opportunity."

On the basis of these considerations I now propose my definition of the tourist role. This definition incorporates several elements found in other definitions but also adds several new ones, which make it more specific and explicit: *A "tourist" is a voluntary, temporary traveller, travelling in the expectation of pleasure from the novelty and change experienced on a relatively long and non-recurrent round-trip.*

In order clearly to demonstrate the derivation of the tourist role from the general category of travellers, and to point out the analytical differences between the tourist role and other types of traveller roles, this definition can be presented in the form of a "conceptual tree" as in Diagram 2.1.

The dimensions appearing in Figure 2.1 are identical with the terms used in the definition, but they are set out in an analytical order, so that the broader characteristics are listed first, and the more specific ones later on. Thereby a cumulative definition of the tourist role is achieved. The conceptual tree indicates clearly the analytical points of difference between the tourist role and other traveller roles. It has to be pointed out though, that only one "branch" of the "tree" has been presented: the diagram develops conceptually only the tourist role, whereas other traveller roles were lumped together on the right hand of the diagram and merely illustrated by a few examples relevant for our purpose. For a fully developed "tree" of specific traveller roles branching out of the general *genus* of traveller, many other roles would have to be added and the analytical differences between

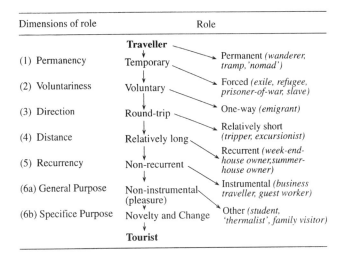

Figure 2.1: "Conceptual Tree" for the Definition of the Tourist Role

them specified. Such an effort might necessitate the introduction of additional differentiating dimensions.

In Figure 2.1, the values for each of the dimensions by which the tourist role is defined has been merely dichotomized. However, most of these dimensions are actually not dichotomies, but continua which can be sub-divided into any number of specific categories. The fuzziness of the concept of the tourist role is the result of the fuzziness of each of the dimensions by which this role is defined. The task of the effort of conceptualization here is to determine the limits of variation on each dimension which one can meaningfully speak of as having a "touristic component," as well as to break the continua into a number of empirically recognizable sub-types of roles with an increasingly diminishing "touristic component."

The Dimensions of the Tourist Role

We shall now discuss each of the analytical dimensions of the tourist role, paying special attention to the roles on the borderline of fully-fledged tourism; such roles will be discussed in the context of that dimension in which their marginality is most pronounced.

(1) *Permanency*. We stated above that a tourist is a temporary traveller, possessing a permanent abode. But what are the limits of temporariness? How long has one to be on the way to become a *permanent* traveller? And how little time should elapse for one to be come even a temporary *traveller*? These questions are intended to determine the upper and lower limits of temporariness in the tourist role.

Let us start with the lower limits. As will be remembered, the U.N. Conference on International Travel and Tourism set the minimum time of sojourn necessary for a traveller to be considered an international tourist at twenty-four hours; travellers on shorter stays were termed "excursionists." This decision has probably been taken primarily for statistical and economic reasons, so as to separate the "real" tourists from persons in transit and the one-day visitors.[15] But it agrees by and large with the implications of findings of recreation studies on the way people spend free-time periods of varying length. Thus Burton (1971:245) established five typical periods of recreational time: (i) very short (up to an hour); (ii) short (a few hours); (iii) a full day; (iv) several days; (v) a week or more (yearly vacations). He found that only periods (iv) and (v), namely those extending beyond a single full day, offer opportunities for travel on the regional or national level (ibid., Table 44, 247). We could therefore claim that a person becomes a fully-fledged tourist only if his trip extends for more than one full day — or in other words, if he spends at least one night away from home. We may term the one-day traveller an "excursionist" if he covers a long distance, and particularly if he crosses an international boundary; or, following Wall (1972), a "pleasure-tripper" if he covers a relatively short distance. These two types represent, respectively, a marginal and a minimal kind of tourism, intermediate between fully-fledged tourism and short-time travelling devoid of any "touristic component."

It is more difficult to determine the upper limits of temporariness in the tourist role. When does a person cease being a tourist and become a wanderer, a tramp or a (modern) "nomad?" As is well known, a fairly large number of mostly young travellers for pleasure in the contemporary world take off for considerable periods of time, up to several years, and wander around the world. Some eventually return and settle down; others continue to travel indefinitely (Chapter 4). Under such conditions it is obviously impossible to put a fixed limit upon the tourist role and to separate it completely from that of the wanderer. I suggest that a traveller be viewed as "temporary," and hence as a tourist, as long as he still possesses a permanent home to which he returns periodically or to which he intends to return eventually, even if he stays away for many years. The "itinerant hippie" (Chapter 4) and other forms of the drifter-wanderer, on the road for an indefinite period of time, is hence a marginal tourist role, intermediate between temporary and permanent travellers.

It should be pointed out that even in the roles of some "permanent travellers," such as tramps, hoboes and other modern "nomads," one can find a "touristic component" of varying intensity. Though many of them took up wandering by force of circumstance, some value highly this kind of existence or are driven to it by an inner urge for new experiences and places, similar to the tourist's quest for novelty and change.[16]

(2) *Voluntariness*. This dimension is, in the context of our discussion, less ambiguous than the others, since the tourist, as a traveller for pleasure, represents an extreme prototype of the voluntary traveller who is neither politically forced nor emotionally compelled to leave his place of abode. In this respect he is the diametrical opposite of the refugee, the prototype of the involuntary traveller. There are, however, as Kunz (1973) has shown, several types of forces which might lead to the emergence of refugee movements, some of which, like deportation, are physically more compelling than others, which include a relatively greater amount of "voluntary" personal decision-making, like flight in fear.[17] Some people (e.g. writers like James Joyce and Thomas Mann) voluntarily exile themselves from a country, and some, owing to favourable personal circumstances, are able to sustain a tourist-like style

of life during their exile. Such "tourist-exiles," then, would represent an intermediate type of marginal tourism on this dimension.

Voluntariness can be contrasted not only with sheer force, but also with socially sanctioned, normative obligations. Social expectations may induce people to undertake a trip, though they perhaps would not do so of their own volition. The institution of pilgrimage, as Turner points out, is an intermediate case in this respect: "It is infused with voluntariness though by no means independent of structural obligatoriness" (Turner 1973:204).

(3) *Direction.* The distinction between a round-trip and a one-way trip is apparently sharp and easily determined. However, there exist several types of travellers who linger around in their host countries, without deciding unequivocally whether to settle there or to return to their country of origin. Hence an element of fuzziness is introduced into this dimension.

Tourist-migrants exemplify this type of traveller: these are people who had originally arrived in their host-country as tourists, but decided to stay on, work and sometimes even to settle there. Such cases are especially prominent in the Bahamas and Hawaii.[18] This is also a common occurrence in Israel, where "tourist-immigrant" (*tayyar-oleh*) is an officially recognized class of residents.

Another example of an intermediate type of traveller on this dimension are the so-called "permanent tourists": these are persons who, though deriving their income in their country of origin, prefer to take up semi-permanent residence in another country. The bulk of this category consists of the retired from affluent countries living in the cheaper, developing ones: Americans in Mexico (Ball 1971), and more recently on some Pacific islands (Tudor 1970) and British on Majorca (Riedel 1972) or Malta (Jones 1972), are good examples of this type. A variety of the poor man's permanent tourism are retired people in the United States settling in trailer camps, where they are permitted to stay as long as they do not engage in gainful employment (Hoyt 1954).

(4) *Distance of Trip.* To qualify as tourism, a trip should be relatively long. "Relative length" is obviously a fuzzy term; it is determined contextually, by taking into account the previous experience of the traveller or the norms of a society or a social group. Thus in many traditional societies or sedentary groups in modern societies, such as peasants,[19] even relatively short trips would qualify as tourism, while among the mobile urban middle and upper-middle classes trips would have to be much longer to acquire this quality. We cannot, hence, put an objective, universally valid limit on the distance one has to travel in order to become a tourist. But we can say that for every society or social group there is a minimal distance the average traveller would have to traverse for him to experience a sense of pleasurable change or novelty. Thus Bonsey suggests that in contemporary Britain there may "... be a

minimum distance which car-owners travel on pleasure excursions and that at distances of less than 'perhaps five miles [8 km]' trippers are not sufficiently removed from their accustomed environment to regard themselves as taking a pleasure trip."[20]

The five-mile limit could, then, be assumed as the inner limit of "minimal tourism" in mobile, Western societies; this inner limit might be very different in other societies. The limit of "fully-fledged," as against minimal tourism would obviously be much further away, but there is no empirical basis on which one could determine the point at which a mere "pleasure-tripper" becomes a tourist, and no clear taxonomy of intermediate types has yet been established.

The distinction which comes closest to dealing with different types of tourists in terms of distance travelled, is that between domestic and international tourists: travel within the boundaries of one's own country as against travel abroad. International tourism is often treated separately from domestic tourism, presumably because the international tourist is formally a foreigner in the country he visits, and because it is assumed that a greater social and psychological distance exists between him and the host environment than in domestic tourism. We have to note, however, that international tourism does not always mean a greater geographical travelling distance, since some places beyond the border may be more accessible to the traveller's place of residence than some places in his own country. Moreover, there are important exceptions to the argument that travelling abroad implies a greater social or psychological distance than travelling at home: visits by white urban U.S. citizens to Indian reservations or by white Australians to an aboriginal area will probably involve a greater social or psychological distance than if these travellers were to visit a Canadian or a European city. The same would be true for upper-class coastal Spanish Latin Americans who, while they are often quite at home in Paris, feel complete strangers in an Andean Indian village in their own back-country. Hence, though the distinction between domestic and international tourism may be quite useful for some purposes, it is both geographically as well as sociologically less clear-cut than is generally assumed.

Is there an outer limit to tourism in the distance-of-trip continuum? Are there culturally determined distances, travel beyond which stops being tourism and becomes something else? It seems that in pre-modern Europe the geographical limits of the area fit for tourism as travelling for pleasure were fairly narrow; and even until recently travel in remote and unknown areas of the world, such as inner Asia and Africa, the Himalayas, Greenland or Antarctica would not have been "tourism," since it was dangerous and uncomfortable — and hence scarcely pleasurable; rather, it was "adventure" or — if it had a serious purpose — "exploration."

Almost all such "distant" areas have by now been sufficiently penetrated to make them accessible to the modern tourist. Indeed, tourism nowadays reaches into the most remote areas of the Earth. Tourism to the less accessible regions of such distant areas often takes the form of what could be termed "touristic exploration": tourist trips are organized like expeditions and the participants often play an intermediary role between the tourist and the explorer (Banks 1972).

In a broad sense virtually every place on earth is at present a potential locale for tourism. The outer limits of tourism have moved to what is beyond the Earth — space and other planets. It is interesting to follow the process by which these too will eventually be "opened up" for tourism — like, for example, the "rush to the moon."[21]

We can conclude, then, that for each culture or historical period there is a range of distances characteristic of touristic travel; travel below and even beyond these distances merges with other types of traveller roles.

(5) *Recurrency*. The tourist is typically on a non-recurrent trip. It is important to point out, however, that the tourist trip has to be non- recurrent, and hence novel, only for the traveller; the fact that many tourist trips are often highly routinized and that virtually millions of tourists tread yearly the same paths is irrelevant in this context. Indeed, the tourist establishment is especially adept at presenting highly routinized trips as offering a "unique experience" to the traveller.

One cannot tell with precision how many times a person has to take a route or visit a place for his trip to become devoid of a "touristic component." We can hence define a few borderline cases, types of travellers whose trips are tangential to the fully-fledged tourist role:

The *habitué* is the vacationer who returns regularly for his holidays to the same region, location or even the same hotel. Though his recurrent trips are spaced out enough in time to preserve an element of change if not of novelty, the "touristic component" of the habitué's trip is reduced with the regularity and frequency of his visits.

The *summer-house owner* possesses a second home at some distance from his regular abode, where he and particularly his family spend prolonged yearly vacations and which they might also frequent for shorter periods during the rest of the year. Since recurrency of visits here is fairly high, the "touristic component" of the visits is relatively small. This is a type of marginal tourist, intermediate between fully-fledged tourism and residence.

The *week-end house owner* possesses a second home near enough to his regular abode for it to be accessible during week-ends. Visits are very frequent so that their "touristic component" is much reduced; this is at most a case of minimal tourism.[22]

(6) *Purpose of Trip.* We have characterized tourism as being travelling for non-instrumental purposes and, specifically, with the expectation of pleasure in the experience of novelty and change. One might argue that this leads to an essentially psychological and hence subjectivistic definition of tourism, which is largely irrelevant for sociological purposes. A person going on a trip out of a desire for social prestige accruing from it will behave like a tourist though he might not derive pleasure from it. It is hence important to point out that it is primarily the socially defined, institutionalized expectation of pleasure — and the role-behaviour correlative to such an expectation — which is of relevance here and not the actual psychological gratification. Thus a person who travels for prestige or is dragged along by his family without actually enjoying his trip will still be a tourist, insofar as his trip is socially defined as pleasurable.

There exists a wide variety of possible kinds of pleasure, even within the realm of the experience of novelty and change, which the tourist can derive from his trip, starting with the absolute passivity of broiling in the sun on a beach and up to the physical exertions of a cross-continental trekking tour. Though tourist promoters and agents are much concerned with the various types of tourist activities and forecast that in the future tourist localities will be catalogued by their suitability for various types of needs and activities rather than by their locations, I am unaware of a systematic sociological typology of tourist activities beyond that distinguishing sightseers from vacationers, to be discussed below.

Though tourism is by no means a novel phenomenon, travelling for pleasure, pure and simple, was not considered in the past a fully legitimate reason for travel, and even today ". . . the suspicion still endures that travel for its own sake is an idle pleasure" (Lowenthal 1962:124). Other, more legitimate, purposes were sought to rationalize a trip, or combined with the seeking of pleasure in order to justify it, like the search for health, education or culture.

Though in our days travel for pleasure in novelty and change is fully legitimate and dominates the tourist scene, there also exist many forms of partial tourism, in which travelling for novelty and change is combined in varying degrees and forms with other non-instrumental or even instrumental purposes. Several of these roles were in fact listed in the broad definition of the "international tourist" by the U.N. Conference on International Travel and Tourism in 1963, quoted above.

The study of the touristic aspect of these roles is a much neglected subject in the sociology of tourism. I am unable yet to present a systematically organized classification of such roles or to specify their precise touristic component. For the present purposes it will suffice to list several types of such partial tourist roles:

(a) *thermalists*: a term used by Lowenthal to indicate people who "take the waters" at the spas, Bäder, etc., chiefly in Britain and Central Europe. This form of travelling had been most popular at a period preceding the institutionalization of modern tourism as a fully legitimate enterprise; it flourished chiefly between the seventeenth and nineteenth centuries. Though the restoration of health served as the major justification of the trip, Lowenthal argues that "localities with hot springs became first health, and then pleasure, resorts. The healthy soon outnumbered the sick . . ." (Lowenthal 1962:124).[23] This form of partial tourism has declined during the twentieth century, though it still enjoys some adherents, mostly among elderly people in Europe.

(b) *students*: education, edification, broadening of personality and the attainment of "culture" were among the most important purposes of early tourism, particularly of the classical "Grand Tour" (Lambert (ed.) 1935; Trease 1967). In modern times, study-trips and more extensive studies abroad became one of the most widespread forms of partial tourism. The conflict between study and tourism seems to be particularly severe with short-time students abroad, who often use their study grants as an opportunity for travel; but the subject has not as yet been systematically investigated from the touristic angle, though there exist innumerable studies of students abroad.

(c) *pilgrims*: another highly interesting group of part-time tourists are pilgrims; indeed, pilgrimages are one of the most important historical antecedents of modern tourism (Sigaux 1966). In modern times the number of pilgrims, though diminished in relation to fully-fledged tourists, has expanded considerably in absolute numbers; a form of "religious tourism," combining elements of pilgrimage with those of ordinary tourism, has developed, so that one authority states that many modern pilgrims ". . . should perhaps be considered as tourists rather than pilgrims per se" (Turner 1973:196).

(d) *old-country visitors*: a peculiar type of partial tourism are trips of emigrants or of their progeny to their old country (Angell 1967); for example, Italians or Irish from the U.S. visiting respectively Italy and Ireland, American Blacks visiting Africa and ex-Corsicans vacationing in their mother island. For the generation of emigrants such trips serve primarily as reunions with kinfolk and friends, though they might also possess a touristic component, in that the returnee explores the changes which have taken place in his old home since his departure or enjoys anew the forgotten pleasures of his youth. When members of second and later generations of emigrants visit the old country of their parents, the touristic component of the trip will be considerably more pronounced.

(e) *conventioneers*: national and international conventions are rapidly becoming one of the more important forms of modern travelling and many cities and resorts have become, or are making major efforts to become, modern "convention centers." A trip to a convention is not, in itself, tourism. But one of the major purposes of the traveller is often to engage in tourism as part of the programme of the convention (e.g. organized sight-seeing), in his free time, or at the expense of attendance at meetings. He can hence be studied as a particular type of partial tourist.

(f) *business-travellers*: business travellers are perhaps the most important group of partial tourists (Angell 1967:112–115; Wilkins 1966). Though the primary, or at least ostensible, purpose of their trip is an instrumental one, many businessmen succeed in combining business-with-pleasure and devote at least part of their free time on the trip to touristic pursuits. The study of business-travellers as tourists, and particularly the comparison of these with conventioneers and pilgrims, should be a fruitful area of study.

(g) *tourist-employees*: this type, first systematically described by Pape under the term "touristry," refers primarily to young professionals who engage in ". . . a form of journeying that depends upon occupation but only in a secondary sense in that it finances the more primary goal, travel itself" (Pape 1965:334). Though engaged in their professions and working for relatively long periods of time with one employer (unlike the drifters, who take up different kinds of occasional employment), these people view their work as a means to "see the world," and not as a basis for an occupational career. Pape cites nursing as one of the occupations which facilitate "touristry," but doctors, younger academic staff and other professionals, particularly at the early stages of their careers, also represent this type of partial tourist. There are also some occupations or types of employment — like air-stewardesses, soldiering and employment in foreign technical assistance — in which the opportunity to engage in "touristry" may provide one of the more important job-inducements.

A marginal example of "touristry" are people on working holidays, such as *au pair* girls, young urbanites working on farms for a summer, or foreign volunteers like those working on an Israeli kibbutz.[24] Such people engage in "touristry" for shorter periods than the professionals or employees mentioned above and do not necessarily work in their occupation;

they are hence an intermediate type between the tourist-employee and the drifter.

(h) *official sightseers*: a type of partial tourist emerged after the Second World War: the person travelling ostensibly on official business, usually of a diplomatic or political nature, but often devoting a major part of his trip to sightseeing, during official or unofficial tours of the country he visits. Many of these official sightseers travel in the opposite direction to the principal tourist flow: namely, from new, developing countries to the developed ones. Though the main purpose of such sightseeing may be defined as educational, it often includes a distinct touristic component.

Sightseers and Vacationers

In the preceding discussion we have shown that tourism is in fact an aspect of a variety of travelling roles, only some of which may be labelled "fully-fledged tourism." Even this category, however, is not a homogeneous one, and can be further analyzed into a variety of more detailed typologies. I have already proposed a sociological typology to tourist roles, based on the extent to which tourists tend to immerse themselves in the novelty and change offered by the host society (Chapter 3). In the present context another typological distinction, namely between "sightseers" and "vacationers," is of more direct relevance. It should be emphasized that these are ideal types, and that actual tourists often combine in varying degrees the characteristics of both types.

Throughout this chapter it has been argued that the essential element in tourism is the pursuit of "novelty and change." These two terms have been used so far indiscriminately, though there is a slight but important difference in their meaning. A novelty is, in principle, new only when one sees or experiences it for the first time. Change, however, does not imply complete novelty: one can experience the transition from office work in the city to leisure on the beach as a welcome change, even though it is one's accustomed way of holiday-making. The primary analytical difference between these two types of tourists is, hence, that sightseers seek novelty, while vacationers merely seek change, whether or not this brings novelty in its train. Sightseeing trips are hence ordinarily non-recurrent, while vacation trips tend to recurrency, as exemplified by the habitué.

There is an important practical implication to this distinction. Using the development of tourism in Israel as an example, we find that tourists tend to be primarily sightseers only on their first visit to the country. On further visits, they tend to become vacationers — to seek out some resort or other leisure facility for holiday-making.

The difference in touristic emphasis also leads to differences in the travelling patterns of sightseers vs. vacationers. Sightseers are "tourists" in the more literal sense of the term, of people "making a tour," in that their trip is typically multi-destinational: they tend to visit a variety of places — countries, regions or localities — on a single trip. The vacationer is typically on a uni-destinational trip, he goes to his resort and returns home from there. Obviously, a person may combine sightseeing and vacationing on a single trip, staying for vacations at one locality, but engaging from there in sightseeing tours; or he may embark on a combined sightseeing-vacationing tour, as in "island-hopping" which is fashionable in the Caribbean (Sargent 1967:69) of in the Pacific.

It follows from the difference in travelling patterns that the emphasis in sightseeing is more on the movement and less on the sojourn, while the opposite is true of vacationing. One can hence hypothesize that with the sightseer, the "traveller" component, in the narrow sense, of the tourist role, becomes more strongly emphasized; while with the vacationer, the "visitor" component becomes dominant.

It is commonly accepted that the development of tourism depends on the attractions, facilities and amenities for tourism which a locality or a country have to offer. An interesting difference in the relative emphasis of sightseeing vs. vacationing tourism should however be noted: the sightseer travels primarily to visit "attractions" — unique features of a country or a locality, which differentiate it from others, and the sight or experience of which gratifies the visitor, such as old towns, archeological sites, natural sights, artistic treasures, etc. The vacationer is more oriented towards facilities and amenities such as good accommodation and food, pleasant beaches, sun,[25] mountain air, opportunities for sports and amusement. One should not conclude from this that the sightseeing tourist is primarily an activist, exerting himself in the search for attractions, while the vacationer tends to linger passively around. True, there was a time, particularly after the Second World War, when vacations were seen as primarily a period of rest and complete loafing; but more recently, as work in affluent countries became less exerting and more monotonous, there was a rising demand for "active vacations," the provision of opportunites for activities and for the pursuit of interests which compensate for the drabness and constrictions of daily life. On the other hand, sightseeing sometimes becomes a completely passive affair, as, for example, when organized mass tourists are shuffled around in air-conditioned buses from one attraction to the other.

Facilities and amenities are, almost by definition, less specialized than attractions: there is less difference between the beaches of the Mediterranean and the Pacific than between their respective cultural attractions or natural sights. According to the principle of intervening opportunities one should therefore expect that vacationers would generally travel to less distant destinations than sightseers. There is some empirical evidence for this hypothesis; Burton, for example, "... found that, in the main people tended to take their holidays within the same general region of the country as their home residences" (Mercer 1970; summarizing Burton 1965).

The roles of sightseers and vacationers differ on several of the dimensions by which we characterized the tourist role; but though the sightseer tends to come closer to the ideal type of the tourist, both should, to my mind, be considered fully-fledged tourist roles. The various partial tourist roles discussed above tend to approximate to one or the other of these roles.

Conclusion

Tourism is a fuzzy concept — the boundaries between the universe of tourist and non-tourist roles are vague and there exist many intermediate categories. Such fuzziness has caused considerable conceptual confusion and empirical distortion in the past. The common-sensical and often ambiguous definitions of the tourist role led researchers and writers to deal only with the central touristic phenomenon — the fully-fledged tourist, and even within this category they often restricted themselves to the modern mass tourist — while they disregarded the wide periphery of partial tourist roles. As a correlate of such an approach, tourism has been treated as a separate field of sociological inquiry unrelated to the broader realm of the sociology of travelling and migration. Accepting Bellman and Zadeh's (1970) dictum that fuzzy phenomena can be precisely defined, we set out to isolate several dimensions characteristic of the phenomenon of tourism; we arranged these into a "conceptual tree" (Figure 2.1), ranging from the more general characteristics to those more specific to the tourist role; thereby a cumulative definition of tourism was derived. This definition is taxonomically systematic in that the same dimensions — when given different values — can be used to define other traveller roles; other "branches" of the conceptual "tree" in the diagram would have to be developed for this purpose. A "conceptual space" for a future sociology of travelling has thereby been proposed. The utility of this conceptual space will be tested when other travellers' roles, such as wanderers or pilgrims, are subjected to a similar conceptual analysis.

The problem of fuzziness has not been resolved by our cumulative definition. To resolve this problem we looked upon each definitional dimension as a continuum, along which varying values characteristic of the fully-fledged, marginal and minimal tourist-roles were distinguished. Such roles were, wherever possible, specified in concrete terms. Thereby the fuzzy boundaries of the concept of tourism were mapped out by ascribing different grades of membership in the set of "tourist" to a variety of intermediary roles. Further refinement in research methods could lead to a transition from the still approximate qualitative terms used here (marginal, minimal) to quantitative terms defining the precise grade of membership of a given type of traveller in the set "tourist."

The introduction of the concept of fuzziness further facilitates the clarification of the conceptual relationships between the variety of traveller roles which we initiated, by the introduction of the "conceptual tree" in Figure 2.1. Since the other traveller concepts, like pilgrim or business traveller, are also fuzzy, one could represent the whole gamut of traveller roles in a multi-dimensional space in which each role would be represented by a well-bound region, representing the fully-fledged role-bearers (those with membership grade 1 in the fuzzy set of that role) and a peripheral region, representing the marginal role-bearers (those whose membership grade varies between 1 and 0). Figure 2.2 exemplifies this conceptual space in a simplified, two-dimensional form.

The marginal areas of the various traveller roles will sometimes intersect, since the different marginal roles may pertain to more than one fully-fledged role (e.g. the tourist-pilgrim will pertain to the marginal area of both, the fully-fledged "tourist" role and the fully-fledged "pilgrim" role). The overlap may occur only along a single dimension or along several dimensions.

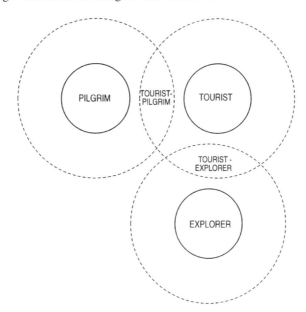

Figure 2.2: A Simplified Conceptual Space for Travellers' Roles

It is recognized that the conceptual effort undertaken in this chapter is but a preliminary step to a more substantive sociological study of tourism and, indeed, of travelling in general. But it is an essential step, since without a clear concept of the subject of our study, we cannot but reach distorted substantive conclusions.

Acknowledgment—This chapter was prepared while I was a Visiting Senior Lecturer in the Department of Sociology, University of Singapore in 1992–1993. Thanks are due to Prof. H. D. Evers, Dr. M. Walters, Dr. P. Weldon, and Mrs. Wong Saik Chin for their useful comments.

Chapter 3

Toward a Sociology of International Tourism

Introduction

In recent decades, there has been an enormous rise in both the number of people traveling for pleasure and the number of countries and places visited regularly by tourists. Sociologists, however, have long neglected the study of tourism as a social phenomenon (but see Boorstin 1962:77–117; Knebel 1960; Waters 1966). Here I should like to propose a general theoretical approach to the phenomenon of international tourism, one which includes a typology of tourists on the basis of their relationship to both the tourist business establishment and the host country.

Varieties of Tourist Roles

> After seeing the jewels at Topkapi, the fabled Blue Mosque and bazaars, it is awfully nice to come home to the Istanbul Hilton.
> (Advertisement in Time magazine)

Tourism is so widespread and accepted today, particularly in the Western world, that we tend to take it for granted. Traveling for pleasure in a foreign country by large numbers of people is a relatively modern occurrence, however, dating only from the early nineteenth century.

It seems that tourism as a cultural phenomenon evolves as a result of a very basic change in man's attitude to the world beyond the boundaries of his native habitat. So long as man remains largely ignorant of the existence of other societies and other cultures, he regards his own small world as the cosmos. What lies outside is mysterious and unknown and therefore dangerous and threatening. It can only inspire fear or, at best, indifference, lacking as it does any reality for him.

A tremendous distance lies between such an orientation and that characteristic of modern man. Whereas primitive and traditional man will leave his native habitat only when forced to by circumstances, modern man is more loosely attached to his environment, much more willing to change it, especially temporarily, and is remarkably able to adapt to new environments. He is interested in things, sights, customs, and cultures different from his own, precisely *because* they are different. Gradually, a new value has evolved: the appreciation of the experience of strangeness and novelty. This experience now excites, titillates, and gratifies, whereas before it only frightened. I believe that tourism as a cultural phenomenon becomes possible only when man develops a *generalized* interest in things beyond his particular habitat, when contact with and appreciation and enjoyment of strangeness and novelty are valued for their *own sake*. In this sense, tourism is a thoroughly modem phenomenon.

Though novelty and strangeness are essential elements in the tourist experience, not even modern man is completely ready to immerse himself wholly in an alien environment. When the experience becomes too strange he may shrink back. For man is still basically molded by his native culture and bound through habit to its patterns of behavior. Hence, complete abandonment of these customs and complete immersion in a new and alien environment may be experienced as unpleasant and even threatening, especially if prolonged. Most tourists seem to need some thing familiar around them, something to remind them of home, whether it be food, newspapers, living quarters, or another person from their native country. Many of today's tourists are able to enjoy the experience of change and novelty only from a strong base of familiarity, which enables them to feel secure enough to enjoy the strangeness of what they experience. They would like to experience the novelty of the macro-environment of a strange place from the security of a familiar micro-environment. And many will not venture abroad but on those well-trodden paths equipped with familiar means of transportation, hotels, and food. Often the modern tourist is not so much abandoning his accustomed environment for a new one as he is being transposed to foreign soil in an "environmental bubble" of his native culture. To a certain extent he views the people, places, and culture of that society through the protective walls of his familiar "environmental bubble," within which he functions and interacts in much the same way as he does in his own habitat.[26]

The experience of tourism combines, then, a degree of novelty with a degree of familiarity, the security of old habits with the excitement of change.[27] However, the exact extent to which familiarity and novelty are experienced on any particular tour depends upon the individual tastes and preferences of the tourist as well as upon the institutional setting of his trip. There is a continuum of possible combinations of novelty and familiarity. This continuum is, to my mind, the basic underlying variable for the sociological analysis of the phenomenon of modern tourism. The division of the continuum into a number of typical combinations of novelty and familiarity leads to a typology of tourist roles. I will propose here a typology of four tourist roles.

The organized mass tourist. The organized mass tourist is the least adventurous kind of tourist and remains largely confined to his "environmental bubble" throughout his trip. The guided tour, conducted in an air-conditioned bus, traveling at high speed through a steaming countryside, represents the prototype of organized mass tourism. This tourist type buys a package-tour as if it were just another commodity in the modern mass market. The itinerary of his trip is fixed in advance, and all his stops are well-prepared and guided; he makes almost no decisions for himself and stays almost exclusively in the micro-environment of his home country. Familiarity is at a maximum, novelty at a minimum.

The individual mass tourist. This type of tourist role is similar to the previous one, except that the tour is not entirely preplanned; the tourist has a certain amount of control over his time and itinerary and is not bound to a group. However, all of his major arrangements are still made through a tourist agency. His excursions do not bring him much further afield than do those of the organized mass tourist. He, too, does his experiencing from within the "environmental bubble" of his home country and ventures out of it only occasionally — and even then only into well-charted territory. Familiarity is still dominant, but somewhat less so than in the preceding type; the experience of novelty is somewhat greater, though it is often of the routine kind.

The explorer. This type of tourist arranges his trip alone; he tries to get off the beaten track as much as possible, but he nevertheless looks for comfortable accommodations and reliable means of transportation. He tries to associate with the people he visits and to speak their language. The explorer dares to leave his "environmental bubble" much mote than the previous two types, but he is still careful to be able to step back into it when the going becomes too rough. Though novelty dominates, the tourist does not immerse himself completely in his host society, but retains some of the basic routines and comforts of his native way of life.

The drifter. This type of tourist ventures furthest away from the beaten track and from the accustomed ways of life of his home country. He shuns any kind of connection with the tourist establishment, and considers the ordinary tourist experience phony. He tends to make it wholly on his own, living with the people and often taking odd jobs to keep himself going. He tries to live the way the people he visits live, and to share their shelter, foods, and habits, keeping only the most basic and essential of his old customs. The drifter has no fixed itinerary or timetable and no well-defined goals of travel. He is almost wholly immersed in his host culture. Novelty is here at its highest, familiarity disappears almost completely.

The first two tourist types I will call institutionalized tourist roles; they are dealt with in a routine way by the tourist establishment — the complex of travel agencies, travel companies, hotel chains, etc., which cater to the tourist trade. The last two types I will call non-institutionalized tourist roles, in that they are open roles, at best only very loosely attached to the tourist establishment.

The Institutionalized Forms of Tourism: The Organized and the Individual Mass Tourist

> 'Where were you last summer?'
> 'In Majorca.'
> 'Where is that?'
> 'I don't know, I flew there.'
>   (Conversation between two girls, reprinted in a German journal)

Contemporary institutionalized tourism is a mass industry. The tour is sold as a package, standardized and mass-produced. All transportation, places to be visited, sleeping and eating accommodations are fixed in advance. The tourist establishment takes complete care of the tourist from beginning to end. Still, the package tour sold by the tourist establishment purportedly offers the buyer the experience of novelty and strangeness. The problem of the system, then, is to enable the mass tourist to "take in" the novelty of the host country without experiencing any physical discomfort or, more accurately, to observe without actually experiencing.

Since the tourist industry serves large numbers of people, these have to be processed as efficiently, smoothly, and quickly as possible through all the phases of their tour. Hence, it is imperative that the experience of the tourist, however novel it might seem to him, be as ordered, predictable, and controllable as possible. In short, he has to be given the illusion of adventure, while all the risks and uncertainties of adventure are taken out of his tour. In this respect, the quality of the mass tourist's experiences approaches that of vicarious participation in other people's lives, similar to the reading of fiction or the viewing of motion pictures. The tourist establishment achieves this effect through two interrelated mechanisms that I will call the transformation of attractions and the standardization of facilities.

Every country, region, or locality has something which sets it apart from all others, something for which it is known and worth visiting: scenic beauty, architecture, feasts or festivals, works of art, etc. In German there is a very appropriate term for these features, *Sehenswürdigkeiten*, or "things worth seeing," and I will call them "attractions." Some attractions are of world renown, and become the trademark of a place; these attract tourists naturally. In other cases, they are created artificially — they are contrived "tourist attractions."

The main purpose of mass tourism is the visiting of attractions, whether genuine or contrived. However, even if they are genuine, the tendency is to transform or manipulate them, to make them "suitable" for mass tourist consumption. They are supplied with facilities, reconstructed, landscaped, cleansed of unsuitable elements, staged, managed, and otherwise organized. As a result, they largely lose their original flavor and appearance and become isolated from the ordinary flow of life and natural texture of the host society. Hawaiian dancing girls have to be dressed for public decency — but not too much, so that they remain attractive; natural sights have to be groomed and guarded until they look like well-kept parks; traditional festivals have to be made more colorful and more respectable so tourists will be attracted but not offended. Festivals and ceremonies, in particular, cease being spontaneous expressions of popular feelings and become well-staged spectacles.[28] Even still-inhabited old quarters of otherwise modern cities are often turned into "living museums" to attract tourists.

While the transformation of attractions provides controlled novelty for the mass tourist, the standardization of facilities serves to provide him with the necessary familiarity in his immediate surroundings. The majority of tourists originate today from the affluent Western countries, the U.S. and Western Europe, and increasingly from Japan. Hence, whatever country aspires to attract mass tourism is forced to provide facilities on a level commensurate with the expectations of the tourists from those countries. A tourist infrastructure of facilities based on Western standards has to be created even in the poorest host countries. This tourist infrastructure provides the mass tourist with the protective "ecological bubble" of his accustomed environment. However, since the tourist also expects some local flavor or signs of foreignness in his environment, there are local decorations in his hotel room, local foods in the restaurants, local products in the tourist shops. Still, even these are often standardized: the decorations are made to resemble the standard image of that culture's art, the local foods are made more palatable to unaccustomed tongues, the selection of native crafts is determined by the demands of the tourist.[29]

The transformation of attractions and the standardization of facilities, made necessary by the difficulties of managing and satisfying large numbers of tourists, have introduced a basic uniformity or similarity into the tourist experience. Whole countries lose their individuality to the mass tourist as the richness of their culture and geography is reduced by the tourist industry to a few standard elements, according to which they are classified and presented to the mass tourist. Before he even begins his tour, he is conditioned to pay attention primarily to the few basic attractions and facilities advertised in the travel literature or suggested by the travel agent, which are catalogued and sometimes even assigned a level of importance. This induces a peculiar kind of selective awareness: the tourist tends to become aware of his environment only when he reaches spots of "interest," while he is largely oblivious to it the rest of the time.[30] As a result, countries become interchangeable in the tourist's mind. Whether he is looking for good beaches, restful forests, or old cities, it becomes relatively unimportant to him where these happen to be found. Transportation by air, which brings him almost directly to his destination without his having to pass through other parts of the host country, contributes to the isolation of the attractions and facilities from the rest of the country — as well as the isolation of the tourist. And so mass tourism has created the following paradox: though the desire for variety, novelty and strangeness are the primary motives of tourism, these qualities have decreased as tourism has become institutionalized.

In popular tourist countries, the tourist system or infrastructure has become separated from the rest of the culture and the natural flow of life. Attractions and facilities which were previously frequented by the local population are gradually abandoned. As Greenwich Village became a tourist attraction, many of the original bohemians moved to the East Village. Even sites of high symbolic value for the host society may suffer a similar fate: houses of government, churches and national monuments become more and more the preserve of the mass tourist and are less and less frequented by the native citizens.

The ecological differentiation of the tourist sphere from the rest of the country makes for social separation; the mass tourist travels in a world of his own, surrounded by, but not integrated in, the host society. He meets the representatives of the tourist establishment — hotel managers, tourist agents, guides — but only seldom the natives. For the natives, in turn, the mass tourist is anonymous. Neither has much of an opportunity to become an individual to the other.

A development complementary to the ecological differentiation of the tourist sphere is the gradual emergence of an international tourist system, reaching across political and cultural boundaries. The system enjoys a certain independence and even isolation from its immediate surroundings, and an internal homogeneity in spite of the wide variations between the countries with which it intersects. The autonomy and isolation could be most clearly seen in those cases where tourists enjoy some special facilities that are out of bounds to the members of the host society, such as spas and nightclubs in communist Eastern European countries which have served exclusively foreigners, or the Berioshka (dollar shops) in the Soviet Union, which catered only to tourists.

The isolation of the mass tourist from the host society is further intensified by a general communication gap. Tourist publications and travel literature are ordinarily written in the spirit of the tourist establishment — and often not by a native of the country — whose prime motive is selling, not merely informing. Such literature colors the tourist's attitudes and expectations beforehand. But probably more responsible than any other single factor mentioned thus far in creating and maintaining the isolation of the tourist is the fact that he seldom knows the language of the country he is traveling in. Not knowing the language makes forming acquaintances with natives and traveling about on one's own so difficult that few tourists attempt it to any extent. Even worse, it may leave the tourist without any real feel for the culture or people of the country.

The sad irony of modern institutionalized tourism is that, instead of destroying myths between countries, it perpetrates them. The tourist comes home with the illusion that he has "been" there and can speak with some authority about the country that he has visited. I would hypothesize that the larger the flow of mass tourists becomes, the more institutionalized and standardized tourism becomes and consequently the stronger the barriers between the tourist and the life of the host country tend to become. What were previously formal barriers between different countries become informal borders within countries.

The Noninstitutionalized Forms of Tourism: The Explorer and the Drifter

Boorstin's (1962:116–117) vivid description of the evolution of the aristocratic traveler of yesterday into the tourist of modern times oversimplifies the issue to make a point. For Boorstin, there exists either the mass tourist or the adventurer, who contrives crazy feats and fabricates risks in order to experience excitement. Even Knebel's (1960) less tendentious analysis postulates little variety in the role structure of the contemporary tourist. Both writers seem to have overlooked the noninstitutionalized tourist roles of explorer and drifter.

While the roles of both the explorer and the drifter are non-institutionalized, they differ from each other chiefly in the extent to which they venture out of their micro-environment and away from the tourist system, and in their attitudes toward the people and countries they visit.

The explorer tries to avoid the mass tourist routes and the traditional tourist attractions, but he nevertheless looks for comfortable accommodations and reliable means of transportation. He ventures into areas relatively unknown to the mass tourist and explores them for his own pleasure. The explorer's experience of the host country, its people, places, and culture, is unquestionably much broader and deeper than that of the mass tourist. He tries to associate with the people he visits and to speak their language, but he still does not wholly immerse himself in the host society. He remains somewhat detached, either viewing his surroundings from an aesthetic perspective or seeking to understand the people on an intellectual level. He does not identify with the natives emotionally or try to become one of them during his stay.

Through his mode of travel, the explorer escapes the isolation and artificiality the tourist system imposes on the mass tourist. Paradoxically, though, in his very attempts at escape he serves as a spearhead of mass tourism; as he discovers new places of interest, he opens the way for more commercialized forms of tourism, the managers of which are always on the lookout for new and unusual attractions. His experiences and opinions serve as indicators to other, less adventurous tourists to move into the area. As more and more of these move in, the tourist establishment gradually takes over. Thus, partly through the unwitting help of the explorer, the scope of the system expands.

As the tourist system expands fewer and fewer areas are left that have mass tourist potential in terms of the traditional kinds of attractions. In recent times, however, the ability of an area to offer a degree of privacy and solitude has, in itself, become a commodity of high value. Indeed, much of the mass tourist business today seems to be oriented to the provision of privacy per se. Obviously, mass tourism here reaches a point at which success is self-defeating.

While the explorer is the contemporary counterpart of the traveler of former years, the drifter is more like the wanderer of previous times. The correspondence is not complete, though. In his attitude toward and mode of traveling, the drifter is a genuine modern phenomenon. He is often a child of affluence, who reacts against it. He is young, often a student or a graduate, who has not yet started to work. He prolongs his moratorium by moving around the world in search of new experiences, radically different from those he has been accustomed to in his sheltered middle-class existence. After he has savored these experiences for a time he usually settles down to an orderly middle-class career.

The drifter seeks the excitement of complete strangeness and direct contact with new and different people. He looks for experiences, happenings, and kicks. His mode of travel is adopted to this purpose. In order to preserve the freshness and spontaneity of his experience, the drifter purposely travels without either itinerary or timetable, without a destination or even well-defined purpose. He often possesses only limited means for traveling, but even when this is not true, he is usually concerned with making his money last as long as possible so as to prolong his travels. Since he is also typically unconcerned with bodily comfort and desires to live as simply as possible while traveling, he will travel, eat, and sleep in the most inexpensive way possible. He moves about on bicycle or motorcycle or hitchhikes rides in autos, private planes, freighters, and fishing boats, he shares rooms with fellow travelers he has met along the way or stays with a native of the area who has befriended him. When necessary, and often when not, he will sleep outdoors. And he will cook his own meals outdoors or buy food on the street more often than eat in a restaurant. If in spite of such frugality, his money runs out before his desire to travel does, he will work at almost any odd-job be can get until he has enough to move on.

The particular way of life and travel of the drifter brings him into contact with a wide variety of people; these usually belong to the lower social groups in the host society. Often the drifter associates with kindred souls in the host society. In my study of a mixed Jewish-Arab town in Israel, I encountered a great deal of association between drifters and local Arab boys who also wanted to travel (Chapter 15).

An international subculture of drifters seems to be developing. In some places drifters congregated and created an ecological niche of their own. On the shore of the Red Sea in Eilat, Israel's southernmost port, there was a "permanently temporary" colony of squatters locally called "beatniks," who drifted there from many parts of the world. Similarly, the National Monument on the Dam, in the very center of Amsterdam, served as a mass meeting place for young people who flocked there from all over Europe and the United States.

The drifter discards almost completely the familiar environment of his home country and immerses himself in the life of the host society. Moreover, as explained above, the drifter differs significantly from the explorer in the manner in which he relates to the host society. The drifter is, then, the true rebel of the tourist establishment and the complete opposite of the mass tourist.

Discussion

So far I have formulated a general approach to the sociology of tourism based on a typology of tourist roles. Here I will develop some implications of this approach and propose several problems for further research.

The fundamental variable that forms the basis for the fourfold typology of tourist roles proposed here is strangeness vs. familiarity. Each of the four tourist roles discussed represents a characteristic form of tourist behavior and a typical position on the strangeness/familiarity continuum. The degree to which strangeness or familiarity prevail in the tourist role determines the nature of the tourist's experiences as well as the effect he has on the host society.

Initially, all tourists are strangers in the host society. The degree and the way they to which affect each other depends largely on the *extent* and *variety* of social contacts they have during their trip. The social contacts of the mass tourist, particularly of the organized mass tourist, are extremely limited. The individual mass tourist, being somewhat more independent, makes occasional social contacts, but his conventional mode of travel tends to restrict them to the close periphery of the tourist establishment, thus limiting their number and their nature. The social contacts of the explorer are broader and more varied, while those of the drifter are the most intensive in quality and the most extensive in quantity.

The extent to which the tourist role is predefined and the social expectations of it spelled out determines to a large degree the manner in which tourists interact with members of the host society, as well as the images they develop of one another. The mass tourist generally does not interact at all, but merely observes, and even that from within his own micro-environment. The explorer mixes but does not become involved. The drifter, however, often becomes both physically and emotionally involved in the lives of members of the host society. Here the length of time spent in one place is as important a determinant of social involvement as attitude. The drifter, unlike the mass tourist, does not set a limit beforehand on the length of time he will spend in any one place; if he finds an area that particularly pleases him, he may stop there long enough for social involvement to occur.

Tourism has some important aggregate effects on the host society, in terms of its impact on the division of labor and on the ecology or the land-use patterns of that society. As he tourist role becomes institutionalized, a whole set of other roles and institutions develop in the host country to cater to his needs — what I have called the tourist establishment. This development gradually introduces a new dimension into the ecology of the host society, as attractions and facilities are created, improved, and set aside for tourist use. This primary impact of tourism has important secondary and tertiary consequences. Predominantly agricultural regions may become primarily tourist areas, as agriculture is driven out by tourist facilities, and the local people turn to tourist services for their living. The "tourist villages" in the Austrian Alps are an example. Conversely, stagnant agricultural areas may receive a boost from increased demand for agricultural products in nearby tourist regions, such as the agricultural boom that has occurred in the hinterland of the Spanish Costa Brava. Without doubt, the impact of large-scale tourism on the culture, style of life, and world-view of inhabitants of tourist regions is enormous.

The explorer and the drifter do not affect the general division of labor in the host society to the same degree as the mass tourist does, and consequently do not have the same aggregate impact on that society. Their effect on the host society is more subtle, but sometimes considerable, as I found in my own study of the impact of drifting tourist girls on Arab boys in a mixed Jewish-Arab city (Chapter 15).

I have dealt here with the role of the explorer in the dynamics of growth of the tourist system, but other mechanisms are undoubtedly at work, such as the planned creation of new attractions to foster mass tourism, like the building of Disneylands. It might be worthwhile to differentiate between the organic and the induced growth of the tourist system and look into the differential effect of the two modes of expansion on the workings of the tourist system and the host society.

Conclusion

Growing interaction and interpenetration between hitherto relatively independent social systems is one of the most salient characteristics of the contemporary world. In K. Deutsch's phrase, the world is rapidly becoming a "global village." No far-off island or obscure primitive tribe manages to preserve its isolation. Tourism is both a consequence of this process of interpenetration and one of several mechanisms through which this process is being realized. Its relative contribution to the process — in comparison to that of the major transforming forces of our time — has been increasing rapidly.

It is interesting to speculate in conclusion about some of the broader sociological consequences of the increase in the scope of tourism for the society of the future. The picture which emerges is complex. On the one hand, as the number of mass tourists grows, the tourist industry will become more and more mechanized and standardized. This, in turn, will tend to make the interaction between tourist and host ever more routinized. The effect of the host country on the mass tourists will therefore remain limited, whereas his effect on the ecology, division of labor, and wealth of the country will grow as the numbers of tourists increases. On the other hand, as host societies become permeated by a wide variety of individually traveling tourists belonging to different classes and ways of life, increased and more varied social contacts will take place, with mixed results for international understanding.

Like-minded persons of different countries will find it easier to communicate with each other and some kind of new international social groupings might appear. Among the very rich such groups existed for a long time; the fashionable contemporary prototype is the international "jet-set." Recently drifter communities have emerged in many parts of the world, comprised of an entirely different kind of social category. The effect of such developments may well be to diminish the significance of national boundaries, though they may also create new and sometimes serious divisions within the countries in which such international groups congregate. Some indication of the emergence of new foci of conflict can be seen in the riots between drifters and sea-men in Amsterdam, the hub of the European "drifter community."

Acknowledgment—This chapter was written while I was a visiting scholar at the Institute of Urban Environment, Columbia University, New York. Thanks are due to the Institute as well as to R. Bar-Yosef, Elihu Katz, and M. Shokeid, for their useful comments.

Chapter 4

Nomads from Affluence: Notes on the Phenomenon of Drifter-Tourism

Introduction

In the growing literature on international tourism, attention focuses primarily on the ordinary mass-tourist, whose sterotyped image and behavior-patterns tend to dominate the thinking of contemporary entrepreneurs, planners and critics of tourism. To redress this imbalance, I have in the preceding chapter (Chapter 3) proposed a distinction between various types of tourist roles ranging from the standardized and highly institutionalized role of the "organized mass-tourist" through the "individual mass-tourist" and "explorer," to the most individualistic and least institutionalized type, the "drifter." When I wrote that chapter, in 1968, I conceived of the drifter as: "... the type of tourist [who] ventures furthest away from the beaten track ... He shuns any kind of connection with the tourist establishment ... He tends to make it wholly on his own, living with the people and often taking odd-jobs to keep himself going. He tries to live the way the people he visits live ... The drifter has no fixed itinerary or timetable and no well-defined goals of travel. He is almost wholly immersed in his host culture." I characterised the drifter as predominantly a child of affluence on a prolonged moratorium from adult, middle-class responsibility, seeking spontaneous experiences in the excitement of complete strangeness.

Since that chapter was written, drifting changed from an interesting but relatively minor phenomenon, embracing but a fraction of the travelling public, into one of the prevalent trends of contemporary tourism.[31] In the process the phenomenon itself was transformed in a peculiar way: on the one hand, it became more closely associated with the "counter-culture"; on the other hand, however, though originally a reaction against routinized forms of travel, it also became institutionalized on a level completely segregated from, but parallel to that of ordinary mass tourism. This change in and institutionalization of an originally highly individualistic phenomenon will be the main theme of the present chapter, in which the development and forms of drifting are examined.

Antecedents

In the recent history of Western societies, there are several antecedents to the modern drifter. On the fringes of society there were always outcasts or marginal groups, such as the American hobos (Allsop 1967; Anderson 1961a) and tramps (London 1967; Spradley 1970), and the Irish "tinkers"[32] who often out of sheer necessity led a shifting nomadic life. At the other end of the spectrum of bourgeois society, there was the well-educated youth of the late Victorian period, who set out on an adventure trip to experience the hidden, strange and exotic life of far-away countries and unknown people. Such youths often submitted themselves voluntarily to extreme hardship, sometimes adopting the way of life of their hosts. A typical, though perhaps extreme, example is provided by the young T. E. Lawrence, who wrote of his 1000 mile walking tour of Syria in 1909: ". . . a most delightful tour . . . on foot and alone all the time, so that I have perhaps, living as an Arab with the Arabs, got a better insight into the daily life of the people than those who travel with caravan and dragomen" (Knightly *et al.* 1969:30). For most of these young men the period of drifting was strictly limited and they settled into "respectable" careers upon completing their travels. Some took up occupations which enabled them to combine work and travel, e.g. commissions in imperial armies and navies. And a few became professional explorers and adventurers, like Richard Burton, for whom traveling was the only meaningful way of life (Brodie 1971).

Another antecedent of a completely different character are the various youth movements flourishing before and after the First World War, particularly the German "*Wandervogel*" (literally "wandering bird") and similar organizations (Knebel 1960:40–44). Touring the open spaces of free nature was experienced by these youths as a liberation form the social and physical oppression of modern city life. The *Wandervogel* was a collective-oriented movement, with strong emphasis on the cameradie between its members. It sustained a patriotic ideology — wandering through one's *Vaterland* was intended to inculcate the youngsters with love for their country and its natural attractions. The Boy Scout movement would be a similar example, but probably less patriotically-minded, for the Anglo-Saxon world.

The fourth and last type of antecedent are the various forms of "working tourism." One of its forms is the "working holiday" in which youths from one country travel into another to work for short-periods, mostly during summer school-vacations. Thus, e.g. a large number of youths tended for many years to come to Israel to work on a kibbutz for a summer. Another form is that adopted by some young professionals, who seek to combine travel with work in their chosen profession as a way of life: this tendency was noted by R. H. Pape, who coined the term "touristry" to designate ". . . a form of journeying that depends upon occupation, but only in a secondary sense, in that it finances the more primary goal, travel itself" (Pape 1964:337). She saw an opportunity for "touristry" in some highly demanded service occupations such as nursing; but she might have added others, such as younger college and university staff taking up visiting appointments in attractive locations abroad.

These different antecedents might to an extent have served as "cultural models" for the modern drifter. Indeed he shares several of their characteristics, and particularly the unwillingness to settle into a sedate, routine and urban way of life and an attraction to simpler, pre-modern, rural life-styles. However, significant differences exist between the drifter as a cultural type and each of his antecedents: the hobo and the tramp ordinarily derived from the lower reaches of society and though they might come to value highly their nomadic way of life, they were often driven into it by necessity; whereas the drifter comes ordinarily from a middle or higher class home and is a tramp by choice. The gentleman-adventurer had often a serious purpose in mind on his travels: discovery perhaps, or exploration or preparation for a future career in which his experience and knowledge could be put to good use. He did not drift around aimlessly. The drifter, however, has no instrumental purpose in mind, and often not even a concrete goal when embarking on his trip. Contrary to the often ideologically and collective-oriented youth-movements, the drifter is an individualist, disdainful of ideologies. He often goes abroad in order to get away from his homeland; he is at best un-patriotic; some contemporary American drifters were even expressly anti-patriotic and combined drifting with an anti-Vietnam war campaign conducted from abroad. Both, the members of the youth movements and the drifters are in a sense escapists: but the escapism of the youth movement was romantic and intended to serve eventually a "constructive" social purpose; the drifter's escapism is hedonistic and often anarchistic. Finally, though drifters might combine work and travelling, work for them is usually more incidental than is the case with "working holidays," or with the young professionals dealt with by Pape. Work is not a goal of the drifter's trip; he considers it, at best, as an unpleasant necessity, and tends to work only when pressed by dire need. He is ordinarily not choosy about the kind of work he engages in: ordinarily, he would take up any odd jobs, well-paid but obnoxious tasks (such as wrapping the bodies of the dead in Sweden), unskilled manual labor in building construction or agriculture (e.g. in Israel), etc. Many of the short-time drifters do not work at all. Others may muddle through considerable periods by begging, scavenging and "sharing" food and lodgings with friends and acquaintances. It is rare to find a drifter engaging in his occupation, though some highly trained student drifters on prolonged trips might intersperse their travel with short stretches of professional work, and thus come close to engaging in "touristry."

Drifting, then, differs in essential respects from other forms of itinerant travelling; hence it has to be understood within its own context, which is essentially that of "postmodern" society.

Motivations

Drifting in its contemporary form made its first appearance some years after the Second World War in Western Europe when students and other middle class youths started to hitch-hike their way through the continent. The scope of drifter tourism expanded numerically and geographically, with the development of cheap forms of surface-travel and lodging opportunities (e.g. the youth hostel). But the major impact upon the growth of drifter tourism was the introduction of cheap air-fares — in itself a realization by the airlines of the enormous potential demand for travel in the younger age-groups. As a result, drifting in the late sixties and early seventies suddenly grew to unprecedented proportions. Millions of youths descended upon the major centers of drifter tourism in Europe, like London, Amsterdam and Copenhagen. Europe remained the center of mass-drifting, but its frontiers are gradually expanding into other areas, such as the Middle East, South and South-East Asia, East Africa, and Latin America, into which individual drifters already started to penetrate in the earlier period.

It is difficult to establish the precise social background of the contemporary drifter. Though Europeans are still the most numerous group, the number of American drifters grows rapidly. There are also increasing numbers of Canadians and Australians. But, though drifting expanded far beyond Europe, it remained a thoroughly "Western" phenomenon; thus, Robinson (1972:572) notes that: "In fact, in poverty stricken Asia, almost the only shoe-string travellers are Europeans." Until recently, drifters were predominantly middle-class students or youths who just completed their studies. Lately, the number of working class drifters seems to be on the increase. While the early drifters were mainly males, the number of females greatly increased in recent years. In general, the contemporary drifters are of more heterogeneous origin than their predecessors, which makes the emergence of a common, international "drifter culture" the more remarkable.

How can one account for the sudden emergence of mass drifting as the most widespread and popular form of travelling of the younger generation in Western societies?

In the absence of systematic research, it is difficult to disentangle the precise factors and motivations underlying the tendency to drifting; but it is possible to outline some of the forces at work.

in accordance with the tastes and interests of contemporary youth. The most well-known of these[34] is the "classic" tour from Turkey through Iran, Afganistan, Pakistan and India to Nepal, with a possible extension to Thailand, Bali and Japan. This trip, the ideal of the modern seeker for the mystique of the Orient, as well as of the hashish-seeker, is, however, still the preserve of the relatively few. Most short-time drifters keep to less ambitious itineraries, through Europe or the Middle East; some of these might not differ much from the itineraries frequented by the ordinary, adult tourist. The drifters and the other tourists thus frequently flow along parallel geographical lines, though through segregated institutional channels.

Institutionalization is not confined to the most frequently travelled itineraries. Even on the far margins of the established system of tourism the pattern is changing: trips through the jungles of South America or of South-East Asia or through deepest Africa were once the preserve of the real adventurer. Some, but few, drifters would venture into these places. Recently, however, enterprising individuals undertook to provide commercialized tours to such far outlying places. An editorial article in the *Geographical Magazine* (1971:242), entitled: "Nomadic Tourists in Search of Adventures," says: "The ease with which travellers . . . fly gently from international airport to international airport, totally protected from all environmental hazards . . . is producing a reaction. A new breed of travellers and holidaymakers is emerging, a breed which demands to see the countries through which it is passing, which demands to participate in the way of life . . . a new industry is developing to cater to that need."

The article goes on to describe the "Encounter Overland Expedition to South Africa" and the Minitrek Company, a pioneer in the area of such organised adventure tours. Other such small companies provide organized tours of the Sahara (like the German Aalto-Touren) (*Spiegel* 1972) or to the Malaysian jungle (Alpha-Malaysia) (Stephen 1971). Some of these tours still preserve the flavor of real adventure; however, as they shade off into out-of-the-beaten-track but conventional mass tours, they become what a German student of tourism aptly described as "adventureless adventures" (*Spiegel* 1972:33). But even if the adventure is still there, as it probably is in the Encounter Overland Expedition, the spontaneous individualism of the original form of drifting is gone.

The guidebook is the hallmark of sedate, middle class tourism. The drifter of earlier days would presumably reject it as spoiling the spontaneity of his experience. With the emergence of semi-fixed drifting itineraries, something which could be called "the guidebooks of the counter-culture" made their appearance: e.g. a booklet called "Project London," a "travelling guide" for the Istanbul-Kathmandu route,[35] and cyclostyled sheets containing useful information on cheap lodgings, food, drugs etc. for Asian countries popular with drifters. The respectable travelling-guide publisher Fodor put out a guide called "Europe Under 25" which is "...selling briskly on American campuses and in head-centers" (Allsop 1967), a neat example of the way in which the tourist-establishment capitalizes on the counter-cultural consumer demands.

Much more information flows by word-of-mouth from the experienced traveller to the newcomer, helping to channelize the aspiring drifters into already well-trodden itineraries.

Infrastructure

As drifter-itineraries coagulate, a separate infrastructure, serving drifter-tourism, gradually comes into existence. Though this infra-structure caters to tastes — and budgets — vastly different from those served by the ordinary tourist establishment, it nevertheless manifests some broadly parallel traits.

The first and most obvious of these is the emergence of a drifter-oriented transportation system, ranging from cheap bus and train fares to special youth air-fares. Private operators of run-down buses in Middle Eastern countries specialize in the transportation of drifters; so do some airlines, e.g. Icelandic Airlines, known as the "hip-hop airline" (*Time Magazine* 1971:52).

But the emergent infrastructure for mass-drifting is not limited to transportation alone. Indeed, its sociologically more important manifestations can be found in the kind of facilities and localities frequented by drifters. When drifters travel as individuals and penetrate outlying areas they make use of such local facilities which are available or which they can afford. When, however, the stream of drifters on an itinerary intensifies, a process of ecological specialisation of drifter-oriented facilities, meeting and lodging places as well as the emergence of whole drifter communities, takes place.

In the beginning of the process drifters will seek out some cheap and conveniently located hostels, eating places, coffee houses and similar establishments, originally catering to the lower-class local population, or some non-commercial establishments, like youth hostels in most European countries, or Sikh temples in South-East Asia. Around such a nucleus, a "drifter tourist-establishment" might develop: local facilities specialise in catering to drifter tastes; new places open, such as "psychedelic" shops, night clubs and coffee-houses, often run by youths who are themselves close to the drifter or hippie culture. Cheap hotels or youth hostels become centers of drifter tourism, where youngsters exchange information, buy and sell their belongings, or smoke pot. In Amsterdam the authorities even permitted the opening of special establishments where pot can be freely smoked. With additional increase in the drifter traffic, whole streets or neighborhoods may become associated with drifters or even dominated by them. Drifters also tend to congregate on or take over public places such as squares or parks to rest or even sleep. The best known examples are the Monument on the Dam in Amsterdam or Picadilly circus in London; but there are many similar, less conspicuous places in the cities on the drifter itineraries, like the area round the Hypodrome in Instanbul.

Perhaps the most interesting development in this respect is the gradual emergence, in different parts of the world, of veritable "drifter communities," permanently-temporary settlements, inhabited variously by drifters, hippies, bohemians and expatriates. There are, or existed in the past, such communities near Kathmandu in Nepal, in Goa in India, on Ibiza in the Baleares, on the French Riviera, outside Eilat on the southern-most tip of Israel, on some Greek islands, in Morocco, on the island of Lamu in northern Kenya, and probably also in other localities. Little systematic information exists on these communities. Here I will draw on information from a short study carried out in Eilat,[36] from which a picture of the structure of such a community emerges, which, judging from informal information, is apparently fairly typical of other such drifter communities around the world.

The drifter community in Eilat in the late 1960s was ecologically dispersed and socially disorganized. It was in fact a random collection of individuals attracted to Eilat as a place where one can lead an unbothered, quiet existence or find work. Since Eilat was a boom town it provided plenty of opportunities for temporary employment in unskilled jobs; and since the town was short on local labor, regulations were relaxed so as to enable foreigners, like the drifters, to be employed.

The drifters were not attracted to Eilat by the existence of a drifter community there; after arrival, however, they found it useful as a source of help and information. The drifter-community did not possess a geographical center. Most of the youths lived alone, in pairs or very small groups, mostly in makeshift shacks, dispersed in the dry river-beds in the desert surrounding the town. A few had hired flats in the housing estates in the town itself. The community could be roughly subdivided into a core of old-timers, mostly hippies, and a periphery composed of a shifting population. However, the core did not provide leadership and was not a focus of social cohesion. The periphery included drifters who stayed for short periods, as well as some Israelis, often of delinquent background,[37] who attempted to gain acceptance into the drifter culture.

There was little social contact with the local population of Eilat, owing mostly to the unwillingness of the locals to associate with the drifters. There existed a basic "drifter-tourist infrastructure" — a coffee-house catering almost exclusively to them and serving as their main recreation center and a youth hostel which provided them with elementary services.

Eilat is also a major center of ordinary tourism in Israel. The drifters were considered a nuisance by the tourist organization and steps were periodically taken by the authorities to restrict their expansion on the beach areas or to reduce their visibility in the town.

Judging from the data on Eilat and information on other drifter communities, their social structure appears to resemble that of American hippie communities as described, e.g. by Yablonsky (1968), except that they are even more heterogeneous, and even less ideological and more individualistic than the latter. The itinerant hippies, staying for longer periods in one place, form the core of these communities; the non-hippie drifters usually stay for shorter periods of time and remain on the periphery of the community.

Relationships

The original drifter was driven by curiosity and a thirst for adventure and experience of the unknown; hence he had a wide range of contacts with the members of the host society, and was almost completely immersed in it. With the *Vermassung* of the drifter phenomenon, this aspect of the drifter role also changes: with the new mass drifter the element of real adventure is drastically reduced. The mass drifter is not really motivated to seek adventure and to mix with the people he visits. Rather, he often prefers to be left alone to "do his own thing," or focuses his attention on the counter-culture, represented by the other drifters whom he encounters on his trip. His social contacts, hence, become progressively narrowed to the company of other drifters. In its social dynamics, mass-drifter tourism develops a tendency parallel to that observed in ordinary mass tourism: a loss of interest and involvement with the local people, customs and landscape, and a growing orientation to the in-group: other drifters in our case, members of the group in the case of the collective mass-tourist.

A new conviviality develops among the heterogeneous assemblage of drifters in their meeting places and on the road. It is an easy, superficial and rather shifting conviviality. However well they may get along with each other, no cohesive, lasting associations take place, not to speak of the emergence of a new collective movement. People meet ephemerally, become intimates very quickly and part again without much ado. They are about the only support to each other upon which they can count and expect help in times of need, on an uncomfortable and arduous trip in an often hostile and dangerous environment (Allsop 1972:132; *Time Magazine* 1971:56–57).

Contacts with the local population under such conditions become highly selective. They are limited predominantly to those members of the lower social classes who cater to the mass-drifters or frequent the same services as they do, as well as to similarly-minded local youths who seek out the drifters and associate with them. So, e.g. in Eilat, foreign drifters and local drop-outs get together; the foreigners, coming from countries with a strong counter-culture, serve as cultural models for the "less advanced" locals. In a similar vein, the Arab boys in the mixed Israeli city which I studied, have been looking forward to meeting the tourists, many of whom were drifters, trying to associate with them, to learn from them, and eventually to travel to their countries of origin (Chapter 15).

Like the mass-tourist, the mass-drifter also gets a biased picture of the host society; the latter's perspective, however, is diametrically opposed to that of the former: the one looks at the host country from the lofty heights of an air-conditioned hotel room; the other from the depths of the dust-bin.

Types

My general description of the *Vermassung* of the drifter phenomenon tends to obliterate some significant differences apparent on the contemporary drifter scene. Not all drifters partake equally in the emergent institutional system of drifting. Some, particularly many Boy-Scout-like Australian and Canadian youngsters, still remain faithful to the original, individualistic type of drifting; while others, e.g. many short-term vacationing students, partake only marginally in the system, in that they use some of its facilities. As it grows in scope, the phenomenon of drifting becomes more heterogeneous. It might be useful, therefore, to draw some distinctions within the general phenomenon of drifting and indicate several emerging sub-types of drifters. In drawing up such a typology, I followed the lead provided by similar typologies developed by Keniston (1968) for "pot-users" and by Yablonsky (1968) for hippies. These authors used as the main dimension of their typology the extent of involvement of the youngster in the pot sub-culture, viz, in the hippie sub-culture. Similarly, the depth of involvement with drifting — measured by the amount of time the drifter devotes to his pursuit and the existence — or non-existence — of any other concerns besides drifting, will here serve as one of the variables in the typology, distinguishing "full-time drifters" from "part-time drifters." But in our previous discussion another dimension of importance has been indicated, namely, the motivation for drifting, and particularly the difference between those drifters who are primarily "outward oriented," i.e. concerned with experiencing the host-country, and those who are primarily "inward-oriented," i.e. concerned with the youth-culture or counter-culture of their co-travellers.

On the basis of these two dimensions, a four-fold typology of drifters can be constructed:

Full-Time Drifters

(1) Outward oriented: The "Adventurer," the original individual drifter, as described in the preceding chapter (Chapter 3).
(2) Inward oriented: The "Itinerant Hippie," the travelling drop-out, on his way to some drug-sanctuary in Europe or Asia or drifting aimlessly from one "hippie" community to another.

Part-Time Drifters

(3) Outward oriented: The "Mass-Drifter," usually a college youth who spends a limited amount of time to see the world, meet people and "have experiences," but tends to stick to the drifter-tourist establishment of cheap lodgings and eating places and cut-rate fares.
(4) Inward oriented: The "Fellow- Traveller," the youth who associates with the "hippies" or other drop-outs, and models his behavior on these roles, but remains marginal to the "hippie" sub-culture. He frequents the pop discoteques and boutiques, dresses "in style," visits the "hippie"-communities for short periods of time, but after his trip he returns to his ordinary pursuits. He is a "part-time drop out,"[38] and parallels the "week-end-hippie" discussed by Yablonsky.

There is little systematic information on the more detailed characteristics and behavior patterns of these sub-types. Here some interesting questions for further investigation emerge, like: What differences exist between the itineraries, use of facilities, and styles of travel of these sub-types? How and where do the different sub-types meet and interact? What is the pattern of socialization into the different sub-types — and particularly, is there a tendency for youths to pass from one sub-type to another? And finally, what is the relationship of the different sub-types of drifters with the broader counter-cultural context? It is hoped that more work on these questions would illuminate a rather surprising gap in our knowledge on the otherwise much investigated field of the contemporary youth culture.

Drifters and Hosts

To round up our discussion, we now turn to the reaction of the host society to the phenomenon of mass drifter tourism.

Tourism thrives on the premise that money earned in one country will be spent in another. The commercialized hospitality of the tourist establishment surrounds the tourist with profit-making amenities and attractions. Inhabitants of the poorer countries, to which much of the tourism from the richer countries flows unilaterally, expect the "rich" foreigners to spend generously and pay often inflated prices for the goods and services they receive.

But these expectations do not hold for the drifter: "The philosophy of the Eurobums is to 'live free,' i.e. to get the maximum distance on the minimum outlay" (Allsop 1972:131). Though the "drifter-establishment" of low-grade and low-rate services may thrive on drifter tourism, the ordinary caterer can expect little benefit from it. Moreover, the intrusion of the drifters into the itineraries and facilities used by ordinary tourists could spell a loss for the tourist establishment, since it antagonises the other tourists, for whom drifters are often anathema. Drifters are believed not to bring in much foreign currency, particularly if they keep going by taking up odd jobs on their trip. Hence they are seen as more of an economic liability rather than a source of income for the economy of the host countries.

But even more important than the economic factors for the formation of attitudes of the host societies toward the drifters, are the cultural ones. Much antagonism toward the drifter, particularly in non-European countries, has been generated by an inability to comprehend their motivation and attitude: being used to well-to-do travellers from the "rich" countries, embodying, so to speak, the affluence of successful modernization, the inhabitants of developing countries were at a loss when they encountered this new breed of tourists.

The original drifter moved among the people and lived with them; these were often ordinary folks, as yet removed from the commercialism and incipient modernism of the more sophisticated sectors of the host-society. They received the drifter as a guest in a traditional manner and he accepted their hospitality. It was only with the *Vermassung* of the drifter phenomenon and the coagulation of fixed itineraries leading necessarily through major urban concentrations that the attitude towards the drifters started to change. Tension between drifters and the local population, and occasional clashes, occurred in several places. The political leadership and the local authorities in many countries became increasingly more hostile: drifters were represented as a nuisance, exasperating the locals by strange and immoral behavior; a source of contamination for the local youth; and a general threat of "cultural pollution" (Chen 1972). They were viewed in the image of the long-haired hippie. Their search for drugs, and particularly their use of some non-European countries, in which drugs are permitted, as drug-sanctuaries, was resented. In an increasing number of countries, drifters were made unwelcome, intimidated, ostracised or barred: they were persecuted in Goa in India while in other localities they were excluded from some catering establishments; restaurants serving them were avoided by regular customers (Srinivasan 1972). Thailand and Nepal took steps to control the drifter traffic. Singapore, afraid to contaminate its society and its progressive, modern image, asked young travellers to cut their hair before entering the country and in general made them feel most unwelcome; similar concern with contamination of the local youth has been expressed in Taiwan and Tanzania, and I myself came across such a concern already in 1966 during field-work in the Israeli town which was a center of attraction for drifters.[39] There were incidents with drifters on Bali; "They have been fired upon on the Costa Brava and clubbed in Ibiza . . . They have been given the bum's rush in Italy and had their communes busted on the French Riviera" (Allsop 1972:103). In the more lenient Western European countries they generally fared better; the Dutch and the Danes went out of their way to cater to their needs. But the European tolerance has also diminished: there were clashes between the drifters and local sailors on the Dam in Amsterdam. And even in tolerant Britain, the London Tourist Board, after the recent summer-invasion of youth established a work group on young travellers. One question it will have to figure out is ". . . how welcome it is going to make this young people" (Beck and Brian 1971:XXIV).

Mass drifter tourism is, hence, under pressure almost everywhere and particularly in developing countries. Such pressure probably serves to increase the drifters' withdrawal and insulation, started with the *Vermassung* of drifter tourism. The emerging drifter is becoming almost the complete opposite of its original prototype. Contemporary drifter communities are probably as much semi-autonomous islands of transplants in an alien and sometimes hostile environment as expatriate communities often tended to be.

Real as the problems engendered by large numbers of drifters in developing countries might be, I still wonder whether they fully account for the intensity of the hostile reaction which they provoked there. After all, there are other means to "contaminate" the local youth — like modern Western mass culture disseminated through the local communication media; and drugs were not invented by the drifters — rather the drifters drew nearer to the traditional sources of supply. Hence, I suspect the existence of some deeper, symbolic motive behind the more concrete reasons for hostility towards the drifters: leaders of developing countries, in spite of their drive for modernization and industrialization, are often ambivalent in their attitude toward Western culture; while urging their countrymen to embrace the "positive" elements, they ask them to reject the "negative" ones. "Hippyism," represented by the drifter, tends to become the symbol and epitome of all that is negative, rejectable or despicable in contemporary Western culture.[40] In a rather paradoxical manner, the very youths who in their way rebelled against their own culture and rejected it, come to be considered as the most fearsome representatives of its "negative" aspects.[41]

Acknowledgment—This chapter was completed when I was Visiting Senior Lecturer at the Department of Sociology, University of Singapore. My thanks are due to H. D. Evers, H. Luther and P. Weldon for their comments on an earlier draft of this chapter.

Chapter 5

A Phenomenology of Tourist Experiences

Introduction

What is the nature of the tourist experience? Is it a trivial, superficial, frivolous pursuit of vicarious, contrived experiences, a "pseudo-event" as Boorstin (1964:77–117) would have it, or is it an earnest quest for the authentic, the pilgrimage of modern man, as MacCannell (1973:593) believes it to be?

Tourists are often seen as "travelers for pleasure";[42] however, though sufficient for some purposes, this is a very superficial view of the tourist. The more precise quality and meaning of the touristic experience have seldom been given serious consideration, either in theoretical analysis or in empirical research. Not that we lack controversy — indeed, the nature and meaning of tourism in modern society became the subject of a lively polemic among sociologists and social critics. In one camp of the polemic, we find those, like Boorstin (1964) and Turner and Ash (1975), for whom tourism is essentially an aberration, a symptom of the malaise of the age. Boorstin bemoans the disappearance of the traveler of old, who was in search of authentic experiences, and despises the shallow modern mass tourist, savoring "pseudo-events." The opposing camp is represented primarily by MacCannell; he criticizes the critics, claiming that ". . . Boorstin only expresses a long-standing touristic attitude, a pronounced dislike . . . for other tourists, an attitude that turns man against man in a they-are-the-tourists-I-am-not equation" (MacCannell 1973:602). He argues that Boorstin's approach, ". . . is so prevalent, in fact (among the tourists themselves as well as among travel writers), that it is a part of the problem of mass tourism, not an analytical reflection on it" (MacCannell 1973:600). As in every polemic, however, the protagonists of the opposing views tend to overstate their case. Thus MacCannell, claiming to confront Boorstin's view with empirical evidence, states that "None of the accounts in my collection [of observations of tourists] support Boorstin's contention that tourists want superficial, contrived experiences. Rather, tourists demand authenticity, just as

Boorstin does" (ibid.:600). But, MacCannell himself is very selective in the choice of his observations: his accounts are mostly taken from young tourists; Boorstin's thesis may well find more support in a different sample, composed primarily of sedate, middle-class, middle-aged tourists. Hence, even if one admits that Boorstin's claims may be too extreme and that some tourists may indeed be in search of "authenticity," it nevertheless appears too far-fetched to accept MacCannell's argument that all tourists single-mindedly pursue "real," authentic experiences, but are denied them by the machinations of a tourist establishment which presents them with staged tourist settings and "false backs." The conflict between these contrasting conceptions of tourists remains thus unresolved, as the proponents of each claim to describe "the tourist" as a general type, while implicitly or explicitly denying the adequacy of the alternative conception.

In my view, neither of the opposing conceptions is universally valid, though each has contributed valuable insights into the motives, behavior and experiences of some tourists. Different kinds of people may desire different modes of touristic experiences; hence "the tourist" does not exist as a type. The important point, however, is not merely to prove that both conceptions enjoy some empirical support, though neither is absolutely correct; rather it is to account for the differences within a more general theoretical framework, through which they will be related to, and in turn illuminated by, some broader views of the relationship of modern man to his society and culture. In this chapter I shall attempt to do so by examining the place and significance of tourism in a modern person's life; I shall argue that these are derived from his total world-view, and depend especially on the question of whether or not he adheres to a "center," and on the location of this "center" in relation to the society in which he lives. Phenomenologically distinct modes of touristic experiences are claimed to be related to different types of relationships between a person and a variety of "centers."

Tourism and the Quest for the Center

The concept of the "center" entered sociological discourse in several over-lapping, but not identical fashions. M. Eliade (1971:12–17) pointed out that every religious "cosmos" possesses a center; this is ". . . pre-eminently the zone of the sacred, the zone of absolute reality" (ibid.:17). In traditional cosmological images, it is the point where the *axis mundi* penetrates the earthly sphere, ". . . the meeting point of heaven, earth and hell" (ibid.:12).

However, the center is not necessarily geographically central to the life-space of the community of believers; indeed, as Victor Turner has pointed out, its ex-centric location may be meaningful in that it gives direction and structure to the pilgrimage as a sacred journey of spiritual ascension to "The Center Out There" (Turner 1973). The "center," however, should not be conceived in narrowly religious terms. E. Shils (1975) has argued that every society possesses a "center," which is the charismatic nexus of its supreme, ultimate moral values. While Shils does not deal explicitly with the location of the symbolic bearers of the charismatic "center," there is little doubt that he considers the locus of its paramount symbols, e.g. the monarch or the crown (Shils and Young 1953), to be ordinarily within the geographical confines of the society. Shils' concept of the center was further developed by S. N. Eisenstadt (1968), who distinguishes between multiple "centers," e.g. political, religious or cultural; in modern society these centers do not necessarily overlap, and their paramount symbols may be differentially located. The individual's "spiritual" center, whether religious or cultural, i.e. the center which for the individual symbolizes ultimate meanings, is the one with which we are concerned in this chapter.

Structural-functionalist theory, particularly in the Parsonian variety, assumes as a matter of course that the spiritual center of the modern individual will be normally located within the confines of his society — he will "conform" with this society's ultimate values. Such conformity may indeed generate tensions and dissatisfactions. These, however, will be taken care of by the mechanisms of "pattern maintenance" and "tension management." The latter will include various types of leisure and recreational activity in which the individual finds release and relief. Such activities take place in segregated settings, which are not part of "real" life; in Schuetz's phenomenological terminology, they may be called "finite provinces of meaning" (Berger and Luckmann 1966:39). Though consisting of activities representing a reversal of those demanded by the central value-nexus (e.g. "play" as against "work"), they are "functional" in relieving the tensions built up in the individual and hence reinforce, in the long run, his allegiance to the "center."[43] The individual may need relief from tensions, created by the values, but he is not fundamentally alienated from them. Tourism, in the Parsonian scheme, is a recreational activity par excellence: it is a form of temporary getaway from one's center, but in relation to the individual's biography, his life-plan and aspirations, it remains of peripheral significance. Indeed, in terms of a functional theory of leisure, tourism only remains functional, so long as it does not become central to the individual's life-plan and aspirations — since only so long will it regulate his tensions and dissatisfactions, refreshing and restoring him, without destroying his motivation to perform the tasks of his everyday life. This means that tourism is essentially a temporary reversal of everyday activities — it is a no-work, no-care, no-thrift situation; but it is in itself devoid of deeper meaning: it is a "vacation," i.e. "vacant" time. If tourism became central, the individual would become "deviant," he would be seen as "retreating," opting-out, or escaping the duties imposed upon him by his society.

The assumption that modern man is normally a conformist, and that he will hence generally adhere to the center of "his" society is, to say the least, simplistic. Many moderns are alienated from their society. What about the "spiritual" center of such alienated people? Several alternatives can be discerned: (a) some may be so completely alienated as not to look for any center at all, i.e. as not to seek any ultimate locus of meaning; (b) some, aware of what to them looks an irretrievable loss of their center, seek to experience vicariously the authentic participation in the center of others, who are as yet less modern and less, in E. Heller's (1961) term, "disinherited"; (c) some, particularly those whom Kavolis (1970) described as "post-modern," often possess a "decentralized personality," and equivocate between different centers, almost turning the quest into the purpose of their life; (d) finally, some may find that their spiritual center lies somewhere else, in another society or culture than their own. I argue that within the context of each of these possible types of attitude to the center, tourism will be endowed with a different significance. In the following I shall develop a phenomenology of modes of touristic experiences and relate them to these alternative forms of relationship between a modern person and various "centers."

The Modes of Tourist Experiences

Traveling for pleasure (as opposed to necessity) beyond the boundaries of one's life-space assumes that there is some experience available "out there," which cannot be found within the life-space,[44] and which makes travel worthwhile. A person who finds relief from tensions within his life space, or does not perceive outside its boundaries any attractions the desire for which he cannot also fulfil at home, will not travel for pleasure.

Risking some over-simplification, I argue that primitive society usually entertained an image of a limited "cosmos," ideally co-terminous with its life-space, surrounded by a dangerous and threatening chaos. Insofar as the sacred center was geographically located within the life-space, primitive man had no reason or desire to venture beyond its boundaries. It is only when a powerful mythological imagery locates the "real" center in another place, beyond the limits of the empirical world, a "paradise" beyond the surrounding chaos, that "paradisiac cults," terminating in large scale voyages, develop (Eliade 1969c:88–111). This is the original, archaic pilgrimage, the quest for the mythical land of pristine existence, of no evil or suffering, the primaeval center from which man had originally emerged, but has eventually lost it.[45] The pilgrimage later on becomes the dominant form of non-instrumental traveling in traditional and particularly peasant societies (Turner 1973). However, the traditional pilgrimage differs from the archaic one, in that the pilgrim's goal, the center, is located within his "world," but beyond the boundaries of the immediate life-space; this contingency is predicated upon a separation between his limited life-space and his "world": the image of the latter is vastly expanded and embraces a large number of life-spaces of individual communities or societies. Thus, Jerusalem becomes the center of the Jewish and Christian "world," Mecca that of the Muslim "world." Traditional pilgrimage is essentially a movement from the prophane periphery towards the sacred center of the religious "cosmos."

Modern mass tourism, however, is predicated upon a different development: the gradual abandonment of the traditional, sacred image of the cosmos, and the awakening of interest in the culture, social life and natural environment of others. In its extreme form, modern tourism involves a generalized interest in or appreciation of that which is different, strange or novel in comparison with what the traveler is acquainted with in his cultural world (Chapters 2 and 3). Hence, it leads to a movement away from the spiritual, cultural or even religious center of one's "world," into its periphery, toward the centers of other cultures and societies.

Pilgrimages and modern tourism are thus predicated on different social conceptions of space and contrary views concerning the kind of destinations worth visiting and of their location in the socially constructed space; hence, they involve movement in opposite directions: in pilgrimage from the periphery toward the cultural center, in modern tourism, away from the cultural center into the periphery.

These differences notwithstanding, the roles of pilgrim and tourist are often combined, particularly in the modern world (Cohen 1992; Dupont 1973). The fusion of the roles does not, however, mean a fusion of the divergent cognitive structures. MacCannell, who views the tourist as a modern pilgrim (1973:593), does not expressly discuss the problem of the cognitive structure of the tourist's "world," in contrast to that of the pilgrim.

Here I shall develop a phenomenological typology of tourist experiences by analyzing the different meanings which interest in and appreciation of the culture, social life and the natural environment of others has for the individual traveler. The degree to which his journey represents a "quest for the center," and the nature of that center will be at the heart of this analysis. The typology, in turn, relates to different points of a continuum of privately constructed "worlds" of individual travelers (not necessarily identical with those prevalent in their culture), ranging between the opposite poles of the conception of space characteristic of modern tourism on the one hand and that of the pilgrimage on the other. I distinguish five main modes of touristic experiences:

(1) The Recreational Mode
(2) The Diversionary Mode

(3) The Experiential Mode
(4) The Experimental Mode
(5) The Existential Mode.

These modes are ranked here so that they span the spectrum between the experience of the tourist as the traveler in pursuit of "mere" pleasure in the strange and the novel, to that of the modern pilgrim in quest of meaning at somebody else's center. Let us now discuss each in some detail.

(1) *The Recreational Mode*: this is the mode of touristic experiences which a structural-functionalist analysis of society would lead us to expect as typical for modern man. The trip as a recreational experience is a form of entertainment akin in nature to other forms of entertainment such as the cinema, theatre, or television. The tourist "enjoys" his trip, because it restores his physical and mental powers and endows him with a general sense of well-being. As the term "recreation" indicates, even this mode of tourist experience is ultimately and distantly related to and derived from the religious voyage to the sacred, life-endowing center, which rejuvenates and "re-creates."[46] Indeed, one can follow the process of "secularization" of tourism historically, e.g. in the change from "thermalists," whose belief in the healing properties of thermal springs was ultimately grounded in mythological images of springs as "centers" from which supernatural powers penetrate the empirical world, to tourists, who "take the waters" primarily as a form of high-class socializing (Lowenthal 1962). Though the belief in the recuperative or restorative power of the tourist trip is preserved, it is a secular, rational belief in the value of leisure activities, change of climate, rest, etc.

While the traditional pilgrim is newly born or "re-created" at the center, the tourist is merely "recreated." In the recreational tourist trip, the intent and meaning of the religious voyage is secularized: it loses its deeper, spiritual content. Though the tourist may find his experiences on the trip "interesting," they are not personally significant. He does not have a deep commitment to travel as a means of self-realization or self-expansion. Like other forms of mass entertainment, recreational tourism appears from the perspective of "high" culture as a shallow, superficial, trivial and often frivolous activity, and is ridiculed as such by Boorstin and other culture critics. A correlate of this view is that the tourist traveling in that mode appears often to be gullible to the extreme (Mitford 1959), easy to be taken in by blatantly inauthentic or outrightly contrived, commercialized displays of the culture, customs, crafts and even landscapes of the host society. His apparent gullibility, however, ought not to be ascribed solely to his ignorance; rather, he does not really desire or care for the authentic (Huetz de Lemps 1964:23); he is "no stickler for authenticity" (Desai 1974:4). Since he seeks recreation, he is quite eager to accept the make-believe and not to question its authenticity; after all one does not need to be convinced of the authenticity of a TV play or a motion picture in order to enjoy it as a recreative, entertaining or relaxing experience.

The recreation-seeking tourist, hence, thrives on what Boorstin (1964) calls "pseudo-events." But the depth of contempt in which he is held on that account by intellectuals and "serious" travelers is misplaced: the tourist gets what he really wants — the pleasure of entertainment, for which authenticity is largely irrelevant. Such recreation-oriented tourists should be looked upon less as shallow, easily gullible simpletons who believe any contraption to be "real," or as stooges of a prevaricating tourist establishment, but rather as persons who attend a performance or participate in a game; the enjoyability of the occasion is contingent on their willingness to accept the make-believe or half-seriously to delude themselves.[47] In a sense, they are accomplices of the tourist establishment in the production of their own deception. Recreation-oriented tourists, like the audience of a play, can completely legitimately enjoy themselves despite, or even — as in the case of some of the more outlandish performances of local custom — because, the fact that the experienced is not "real"; the real thing may be too terrifying or revolting to be enjoyable. For the recreation-seeking tourist, the people and landscapes he sees and experiences are not part of his "real" world; like other recreational settings, they are "finite provinces of meaning" separate from reality, though this is not explicitly admitted by either the tourists or the staff of tourist establishments. Indeed, tourists as well as staff, may be mutually aware of the fact that each is playing a role in order to keep up an inauthentic, indeed artificial, but nevertheless enjoyable, "construction of (touristic) reality." If this is openly admitted, the tourist situation would be homologous to that of mass entertainment. The distinguishing trait of the tourist situation, however, is that such an admission would spoil the game.

Tourism as recreation is, in itself, not a "serious business"; rather it is an "idle pleasure" (Lowenthal 1962:124), and as such had a hard time in gaining recognition as a legitimate reason for travelling. It achieved such legitimation, indeed, not because it is enjoyable in itself, but rather on the strength of its recuperative powers, as a mechanism which recharges the batteries of weary modern man (Glasser 1975:19–20), refreshes and restitutes him so he is able again to return to the wear and tear of "serious" living. Such tourism serves as a "pressure-valve" for modern man. When he cannot take the pressures of daily living any more, he goes on a vacation. If he overdoes it, or fails to return to serious living, his behaviour becomes "dysfunctional," in its extreme anomic escapism. But ordinarily it is "functional" because it manages the tensions generated by modern society and hence helps to preserve the adherence of the individual to it — in a similar way in which the Carnival (e.g. Baroja 1965:23–24) and other forms of legitimate debauchery, normatively circumscribed in time and place, served as a "pressure-valve" of traditional Christian society. In the functionalist view, recreational tourism is chiefly caused by the "push" of the tourist's own society, not by the particular "pull" of any place beyond its boundaries. The recreational tourist is primarily "getting away." Hence, he is often equanimous as to the choice of possible destinations for his "holiday," thus providing the advertisement industry with plentiful opportunities to tilt his decision in a variety of competing directions.

Though not serious business in itself, recreation, then, performs a serious "function" — it restitutes the individual to his society and its values, which, despite the pressures they generate, constitute the center of his world. Insofar as he is aware of this function and values it, it becomes, in an oblique sense, the meaning of his trip. If it were not for the pressures generated in his daily life at home, or if the pressures were resolved by alternative mechanisms, as, e.g. they are in traditional societies, he may find no need to travel; he would stay at home. Here we have one of the main reasons for the tremendous upsurge of tourism in modern, and particularly in urban society (Dumazdier 1967:125–126): this society generates pressures, which it has few means to resolve; peasants, even in modern societies, travel little.

(2) *The Diversionary Mode*: Recreational tourism is a movement away from the center, which serves eventually to reinforce the adherence to the center. Hence, it may possess a meaning for the person oriented to that center.

As we pointed out above, however, modern men are often alienated from the center of their society or culture. Some of them may not be seeking alternative centers: their life, strictly speaking, is "meaningless," but they are not looking for meaning, whether in their own society or elsewhere. For such people, traveling in the mode just described, loses its recreational significance: it becomes purely diversionary — a mere escape from the boredom and meaninglessness of routine, everyday existence, into the forgetfulness of a vacation, which may heal the body and sooth the spirit, but does not "recreate" — i.e. it does not re-establish adherence to a meaningful center, but only makes alienation endurable. Diversionary tourism is then, in terms of what Glasser calls the "Therapy School" of sociology of leisure, ". . . a healing balm for the robots . . . It accepts that for most people work will always be emotionally uncommitting and therefore unrewarding, and that they are condemned to seek in their leisure temporary oblivion and comfort for abraded nerve endings . . . the Therapy School . . . [puts] emphasis on immediate diversion . . ." (Glasser 1975:21).

The diversionary mode of tourist experience, hence, is similar to the recreational, except that it is not "meaningful," even in an oblique sense. It is the meaningless pleasure of a center-less person.

The recreational and diversionary modes of touristic experience have been the target of the savage criticism of tourism by culture critics such as Boorstin (1964) and Turner and Ash (1975). They are apparently characteristic of most mass tourists from modern, industrial urban societies. On this point I tend to agree with Boorstin, rather than with MacCannell. Even then, however, an interesting question remains unresolved: which one of these two modes is the prevalent one? One cannot approach this question without first taking a stand on that most basic problem: how deeply is modern man alienated? Even the critics of tourism may not be unanimous on this question. Hence, even the criticisms may differ: if modern man is conceived of as adhering to a central nexus of "Western values," his prevailing mode of travel is recreational; he may then be criticized for his narrow "parochialism," his lack of readiness to relate to the values of others except in a superficial, casual manner. If modern man is conceived of as alienated, then his prevailing mode of travel is diversionary; tourism is then criticized primarily as a symptom of the general malaise of modern society.

The two modes of tourism discussed above, however, do not exhaust the field; some tourists, primarily the minority of noninstitutionalized types of tourists (Chapter 3), indeed derive a deeper meaning from their travels, of the kind MacCannell finds characteristic of tourists in general. The remaining three modes of touristic experience represent different levels of depth of meaning which tourism may possess for the individual.

(3) *The Experiential Mode*: the recreational tourist adheres to the center of his society or culture; the diversionary tourist moves in a center-less space. But what happens when the disenchanted or alienated individuals become growingly aware of their state of alienation, and the meaninglessness and fatuity of their daily life, as many younger members of the middle classes in the contemporary society have become?

One direction which their search for meaning might take is the attempt to transform their society through revolution; another, less radical alternative is to look for meaning in the life of others — tourism (MacCannell 1976:3).

The renewed quest for meaning outside the confines of one's own society is commenced, in whatever embryonic, unarticulated form, by the search for "experiences": the striving of people, who have lost their own center and are unable to lead an authentic life at home, to recapture meaning by a vicarious, essentially aesthetic, experience of the authenticity of the life of others (MacCannell 1973). This mode of tourism we shall call "experiential."[48]

The "experiential" mode characterizes the tourist as he emerges from MacCannell's description. If Boorstin is among the most outspoken critics of recreational and *a forteriori* diversionary tourism, which in his view encompass all modern tourism, MacCannell attempts to endow tourism with a new dignity by claiming that it is a modern form of the essentially religious quest for authenticity.

But though he puts forward his view of the tourist against that of the "intellectuals" (MacCannell 1973:598–601), implying that it holds for "the tourist" in general, it is clear that his claim is based on a view of modern man who, alienated from the spiritual center of his own society, actively, though perhaps inarticulately, searches for a new meaning. Indeed, MacCannell argues that "The concern of moderns for the shallowness of their lives and inauthenticity of their [everyday] experiences parallels concern for the sacred in primitive society" (MacCannell 1973:589–590). Unlike in situations where such shallowness engenders a desire for an internal spiritual revolution, the modern tourist turns elsewhere for authenticity: "The more the individual sinks into everyday life, the more he is reminded of reality and authenticity elsewhere" (MacCannell 1976:160). MacCannell claims that "Pretension and tackiness generate the belief that somewhere, only not right here, not right now, perhaps just over there someplace, in another country, in another life-style, in another social class, perhaps, there is genuine society" (MacCannell 1976:155). Therefore, "Authentic experiences are believed to be available only to those moderns who try to break the bonds of their everyday existence and begin to 'live' " (MacCannell 1976:159). The search for authentic experiences is essentially a religious quest: therefore, it follows that ". . . tourism absorbs some of the social functions of religion in the modern world" (MacCannell 1973:589). However, since "Touristic consciousness is motivated by the desire for authentic experience. . . ." (ibid.:597), rather than trivial ones, the chief problem facing the tourist becomes ". . . to tell for sure if the experience is authentic or not" (ibid.:597). As against Boorstin and others who maintain that the tourist is content with contrived experiences, or is a mere superficial stooge, MacCannell endeavors to prove that the tourist is in fact a serious victim of a sophisticated deception: the tourist establishment "stages authenticity," so that tourists are misled to believe that they succeeded in breaking through the contrived "front" of the inauthentic, and have penetrated into the authentic "back" regions of the host society, while in fact they were only presented with "false backs," staged by the tourist establishment, or, in Carter's (1971) term, "fenced in." The problem is not the cultural shallowness of the tourists but the sophisticated machinations of the tourist establishment. However, though critical of the tourist establishment as the progenitor of a "false [touristic] consciousness" (MacCannell 1973:589), MacCannell is nevertheless convinced of the "functional" importance of tourism. Indeed, in an admittedly Durkheimian mode, he claims that tourism ". . . is a form of ritual respect for society" (MacCannell 1973:589) and hence, apparently, reinforces social solidarity. But he probably means "Society" in general (and not necessarily the one of which the tourist is a member), since it was precisely the inauthenticity of life in his own society, coupled with the ". . . reminder [through the availability of souvenirs] of reality and authenticity elsewhere" (MacCannell 1976:160) and the ". . . availability of authentic experiences at other times and in other places" (ibid.:148) which motivated the tourist for his quest in the first place. MacCannell likens tourism to the religious pilgrimage: "The motive behind a pilgrimage is similar to that behind a tour: both are quests for authentic experiences" (MacCannell 1973:593). But, the similarity he points out notwithstanding, there are some important, and to my mind crucial, differences: first, the pilgrim always undertakes his journey to the spiritual center of his religion, though that center may be located far beyond the boundaries of his life-space or society. It is true that the tourist, too, may travel to the artistic, national, religious and other centers of his own society or culture and pay them "ritual respect." But one of the distinguishing characteristics of modern tourism is precisely the generalized interest in the environment, and the desire for experiences far beyond the limits of the traveler's own cultural realm; indeed, it is often the sheer strangeness and novelty of other landscapes, lifeways and cultures which chiefly attract the tourist (Chapter 3).

Secondly, in contrast to the pilgrim, the experience-oriented tourist, even if he observes the authentic life of others, remains aware of their "otherness," which persists even after his visit; he is not "converted" to their life, nor does he accept their authentic lifeways. The pilgrim senses spiritual kinship with even a geographically remote center; the "experiential" tourist remains a stranger even when living among the people whose "authentic" life he observes, and learns to appreciate, aesthetically. The pilgrim's experience is "existential": he participates in, partakes of and is united with his co-religionists in the *communitas* created by the sacredness of the center (Turner 1973). He is fully involved in and committed to the beliefs and values symbolized by the center. MacCannell's tourist, however, experiences only vicariously the authenticity of the life of others, but does not appropriate it for himself. Hence, though his quest may be essentially religious, the actual experience is primarily aesthetic, owing to its vicarious nature. The aesthesis provoked by direct contact with the authenticity of others may reassure and uplift the tourist, but does not provide a new meaning and guidance to his life. This can best be seen where "experiential" tourists observe pilgrims at a pilgrimage center: the pilgrims experience the sacredness of the center; the tourists may experience aesthetically the authenticity of the pilgrims' experience. The "experiential" mode of tourism, though more profound than the "recreational" or "diversionary" ones, does not generate "real" religious experiences.

MacCannell provides the clues for an analysis of the search for new meaning through tourism. But his work falls short of accomplishing that task; an extension of his approach leads to the distinction of still more profound modes of touristic experiences, and to the eventual closure of the gap separating the mode of experience of the modern mass tourist from that of the traditional pilgrim.

(4) *The Experimental Mode*: this mode of the touristic experience is characteristic of people who do not adhere any more to the spiritual center of their own society, but engage in a quest for an alternative in many different directions. It is congenial to the more thoughtful among the disoriented contemporary travelers, particularly the more serious "drifters" (Chapter 4), who, endowed with a "decentralized personality" (Kavolis 1970:438–439) and lacking clearly defined priorities and ultimate commitments, are pre-disposed to try out alternative life-ways in their quest for meaning. Travel is not the only possible form of their quest; mysticism, drugs, etc., may serve as alternative paths to the same goal; indeed, Eliade considers that the internal and external quests for the center are homologous (Eliade 1971:18). But for those who do travel in quest of an alternative spiritual center, travel takes up a new and heightened significance. While the traveler in the "experiential" mode derives enjoyment and reassurance from the fact that *others* live authentically, while he remains "disinherited" (Heller 1961) and content merely to observe the authentic life of others, the traveler in the "experimental" mode engages in that authentic life, but refuses fully to commit himself to it; rather, he samples and compares the different alternatives, hoping eventually to discover one which will suit his particular needs and desires. In a sense, the "experimental" tourist is in "search of himself," insofar as in a trial and error process he seeks to discover that form of life which elicits a resonance in himself; he is often not really aware of what he seeks, of his "real" needs and desires. His is an essentially religious quest, but diffuse and without a clearly set goal.

Examples of such seekers who experiment with alternative lifeways abound among the younger set of travelers: urban American, European or Australian youngsters who taste life in farming communities, the Israeli *kibbutzim*, the Indian *aśrams*, in remote Pacific villages or hippie communes, engage in the experimental mode of tourism. An enlightening example is a short story, apparently written by a foreign student in an Israeli student paper, entitled "In search of, in search of . . ." (Coven 1971), which commences: "I was in search of religion. I was in the depths, the bitter waters. No future, no meaning, loneliness, and boredom. I wanted religion, any religion" (ibid.:22); after describing several attempts to find religion in different Christian and Jewish settings in Israel, the story ends inconclusively; the search goes on.

Indeed, in extreme cases the search itself may become a way of life, and the traveler an eternal seeker. Such may be the case with those "drifters" who get accustomed to move steadily between different peoples and cultures, who through constant wandering completely lose the faculty of making choices, and are unable to commit themselves permanently to anything. If the "seeker" attitude becomes habitual, it excludes the very possibility of that essentially religious "leap of faith," which commitment to a new "spiritual" center consists of; the habitual seeker cannot be "converted."

(5) *The Existential Mode*: if the preceding mode of touristic experience characterizes the "seeker," the "existential" mode in its extreme form is characteristic
of the traveler who is fully committed to an "elective" spiritual center, i.e. one
external to the mainstream of his native society and culture. The acceptance of
such a center comes phenomenologically closest to a religious conversion, to
"switching worlds," in Berger and Luckmann's (1966:144) terminology, though
the content of the symbols and values so accepted need not be "religious" in the
narrow sense of the term. The person who encounters in his visit to an Israeli
kibbutz a full realization of his quest for human communion; the seeker who
achieved enlightenment in an Indian *aśram*, the traveler who finds in the life of
a remote Pacific atoll the fulfillment of his cravings for simplicity and closeness
to nature; all these are examples of "existential" touristic experiences.

For the person attached to an external "elective" center, life away from it is,
as it were, living in "exile"; the only meaningful "real" life is at the center.[49]
The experience of life at the center during his visits sustains the traveler in his
daily life in "exile," in the same sense in which the pilgrim derives new spiritual
strength, is "re-created," by his pilgrimage.

Those most deeply committed to a new "spiritual" center may attach themselves
permanently to it and start a new life there by "submitting" themselves completely
to the culture or society based on an orientation to that center: they will desire to
"go native" and to become, respectively, Hindu recluses, Israeli kibbutz members,
Pacific islanders, etc.

However, what makes "existential" experiences a touristic phenomenon is the
fact that there are many people — and their number is increasing in a growingly
mobile world — who, for a variety of practical reasons, will not be able or
willing to move permanently to their "elective" center, but will live in two worlds:
the world of their everyday life, where they follow their practical pursuits, but
which for them is devoid of deeper meaning; and the world of their "elective"
center, to which they will depart on periodical pilgrimages to derive spiritual
sustenance. Thus, e.g. there are some non-Jewish tourists who every year return
to live for a few months on a kibbutz, while spending the rest of the year in their
home country.

The visit to his center of the tourist traveling in the existential mode is
phenomenologically analogous to a pilgrimage. Indeed, Turner (1973:193–194)
refers to the community of pilgrims as an "existential *communitas*." In terms of
the relationship of their existential quest to the culture of their society of origin,
traditional pilgrimage and "existential" tourism represent two extreme configu-
rations: the traditional religious pilgrimage is a sacred journey to a center which,
though geographically "ex-centric" is still the center of the pilgrim's religion; it is
the charismatic center from which the pilgrim's life derives meaning, the spiritual
center of his society. Hence, though living away from the center, the pilgrim is

not living in "exile." His world and daily abode is hallowed, or given meaning through the center. The center, however, is given; it is not elective, not a matter of choice.

The center of the "existential" tourist, however, is not the center of his culture of origin; it is an "elective" center, one which he chose and "converted" to. Hence, it is not only ex-centric to his daily abode, but beyond the boundaries of the world of his daily existence; it does not hallow his world; hence, he lives in "exile." His pilgrimage is not one from the mere periphery of a religious world toward its center; it is a journey from chaos into another cosmos, from meaninglessness to authentic existence.

Between these two extremes, the pilgrimage to a traditionally given center and to an "elective" one, different intermediate types can be discerned. There exist other than purely religious traditional centers of pilgrimage — such as cultural, aesthetic (artistic or natural) or national ones. Visits to the great artistic centers of the past, the heritage of one's own culture, such as were included, e.g. in the Grand Tour (Lambert (Ed.) 1935; Trease 1967), or any visit by people of "Western" culture to the sites of classical antiquity may take on the quality of *cultural* pilgrimages. Visits to the shrines of the civil religion (Bellah 1967), such as the Capitol or the Lincoln Monument by U.S. citizens, or those of the official state religion, e.g. Lenin's Tomb by Soviet citizens (MacCannell 1976:85) are forms of *political* pilgrimage. A person's culture may include, in addition to the religious, any number of primary and secondary cultural, aesthetic and national centers, visits to which may be conducted in the existential mode of pilgrimages. Indeed, in the complexities of the modern world, the "world" of any given culture and society is not clearly bounded; the cultural inheritance of one society is often appropriated by, and made part of other cultures. Many Westerners consider the centers of the ancient Greek or Hebrew cultures as part of "their" tradition. Hence, what is today an "elective" center of a few individuals, outside the confines of their culture of origin, may tomorrow be appropriated by that culture; centers are "traditional" or "elective" only relatively to a given point in history.

We spoke of the "existential" tourist as one who adheres to an "elective" center. Such a center may be completely extraneous to his culture of origin, the history of his society or his biography. But it may also be a traditional center to which he, his forebears or his "people" had been attached in the past, but became alienated from. In this case, the desire for a visit to such a center derives from a desire to find one's spiritual roots. The visit takes on the quality of a home-coming to a historical home. Such travelers, so to speak, re-elect their traditional center. This conception is perhaps most clearly articulated in the ideology of Zionism. The full realization of the Zionist ideal is "*aliyah*," literally "ascension," the essentially religious term used to describe the act of permanent migration of a Zionist Jew to Israel.

Many Zionists, however, though Israel is their center, do not take the ultimate step of *"aliyah."* Their commitment to the "center" is expressed in a variety of less radical forms of behavior, one of which are repeated sojourns in Israel, differing in content, frequency and length: periods of study and volunteer work on kibbutz settlements, yearly visits as private persons or in groups organized by different Zionist organizations, or eventual retirement to Israel, etc. All of these are, in various degrees, forms of "tourism" (Chapter 2). Particularly those who return yearly for relatively short visits for no other reason but to live for a while in Israel, exemplify the "existential" mode of tourism, in the form of a renewed relationship to a historical center.

In recent years, the motivation for "existential" tourism to Israel has widened to include not only Zionists in the narrow sense, but also Diaspora Jews who desire to taste "genuine" Jewish communal life; the borderline between these and Jews who come for religious reasons, i.e. pilgrims in the narrower traditional religious sense has thus become blurred. Even people who are not pilgrims in any sense, may be overcome by an "existential" experience at the center. This comes through powerfully from a review of S. Bellow's book, *To Jerusalem and Back*: "The most saline of American writers finds himself unable to escape the tenebrous undertow of Jewish mysticism. 'My inclination is to resist imagination when it operates in this way' he writes. 'Yet I, too, feel that the light of Jerusalem has purifying powers and filters the blood and the thought. I don't forbid myself the reflection that light might be the outer garment of God' " (*Time Magazine* 1976a:62).

A craving for an existential experience at one's historical sources probably motivates many old-time immigrants — and their progeny — who travel from their country of abode to visit the "old country," from which they or their parents once departed: e.g. the American Italians or Irish visiting Italy or Ireland, the Corsicans in France visiting Corsica, the American Chinese visiting mainland China, etc. Perhaps the most interesting recent example of the sudden awakening of such cravings among a long-exiled people is the renewed interest of American blacks in Africa as the land of their fathers (*Spiegel* 1973). Though I have to add, a point to be discussed more fully below, that the mere desire for such an experience is not a guarantee for its fulfillment, as many American blacks who visited Africa, and for that matter Jews who visited Israel, learned to their sorrow.

The various modes of tourist experience were here presented in an ascending order from the most "superficial" one motivated by the desire for mere "pleasure," to that most "profound," motivated by the quest for meaning. The modes were separated for analytic purposes; any individual tourist may experience several modes on a single trip; a change from one mode to another may also occur in the "touristic biography" of any individual traveler. The mix of modes characteristic of different types of trips and the changes in the desired modes of experience during a person's "touristic biography" are empirical problems for further investigation.

One particular conceptual problem, however, remains to be clarified: the problem of "multiple centers." I have throughout proceeded on the tacit assumption that the individual adheres to only one principal "spiritual" center. If he is alienated from the center of his society or culture, he may look for it elsewhere.

This, however, is an over-simplification, which needs two qualifications: first, some people, we may call them "humanists," entertain extremely broad conceptions of "their" culture and are willing to subsume under it everything, or almost everything human, on the principle of Goethe's famous statement "Nichts Menschliche ist mir fern" ("Nothing human is alien to me"). For such people, there is no single principal "spiritual" center: every culture is a form in which the human spirit is manifested. They may thus travel in the experiential or even existential modes, without being alienated from their culture of origin; for them, the culture they happen to have been reared in, is just one of the many equally valid cultures.

Secondly, there are people, we may call them "dualists" or more broadly "pluralists," who adhere simultaneously to two or more heterogeneous "spiritual" centers, each giving rise to different forms of life. Such persons may feel equally at home in two or more "worlds," and even enjoy "existential" experiences from their sojourn at another center or centers, without being alienated from their own. American Zionists, for example, must not necessarily feel in "exile" in the United States, but may adhere simultaneously to the "American Dream" and to Israel as the Zionist center, and be equally committed to both.

"Humanists" and "dualists" or "pluralists" qualify the underlying hypothesis of this chapter, that a person seeks and ultimately adheres to "spiritual" centers of others only after he realizes the discomfort of his alienation from the center of his own culture and society. They indicate the necessity for a more thorough phenomenological investigation of the variety of complex world-views which developed in the contemporary world, for the analysis of which Eliade's or Shils' basic models do not suffice any more.

Conclusion

The typology of modes of tourist experiences presented above reconciles the opposing views of *"the tourist"* in the current polemic on tourism and thereby prepares the way for a more systematic comparative study of touristic phenomena. Our discussion shows that, depending on the mode of the touristic experience, tourism spans the range of motivations between the desire for mere pleasure characteristic of the sphere of "leisure" and the quest for meaning and authenticity, characteristic of the sphere of "religion"; it can hence be approached from both, the perspective of the "sociology of leisure" as well as that of the "sociology of religion." But neither of these approaches will exhaust the whole phenomenon, owing to the differences in the modes of experiences desired by different tourists. The context within which the typology has been developed was borrowed from the sociology of religion: my point of departure was a tourist's fundamental world-view, and specifically, his adherence to, or quest for, a "spiritual" center. I assumed that different world-views are conducive to different modes of the touristic experience. In fact I tackled the same problem which MacCannell addressed himself to, but, instead of assuming that all tourists are "pilgrims," I attempted to answer the question, under what conditions and in what sense tourism becomes a form of pilgrimage? It now remains to work out some of the implications of the typology developed in response to this question.

By claiming that tourists pursue different modes of experience, I did not imply that these are invariably realized in their trip. Two problems can be discerned here: first, from the viewpoint of the tourist, what are the chances of *realization* of the different modes of touristic experience? Second, from the point of view of the external observer, what are the possibilities of *falsification* of such experiences by the tourist establishment? Again, I raise questions which MacCannell has been concerned with, but my answers are somewhat different.

While MacCannell takes a lofty view of the desires of the tourists, and a pessimistic view of their realizability, I claim that the various modes of touristic experiences differ in the ease of their realization; generally speaking, the more "profound" the mode of experience, the harder it becomes to realize it. The "diversionary" mode is the easiest to realize: as with any kind of entertainment, it suffices if the travel experience has been pleasurable. The realization of the "recreational" mode demands, in addition, that the experience perform a restorative function for the individual. Since the traveler in these two modes has no pretensions for authenticity, his experience cannot be falsified. He can achieve his aim even when he is fully aware that his experience was staged in a "tourist space." As in other forms of entertainment, there is no need fully to camouflage the staging. The art of the tourist "producer" is to create in the tourist a semi-conscious illusion, and to engage his imagination until he is turned into a willing accomplice, rather than a stooge, of the game of touristic make-believe. The tourist and the touristic entrepreneur may agree that they deal in contrivances; indeed, the fact that these are contrivances often ensures their enjoyability. Insofar as much of what tourists around the world come in touch with in their sightseeing tours, e.g. on visits to "native villages," or at performances of "folkloristic dances and ceremonies" becomes explicitly defined as entertainment, rather than authentic culture, no falsification of the experience of the unpretentious "diversionary" or "recreational" tourist is involved.

The situation is completely different for tourists traveling in the other modes of touristic experience; for them, the authenticity of the experience is crucial for its meaning. This is true not only for the "experiential" tourist, who is reassured by the authentic life of others, and for whom authenticity is obviously a *sine qua non* for the realization of his experience. It is equally true for the "experimental" and "existential" tourist: one can hardly experiment with alternative ways of life if these are merely contrived for one's convenience, nor can one derive existential meaning from a "spiritual center" outside one's society or culture, if such a center is only a chimera, advertised to lure tourists in quest of existential experiences. No wonder that MacCannell, who discusses mainly what I termed "experiential" tourism, emphasizes that the tourist constantly faces the danger of a "false" [touristic] consciousness," by becoming the victim of the machinations of the tourist establishment, which presents him with a "... false back [which] is more insidious and dangerous than a false front; [hence] an inauthentic demystification of social life [of the hosts] is not merely a lie but a superlie, the kind that drips with sincerity" (MacCannell 1973:599). In MacCannell's view, the prevalent fate of tourists is to become entrapped in "tourist space," never able to realize their craving for authenticity: "... there is no way out for them so long as they press their search for authenticity" (MacCannell 1973:601). This claim attains with MacCannell almost the status of a "touristic condition" reflecting a generally absurd human condition captured in works of existentialist philosophers. If for Sartre, there is "No Exit" from the human existence and no way to penetrate the subjectivity of others, for MacCannell there is no way for the tourist to penetrate the others' authenticity. Taken to its extreme, the quest of MacCannell's tourist, like that of Camus's or Sartre's heroes, is absurd.

I do not subscribe to this view and believe that at least some modern tourists, particularly the explorer and the original drifter (Chapters 3 and 4) are capable of penetrating beyond the staged "tourist space" and its false backs and observe other people's life "as it really is." But this demands an effort and application, and a degree of sophistication which most tourists do not possess. There is hence a high chance that any of those tourists who desire authenticity, will be misled by the tourist establishment, and their experience will be falsified; as long as they do not grasp the falsification, they may labour under the illusion that they have realized their aim; if and when they penetrate the deception, they will be both enlightened and disenchanted; their resentment will give rise to demands for "honesty in tourism."

The mechanisms which support the constitution of the touristic illusion and the processes of its denouement have yet to be studied in detail. Such a study would, in MacCannell's neo-Marxist terminology, represent the examination of the processes through which "false [touristic] consciousness" is created and those through which "[touristic] class consciousness" emerges. MacCannell has done some pioneering work in this field, but much more systematic study is needed.

The tourist traveling in the experimental mode also faces the problem of authenticity. The danger of delusion will be less serious in his case, since his desire to experiment with other forms of life and not just experience them, leads him off the beaten track and sharpens his critical faculties. Being inquisitive and uncommitted, he is tuned to discover deception. His major problem, however, is to achieve commitment to any of the lifeways with which he experiments. What originally appears as experimentation with a view to an ultimate commitment to one of the alternatives, may turn into a predicament. An "experimental" tourist with a decentralized personality, may easily become an "eternal seeker." If false consciousness is the danger faced by the "experiential" tourist, total disorientation, and ultimate alienation from all human society, is the threat to the "experimental" tourist. The fate of some modern drifters strongly supports this argument.

The tourist traveling in the existential mode faces the most serious problem of realization. Commitment to and authenticity of the experience of the "elective" center are not enough; the ultimate problem is that of "commensurability": is the "true" life at the center indeed commensurable to his high hopes and expectations? Does it enable the traveler to live authentically, to achieve self-realization? This is a problem which existential tourists share with pilgrims. The center, of course, symbolises an ideal. Ideals are not fully realizable, but can only be approached "asymptotically."[50] The geographical center symbolizes the ideal one; between the two, however, there is necessarily a discrepancy: Jerusalem may be the Holy City, but ordinary human life in Jerusalem is far from holy. The pilgrim or the existential tourist "ascends" spiritually to the ideal center, but he necessarily arrives at the geographical one. How does he handle the discrepancy? For example: a person adhering to the ideal of voluntary collectivism, may go to live on a kibbutz, as an "elective" center embodying his ideals; soon, however, he will realize that life on the kibbutz is far from ideal. He will thus encounter a discrepancy between the ideal conception and actual life, which, if not dealt with satisfactorily, may provoke a personal crisis of meaninglessness, futility and disenchantment.

I distinguish three kinds of "existential" tourists in terms of the manner in which they deal with the perceived discrepancy:

(a) "Realistic idealists," who are willing to concede that even the most ideal place, society or culture have shortcomings, and are thus able to achieve self-realization at the center without deluding themselves of its faultlessness. I suggest that these are often people who became committed to their "elective" center after a prolonged quest and experimentation, and are thus bereft of illusions.

(b) "Starry-eyed idealists," those "true believers" (Hoffer 1952) who will see perfection in whatever they find at the center and refuse to face the reality of life in it, inclusive of its shortcomings. From the point of view of the external observer, their self-realization will be based on self-delusion. I suggest that these are often people whose commitment to an "elective" center was a result of a sudden conversion, of a precipitous "switching of worlds" in the certainty of discovery of a panacea.

(c) Finally, there are the "critical idealists" who oscillate between a craving for the center from afar, and a disenchantment when they visit it. They are attached to the ideal which the center is meant to represent, but reject the reality they found at it. For these, the center has meaning when they are remote, but tends to lose it when they approach it. Their attitude has been forcefully expressed by the Jewish writer Elie Wiesel, at a Conference on Jewish Intellectuals in New York in 1971: "I am at home in Jerusalem when I am not there."[51] I suggest that the "critical idealists" tend to be people who adhered to the center for a long time from afar, and for whom the trip was a realization of a long-cherished dream. They may preserve their dream, while denying the adequacy of its earthly embodiment, and advocating a reform of the actual center to bring it closer to the ideal.

The problem of discrepancies, however, can be "resolved" in another way — at the expense of the authenticity of the tourist's experience, i.e. by straightforward falsification. As demand for existential experiences increases, the tourist establishment and other bodies may set out to supply it. The existential mode of the tourist experience, based as it often is on a prior commitment, is particularly amenable to falsification. The tourist, expecting the ideal life at the center, is easily taken in; he is helped, as it were, to become a "starry-eyed idealist." Like traditional pilgrimage centers, centers of "existential" tourism are advertised and embellished; tours through "existential tourist space," like traditional pilgrimages, are staged. New centers may even be straightforwardly invented. The purveyance of existential experiences becomes big business. Tourist-oriented centers of Eastern religion, catering for "instant enlightenment" may be one example.[52] Another are the massive "Zionist pilgrimages" staged by the Israeli governmental and national institutions, in which the visitors are brought to a pitch of Zionist ecstasy at the height of a well-planned and organized tour through staged "Zionist tourist space." The largest of these pilgrimages, equal in everything to its religious counterpart, was the massive United Jewish Appeal "This Year in Jerusalem" tour of 1976, which brought several thousand people to the country and large contributions to the U.J.A. The study of staging the "existential" touristic sites and tours, such as the U.J.A. pilgrimages, is just commencing, but promises rich and interesting data for comparison with traditional religious pilgrimages.[53]

One last word on the relationship between the modes of touristic experiences and the problem of strangeness. It is generally assumed that tourists, when leaving their familiar environment, expose themselves to increasing degrees of strangeness, against which the more routine, less adventurous mass tourists are protected by an "ecological bubble of their home environment" (Chapter 3), so as not to suffer a disorienting culture shock which would spoil the pleasure of their trip. This argument is based on a tacit assumption that the tourist, adhering to the "spiritual center" of his own society or culture, prefers its lifeways and thought-patterns, and feels threatened and incommoded when faced with the different, unfamiliar ones of the host country. Strangeness, however, may be not only a threat, but also a lure and challenge. This seems particularly true for those travelers for whom the above assumption does not hold and who have either lost their "center" and travel in the experiential or experimental mode, or adhere to a new "elective" one outside their society (existential mode). Such travelers may well desire exposure to strangeness and not shun it, but rather seek to "submit" to it. Unlike the mass tourist, they will not suffer from a culture shock when exposed to the host environment, but may rather experience what Meintel (1973:52) calls a "reverse culture shock" upon return home. Talking of the personal experience of anthropologists, Meintel observes: "Desirable values. . . . which were not experienced before and which may have been attained as a stranger in a foreign setting may appear unrealizable in the home situation. Nash attributes the fact that 'many anthropologists come alive only when a field trip is in prospect for them' to the attractions of the stranger role (Nash 1963:163), but perhaps, desirable personal ends attained to a significant degree elsewhere are actually unattainable in the situations to which these individuals return" (Meintel 1973:3). Her observation may well apply to "existential" tourists as well, provided that they succeeded in realizing the desired experiences. The problem of such travelers is, however, that being the most committed and nurturing the highest expectations, they may indeed experience a "shock" upon arrival at their "elective" center — but not one emanating from the contrast between home and their "elected" external center, but rather from the fact that this "center" is too much like home and hence does not correspond to their idealized image.

Acknowledgment—The collection of material on which this chapter is based was facilitated by a grant of the Basic Research Unit of the Israel National Academy of Sciences and Humanities. Thanks are due to the Academy for its support and to Dr. J. Dolgin and J. Michalowicz for their comments on an earlier draft of this chapter.

Chapter 6

Tourism as Play

Play becomes the root metaphor of the study of religion under the conditions of the 'death of God' (Miller 1973:XXIX).
At a time when some proclaim that God is dead, North Americans may take comfort in the truth that Mickey Mouse reigns at the baroque capital of the Magic Kingdom and that Walt Disney is his prophet (Moore 1980:216).

Introduction

The message of Turner's opus is that, whatever its concrete manifestations, the fundamental nature of the "ritual process" is a universal one. Generalizing the long neglected ideas of van Gennep, Turner argued that individuals, groups and whole societies move through various manifestations of a basic form of "rites de passage," fluctuating between normal, structured, mundane states and their dissolution into extraordinary, liminal, antistructural situations of "communitas"; these, in turn, eventuate in structural reintegration in the form of a new personal status or social state (Turner 1974:80–154; Turner and Turner 1978:2–3).

The middle, liminal stage of the process is crucial, since here is given "recognition to an essential and generic human bond, without which there could be no society" (Turner 1974:83). It emerges from Turner's writings that this bond is effected through the incumbents' communion, in the state of liminal dissolution, with some "sacred" transcendent reality, an experience largely analogous to what R. Otto (1959) called "numinous." Indeed, like Otto, Turner's concern throughout is with the striking common, universal traits of liminal phenomena, which he discovers in a bewildering variety of situations, rather than with the particular traits of concrete manifestations of liminality.

While Turner's insights proved fruitful for surprisingly diverse areas of research, the comparative dimension of his conceptual scheme has been largely neglected. His major comparative contribution was the distinction between full-fledged "ludergic" liminal, and the more specialized and voluntary "ergic" liminoid situations (Turner and Turner 1978:36). This distinction relates to the transition from relatively simple undifferentiated tribal societies to the more complex, differentiated historical and modern ones (ibid.:34–36). Liminoidity is, however, only a weakened or impoverished variety of liminality; its social significance remains unaltered and so does the nature of the ritual process. Liminality, in its strong or weakened variety, has thus the same "function" in all societies — tribal, historical, or modern.

The tacit assumption of Turner's work is that all societies do recognize, in their own "social construction of reality," some sacred, transcendent realm, a "beyond," with which the incumbents are in communion, in their extra-ordinary state of liminality. This explains the power of such situations to effect personal or societal transitions in the ritual process. Hence a question of fundamental importance emerges: what is the nature of liminality and of the ritual process in societies, such as the modern, secular Western ones, which are based on immanentistic values, such as achievement, freedom and social opportunity, and whose construction of reality does not explicitly recognize the existence of an ontologically real, transcendent realm, a reality with which the modern individual may communicate.

It is this theme which I want to tackle, using the concrete example of tourism as play in modern secular society.

The Background

While an earlier generation of social critics, such as Boorstin (1964:77–117), tended to dismiss tourism as a frivolous activity, reflecting the superficiality of contemporary mass culture and devoid of any intrinsic significance, a later generation of social scientists, guided essentially by a structuralist approach, tended in the opposite direction — and identified the tourist as the pilgrim of modernity in a serious quest for authenticity (MacCannell 1973, 1976). MacCannell's ingenious analysis of tourism provided an important correction of the earlier view, but his claims were too far-fetched. In particular, he failed to account convincingly for the fact that so many blatantly inauthentic attractions do, in fact, attract many tourists. His principal explanation, which doubtlessly applies in many instances, is that the touristic establishment stages the authenticity of attractions, thus creating a contrived "tourist space," which appears genuine to the unwary tourist (MacCannell 1973). But many attractions are so obviously staged, and their inauthenticity is so easily recognizable, that one has to assume that tourists must be inordinately stupid or naive to accept them seriously as authentic. Moreover, there is one class of attractions, the overtly staged ones (Cohen 1979b:26–28), which make no claim to authenticity, and still attract great numbers of visitors: Disneyland and Walt Disney World are perhaps the most outstanding examples.

For social critics like Boorstin, the popularity of such attractions is just another manifestation of the superficiality of contemporary mass culture. MacCannell, however, would be hard put to explain this popularity, as long as he continues to claim that all tourists seek authenticity (MacCannell 1973:600; 1976:104). Recently, however, processually (rather than structurally) oriented anthropologists, taking their lead from Turner's analysis of ritual and pilgrimage, set out to explain the "ludic" (playful) element in tourism which MacCannell missed. Their approach throws new light on the popularity of such phenomena as Disneyland — beyond the obviously "staged" surface of which they claim to discover some deep symbolic themes.

In an earlier attempt to resolve the controversy between the socio-critical and the structuralist approaches, I suggested a distinction between the deep-structural and phenomenological levels in the analysis of tourism (Chapter 5, Cohen 1992b). I claimed that, while on a deep-structural level, tourism may indeed be analogous to the pilgrimage, different phenomenologically distinct modes of the touristic experience should be distinguished by the extent to which they reflect, in the tourists' "desired mode of experience," the deep structural themes. It turned out that authors like Boorstin and MacCannell referred to phenomenologically distinct types of tourists. Here I shall further extend this analysis to incorporate the "ludic" tourist of the Turnerians, and to distinguish his from the other types of the touristic experience. To do this, a brief recapitulation of my earlier typology (Chapter 5) is in order.

The typology consists of five modes of the touristic experience. The "Diversionary mode" was conceived as characteristic of the modern man who, though alienated from the "center" of his socio-culture, does not seek a new, alternative center. His life is, strictly speaking, "meaningless," and this meaninglessness also reflects on the mode of experience he seeks in tourism: he travels for mere entertainment or "diversion" as an escape from boredom and routine, but does not actively seek "authenticity."

The "Recreational mode" was conceived as characteristic of the tourist who altogether identifies with the mundane centers of modern, secular Western society — i.e. with the work-ethic, belief in techno-economic progress, personal achievement, etc. — but travels essentially in search of a physical and mental restoration from the stresses of modern life. The recreational tourist, therefore, is not much concerned with genuine authenticity, and may well thrive on "pseudo-events" (Boorstin 1964). In comparison with e.g. the religious pilgrimage, recreational tourism is apparently a superficial, frivolous activity. Turnerian symbolic anthropologists have recently undertaken to uncover the deeper significance of such tourism — and it will be their analyses from which I shall depart in the body of this chapter.

The "Experiential model" was conceived as characteristic of those alienated modern men, who, in the spirit of MacCannell's conception of the tourist, look for authenticity, i.e. meaning (which they miss in their own world), in the life of others: "The more the [modern] individual sinks into everyday life, the more he is reminded of reality and authenticity elsewhere" (MacCannell 1976:160). The quest for authenticity is, for MacCannell, essentially analogous to a religious quest, i.e. a quest for a Center or transcendent Reality. Though, in the tradition of structuralist analysis, MacCannell refrains from discussing the quality of the tourist's experience, he leaves little doubt that the tourist engages in a serious, rather than playful, quest: the tourist believes that the authenticity he seeks in fact does exist, ". . . only not right here, not right now, [but] perhaps just over there, someplace, in another country, in another life style, in another social class . . . there is genuine society" (ibid.:195). To be precise: the experiential tourist is aware of the authenticity in the life of others and may infer from it that, at least for them, there still exists a transcendent Center, a meaning-conferring Reality, lost or barred for the moderns, who are hence condemned to live a spurious, meaningless life. But he does not seek to experience that Center directly — rather, remaining modern, he merely experiences it vicariously (MacCannell 1973); at most he strives to "museumize" the authentic pre-modern and non-modern into modernity (MacCannell 1976:8, 83—84).

In my own presentation of the varieties of touristic experiences (Chapter 5), I went beyond MacCannell in that I conceptualized two additional modes: an "Experimental mode," characteristic of the tourist who, alienated from modernity, engages in a quest for an alternative lifestyle or "elective center," outside modernity, which suits his needs and desires; and finally, an "Existential mode," characteristic of the traveller who "arrived" at his goal — i.e. found his "elective center" and underwent an experience of "switching worlds" (Berger and Luckman 1966:144). By encountering Reality, he also discovers his real self and meaning in his life; he is reborn or "re-created" at the center, like the prototypical pilgrim. While he may not be able to stay indefinitely at his elective center, the existential tourist remains oriented toward it, feeling as if he were in exile when he returns to his ordinary place of abode.

In this chapter I shall deal primarily with the recreational mode; but I shall contrast it to some of the others, in an attempt not only to clarify the subtle phenomenological differences between them, but also to relate them comparatively to the varying "social constructions of reality" characteristic of the different stages of development of the modern world.

"Playing at Reality" in Recreational Tourism

My chief concern in this chapter is with recreational tourism. I argue that this type of tourism is essentially, a "play at Reality" — i.e. the tourist "plays" as if the attractions (even the overtly contrived ones) represented or symbolized some independent, ontologically present but transcendent Reality — even as he "knows" that such a Reality does not or cannot exist anymore according to his own, immanentistic construction of the world. Moore perceived this clearly in his analysis of Disney World:

> Traditional pilgrimage centers evoke the supernatural . . . Walt Disney World . . . evokes the supernatural in a context within which the supernatural has been banished (Moore 1980:215).

The loss of transcendent Reality is perceived by many moderns as the price of the "disenchantment of the world," the process of progressive rationalization and ever more radical secularization[54] which eventually eliminated "transcendence" as an independent realm of being from the modern worldview. Recreational tourism is thus essentially "nostalgic," a playful pilgrimage to a by now fictive Center, experienced both joyfully and sadly as if it were real.

My argument concerning the nature of recreational tourism is construed in precise analogy to that of "play theology" (Miller 1983), which "plays theology" *as if* its subject, God (who is in fact dead) really existed. The essence of both phenomena consists in their "as if" character: it is this which distinguishes the play of recreational tourism from the mere entertainment of diversionary tourism on the one hand, and from the more serious quests of the experiential, experimental or existential tourists on the other. The essence of the "as if" attitude of the recreational tourist consists of his playful acceptance of the make-believe presented by the attractions — in contrast to the experiential tourist, who seeks to discover "authenticity," some ontologically present, basically transcendent Reality in the life of others. To put it in the language of the later Schuetzian phenomenology: "play," according to this approach, could be seen as a "finite province of meaning" (Schuetz 1973, vol I: 229ff), set apart from the surrounding "paramount reality" by spatio-temporal boundaries (Huizinga 1955). In the touristic "play at reality," however, the situation of play, which, looked at from the perspective of the outside observer, is set apart from the paramount reality of everyday life, is experienced by the player for the moment as if it were real, as a reflection or symbolization of some transcendent Reality.

It is this readiness for playful self-deception, the willingness to go along with the illusion that an often obviously contrived, inauthentic situation is real, or represents Reality, that escaped MacCannell in his analysis of the tourist as the modern pilgrim, whose sightseeing has the obligatory nature of paying homage to attractions as differentiations of (modern) Society (MacCannell 1976:42−43).[55] Experiential tourism is thus a "serious" quest, akin to that of the pilgrimage; recreational tourism, in contrast, is playfully "frivolous" rather than "serious" (Pfaffenberger 1983:61). Although, as Turner has shown, ludic activities may accompany a pilgrimage, the truly religious pilgrim never has a merely playful, "as if" attitude to the "Center out there" itself, his ultimate goal, which for him embodies Reality. Moore's (1980) analysis of Walt Disney World as a "playful pilgrimage center," is, phenomenologically seen, merely an analogy: the differences between a religious and a playful pilgrimage center is as significant as the similarities between them — and consists precisely in the difference between serious theology (i.e. one which proceeds from the belief in a living God), and "play theology" (which "plays theology," although God is, in fact, dead).

Even more interesting than the still formally bounded ludic space of Walt Disney World, is the "play at reality" in some other, less formally segregated situations of recreational tourism, studied by authors who followed Turner's processual approach. Most enlightening in this respect are the studies by Wagner (1977) on Swedish mass tourism in a Gambian resort, Lett (1983) on charter yachting in the Caribbean, Gottlieb (1982) on "Americans" Vacations' and Buck (1978a, 1978b) on nostalgic tourism in Amish communes. Some of the themes raised in these studies can also be found, in an attenuated form, in my study of the "marginal paradises" on the beaches of the islands in southern Thailand (Cohen l982b). Here the grounds of recreational touristic play are apparently part of the surrounding "paramount reality," with no markers to set them off as "mere playgrounds."

It is this ambiguous status of such places which enables the recreational tourist to savour his experience as if it was "real" — while subconsciously aware of the fact that it is not so. This insight accounts for the success, e.g. of touristic "paradises": tourists enjoy the paradisiac play knowing very well that they cannot be but fictitious paradises (cf. also Chapter 16).

To conclude, students following Turner's approach generally strove to show the analogy between religious ritual and ludic tourism, usually concluding that touristic play assumes in modern secular society a function similar to that of ritual or pilgrimage in traditional societies (Moore 1980:207). While I do not necessarily dispute their claim, its too general and sweeping nature led to the loss of what appears to me a tragic trait in the predicament of modern secular man: namely that for him transcendence can only be playfully imagined, but can no longer claim reality. By assimilating the analysis of touristic play to the Turnerian analysis of ritual, these authors erased the distinctive quality of secular "recreational" tourism as against religious ritual or pilgrimage — which, in turn, derives from a crucial difference between secular modernity and traditional society, based on a religious world view. It is this difference which I shall attempt to explicate and illustrate below.

Ritual, Play and Reality

Turner has repeatedly pointed out that there are important integral ludic (playful) elements in tribal ritual and historical pilgrimage (Turner and Turner 1978:35). Significantly, however, he claims that with growing social differentiation the ludic element recedes in favor of the ritual element; in the highly differentiated post-industrial societies ritual and pilgrimage lose much of their ludic character, thus becoming "liminoid" (ibid.:36–39). Simultaneously, play becomes a separate realm of human activity, which, according to Moore (1980:207), achieves preponderance over ritual in contemporary secular society.

For our purposes the important difference between ritual and play rests on their respective underlying ontological assumptions; even for the modern religious individual, that which is experienced in ritual or pilgrimage is considered to be real; for the secular individual that which is experienced in play is not — although he may enjoy imagining that it was.

Let me briefly explicate the difference: the prototypical pilgrim at the Center has an "existential" experience: he is renewed, rejuvenated, born-again — in brief re-created there. His visit to the Center can be interpreted in Eliade's (1971:35) sense, as a projection of the mythical theme of Creation, a moment of eternity in time — on the biographical rather than the cosmological level. Such an experience is, phenomenologically seen, "deep" — the ecstatic and mystical encounter at the Center with the numinous or "Wholly Other" (Otto 1959:39–44). The "existential" tourist undergoes a similar experience at his "elective" center in the recesses of the Other (Cohen 1992b). His experience is, in an analytical sense, also religious; that of the "recreational" tourist, however, is not. The difference in the quality of their respective experiences, in turn, relates to the different ontological status of the experienced, from the perspective of the experiencer's own world view.

In the religious world view, following Eliade (1971), only that which is non-contingent is really real. Such, indeed, is the Center as a transcendent singularity in space, the point of penetration of eternity into time. The Center may well be "anti-structural" in Turner's sense, an antidote to the routine of the mundane world, but it has Reality, precisely because the religious world view admits the ontological reality of transcendence.

The modern secular world view leads progressively to the denial of transcendence, eventuating in the view that there is nothing "out there" in the recesses of the world but the void (Bell 1977:427), which, in contrast to, e.g. Buddhism, is *not* given religious significance (and does not, therefore, as in Buddhism, paradoxically become *the* Ultimate Reality). Modern man is thus caught in a Sartrian predicament of "no-exit" from the immanence of his "disenchanted" world, while continuing to long for a transcendent Reality. I submit that, just as the "death of God" theology plays as if a non-existent God was real, so the recreational tourist plays at the reality of a Center, the existence of which is denied by his own secular "construction of reality." The success of this "play at Reality" is precisely what endows this kind of tourism with its distinctive recreational quality — in the sense in which this term is usually used in modern functionalist leisure studies. Such a view of recreational tourism also distinguishes it, on the one hand, from ritual and pilgrimage — which explicitly relate to an ontologically affirmed transcendent Reality, and on the other, from the mere entertainment of "diversionary tourism" — which does not "play at Reality," and which is essentially meaningless.

This interpretation goes a long way to explain one of the outstanding characteristics commonly attributed to the mass tourist: his easy gullibility (e.g. Mitford 1959). Tourists are said to be easily taken in by blatantly contrived sights; that they accept unquestioningly obviously fabricated accounts and explanations; and that they can be easily cheated. Several explanations have been proposed for this alleged gullibility: the most charitable is that by Adams (1972), who attributed it to the tourist's ignorance and confusion in a new and strange situation. The social critics of tourism tended to see in the gullibility a reflection of the superficiality of modern mass culture (Boorstin 1964); while MacCannell attributed it to the prevarications of a tourist establishment which cunningly "staged authenticity" (MacCannell 1973; cf. Loeb 1977). The approach here proposed permits an alternative interpretation which makes superfluous a recourse to either the tourist's ignorance and superficiality, or the cunning of the touristic establishment. The playful attitude of the recreational tourist creates a predisposition to believe, akin to that found in a theatricial audience which is wholly involved with the action on the stage. Both involve a suspension of disbelief, a readiness to give oneself up to the experience. There is, however, a crucial difference: in the theatrical performance, the separation of the playful situation from its surroundings is institutionalized; the concrete expression of such institutionalization is the spatio-temporal separation of the performance from the surrounding mundane "paramount reality." Such a separation still exists in some overtly staged tourist attractions, such as the Disneylands, which are "bounded liminal spaces" (Moore 1980:216) and whose playful character is openly acknowledged. The distinguishing characteristics of covertly staged touristic attractions, however, is precisely that they are not, or, at least superficially, appear not to be, so separated from the surrounding environment — rather they are, or are made to appear, an integral part of it. Their touristic attractiveness consists precisely of their appearance *as if* they were real; though they may be half aware of their staged character, recreational tourists playfully accept their apparent reality. The tourist "believes," not because he is ignorant, superficial or cheated, but in order to playfully experience their apparent reality — and through them a transcendent Reality beyond, which is symbolized or embodied by the attractions. Only thus can we understand the success of the game, prescribed by the expert on tourist management, L. G. Crampon, to transform a tourist into a Hawaiian in three easy steps:

> '*Stage One* — Get the visitor to dress Hawaiian
> *Stage Two* — Get the visitor to speak Hawaiian
> *Stage Three* — Get the visitor to act Hawaiian'

(Crampon n.d.:53–4). These steps are accomplished, respectively, by having the visitor put on an *aloha* shirt, say "Aloha!" instead of "Goodbye," and make him love Hawaii (since that is the way the *kamai'ina*, i.e. the locals, do) (ibid.:53–54). And there is probably no exaggeration in Crampon's statement to the effect that "probably this visitor is not 'acting.' He does like Hawaii. He is convinced that Hawaii is a paradise" (ibid.:54). Vacationing tourists in the studiously primitive surroundings of a Club Méditerranée resort and other less formally informal "touristic" paradises undergo similarly simplified rituals through which they playfully become natives or primitives for the duration of their vacation. Gottlieb (1982) has put such touristic metamorphoses in a comparative framework in her analysis of the process through which higher class Americans become a "Peasant for a Day," while lower-class ones become a "Queen (King) for a day" during their vacations.

C. Graña, in his spirited article on the modern museum as a palace (1971), uses the example of a little known picture by Louis Gabl entitled "The Peasant Visits the Castle," to illustrate succinctly this playful touristic transformation of identity discussed by Gottlieb: The picture ". . . shows the interior of a baronial house which has . . . been recently opened to the public . . . in the foreground . . . a peasant woman sits in a monumental and splendidly carved chair . . . the expression on her face makes us partners in the game of 'Look at me, I'm a Queen!' . . ." (ibid.:110). Graña continues: "The anecdote related in the painting carries two implications. On the one hand there is a mocking of the vanity of princely pomp; kings and nobles are after all made of the same stuff as the rest of us. But on the other hand it clearly proclaims and relishes the glorious folly of playing 'Queen for a day' . . . .

There is an appropriation of privileged glory by the popular customer-invader. But the thrill and the joy of this capture could not be what it is if it did not contain an act of secret veneration for a state of spiritual *and* material splendor which has never in actuality been part of our lives" (ibid.:110). The last point is crucial, and can be further expanded: in Graña's view, the (recreational) tourist playfully acts out something which in actuality he is not or cannot be. One can generalize Graña's insight and apply it to man living in a secularized world; the recreational tourist strives to recapture and re-enact playfully the sense of enchantment of the encounter with some transcending Reality, even as he "knows" that according to his own worldview such a Reality does not, in fact, exist. In that he differs from the experiential tourist, who vicariously, but seriously, experiences other people's Reality. The experiential tourist "knows" that there is such a Reality — for other cultures or in other times (MacCannell 1973:160), unaccessible to him as long as he remains modern; indeed, his efforts to make it accessible may turn him into an "experimental" or "existential" tourist; the recreational tourist, however can only mournfully regret the loss of that Reality, and enjoy its playful reenactment. This, I submit, is nostalgia in the deepest sense of the word. Students of recreational tourism, such as Moore (1980:211) and Buck (1978b) indeed dwelt upon nostalgia as a central theme in the touristic experiences of replications or stagings of the (American) past. But these are only concrete, minor instances of a general and profound nostalgia characteristic of modern man as recreational tourist; a nostalgia which is a modern version of Eliade's (1968:57–71) "nostalgia for Paradise" — just that their worldview tells them that there is no such place — and the only recourse left to them, *within the confines of that worldview*, is to recreate themselves playing as if there were — precisely like the play theologian plays as if God existed.

Tourist Experience and Modern Society

Recreational tourism is the most "functional" of the different modes of the touristic experience for modern, secular, society: it permits a playful outlet to modern man's longing for Reality, without endowing the object of his longing with ontological substance and thus threatening the modern, secular world view. He may thus play at what is not, or is not any more, even as he preserves his allegiance to the mundane, immanentistic centers of modernity. Man is thus "recreated" by his touristic activities, without becoming alienated from modernity.

Modernity, however, has a dynamics of its own: as the process of rationalization and disenchantment of the modern world ineluctibly proceeds, it eventually gnaws at the very centers of secular modern society: the modern secular religions of "progress," whether in their capitalist or socialist varieties, are eventually undermined by that very process and lose their attractiveness (cf. Weisskopf 1983:98). Contemporary "late modern" society is marked by growing alienation of its members, even as its center disintegrates; it faces the threat of becoming a centerless world, verging on nihilism (Ferrarotti 1979). This development may eventuate in contrary outcomes: alienated man may either accept the meaninglessness of his predicament and "give up" — a mood which, in the realm of tourism, leads to the "diversionary" mode. Or contrariwise, he may strive to retrieve meaning in the face of the threat of ultimate meaninglessness: this leads to a renewed, serious (and not merely playful) quest for novel "elective centers" (Chapter 5; Cohen, Ben-Yehuda and Aviad 1987). The first stirrings of this renewed quest find expression in experiential tourism: here the tourist seeks to ensure himself of the existence of a Reality — but elsewhere, beyond the limits of modernity. The experiential tourist, however, does not identify with the centers of other people's Reality, which remain inaccessible to him; rather he merely experiences their lives vicariously, remaining throughout an alienated modern. The outcome of such tourism, as MacCannell (1976:9, 83–84) shrewdly noted, consists of the incorporation or "museumization" of the non-modern and pre-modern "attractions" into modernity. They thus become "living museums," guarantors of the possibility of Reality. As, however, in this very process of museumization, they lose their authentic character and become progressively "staged," the experiential tourist loses interest in them. Such attractions then become the playgrounds of the recreational tourist, who, since he accepts the modern secular worldview, is satisfied with their "as if" character. The serious seekers of authenticity, on their part, move further afield.

As the consciousness of their alienation and the decentralization of their world deepens, late moderns realize the insufficiency of the merely vicarious experience of the Reality of others, and set out to seek new "elective" centers of their own; they become experimental or, insofar as they embrace such a center, existential tourists. Unlike experiential tourists, however, the latter do not incorporate their "elective" centers into modernity — rather they themselves abandon modernity (e.g. Blakeway 1980; Schneebaum 1970). Thereby they create touristic models for alternative life-styles, which may in the future attract like-minded moderns. In this the "existential" tourist who discovered or popularized an "elective" center resembles the initiators or founders of "countercultural" movements, such as sects, cults and communes, the emergence of which signifies the transition from an increasingly centerless late modernity into a multi-centered, post-modern, future world. For those who embrace a new "elective" center, transcendent Reality has been recovered — and they cease to relate to it playfully, whether in religion or in tourism.

To conclude: ludic, recreational tourism characterizes those moderns who have lost their belief in a transcendent Reality and give allegiance to the mundane, secular centers of the modern world (i.e. to the "religions" of progress, achievement and similar secular utopias), but still long for an apparently unretrievably lost transcendent Reality; it is this longing which motivates them to play at Reality, thus giving substance to Moore's (1980:207) statement: "Play lost importance to ritual in primitive cultures and archaic civilizations . . . but in our post modern world [i.e. late modern in my terminology] play seems to be gaining importance at the expense of both organized religion and obligatory ritual." Playful recreational tourism is an "as if" substitute for serious ritual in a secular, modern world for which God is dead. Serious experiential tourism to the Reality of others characterizes those moderns who are alienated from their late modern world, as it increasingly inclines towards centerlessness. These individuals seek to experience authenticity in the life of non-moderns, while themselves remaining (alienated) moderns. Experimental and existential tourism, finally, characterizes those who actively seek an alternative to modernity — an "elective" center. By identifying with it, they may eventually contribute to the transition of the late modern to a pluralistic post-modern world, in which transcendent Reality will again be retrieved, albeit in a multiplicity of ways.

Conclusion

The preceding analysis suggests an important general conclusion for the study of "comparative liminality": unlike societies recognizing an ontologically separate, transcendent Reality, even structured, liminal (and not merely liminoid) situations in the modern secular, immanentistic world do not sustain a full-fledged "ritual process." To put it bluntly: the tourist's "comfort in the truth that Mickey Mouse reigns at the baroque capital of the Magic Kingdom" is simply not the same as the pilgrim's existential rebirth through his communion with the Divine at the very Center of the world. Mickey Mouse may recreate but does not effect communion with transcendence; hence the third, crucial stage of the *rite de passage* is missing: the reintegration into a new (and higher) status in the mundane social structure. Moore's (1980) and Wagner's (1977) studies do not show that the alleged modern *rite-de-passage*, whether through Disneyland or touristic paradise, leads to any perceptible change in the tourist's status in his home society. The attraction may feature "passages" (Moore 1980:212–213), but these lead nowhere; there is no rebirth.

The recreational touristic play may help the tourist return, refreshed, to his mundane existence, but does not spiritually change his life. The playful experience is marginal in the life plan of the "recreational" tourist, whereas the *rite-de-passage* is central to the life plan of the religious pilgrim. It is this crucial difference which I sought to capture in the title of my paper on tourism on the beaches on the islands of southern Thailand (Cohen 1982b). But the folksy wisdom of the anonymous German poet of the early modern age captured the same idea much earlier in his description of the "recreational" attitude to religion of the fishes to whom, upon finding his church empty, St Anthony of Padua turned to preach:

> '*Die Predigt geendet*
> *Ein jedes sich wendet*
> *Die Hechte bleiben Diebe*
> *Die Aale viel lieben*
> *Die Predig hat g'fallen*
> *Sie blieben wie alle'*
> *(As the sermon ended*
> *Each turned his own way*
> *The pikes remained thieves*
> *The eels made much love*
> *They all liked the sermon*
> *But remained like all (i.e. unchanged)*
> Arnim and Brentano (comp. 1921:140)

Chapter 7

Authenticity and Commoditization in Tourism

Introduction

Much of the contemporary literature on the nature of modern tourism and its impact upon host societies relies on several important assumptions. In a most general way, these assumptions can be formulated as follows: First, tourism is said to lead to "commoditization" (Greenwood 1977) of areas in the life of a community which prior to its penetration by tourism have not been within the domain of economic relations regulated by criteria of market exchange (cf. Appadurai 1986). Local culture generally serves as the principal example of such commoditization. In particular, "colorful" local costumes and customs, rituals and feasts, and folk and ethnic arts become touristic services or commodities, as they come to be performed or produced for touristic consumption. Sexual services, in the form of tourist-oriented prostitution, are another major example of commoditization. The critical issue is that commoditization allegedly changes the meaning of cultural products and of human relations, making them eventually meaningless: "We already know from world-wide experience that local-culture . . . is altered and often destroyed by the treatment of it as a touristic attraction. It is made meaningless to the people who once believed in it . . ." (Greenwood 1977:131). Furthermore, according to the same source, since local culture can be commoditized by anyone, without the consent of the participants (1977:137), it can be expropriated, and the local people exploited.

    Second, commoditization is said to destroy the authenticity of local cultural products and human relations; instead a surrogate, covert "staged authenticity" (MacCannell 1973) emerges. As cultural products lose their meaning for the locals, and as the need to present the tourist with ever more spectacular, exotic and titillating attractions grows (Boorstin 1964:103), contrived cultural products are increasingly "staged" for tourists and decorated so as to look authentic. Fake "airport art" (Graburn 1967) is sold to tourists as if it were a genuine cultural product. Above all, tourists, who are apparently permitted to penetrate beyond the "front" areas of the visited society into its "back" (MacCannell 1973:597–598), are in fact cheated. Such back regions are frequently inauthentic "false backs," insidiously staged for tourist consumption. Thus, for example, localities may be staged as being remote, or "non-touristic" in order to induce tourists to "discover" them (MacCannell 1973:594); and native inhabitants of "exotic" places are taught to "play the native" in order to appear "authentic" to the tourists (cf. Chapter 16).

Third, "staged authenticity" is said to thwart the tourist's genuine desire for authentic experiences. MacCannell (1973:597) argued that "Touristic consciousness is motivated by the desire for authentic experiences, and the tourist may believe that he is moving in that direction . . . However, it is often the case that . . . what is taken to be entry into a back region is really entry into a front region that has been totally set up in advance [i.e. has been staged] for touristic visitation." According to MacCannell (1973:593), the tourist, in his desire for authentic experience, is the modern embodiment of the religious pilgrim. Tourism thus appears to become a modern surrogate for religion (MacCannell 1973:589; cf. also Cohen 1992b). However, it is implicit in MacCannell's analysis that there is no salvation in tourism: the tourist establishment dominates the tourist industry, and by misleading tourists to accept contrived attractions as "authentic," creates a "false touristic consciousness." A fully developed mass tourist system surrounds the tourist with a staged tourist space, from which there is "no exit." The modern tourist-pilgrim is thus damned to inauthenticity: "Tourists make brave sorties out from their hotels hoping, perhaps, for an authentic experience, but their paths can be traced in advance over small increments of what is for them increasingly apparent authenticity proffered by [staged] tourist settings. Adventurous tourists progress from stage to stage, always in the public eye, and greeted everywhere by their obliging hosts" (MacCannell 1973:602).

It follows from these assumptions that commoditization, engendered by tourism, allegedly destroys not only the meaning of cultural products for the locals but, paradoxically, also for the tourists. It thus emerges that, the more tourism flourishes, the more it allegedly becomes a colossal deception. These assumptions are highly persuasive and appealing to both sociologists and critics of modern society. But the conclusion seems far-fetched and hard to accept; unless, of course, one adopts a view of modern society as completely absurd and dominated by sinister powers, so that its members are surreptitiously misled to believe that they have genuinely authentic experiences, while in fact being systematically debarred from having them. However, before one goes to that extreme, it would be prudent to examine critically the above assumptions, in order to reach perhaps some more realistic conclusions.

Authenticity

"Authenticity" is an eminently modern value (cf. Appadurai 1986:45; Berger 1973; Trilling 1972), whose emergence is closely related to the impact of modernity upon the unity of social existence. As institutions become, in Nietzsche's words, "weightless" and lose their reality (Berger 1973:86; Trilling 1972:138), the individual is said to turn into himself. "If nothing on 'the outside' can he relied upon to give weight to the individual's sense of reality, he is left no option but to burrow into himself in search of the real. Whatever this *ens realissimum* may then turn out to be, it must necessarily be in opposition to any external [modern] social formation. The opposition between self and society has now reached its maximum. The concept of authenticity is one way of articulating this experience" (Berger 1973:88).

Modern man is thus seen, from the perspective of a contemporary existential philosophical anthropology, as a being in quest of authenticity. Since modern society is inauthentic, those modern seekers who desire to overcome the opposition between their authenticity-seeking self and society have to look elsewhere for authentic life. The quest for authenticity thus becomes a prominent motif of modern tourism, as MacCannell (1973, 1976) so incisively showed. However, here is also found the source of the confusion which the unexplicated use of this term introduced into tourism studies. In MacCannell's writings, as indeed in those of the researchers who followed his line of analysis (e.g. Redfoot 1984), the "quest for authenticity" is a "primitive" concept, which is at best illustrated, but left undefined. However, one appears to understand intuitively what is meant by it. It is a quest for that unity between the self and societal institutions, which endowed pre-modern existence with "reality" (Berger 1973:85). The alienated modern tourist in quest of authenticity hence looks for the pristine, the primitive, the natural, that which is as yet untouched by modernity. He hopes to find it in other times and other places (MacCannell 1976:160), since it is absent from his own world.

The difficulty with this use of the concept of "authenticity" in tourism studies is that it is a philosophical concept which has been uncritically introduced into sociological analysis. Furthermore, in tourism studies, the concept is used to characterize a criterion of evaluation used by the modern tourist as observer. The question, whether the "tourees" observed by the tourist at all possess such a concept, and if so, which traits of their own culture they consider to be "authentic" is rarely, if ever raised. Finally, the social analyst is tacitly assumed to understand the tourist's quest for "authenticity" because both belong to the modern world; they both appear to conceive of "authenticity" in similar, unproblematic terms. "Authenticity" thus takes up a given or "objective" quality attributable by moderns to the world "out there." The only apparent difference between the tourist and the social analyst is that the latter is more circumspect than the former. He is therefore assumed to be able to penetrate beyond appearances, and discover the deception of "staged authenticity" (MacCannell 1973) perpetrated by the tourees, or the tourist establishment. The unsuspecting tourist, who is less sophisticated and knowledgeable than the analyst, is assumed to be taken in by such prevarications. It then follows that, if the tourist had the analyst's debunking knowledge, he would reject the "staged authenticity" of the sights as contrived and lacking in authenticity. MacCannell and others who adopted his conceptual framework did not raise the possibility that the tourist and social analyst may conceive of authenticity in different terms.

In contrast to MacCannell, it is suggested that "authenticity" is a socially constructed concept; its social (as against philosophical) connotation is, therefore, not given, but "negotiable." The manner of the negotiation of its meaning should hence be made a major topic in the sociological and anthropological study of tourism. Several specific issues have to be distinguished.

Differential Conceptions of Authenticity

According to Trilling (1972:93) the provenance of the word "authenticity" ". . . is in the museum, where persons expert in such matters test whether objects of art [and by extension, ethnographic objects] are what they appear to be or are claimed to be, and therefore . . . worth the admiration they are being given." The approach to "authenticity" current until recently among curators and ethnographers will hence help to clarify the socially constructed nature of the concept. One of the paradoxes of the progressive professionalization of curators of primitive and ethnic art in the world's museums has been that a growing number of objects were declared to be "fakes," not because any new information had been discovered on the objects themselves, but rather because the connotation of the concept of fakery had been gradually extended. "Purist" curators and art historians tended to conceive of authenticity in primitive and ethnic art in ever more rigorous terms. Thus, McLeod, the director of the Museum of Mankind and an expert on African art, defined "genuine" (i.e. authentic) African art as ". . . any piece made from traditional materials by a native craftsman for acquisition and use by members of local society (though not necessarily by members of his own group) that is made and used with no thought that it ultimately may be disposed of for gain to Europeans or other aliens" (McLeod 1976:31).

Another author, also discussing African art, declared as authentic "Any object created for a *traditional purpose* and by a *traditional artist* . . .," but only if it "...conforms to *traditional forms*" (Cornet 1975:52, 55; emphases in the original). Like McLeod, Cornet also argues that, in order to be acceptable as authentic, the product should not be manufactured "specifically for the market" (ibid.:52).

Both authors hence emphasize the absence of commoditization as a crucial consideration in judgments of authenticity. It is noteworthy that Cornet proposes his definition despite his observation that there are cases where "...fakes [inauthentic objects] have become authentic" (ibid.:54), and cites as example objects produced by African artisans, in the past, for European patrons.

Such strict attitudes to authenticity, while in one sense professional, reflect in another the general modern preoccupation with authenticity which, indeed, appears to have contributed to the growing rigour of professional attitudes. Authenticity, for curators and ethnographers, is principally a quality of pre-modern life, and of cultural products produced prior to the penetration of modern Western influences: hence the common emphasis on cultural products which were "hand made" from "natural" materials. This emphasis obviously reflects the alienation of modern man from artificial and machine-made products. "The machine ... could make only inauthentic things, dead things..." (Trilling 1972:127). The same is essentially true for those anthropologists who, in quest of an "ethnographic present," seek to recapture the society and culture of the people whom they study as these had been before the "contaminating" contact with the Western world.

Here, too, scientific consensus mingles with the more personal, modern quest for the "pristine" and "authentic." Curators, ethnographers, and anthropologists thus constitute the most fitting prototypes of MacCannell's tourist who seeks authenticity in other times and other places. Redfoot (1984:299–301), indeed, classifies anthropologists as "third order tourists" who, according to Levi-Strauss, "...reject the artifices in their own culture and seek an alternative reality in 'quest' "; once there, however, they (unlike Redfoot's "fourth-order tourists") "...refrain from 'going native' " (1984:300). The anthropologist, thus "...digs deeper [than other tourists] in a quest for authenticity ... " though, his quest "... is doomed to failure because of the subjective distancing from the 'primitive' built into the anthropologist's role" (ibid.:301).

Anthropologists, like curators and ethnographers, even if paradigmatic of the modern tourist, appear to entertain more rigorous criteria of authenticity than do ordinary members of the traveling public. They belong to the wider category of modern, alienated intellectuals — indeed, their alienation from modernity often induces them to choose their respective professions.

Alienation may well be a structural consequence of the pluralization of modern life-worlds and the "weightlessness" of modern institutions (Berger 1973; Berger *et al.* 1973). However, not all moderns are personally equally alienated or aware of their alienation. Those who continue to identify unreflectively with one or another of the centers of modernity such as the work-ethic or the ethos of material and occupational achievement, are personally less alienated than those who are not so identified. Those who are disposed to reflect upon their life-situation are more aware of their alienation than those who do not tend to such contemplation.

Intellectuals, here exemplified by curators, ethnographers, and anthropologists, will be generally more alienated, and more aware of their alienation, than the rank-and-file middle-classes, and especially the lower middle class, who still strive to attain the material gains which those beyond them already enjoy.

Alienation and the quest for authenticity, however, appear to be positively related (cf. Chapter 5). It follows that intellectuals and other more alienated individuals will engage on a more serious quest of authenticity than most rank-and-file members of society. It is hypothesized further that, the greater their concern for authenticity, the stricter will be the criteria by which they conceive of it. Less alienated and hence less concerned individuals, including most rank-and-file tourists, will be content with much wider, less strict criteria of authenticity. This was probably meant by Nettekoven (1973) when he argued that "tourists are not ethnologists" and by Desai (1974:3) when he observed that the tourist is not a "stickler for authenticity."

However, though most tourists may not seek "authentic experiences in any ethnographic sense," Goldberg (1983:486) cautions that "neither are they content with mere entertainment...." Tourists indeed appear to seek authenticity in varying degrees of intensity, depending on the degree of their alienation from modernity. Following the preceding analysis, it can be argued that they will also conceive "authenticity" in different degrees of strictness. In other words, individuals who are less concerned with the authenticity of their touristic experiences, will be more prepared to accept as "authentic" a cultural product or attraction which more concerned tourists, applying stricter criteria, will reject as "contrived."

This argument can be restated in terms of the author's earlier typology of "modes of touristic experience" (Chapter 5) in which five types of such modes were proposed, according to the depth of experience the individual seeks in tourism. Tourism typically involves some encounter with the "Other." The deeper the experience sought by the tourist, the more strongly will he tend to embrace this "Other" and to turn it into his "elective center." But, since the salience of that Other-turned-Center thereby increases for the tourist, his concern with its authenticity will grow proportionately. This, in turn, will induce the tourist to adopt stricter criteria for the judgment of authenticity than do those tourists for whom the experience is less salient. It follows that "existential" tourists (Chapter 5) who tend spiritually to abandon modernity and embrace the Other as their elective center and, as it were, "switch worlds" (Berger and Luckmann 1966:144), or "go native" (Redfoot 1984:299 ff) will be the most "purist" of tourists. They will strive to move furthest away from the beaten track and to get in most closely with the natives (e.g. Blakeway 1980; Schneebaum 1970). In that, they resemble the anthropologist, curator, and ethnographer. However, unlike the latter, they do not take up the attitude of subjective detachment (Redfoot 1984:299) to the cultural products they encounter. While their experience may thus be fuller and more spontaneous, they also lack the professional attitude and critical capacity necessary to determine whether the traits by which they determine the "authenticity" of an object or an attraction are genuine or false. Hence they will more easily fall prey to sophisticated forms of covertly "staged authenticity" (MacCannell 1973). Here, the locals or the tourist establishment "stage" precisely those aspects of the cultural product which serve the existential tourists as marks of authenticity, according to their own, strict criteria. Indeed, authenticity-eager tourists, like Hollander's (1981) "political pilgrims," may tend to idealize the destination, and thus eagerly embrace as genuine the very prevarications with which they are served. This kind of staging is particularly insidious, because it acts upon the profound will to believe of serious tourists, and not on the make-believe attitude of the more frivolous ones. The disenchantment of such existential tourists may therefore be particularly bitter (cf. Chapter 5).

The further one moves down the scale of modes of touristic experiences, the less strict the criteria of authenticity employed by the tourist will tend to become. The criteria of "experimental" tourists who experiment with various potential elective centers will still resemble those of existential tourists. "Experiential" tourists, who seek to participate vicariously in the authentic life of others, will also tend to employ fairly strict criteria of authenticity, close to those of "existential" tourists. However, "recreational" tourists, who seek in the Other mainly enjoyable restoration and recuperation, and hence tend to approach the cultural products encountered on their trip with a playful attitude of make-believe (Chapter 6), will entertain much broader criteria of authenticity. Indeed, they might well be prepared playfully to accept a cultural product as authentic, for the sake of the experience, even though "deep down" they are not convinced of its authenticity (Chapter 6; cf. also Goldberg 1983:485). Hence, a less ingenuous "staging of authenticity" will be sufficient to make this kind of tourist accept a product as authentic — though their conviction of its authenticity may also be less than that of "existential" tourists. Finally, "diversionary" tourists, who seek mere diversion and oblivion on their trip, will remain totally unconcerned with the problem of authenticity of their experiences.

Differential Symbolizations of Authenticity

In the view of some experts on ethnic art (e.g. Willett 1976), authenticity and falseness are not a dichotomous pair of concepts. Rather, there exists a continuum leading from complete authenticity, through various stages of partial authenticity, to complete falseness. The question therefore arises: Which are the diacritical traits which, for a given individual, in particular a tourist, make a cultural product acceptable as "authentic?" The question here is *not* whether the individual does or does not "really" have an authentic experience in MacCannell's (1973) sense, but rather what endows his experience with authenticity in his own view. Thus one can follow Gottlieb's approach: she ". . . assumes that the vacationers' own feelings and views about vacations are 'authentic,' whether or not the observer judges them to match the host culture" (Gottlieb 1982:168). However, while Gottlieb does not make any further inquiries into the bases of tourists' feelings and views, it is proposed here to open these to investigation. According to the approach developed above, tourists will differ in the number and kinds of traits necessary to their mind to authenticate a cultural product.

As the preceding section notes, for the purist professional expert, only a cultural product which appears authentic in all of its varied aspects, would be acceptable as "authentic." This may also be the case with deeply concerned tourists. Thus, on one of the trekking trips in which this author participated in the course of his study of the penetration of tourism into the hill-tribe area of northern Thailand, a French tourist, a teacher by profession, complained about the fact that the people in a tribal village, which had been opened to tourism only a few weeks earlier, used industrially produced plastic cups instead of indigenously produced bamboo cups. The mere adoption of plastic cups, although unrelated to the penetration of tourism, already offended his sense of cultural authenticity.

While this kind of tourist often serves as the prototype of the ideal tourist, he is, statistically speaking, a minority among the huge population of contemporary mass tourism. Such a demand for "total authenticity" will be most prominent among "existential" or "experimental" tourists, seriously concerned with the Other as at least a potential elective center. The vast majority of tourists do not demand such a "total authenticity." Even "experiential" tourists, though seriously concerned with the authenticity of their experience, and entertaining strict criteria for judgments of authenticity, will often focus in such judgments on some traits of the cultural product and disregard others. Hence, they will be prepared to accept a cultural product as authentic, insofar as traits, which they consider to be diacritical, are judged by them to be authentic. These traits are then considered sufficient for the authentization of the product as a whole. One could say that they symbolize metonymically the authenticity of the tourist-oriented cultural product as a whole. Therefore, such tourists will accept a commercialized object as "authentic," insofar as they are convinced that it is indeed ornamented with "traditional" designs and "hand made" by members of an ethnic group (even though it may have been made of different materials or in a different form than the "traditional" product and was produced expressly for the market). They may similarly accept as "authentic" a commercialized replication of local customs, such as a dance or a ritual, in so far as it tends to be performed identically by members of the local group, as is its non-commercialized counterpart. A recent study by Moscardo and Pearce (1986) provides some empirical evidence on this point. They have studied visitors perceptions of Australian historic theme parks. Since such parks "preserve or restore some aspects of a nation's or a region's heritage" (1986:471), they are almost by definition not "authentic" in MacCannell's sense. However, the visitors generally did perceive them as "authentic" — in the sense of being accurate reconstructions of Australia's past (ibid.:474–476), rather than genuine historical remains. Contrary to the authors' claim (ibid.:472), park operators — and some tourists — appear thus to be using the word "authenticity" differently from social scientists. However, the point of this argument is that by accepting a particular trait of the site, namely "verissimilitude," as authenticating the site as a whole, the tourists become neither superficial fools satisfied with the spurious, in Boorstin's (1964) sense, nor victims of a prevaricating touristic establishment which "stages" authenticity in MacCannell's (1973) sense.

Recreational tourists, whose concern with authenticity is relatively low, may well accept even a substantially staged product and experience as "authentic." This would not be necessarily because they have been misled by the staging, but because even the faintest vestige of, or resemblance to what experts would consider an "authentic" trait of the product, may suffice for them to play the make-believe game of having an "authentic" experience. Therefore, such tourists may playfully consent to buy fake products or experiences as if they were genuine, merely because their resemblance to the genuine thing gives these tourists an inkling of authenticity. The recreation which Gottlieb's (1982) tourists derive from being a "King for a Day" or a "Peasant for a Day," one may argue, derives from their feeling "how it must have been to be a king (or a peasant)"; even though they are perfectly aware of the fact that their own, purchased experience has been staged for their benefit.

Finally, diversionary tourists may enjoy touristic products even if these are, in their own view, completely contrived, insofar as they appeal to them merely as "funny," "cute," or "lovely."

Emergent Authenticity

Since authenticity is not a primitive given, but negotiable, one has to allow for the possibility of its gradual emergence in the eyes of visitors to the host culture. In other words, a cultural product, or a trait thereof, which was at one point generally judged as contrived or inauthentic may, in the course of time, become generally recognized as authentic, even by experts, as Cornet's (1975:54) equivocation quoted above demonstrates. Thus, for example, an apparently contrived, tourist-oriented festival (such as the Inti Raymi festival in Cuzco, a "revival" of an ancient Incaic custom) may in due time become accepted as an "authentic" local custom. Similarly, craft products initially produced merely for sale to visitors and tourists, may eventually become "authentic" products of an ethnic group or region — as happened with, for example, the Eskimo soapstone carvings (Graburn 1976b) or the Haida argillite carvings (Kaufmann 1976). Greenwood (1982:27) remarked that "all viable cultures are in the process of 'making themselves up' all the time." One could call this process "emergent authenticity" just as a parallel process in the ethnic realm was termed "emergent ethnicity" (Yancey *et al.* 1976). "Emergent authenticity" stresses one aspect or refers to one manifestation, of the wider phenomenon of "invention of tradition," whose ubiquitousness has been so impressively documented in Hobsbawm and Ranger's (1983) volume. In principle it is possible for any new-fangled gimmick, which at one point appeared to be nothing but a staged "tourist trap," to become over time, and under appropriate conditions, widely recognized as an "authentic" manifestation of local culture. One can learn about this process of gradual "authentication" from the manner in which the American Disneylands, once seen as the supreme example of contrived popular entertainment, became over time a vital component of contemporary American culture (e.g. Johnson 1981; King 1981). They will, no doubt, in the future be perceived even by historians and ethnographers, as an "authentic" American tradition (cf. Moore 1980).

One further point, closely related to the concept of "emergent authenticity" ought to be noted. The new, "external public" (Graburn 1976a; Shiloah and Cohen 1983:237) provided by the tourists, may offer an opportunity to the producers of cultural products to incorporate in them novel but "authentic" messages, differing from those incorporated in cultural products intended solely for the "internal" local or ethnic public. Thus, Silver (1979) claims to have detected such messages hidden in the apparently exaggerated, "exotic" features of commercialized African sculptures. This author also found such messages explicitly stated in the commercialized figurative embroideries of Hmong (Meo) refugees from Laos (Cohen 1990). The Hmong from whose "traditional" arts figurative representations were absent, nostalgically depict in these embroideries the richness of their traditional customs to the world at large, as well as seek to draw its attention to their sufferings in recent history and to their present dire predicament. Such messages thus become new cultural expressions, which are recognized as "authentic" even by experts, such as anthropologists or ethnographers interested in cultural change.

Commoditization

"Commoditization" is a process by which things (and activities) come to be evaluated primarily in terms of their exchange value, in a context of trade, thereby becoming goods (and services); developed exchange systems in which the exchange value of things (and activities) is stated in terms of prices form a market. Though trade systems and gift systems were apparently even in the past less unequivocally segregated than previously claimed, markets have expanded throughout the world in the modern era, bringing about the commoditization of an ever wider range of things and activities (cf. Appadurai 1986). The principal question in this context is, what happens to the other meanings (particularly religious, cultural, and social) of things (and activities) once they become commoditized, particularly under the impact of tourism.

It is generally the case that "Dealings with strangers . . . provide contexts for the commoditization of things that are otherwise protected from commoditization" (Appadurai 1986:15). Tourists in the modern world are particularly ubiquitous types of strangers, notorious for their propensity to precipitate, directly or indirectly, the commoditization of an ever wider range of things (and activities), many of which have been kept out of the domain of the market prior to the penetration of tourism, by rigorous normative prohibitions and taboos.

According to Greenwood (1977), who made one of the first studies of commoditization of culture through tourism, the commoditized cultural products lose in the process their intrinsic meaning and significance for the local people, who in turn lose their enthusiasm for producing them. Thus, Greenwood argues, as the public ritual of the *Alarde* in the Spanish-Basque town of Fuenterrabia became a major touristic attraction, and the authorities declared that it should be performed twice on the same day to accommodate the large number of visitors, the local participants lost interest in it. Consequently, ". . . the municipal government was considering payments to people for their participation in the Alarde . . . just as the gypsies are paid to dance and the symphony orchestra is paid to make music. The ritual has become a performance for money. The meaning is gone" (Greenwood 1977:135). In other words, the once "authentic" public ritual became a staged performance, a cultural "commodity."

Such processes of commoditization of culture for touristic purposes are doubtlessly quite common all over the Third World and in the ethnic areas of both Western and communist countries. Rituals, ceremonies, costumes, and folk arts may all be subjected to commoditization. Moreover, since the process is frequently initiated by culture-brokers and touristic entrepreneurs from outside the local community, it may well lead to the exploitation of the locals and of their cultural resources by outsiders. Finally, the process of commoditization also tends to affect the cultural products themselves. As they become increasingly oriented to an "external public," rituals may be shortened, embellished, or otherwise adopted to the tastes of the tourists (cf. Boorstin 1964:103). Art and craft products may also be changed in form, materials, or colors (cf. Cohen 1983a, 2000), ". . . in response to the impositions or temptations from large-scale and sometimes far-away consumers" (Appadurai 1986:47) such as in the case of "indirect tourism" (Aspelin 1977). Indeed, the emerging genre of "tourist arts" (Appadurai 1986:47; Cohen 1992c; Graburn ed. 1976) is perhaps the most salient example of the commoditization of a range of cultural products through tourism.

All these developments and sometimes radical changes in the form and content of the commoditized goods and services notwithstanding, however, Greenwood's categorical assertion that, once a cultural product is commoditized "the meaning is gone," appears to he an overgeneralization. Counter-examples may be easily found. For example, folk musicians, who play for money to an external audience, may be excited by the opportunity to present their art and proud to display their competence. There is no reason to assume that their music lost all meaning for them, merely because they have been paid for performing it. It would be absurd to argue that all popular music is meaningless for the artists merely because it is commercialized. Greenwood appears to have assumed that the immediate negative reaction of the local population to the commoditization of the *Alarde* will become its permanent attitude to the festival. This assumption, however, contradicts an implication of his own later insight regarding "emergent authenticity" cited above.

For, just as a new cultural product can become with time widely accepted as "authentic," so it can, although changed through commoditization, acquire a new meaning for its producers. Thus, what used to be a religiously meaningful ritual for an internal public, may become a culturally significant self-representation before an external public. Moreover, the two kinds of meanings are not necessarily mutually exclusive but could be additive: new meanings may be added to old ones, which persevere into the new situation. According to McKean (1976b:241–243), Balinese ritual performances have three separate audiences, a divine, a local, and a touristic. This last one does not necessarily spoil the meaning of the performance for the two others. "The touristic audience is appreciated for the economic assets it can bring . . . but its presence has not diminished the importance of performing competently for the other two audiences, the villagers and the divine realm" (ibid.:244). Moreover if Balinese performances are staged specifically for tourists, ". . . the funds, as well as the increased skills and equipment available have enriched the possibility that the indigenous performances will be done with more elegance, in effect conserving culture" (ibid:244).

One has to bear in mind that commoditization often hits a culture not when it is flourishing, but when it is actually already in decline, owing to the impingement of outside forces preceding tourism. Under such circumstances, the emergence of a tourist market frequently facilitates the preservation of a cultural tradition which would otherwise perish. It enables its bearers to maintain a meaningful local or ethnic identity which they might otherwise have lost. This is particularly the case in the sphere of folk arts and crafts, many of which are in decline in Third World countries owing to the penetration of industrial goods and Western consumer tastes — but some of which have been salvaged or revived through demand by the tourist market (cf. Graburn ed. 1976). Finally, even where a cultural tradition still flourishes, its commoditization may well be emically perceived by its members as less of a change than it appears to an external analyst. While to the external observer, commoditization may appear to involve a complete transformation of meaning as a cultural product is being reoriented to a new, external audience, the performers themselves may not necessarily perceive that such a transformation had in fact occurred. Rather, despite the changed context, they may perceive an often astonishing degree of continuity between the old and the new situation. Thus, performers of tourist-oriented Voodoo shows in Haiti, do still go into a trance (Goldberg 1983:488); and tourist-oriented prostitutes in Bangkok bring many traditional attitudes towards Thai men into their relationships with tourists (Cohen 1993b). Local people frequently interpret novel situations in traditional terms, and thus perceive a continuity of cultural meaning which may escape the observer (cf. Smith 1982).

Conclusion

This analysis leads to a conclusion which is, in the main, the opposite of that deduced from the basic assumptions prevalent in much of the contemporary literature on tourism, as presented at the beginning of this chapter. Commoditization does not necessarily destroy the meaning of cultural products, neither for the locals nor for the tourists, although it may do so under certain conditions. Tourist-oriented products frequently acquire new meanings for the locals, as they become a diacritical mark of their ethnic or cultural identity, a vehicle of self-representation before an external public. However, old meanings do not thereby necessarily disappear, but may remain salient, on a different level, for an internal public, despite commoditization — as the case of Balinese ritual performances exemplifies. Neither does commoditization necessarily destroy the meaning of cultural products for the tourists, since these are frequently prepared to accept such a product, even if transformed through commoditization, as "authentic," insofar as some at least of its traits are perceived as "authentic." Such traits can then be taken to authenticate, metonymically, the product as a whole. The breadth of such authentic traits necessary to satisfy the tourist will, in turn, depend on the depth of the touristic experience to which each individual tourist aspires. Since most rank-and-file tourists do not aspire to much depth, a few traits of a cultural product which appear "authentic" will in most cases suffice for its acceptance as an "authentic" product. Hence, mass tourism does not succeed because it is a colossal deception, but because most tourists entertain concepts of "authenticity" which are much looser than those entertained by intellectuals and experts, such as curators and anthropologists. Indeed, for many tourists, tourism is a form of play (Chapter 6), which like all play, has profound roots in reality, but for the success of which a great deal of make-believe, on part of both performers and audience, is necessary. Tourists willingly, even if often unconsciously, participate playfully in a game of "as if," pretending that a contrived product is authentic, even if deep down they are not convinced of its authenticity.

This re-examination of some of the assumptions prevalent in the tourism literature has some important implications for the study of the social and cultural impacts of tourism. In particular, rather than assuming the destructive impact of commoditization on the authenticity and meaning of cultural products, such impact should be submitted to a detailed empirical examination, if possible within an emic, processual, and comparative framework (Cohen 1979b:31–32). Such an approach will make it possible to gauge over time the permutations of meaning and authenticity as perceived by locals and tourists alike; it will also make it possible to determine the conditions under which cultural meanings are preserved or newly emergent, and distinguish them from those under which they are practically destroyed through the impact of tourism. Such an examination will, in turn, forge the intellectual instruments necessary for the formulation of a prudent policy approach to tourism, as both a branch of economic development and as a major cultural manifestation of the modern world, which will avoid the extremes of a total condemnation of tourism as well as of its uncritical approbation.

Chapter 8

Traditions in the Qualitative Sociology of Tourism

Introduction

While quantitative methods enjoy much prestige in contemporary sociology, preoccupy the methodologists, and are taught at universities to the virtual exclusion of everything else, it is nevertheless correct that "much of the best work in sociology has been carried out using qualitative methods and without statistical tests" (Collins 1984:340). Qualitative methodology has recently attracted growing attention (e.g. Schwartz and Jacobs 1979). However, sociologists of tourism have given it but scarce, if any, explicit consideration, although in this field, the most significant and lasting contributions have also been made by researchers who employed an often loose qualitative methodology. Not only were their research methods often ill-defined and their data unsystematically collected, but even their definition of theoretical concepts, and the operationalization of the latter, leaves much to be desired. Nevertheless, their often acute insights and the theoretical frameworks in which these have been embodied, provided the point of departure for several "traditions" in the sociological study of tourism, which endowed the field with its distinctive intellectual tension, even as the much more rigorous and quantitative "touristological" studies often yielded results of rather limited interest.

In this chapter three such emergent "traditions" will be examined: those departing from the work of Boorstin, MacCannell and Turner. Though their disciplinary backgrounds differ — Boorstin a historian, MacCannell a sociologist, and Turner an anthropologist — the impact of each of these major figures on the sociological study of tourism was considerable. The fundamental intellectual problem which drew the attention of each to the field of tourism, their basic approaches, and the "research program" which emerged from them are examined and compared. This is followed by the unfolding of these research programs by their followers and critics, paying particular attention to the empirical studies which they informed. The article concludes by a comparative examination of the three approaches and of possible ways of their mutual accommodation.

Boorstin and Touristic "Pseudo-Events"

Boorstin's principal intellectual concern is with the contrived and illusory nature of the human experience in contemporary American society, with the "thicket of unreality which stands between us and the facts of life" (Boorstin 1964:3). His principal argument is that contemporary Americans do not experience "reality," but thrive on "pseudo-events." The modern mass tourist serves as a prime illustration of his argument. Boorstin's (1964:77−117) chief claim in his essay on "the lost art of travel" is that the modern tourist (in contrast to the traveler of yore) is just a passive onlooker who seeks to enjoy the extravagantly strange from the security of the familiar. Isolated from the host environment and the local people, he travels in guided groups and thrives on contrived "attractions" gullibly enjoying the "pseudo-events," while blithely disregarding the "real" world around him. This attitude, in turn, induces both the tourist entrepreneurs and the natives to produce ever more extravagant contrivances for touristic consumption, thus increasing the gulf between the tourist and the real life at his destination. Eventually, the (contrived) image of the destination becomes, promoted by commercial advertisements, the criterion by which the tourist selects and evaluates the sights at his destination. Tourism thus turns into a closed, self-perpetuating system of illusions. While Boorstin draws his witty and often caustic conclusions from acute observations of the modern scene, he does not — like, for example, Turner and his followers at a later stage — ask whether the illusory experience of the modern tourist may have some deeper, unsuspected human or cultural meaning. His primary concern is to criticize the prevailing tenor of modern society. Moreover, it is this critical stance which he shares with other students of tourism who directly or indirectly followed his lead.

   Several observations on Boorstin's approach are necessary. First, Boorstin is not a "detached" analyst, but an ironic observer who freely mixes opinions with facts, thus providing a fascinating but wholly one-sided argument. Secondly, while his conclusions are original, his opinions are not. In fact, they are widely held prejudices about the nature of modern tourism. As MacCannell (1973:600) acutely observed, Boorstins attitude to tourism "... is commonplace among tourists and travel writers," rather than a privileged perspective of the researcher. Thirdly, Boorstin presents a general characterization of what he sees to be the tourist, disregarding any differences which may exist in the motivation, conduct, and experiences of actual tourists. Finally, the empirical illustrations, which he marshals to buttress his argument, though often intriguing, are far from giving a systematic or well-balanced picture of modern tourism.

Boorstin's was the first in a long line of socio-critical publications on tourism both in America and Europe (e.g. Adler 1980; Armanski 1978; Fussell 1979; Lewis and Brissett 1981; Turner and Ash 1975). Some of these referred expressly to Boorstin; others did not; yet all were written in the same spirit. Most, unfortunately, exemplified little theoretical rigor or methodological sophistication and did not substantially advance or develop Boorstin's approach. Nevertheless, Boorstin's brief essay served as an important point of departure for more disciplined writings in the sociology of tourism. Indeed, it could be argued that it provoked the serious sociological study of tourism in the English-speaking world. Most of this work, however, emerged from a polemic with both Boorstin's perspective and his characterization of the tourist, rather than from an unquestioning acceptance of his premises and conclusions.

Boorstin (1964:94–99) argued that the tourist seeks to observe the strangeness of the host environment from the security of his immediate surroundings, such as American-type hotels. The present author, in an early article (Chapter 3), turned this general insight of Boorstin's into a variable which served as the basis for the construction of a typology of tourist roles, thus breaking down Boorstin's global image of the tourist into more specific, empirically identifiable types. Four such types were conceptualized and ordered by the extent to which they tend to travel within the familiarity of the "environmental bubble" of their home environment, as against their readiness to expose themselves to the strangeness of the host environment. Two "institutionalized" (or better, "conventional") types were distinguished: the "organized mass tourist," in whose role familiarity is most, and exposure to strangeness least emphasized, and whose trip is virtually completely ensconced by the environmental bubble of the tourist establishment; and the "individual mass tourist" who is similarly ensconced but, traveling on his own, tends to expose himself somewhat more to the strangeness of the host surroundings. These two types were contrasted with "non-institutionalized" (or "non-conventional") types of tourists, the "explorer" who takes only residual recourse to the familiarity of the services provided by the tourist establishment, and the "drifter," who travels outside the orbit of these services and who is most exposed to the strangeness of the host environment. It was further argued that the type of the tourist's role influences the nature of his experiences on his trip, the extent and variety of his contacts with members of the host society, and even his impact on the destination (Chapter 3). At a later stage, this typology was further related to other, more specific topics, such as language usage in touristic situations (Chapter 14).

The typology helps to qualify Boorstin's general argument that all modern tourists seek illusory "pseudo-events." This may be to some extent true of the two conventional types of mass tourists who are both more exposed to such events and more prepared to accept them, even though the deeper meaning of these tourists' quest for illusions may have escaped Boorstin (see below and Chapter 6). It is true to a much smaller extent of the two non-conventional types of tourists, the explorer and the drifter, and certainly not of the "original drifter" (Chapter 4) who is the contemporary counterpart of the traveler of the past.

This further development of Boorstin's basic idea involves a change of perspective. Boorstin's approach was essentially "diachronic." He proposed a model for a historical transition from "Traveler to Tourist." This was transformed by the author into a synchronic typology of contemporary tourists, one pole of which, the "drifter" corresponded to Boorstin's (historical) traveler, while the other, the "organized mass tourist" corresponded to his description of the (contemporary) tourist. Such a typology was intended not only to qualify the widely disseminated stereotype of "the tourist," but also to create the basis for a comparative study of tourism.

Similar typologies have been proposed by other students of tourism, especially Smith (1977:8–13). Her typology is in a sense a further refinement of the author's and thus continues the line of analysis initiated with the criticism of Boorstin's ideas. The typologies of Cohen and Smith have been further examined in several empirical studies (cf. Cohen 1984b:378).

Despite the impression of continuity emerging from the preceding discussion, it could hardly be said that Boorstin's work engendered a full-fledged "tradition" in the study of tourism. Yet his short essay remains one of the most frequently cited works in the field — it was cited 15 times in the articles appearing in *Annals of Tourism Research* in the last ten years (1977 to 1986). However, only rarely did his ideas generate specific research projects or even help much in the formulation of theoretical problems (but see Papson 1981). References to his work were generally critical. For example Schmidt (1979:445) calls his position a caricature, and Buck (1977:198) comments that Boorstin "chooses to compare the worst . . . of current travel trends, with the best . . . of another time" (but still finds his argument "convincing"). Moreover, those who confronted his position with that of others, especially with MacCannell's (e.g. Graburn 1983a:15) usually tended more towards the latter. Boorstin's importance for the sociology of tourism lies in the fact that he gave it an initial impetus — even though the work of his successors denied the validity of the image of the contemporary tourist, which he had so wittily painted in his essay.

MacCannell and Touristic "Authenticity"

MacCannell was the first sociologist to anchor the study of tourism in the mainstream of sociological theory, by relating his analysis to the work of Marx,

Durkheim, Levi-Strauss, and Goffman in an effort to develop an "ethnography of modernity" (MacCannell 1976:1). This is closely related to his principal intellectual concern which is in fact similar to that of Boorstin: the inauthenticity of modern life. However, MacCannell looks for the ways in which modern man seeks to overcome his predicament, and here his interest turns to the tourist. The image of the tourist which emerges from his work contrasts sharply with Boorstin's. Indeed, it is almost a studied reversal of it. For Boorstin, the tourist expresses the inauthenticity of modernity; for MacCannell he embodies the quest for authenticity. In MacCannell's (1973:589−590) view, indeed, this quest represents the modern version of a universal human concern with the sacred. The tourist is seen as the pilgrim of the contemporary secular world (MacCannell 1973:593), paying homage to "attractions," the symbols of modernity, just as the traditional religious pilgrim paid homage to a sacred center. However, since the symbols of modernity are many and varied, reflecting the differentiations of modern society, they are represented by a multiplicity of "sanctified" attractions. Moreover, modernity, in MacCannell's (1976:8) view greedily incorporates the "pre-modern" and "museumizes" it, to be displayed for viewing by modern man, so that the touristic "attractions" are a heterogeneous mix ranging from modern phenomena, such as various "work-displays" (MacCannell 1976:62ff.), down to strange and exotic primitive customs. The aggregate of the attractions is the modern equivalent of the traditional pilgrimage center. MacCannell (1976:109−133) goes on to develop a "semiotic" of attractions, with the express intention to link the study of tourist attractions, as signs, to the structuralist approach of theorists of culture, such as Levi-Strauss. This, indeed, appears to be the heart of MacCannell's program (cf. van den Abbeele 1980), although his semiotic analysis remains, on the whole, only loosely integrated with the other main themes of his work.

While for Boorstin (1964:103) attractions are "of little significance to the inward life of a people, but wonderfully saleable as tourist commodity," for MacCannell they are highly significant social symbols. Boorstin (1964:103) takes it for granted that "attractions" are inauthentic; he states that "Tourist attractions serve their purpose best when they are pseudo-events," since in his view tourists seek illusions. MacCannell's tourist, however, is concerned with the authenticity of the attractions. The quest for authenticity, indeed, rather than the search for contrived illusions, is said to be the fundamental motivation of modern tourists. Since, however, modern man is alienated from his own inauthentic and shallow world, he seeks authenticity elsewhere in other times and other places (MacCannell 1976:3; cf. Chapter 7). He displays a "fascination for the 'real life' of others" (MacCannell 1976:91), which possesses "reality," in contrast to his own spurious existence. Moderns are attracted by "reality." Borrowing an idea from Goffman (1959) and applying it to the study of tourism, MacCannell (1973:594) argues that moderns do not find "reality" in the "front" of their destinations, but discover it in the "back" regions. However, as the right of tourists to look into these "back" regions, into the inner workings of the host society and its institutions, becomes institutionalized (MacCannell 1976:49), so the locals — whether in self-defense or owing to commercial interests — create contrived "tourist spaces" in which spurious attractions are decorated and presented as if they were "real." In other words, they "stage authenticity" for touristic consumption. MacCannell (1973:601) claims that ". . . once tourists have entered touristic space, there is no way out for them as long as they press their search for authenticity." The resulting inauthenticity of tourist experiences is, hence, not a consequence of the tourist's superficial desire for the spurious and illusory, as Boorstin argued, but rather a structural consequence of the development of tourism.

The principal advance of MacCannell's approach over Boorstin's consists in his distinction between the touristic perspective and that of the social scientist. MacCannell (1976:10) ". . . uses critical statements such as Boorstin's [regarding modern tourism] in the same way as the ethnographer uses the explanations of social life volunteered by his native respondents: as part of the puzzle to be solved, not as one of its solutions." MacCannell thus opened new vistas on tourism, precisely because he has separated current opinions on tourism from the sociological study of touristic phenomena, and made the former a subject of the latter. This distinction, in turn, by introducing an allegedly unbiased view of the tourist into sociological discussion made it possible, in principle, to distinguish between the socio-structural characteristics of tourism and the personal motivation of individual tourists (which, owing to his prejudiced view of tourism, remained fused in Boorstin's analysis).

However, while MacCannell's approach is stunningly innovative, his portrait of the tourist is no less a "positive caricature" than Boorstin's was a negative one (Schmidt 1979:445). He criticizes Boorstin for falling back from an attempt at a structural analysis of "sightseeing and touristic phenomena . . . onto individual-level interpretations" (MacCannell 1973:600), that is, for interpreting the illusory character of the attractions as an indication that tourists are motivated to seek illusory experiences. But he appears to be committing a similar error. Having discovered, like Trilling (1972) and Berger (1973) before him, "authenticity" as a basic value of modern culture, deriving from the peculiarly fragmentary and alienating nature of modern social structure, MacCannell (1973) goes on tacitly to ascribe such a quest to each and every individual modern tourist: "None of the accounts in my collection support Boorstin's contention that tourists want superficial, contrived experiences. Rather, tourists demand authenticity, just as Boorstin does." MacCannell's collection, however, was hardly systematic or representative, being based on informal methods. He collected his data by ". . . follow tourists, sometimes joining their groups, sometimes watching them from afar, through writings by, for and about them" (1976:4). Such informal methods may be highly useful to gain basic insights. They do not, however, lead to balanced conclusions any more than Boorstin's spirited quotations. Indeed, the idea that all tourists engage equally seriously in a quest for authenticity offends one's common sense (Schudson 1979:1252).

MacCannell's work had a more significant impact on the sociological study of tourism than that of any other researcher before him. An indication of his influence is the fact that it was cited 50 times in the articles appearing in *Annals of Tourism Research*, in the ten-year period of 1977–1986, as well as in most other sociological publications on tourism during that period. Moreover, the reaction to MacCannell's approach was less critical than that to Boorstin's. Indeed, many authors have found that MacCannell's concepts — and particularly his twin ideas of "staged authenticity" and "tourist space" — helped to illuminate some of their specific research findings (e.g. Adams 1984:478–479; Buck 1977:191–200; Ichaporia 1983:85; LaFlamme 1979:145–146; Moore 1985:639–640; Schmidt 1979:445; Schuchat 1983; Richter and Richter 1985). Others have employed his ideas creatively in the formulation of their research designs and thus amplified and examined empirically some of MacCannell's theoretical concepts. Among the more important empirical studies based on MacCannell are Buck's (1978b) study of boundary maintenance in an Old Order Amish community and Fine and Speer's (1985) examination of the rhetoric of "sight sanctification." Even as MacCannell's approach found wide acceptance and application, thus indeed giving rise to a veritable "tradition" in tourism studies, several critical voices were heard which qualified, reformulated, and further developed his approach. Some critics found his data collection rather unsystematic (e.g. Moore 1985:662), though it should be pointed out that the specific studies which closely followed MacCannell's approach made up much of that deficiency and found his claims — in contrast to those of Boorstin's — generally confirmed. Others, however, criticized MacCannell's theoretical approach. Indeed, their work endowed the "tradition" which emerged from it with its vital and dynamic quality.

MacCannell's, like Boorstin's, characterization of the tourist was too global to be realistic. Hence, it had to be qualified. Just as "strangeness and familiarity" provided a useful point of departure from Boorstin's paradigm of the tourist to develop a typology of tourist *roles*, so the concept of "authenticity" in MacCannell's work provided this author with a starting point for a typology of tourist *experiences*. A systematic elaboration of this idea (Chapter 5) departed from MacCannell's claim that modern man, in his alienation from his own environment, seeks authenticity elsewhere and so, in fact, becomes a tourist. Assuming, however, that not all moderns are equally alienated, one can hypothesize that they also will not seek authenticity with equal intensity. Rather, these two variables will be directly related: the greater the alienation, the more intensive the quest for authenticity. A five-fold typology of "modes of (desired) touristic experiences" was therefore developed on the basis of this hypothesis. In order to relate MacCannell's approach to a broader theoretical framework in the study of religion, and expand the typology even further, MacCannell's approach was rephrased in terms of a pair of concepts not utilized by him, but germane to his general perspective: the concepts of "the Center" (Eliade 1971:12−17; Shils 1975) and of its opposite, "the Other." The gist of the argument developed on this background is as follows. A modern individual who is attached to the Center of his own society (and not alienated from it) will strive to "recreate" himself from the strains which it provokes in the recesses of the Other, beyond the boundaries of his world. He will seek *recreational* experiences with little concern for their authenticity. Recreational tourists will resemble Boorstin's image of *the* tourist. By contrast, a modern individual who is completely alienated from his own society, and seeks an alternative to it, will tend to embrace the Other beyond the boundaries of his world, and turn it into his "elective Center." Such a tourist will seek *existential* experiences, and will be deeply concerned with their authenticity. Indeed, he will come closest to the prototypical pilgrim (cf. Turner 1973:214). This type, however, goes beyond MacCannell's conception of the tourist. His tourist merely seeks a vicarious experience of the authentic life of others, without, however, embracing their life as his own "elective Center." With all his alienation, MacCannell's tourist does not strive to abandon modernity. He is the *experiential* tourist par excellence, an observer, who, though concerned about the authenticity of the Other, which he experiences, does not identify with it. He, therefore, occupies a middle position between the recreational and existential types. Two additional intermediate types are the *diversionary* tourist (located between the recreational and experiential types) who, though alienated, does *not* seek authenticity; and the *experimental* tourist (located between the experiential and the existential types) who seeks, but has not yet found, an "elective center" in the Other, and is much concerned with the authenticity of his experiences. This typology was, in turn, further elaborated by Redfoot (1984) and utilized in several empirical case studies (e.g. Cohen 1982b:221; Goldberg 1983:485ff; Graburn 1983b).

Another of MacCannell's ideas which was taken up and further developed by others is that of "tourist space." MaeCannell's general concept was developed in Cohen (1979b:26−27) into a four-fold typology based on the distinction between covert and overt tourist spaces on the one hand, and the tourist's impression of whether or not he faces staged tourist space, on the other. Pearce (1982:100−101, cf. also Moscardo and Pearce 1986) further developed and operationalized this typology for empirical research.

While these typological refinements and empirical examinations of Mac-Cannell's work continued, his position was attacked from a more fundamental perspective — one which indeed leads to the transition to the paradigm of the tourist developed on the basis of Turner's approach. This process involved, at the outset, a reformulation of the concept of "authenticity" as conceived by MacCannell. Greenwood (1982:27), without referring expressly to MacCannell, has shown that "authenticity" is a dynamic, emergent phenomenon rather than a static one — and, hence, today's "staged" attractions may turn into "authentic" ones tomorrow. "Authenticity" is thus shown not to be a given, unchanging quality, as implicit in the usage of MacCannell (or of Trilling 1972), but rather a "negotiable" quality of objects or attractions. From here, it is but a short step to the transition from an "etic" view of authenticity, that is, one involving "the interpreter's conceptual apparatus" (Feleppa 1986:243–244), to an "emic" one, that is, one involving "the adoption of the subjects viewpoint by the [researcher]." This transition from the researcher's to the subject's (the tourist's) point of view which lies beyond the limits of the research program deriving from MacCannell's approach, was pioneered by Gottlieb (1982). Departing from MacCannell's and Cohen's alleged view ("... that the touristic experience can be 'meaningless,' 'superficial' or worse, based on 'false consciousness' ") she argued that her approach "... proceeds from the premise that what the vacationer experiences is real, valid, and fulfilling, no matter how 'superficial' it may seem to the social scientist" (1982:167). She hence assumes "... that the vacationers' own feelings and views about vacations are 'authentic' whether or not the observer judges them to match the host culture" (1982:168). This formulation changes the direction of the research program as implied in MacCannell work. Instead of asking whether the tourist's experience is authentic, one can now ask what is the connotation and denotation of authenticity in the tourist's own eyes: that is, what he considers to be the essential marks of authenticity, and which sites, objects, and events on his trip do, in his opinion, possess these marks (cf. Chapter 7). This reorientation of the research program, in turn, links up with the third and most recent tradition in the study of tourism, which derives from the work of Victor Turner.

Turner and the Touristic "Center Out There"

Of the three theoreticians under review, Turner is exceptional in that he himself did not make any direct contribution to the study of tourism. However, his work on pilgrims (Turner 1973; Turner and Turner 1978) and his "processual" approach in anthropology, and particularly his ideas about liminality, anti-structure (Turner 1974) and, eventually, "world reversals" (Turner 1978), provided an important point of departure for some of the more recent work in the sociology of tourism.

In a concise and somewhat simplified manner, Turner's approach can be summarized as follows. People in ordinary, profane life live in social, economic, and political structures. In ritual, and particularly the *rites-de-passage* originally described by van Gennep (1960, original edition 1908), the individual is torn out of this structural context. He typically goes through the following three-stage ritual process: First is *Separation*, both spatial and social. The individual is taken to an unfamiliar place, peripheral to his ordinary place of abode, and separated from his ordinary social group. Second is *Liminality*: Through the separation, the individual has crossed the threshold (Latin *limen*) of his ordered world, and finds himself in a state of "anti-structure," "out of time and place," where his ordinary role and status obligations are suspended and where general human (rather than particular social) bonds are emphasized. He experiences "communitas," an intensive and undifferentiated bond with the group undergoing the ritual. In this liminal stage, he is confronted with the fundamental symbols of his culture and undergoes a "direct experience of the sacred, invisible, supernatural order" (Turner 1973:214). Third is *Reintegration*: The individual is reintegrated into his ordinary social group usually in new roles and at a higher social status.

While this model fits most closely simple or "archaic" tribal societies, Turner also applied it to the analysis of the pilgrimage, a phenomenon prevalent in large-scale, traditional peasant societies, whose members profess one of the major world religions (such as Christianity, Islam, Hinduism, or Buddhism). The pilgrim is conceived as leaving his ordinary daily surroundings and departing on a journey to the "Center Out There" (Turner 1973), a journey which is not only a movement in space from the familiar to the unfamiliar, but concomitantly also a spiritual ascent (as manifested in the Hebrew term for pilgrimage *"aliyah le'regel"* — an "ascent to the festival" [in Jerusalem]). During the journey, the pilgrim is removed "from one type of time to another" (Turner 1973:221). But, while in a liminal state he also participates in a sacred existence and achieves a step toward holiness and wholeness (Turner 1973:221), which reaches its climax in the existential experience of the center itself. At a later stage, Turner and Turner (1978:1–39), distinguished between liminal situations which are obligatory and typically appear in a religious context, and liminoid situations, which are optative, and hence characteristic of modern secular contexts, such as leisure. This distinction made it possible to apply Turner's general theoretical approach to modern touristic phenomena.

Turner's processual model and especially his paradigm of the pilgrimage were attractive to students of tourism, who, from the late 1970s onward, began to adopt it to the study of touristic phenomena. His work was cited, only from 1979 onwards, 11 times in the articles appearing in *Annals of Tourism Research* between 1977 and 1986, but several of these articles (e.g. Gottlieb 1982; Lett 1983; Pfaffenberger 1983) are permeated by Turner's approach more thoroughly than most studies which referred to the founders of the other two "traditions" here reviewed.

Turner's approach opens completely new and unsuspected perspectives and interpretative possibilities on touristic phenomena. The tourist, like the pilgrim, also moves from a Familiar Place to a Far Place and returns to the Familiar Place (Turner 1973:213). The tourist's respectful visits to attractions at the Far Place, resemble the pilgrim's ascent to the "Center Out There." Up to this point, the analogy is common to the approaches of both MacCannell and Turner. Turner, however, goes beyond MacCannell's rather narrow Durkheimian premises in a manner which makes his approach more adequate for the interpretation of concrete touristic behavior. For MacCannell's approach necessarily leaves unexplained an essential aspect of behavior in touristic situations: the suspension of everyday obligations, the freedom enjoyed by tourists, and their license for permissive and playful "non-serious" behavior in the Far Place (Lett 1983). Such behavior witnesses to the "looseness" of touristic situations, which is well captured in Turner's concepts of liminality and particularly liminoidity, characteristic of the Center in the Far Place. For Turner's Center is not just a Center. It is a "Center Out There" at once central and peripheral; it is marked by a "sacred peripherality" (Turner 1973:212). Hence, it embodies the characteristics of both, the Center and the Other (Pfaffenberger 1983). Indeed, precisely in its otherness the Center expresses those general human values, which the differentiations of everyday life tend to repress: spontaneity, personal wholeness, and social togetherness, embodied in Turner's concept of "communitas" (Turner 1974:80–154). Particularly in modern society, where leisure takes the place of ritual, and obligatory liminality becomes optative liminoidity, the expressive, playful ("ludic" in Turner's terminology) aspects of touristic behavior in the Far Place will become particularly prominent. Furthermore it is this ludic aspect of tourism which researchers in the Turnerian "tradition" most commonly emphasize. The tourist seeks freedom from structure in the liminal state of being "out of time and place," the title of Wagner's (1977) study of Swedish mass tourists in a Gambian beach resort. He tends to be playful and frivolous, often to a consciously exaggerated extent (Lett 1983), and to enjoy the illusions of the make-believe of overtly staged touristic attractions (Chapter 6). But, while he is not MacCannell's serious seeker, the tourist does not thereby become Boorstin's gullible and superficial half-wit. For the liminal playfulness of tourists is deceptive. Though apparently superficial, the Turnerian analysis points to its deeper and unsuspected significance. Specifically, the playfulness of touristic liminality is said to give access to valuable compensatory experiences of an existential or social nature. Thus, Wagner (1977:44) comments with regard to the liminal existence of Swedish tourists in Gambia: "On the psychological and existential level [the] normless living . . . may liberate the individual from the stresses and pains imposed by the formal structure of his own society and give him a chance to recuperate, to recharge his inner being, even to make it pleasurable to get back . . . to work." The religious pilgrim's "re-creation" at the Center here becomes the secularized "recreation" of the modern tourist (Chapter 5). But the emphasis here is not merely on the "functional" value of recreation for daily life; rather it is on the existential significance of the liminal experience for the individual tourist.

The compensatory significance of liminal touristic experiences is similarly emphasized in the work of Lett (1983), who showed how charter yacht tourists consciously, though playfully, invert the norms and behavior patterns of daily life, within a strictly limited spatio-temporal setting. The tourists enjoy themselves in an exaggerated, unrestrained manner, which stands in sharp contrast to the conventions of everyday American middle-class life. They indulge in unlimited hedonism of sex and drink in an atmosphere of chumminess, resembling Turner's "communitas." Such conduct, according to Lett (1983:53—54), is primarily of a restitutive and compensatory significance, recreating and restoring the tourists for their return to their structured everyday life. Lett emphasizes the temporary nature of the inversion. His subjects are definitely not "existential" tourists who would embrace the liminal existence in the Caribbean as a way of life. Rather, "the ludic and liminoid licence provides [for the tourists] a temporary release from, but not a permanent alternative to, everyday life" (Lett 1983:54), as it does, for example, for "drop-outs" (Cohen 1984a). Other students in the Turnerian "tradition" go beyond this functionalist interpretation of touristic liminoidity. Moore (1980:215) shows how the playful nature of Walt Disney World (generally dismissed as perhaps the most contrived of staged touristic attractions) "evokes the supernatural in a [modern] context within which the supernatural has been banished" and thus makes accessible experiences which are otherwise barred to secularized moderns (Chapter 6).

Gottlieb (1982) shifts the emphasis on the compensatory significance of tourism from the psychological and existential to the social sphere, thus introducing a novel, class-related structural component into the Turnerian "tradition." Approaching tourism ("vacations" in her terminology) as an "inversion" of everyday reality (cf. Babcock 1978), she attempts to show that middle-class vacationers play at being a "Peasant for a Day," while lower-middle-class vacationers play at being "King (Queen) for a Day." Both thus seek in vacations that experience of the total social existence which they are denied in their everyday life. Inversion is, therefore, seen not merely as a global reversal of social existence per se but as patterned by the specific characteristics of the structural conditions of the life of a social group or class. A similar argument on the level of culture, rather than social structure, is presented in Passariello's (1983:120) study of Mexican vacations: "As weekend tourists, the Mexicans are seeking to experience in a short time something different from their ordinary, daily lives. What is considered 'different' ... seem to vary culturally in structure, with the cultural variation depending ... on the point of historical development of the tourist-producing culture." Gottlieb's and Passariello's studies thus make an important advance over the earlier work in the Turnerian "tradition" the need for which was first alluded to by Graburn (1983a:21). By detailing the characteristics of the touristic inversion in terms of the social or cultural specifics of the tourist's daily existence, they endow such general and unspecified existential Turnerian terms as "liminality" and "inversion" with a more definite and concrete meaning. Thereby the way is opened to a systematic comparative study of liminal touristic phenomena which goes beyond the mere demonstration of the applicability of Turner's approach to the study of tourism.

Just as MacCannell's approach was a conscious reaction to Boorstin's, so the Turnerian approach constitutes an (implicit) reaction to MacCannell. However, as it is the most recent of the three "traditions" discussed here, its limitations have not yet been submitted to much systematic criticism (but see Nash 1984). What directions this criticism will take in the future is difficult to predict. One point, however, appears to be obvious. While the emphasis on the liminal and ludic aspect of tourism and on the inversions of daily life in "vacations" is an important corrective to earlier views of the tourist, not all tourists are "ludic." It, therefore, becomes necessary to incorporate the concepts of liminality and inversion into a comprehensive, comparative theoretical approach to tourism, which will take account of the variety of touristic phenomena, ranging between the poles of the "serious" tourist and that of the "frivolous" vacationer. The development of such an approach, however should go hand-in-hand with a systematic critical treatment of Turner's seminal, but global, concept of the "Center Out There" in which the qualities of Center and Other are dialectically intertwined. Pilgrimage goals and touristic destinations differ in the extent to which they embody the Center or the Other — and hence in the degree to which they grant the prospective visitors the license to indulge in liminal and "ludic" activities. The study of the relationship between different kinds of destinations defined in these terms, and types of tourists defined in terms of the seriousness or licentiousness of their conduct, could, then, significantly extend the research program for the study of tourism in the Turnerian "tradition."

Conclusion

A comparative examination of the three research "traditions" in the qualitative sociology of tourism leads to several interesting conclusions. Four important developments can he noted as one moves from the earliest of these "traditions," Boorstin's, to the latest, Turner's.

First, the traditions become progressively more continuous and rigorous. Boorstin can hardly be said to have founded a "tradition." His impact consists mainly in that he formulated a challenging thesis which was then mostly criticized by sociologists. However, even this criticism did not lead to much systematic research. MacCannell had many followers who borrowed his various original ideas and concepts, but very few studies have adopted his approach as the theoretical basis of their design. Turner, though not directly engaged in the study of tourism, created a "tradition" in the fullest sense of the term, with several important empirical studies, conducted mostly with anthropological research methods, adopting an expressly Turnerian theoretical approach.

Second, the approach to tourism was gradually de-ideologized. Boorstin's was an expressly socio-critical position which analyzed tourism in terms of a sophisticated, but biased, critical view of modern man. One of MacCannell's major contributions consists of the fact that he distinguished between a sociological and an ideological approach to tourism. Thus, in principle, he opened the field to analysis from an unbiased sociological and anthropological perspective — although his own perspective did not necessarily fully live up to this ideal. Turner's followers, finally, appear to be fairly uninhibited by an ideological, but not necessarily a theoretical, bias.

Third, there was a progressive theoretical consolidation. Boorstin had no express theoretical approach to tourism. MacCannell ingenuously combined several theoretical approaches which, however, remained in an uneasy tension in his work. Turner and his followers, finally, integrated the study of tourism most fully with a general theoretical approach — Turner's "processual" anthropological theory.

Finally, and largely as a consequence of the developments mentioned above, there was a change from an etic to an emic perspective on the tourist: from one looking at the tourist from the outside and evaluating the nature of his experiences (e.g. regarding their "authenticity") by an extraneous yardstick, to one which tries to comprehend them from within. Boorstin's and MacCannell's approaches are essentially etic. The transition to an emic approach took place in the criticism of MacCannell's position and is, at least implicitly, characteristic of the approach of Turner's followers.

One can thus conclude that something approaching a "research program" gradually emerged as the focus of interest in the study of tourism moved from one "tradition" to the other. However, even in the Turnerian "tradition" such a program still remains on the whole implicit.

Turning now to a more substantive comparison between the three "traditions," they stand in an interesting relationship which could be represented in the form of a triangle, as in Figure 8.1. Boorstin's and MacCannell's approaches to tourism

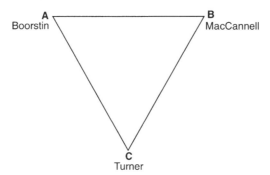

Figure 8.1: The Relationship Between the Three Major "Traditions" in the Qualitative Sociology of Tourism

form a pair of opposites, with Turner in a mediating position. This opposition — and mediation — is reiterated in several issue-areas in the respective approaches of the three traditions:

Image of the Tourist: While Boorstin's image is expressly negative and MacCannell's is implicitly positive, the image of the tourist in the Turnerian "tradition" is on the whole neutral.

Analytical Focus: Boorstin's approach focuses on the individual; MacCannell's, at least nominally, on the social structure (though he also relates to the tourist as an individual); and Turner's on the social process, integrating the analysis of individual experience with social dynamics.

Level of Analysis: Boorstin's analysis relates primarily to the superficial psychological motives behind the modern touristic experience; MacCannell's to the structural, semiotic significance of tourist settings; while Turner and his followers to the deeper, cultural symbolic meaning of the touristic experience within the broader social process.

Direction of the Touristic Quest: All three traditions refer, at least implicitly, to the Center-Other continuum, albeit in different senses, and with contrasting intentions. Boorstin can be interpreted as arguing that modern tourists seek recreation in the Other, but do not engage upon a serious quest for a Center. MacCannell sees dispersed centers of modernity in all attractions, but no single Center which would be the tourist's goal. The plurality of centers, reflecting the differentiations of society to which the tourist pays homage, constitute in their aggregation the Center of modernity. Turner, ingeneously, mediates between these positions. The "Center Out There" being a peripheral Center, combines the qualities of both, the Center and the Other. Indeed, the liminal inversions characteristic of conduct at this peripheral center, in one sense express its otherness, but in another they also express some central human (or social) concerns and values, repressed in everyday life. The anti-structural Other hence becomes a sacred Center in a profound (and unsuspected) sense.

The three traditions thus stand in an intriguing, and often ironic contrapunctal relationship. They relate to touristic phenomena on different levels and from varying perspectives which lead to widely different interpretations of the same empirical data. Any facile attempt at their integration faces certain failure. But none of the perspectives is in itself sufficient for the comprehension of the wide variety of touristic phenomena. Indeed, at the extreme, the images of *the* tourist emerging from each is no more than a caricature.

One way to accommodate the various approaches and moderate their extreme images of the tourist is to bring them to a common ground and build typologies which would bridge them. Some attempts at such typologies were described above. Typologies, however, do not resolve the problem, precisely because they reduce to a common ground the essential differences in analytical focus characteristic of each approach. Hence, an alternative strategy appears to be more appropriate: a research program which would simultaneously take account of, and compare, the tourist's psychological needs and experiences, the socio-structural features of tourist settings, and the cultural symbols expressed in the touristic process. Such a theoretically complex and sophisticated research program, translated into comparative empirical research projects, could help to resolve many of the misunderstandings and at least apparent controversies which presently beset the sociological study of tourism.

Chapter 9

Contemporary Tourism: Trends and Challenges

Introduction

Tourism is essentially a modern western phenomenon. Although travel for religious, cultural, educational and medical purposes, and even for entertainment, can he found throughout human history, I claim, in contrast, for example to Nash (1981), that the motivations, roles and institutional structures of modern tourism differ significantly from those of pre-modern and non-western forms of travel, and are closely related to some other crucial characteristics of modernity (Chapter 3). These motivations and structures have changed and continue to change over time as tourism itself changes. This chapter examines, from a sociological perspective, the changing nature of tourist attractions and places, noting their shift from the natural and authentic to the artificial and contrived, and the implications of related changes in tastes and preferences of tourists in contemporary society. It cannot be denied, however, that modern tourist travel has spread in recent decades virtually throughout the world. Contemporary Japanese, Taiwanese, Koreans and members of many Third World societies are also tourists in the western sense of the term, even though their specific mode of traveling may incorporate elements from their own cultural traditions (Graburn 1983b; Ikkai 1988).

The early work in the sociology of tourism, therefore, focused on the modern western tourist. This work was concerned at first with the changes which occurred in the motivation and role of pre-modern travelers as they became modern tourists (Boorstin 1964:77−117; Knebel 1960), and, later on, with the nature of the relationship between tourism and modernity (MacCannell 1973, 1976). Here, the principal question of concern became that of the "authenticity" of the tourist experience (MacCannell 1973; Chapter 7): in effect, to what degree modern tourists are in quest of authenticity and, if they are, whether they are able to realize their aim. The destination, the site of their experience, was in this early work seen mainly as the medium for the realization of the tourists' motivations. To be sure, there existed from early on a wider concern with the "impacts of tourism," the balance of desirable and undesirable consequences of tourism for destinations in the ecological, economic, social, political and cultural domains (Cohen 1984b:383–388; Noronha 1977). However, in the spirit of the focus on the tourist and the quality of his or her experience, much of this work, within the confines of the sociology of tourism, was concerned with the changes that tourism imparts to destinations, changes which may eventually have a negative feedback impact on their touristic attractiveness.

A major theme informing the sociological discourse on tourism impact was that of "staged authenticity," a term coined by MacCannell (1973) to describe the artful presentation of contrived sites and sights as if they were authentic, when, in fact, they had already been transformed, partly by tourism itself. Such staging was seen to lead eventually to the emergence of a "tourist space," which separates the sphere of tourism from the ordinary flow of local life, and thus prevents the tourist from experiencing its authenticity. The tourist was seen as caught in such a space, as if in a trap. Since the quest for authenticity was presented as a modern, secular substitute for the pre-modern religious quest, the denial of its fulfillment was at least implicitly seen as a negative consequence. It followed that tourism, by virtue of its very development, blocks the route to secular salvation, which it had initially promised (Dumont 1984:140; Chapter 7).

This trend of investigation at a later stage led to a growing concern with alternative tourism (Cohen 1987a; Holden 1984; Pleumarom 1990; Singh *et al.* 1989; Smith and Eadington 1992). That concept has several connotations, each of which conceives a different variety of this kind of tourism (Cazes 1989). I called one of these varieties "counter-cultural" alternative tourism (Cohen 1987a), to indicate the opposition of its practitioners to the tourist establishment, and their desire to develop a style of travel studiously contrasting with that of routine mass tourists. This kind of tourism was supposed to re-open the path to salvation — enable the tourist, traveling alone or in small groups in the touristically unchartered territory beyond the limits of the "tourist space," to have "authentic" experiences. Such alternative tourism is often at least implicitly considered by its protagonists to he "sustainable" — it is assumed that is does not significantly impinge upon the destination, and could therefore go on indefinitely. Alternative tourism, however, has a negligible impact only as long as its density is low — as long as few tourists visit remote locations at low frequencies. As the number of such tourists grows, they can engender considerable, though perhaps unsuspected, damage, precisely to sensitive outlying, as yet "authentic," natural and cultural environments (Burns 1991; Butler 1992).

Under the impact of growing numbers of alternative tourists, their chosen destinations undergo a process of change. Tourism to such destinations, as

Dearden and Harron (1994) have recently shown, then remains "sustainable" only if the motivation of tourists to visit the destinations changes concomitantly. "Sustainability," rather than indicating a static, unchanged state of affairs, thus becomes a dynamic concept: it comes to refer to the existence of some degree of congruence between two sets of changes, in the destination as well as in the motivations of tourists; the ultimate consequence of this process is frequently that ordinary tourists enter the area which has initially been opened by alternative tourists, while the latter penetrate ever deeper into as yet "unspoilt" areas.

It turns out, then, that the idea of developing alternative tourism harbours a contradiction, and that this kind of tourism in fact often serves as the spearhead of ordinary touristic penetration. Indeed, it is this dynamic element of tourism expansion which raises a fundamental question of social policy: namely, should tourists, even alternative ones, be encouraged, or even allowed, to roam freely around and invade any new area, or should they be contained within set confines, even if this might preclude their having "authentic experiences?"

This question reflects a gradual shift in public concern in many countries from tourism development to the protection of local nature and culture from tourism impacts. This concern is in turn reflected in a gradual refocusing of the principal interest of sociologists of tourism, from the tourists and their experiences to the destination: not just a preoccupation, common in any comprehensive touristic planning process, with the problem of how the more undesirable consequences of tourism development could he ameliorated, while developing a destination for tourism; rather, it is a more radical concern with how the local environment and people could he protected from the "tourist gaze" (Urry 1990, 1992:12) in all its various manifestations, This, however, should not be construed to mean that sociologists, or anyone else, suggest that tourism should be stopped altogether — an impossible and preposterous proposition; rather, it means that they seek to deflect tourism to different kinds of destinations — primarily to the man-made ones, created specifically for tourism. Ironically, these are the very "contrived" attractions (Chapter 3) which, at an earlier stage, have been condemned as embodiments of inauthenticity. This term will he used in the following discussion, but in a neutral and not in a derogatory sense.

"Natural and Contrived" Attractions

Two polar types of attractions can he distinguished: the "natural" and the "contrived." As an ideal type, "natural" attractions are completely "unmarked" — sites and sights which have not yet undergone any intervention — physical or symbolic — to make them more appealing, accessible, or even more easily noticed by tourists. The polar type of "natural" attractions is exemplified by physical, cultural, ethnic or archaeological sites which have not been tampered with for touristic purposes. On the other hand, "contrived" attractions, as a polar type, are exemplified by sites and sights which were specifically created for touristic purposes and are wholly artificial in character — that is, they do not contain any "natural" elements.

The polar extremes define a continuum of different admixtures of natural and artificial elements: thus, many basically "natural" attractions may have some "contrived" traits. National parks, even if essentially "natural" attractions, are symbolically marked and sometimes physically fenced off. They are also regulated — for example, the populations of some animal species may have to be controlled artificially, since hunting by surrounding native human populations has been prohibited. All these are "contrived" traits. Similarly, archaeological sites are often marked, reconstructed and adapted for touristic visitation. Museums, though they may collect "authentic," "original" objects of ethnic, cultural or historical significance, often display them in artfully "contrived" settings. Moreover, some contemporary museums do not display "original" objects at all, but only copies or reconstructions of historical or natural environments. Here we approach the pole of completely "contrived" attractions.

Certainly the best-known "contrived" attraction, emblematic of the type, is Disneyland. This kind of attraction was looked down upon as a tourist destination by some researchers in the past. Indeed, when Khrushchev visited the United States in the 1960s, *Time Magazine* poked fun at his corny taste, since he asked to see how Americans grow corn, and to visit Disneyland. Since then the assessment of Disneyland has changed considerably. Precisely because of its emblematic status it is instructive to consider the reasons for that change, since it may throw some light on the changing status of other "contrived" attractions.

There is, first, the patina of age. Although created for commercial touristic purposes, Disneyland over time became an American cultural landmark. Despite its "contrived" origins, it acquired a measure of "authenticity." Second, the analysis of the structure and symbolism of Disneyland has disclosed its deep-structural meaning in American culture (Gottdiener 1982; Johnson 1981; King 1981; Moore 1980). The fact that it is a "contrived" attraction no longer automatically implies that it is meaningless. Finally, and most relevant for present purposes, attitudes to contrived attractions have changed with the emergence of a "post-modern" touristic ethos: tourists, less concerned with authenticity and the hierarchy of attractions, seem to care less for the origins of all attraction as long as the visit is an enjoyable one.

It is this last point which is of particular interest for this discussion, since it indicates a trend away from the paradigmatic dominance of the quest for "authenticity" as the principal culturally sanctioned motivation for modern tourists, and towards a "nivellation" of all attractions, "natural" and "contrived," realistic or fantastic, historical or futuristic, original or recreated, characteristic of the post-modern ethos (Feifer 1985:259–279; Urry 1990:83–103). This nivellation finds expression, among other things, in touristic markers (MacCannell 1976:110–111) on recently established "contrived" attractions. It is strikingly illustrated by the manner in which the "Many Worlds" (Sentosa 1992), the various groups of sights on a recently established major tourist complex, the island of Sentosa in Singapore, are marked. The island features such sights as a secondary rain forest on the "Nature Walk," a fantastic "Dragon Walk" and fictional monuments of an ancient "Ruined City" and a "Lost Civilization." The markers on both the realistic nature sights and the fantastic fictional ones are formulated in the same serious, matter-of-fact language which could easily convince any undiscerning visitor of the reality of the historical existence of dragons.

While it is not the purpose of this chapter to explore in depth this post-modern touristic ethos, it should be noted that it is congruent with the idea, broached at the end of the preceding section, that tourism should be deflected from intruding upon the environment and culture of people towards specifically created, "contrived" attractions.

Modern criticism of mass tourism is generally inimical to "contrived" attractions. The (covert) staging of attractions to which tourists are then surreptitiously directed, and in which they are presented with an allegedly authentic rendition of a people's life and culture, is generally condemned in the literature as an expression of crass commercialism, and of a double deception in which a falsified reality is made to confirm and satisfy the false expectations engendered by images of the destination in the promotional brochures and advertisements (Adams 1984:472). Indeed, much of MacCannell's work was intended to show, on the one hand, how the tourist establishment succeeds in staging authenticity, and on the other, how tourists seek to break through the "front" so established, to the "back," the real life at the visited destination (MacCannell 1973).

However, there is another way to look at staged attractions. Buck (1977:207, 1978), in his study of tourism in an Old Order Amish community, was the first anthropologist to use MacCannell's concept from a different perspective. Instead of focusing upon the tourists' desire to break through the staged front presented by the Amish in order to experience their authentic life in the "back," Buck drew attention to the role which staging plays "in maintaining their way of life in spite of the seemingly pervasive presence of tourists" (1978a:225).

Staged representations may thus be seen to play an important, though perhaps often unintended role, that of keeping the authenticity-seeking tourists out, to prevent their "gaze" from disturbing the life and culture of the community. This role of staged attractions is becoming increasingly important for precisely the most vulnerable and touristically exploited people: the "Fourth World" ethnic minorities, tribal groups and remnants of hunter-gatherer bands whose "real" life is threatened to become a show for organized touristic visits. Regulation of tourist visits to such sensitive sites, and the creation of contrived and staged representations of the toured group's life and culture, is, under these circumstances, an alternative policy to unbridled penetration, and may enable the toured group to derive some benefit from tourism, while protecting it from disruption by outsiders.

Staged attractions may thus play a beneficial role with regard to ethnic and tribal groups which still maintain a viable culture. One could develop a parallel argument regarding physical attractions, namely that valuable environments, harbouring rare flora and fauna, can be protected from detrimental touristic penetration by the creation of regulated and segregated areas in which the most attractive features of the environment are presented to visitors, while the rest is closed to them. To some degree this is the philosophy behind the concept of zoning in national parks and other protected areas.

Not all "contrived" attractions, however, are covertly staged. Indeed, one of the important trends in contemporary tourism development is the growing number of attractions which are admittedly and overtly staged.

There is a growing scarcity and diminishing attractiveness of "natural" attractions. With the rapid penetration of western technology, industrial products and lifestyles into the remotest parts of the world, ever fewer ethnic and tribal groups are able to preserve unaltered their inherited culture and ways of life, and ever fewer natural environments remain pristine and untouched. A growing gap has opened between the image of native people or wild nature in the advertised destinations and the reality which exists there (Cohen 1992a).

While the transformations which the cultural world and the natural environment of the more remote parts of the world undergo are of consuming interest to researchers, they are of diminishing interest to tourists, even to those alternative tourists who are in quest of authenticity. Under these circumstances, the establishment of living museums, reconstructed ethnic or tribal villages, theme parks, wildlife and nature parks, and similar partly or wholly contrived attractions become an increasingly acceptable substitute for "natural" attractions. The establishment of such attractions is a matter of growing concern for developers and policy makers, not only in developed countries such as Japan and Singapore, but increasingly also in developing countries.

The tendency for reconstruction can he found not only in the domain of nature and ethnic or tribal culture, but also, and perhaps even more strongly, in the domain of history. MacCannell (1976:148) argued that the alienated moderns seek authenticity not only in other, that is, non-modern, places but also in other times, that is, in the past. Indeed, archaeological sites and monuments of ancient civilizations have been leading touristic attractions from the very inception of modern tourism. However the accelerated rate of change of the contemporary world destroys at a rapid rate the remnants of even the recent past, both material and cultural, even as it uproots the individual and produces a sense of irretrievable loss. This loss finds its cultural expression in the theme of "nostalgia" (Frow 1991), which is a significant motive for tourism. A powerful motive for the preservation and recreation of the past thus emerges, leading in part to the proliferation of local history museums, protected buildings and neighborhoods, and the designation of various remnants of the past as "heritage centres" (Urry 1990:104−134). As this growing concern with the past becomes exploited by the tourism industry, the past itself is "commoditized" (Evans-Pritchard 1993). As a result, a "heritage industry" emerges (Hewison 1987; Urry 1990:104−112).

Not only have growing numbers of archaeological and historical sites been adapted, and often also at least partly reconstructed, for touristic visitations, but a new type of "contrived" attraction has emerged. This takes the form of historical reconstructions such as the "historic theme parks" (Moscardo and Pearce 1986), in which not only the material remnants of the past, but also the environment, culture, and way of life of bygone eras are conjured up by modern technological devices. These reconstructions of the past are thus a counterpart, in the historical realm, to "living museums," staged ethnic villages and similar "contrived" attractions in the ethnic and cultural realm. The most recent development in this area is the partly imaginary "reconstruction" of prehistoric environments, such as the "Jurassic Parks," which proliferated in the wake of the phenomenal success of Spielberg's film.

In what sense can "contrived" historical reconstructions be considered "authentic" (Moscardo and Pearce 1986)? The problem arises from their paradoxical nature: on the one hand they are obviously and admittedly staged attractions. On the other hand, however, their claim to legitimacy consists precisely in the allegation that, within the constraints of technical possibilities, they are "correct" reproductions of the past, and in this sense may be considered "authentic": they are "authentic reproductions." Research on local history museums and similar contrived historical attractions, however, indicates that a kind of "secondary staging" usually occurs. Rather than being neutral reproductions, such attractions often embody the cultural values, ideological perspectives (Katriel 1997) or commercial interests (Urry 1990:132) of their creators. They are in themselves "cultural productions" of our own time.

"Contrived" natural, ethnic and historical reconstructions have become increasingly popular with the traveling public. A variety of factors may have contributed to their growing popularity, but only two are directly relevant to the present discussion. On the one hand, such attractions, as was already pointed out, are a substitute for "natural" attractions, which are becoming ever scarcer and ever more despoiled in the contemporary world. The "authentic" reproductions of the past also seem to satisfy the nostalgic cravings of contemporary tourists for the past, the remnants of which are being rapidly destroyed. In this sense, the "contrived" reproductions may satisfy the modern "quest for authenticity," in MacCannell's sense, though in fact they may be doubly staged.

On the other hand, however, such attractions are also a show: they therefore bespeak the tourist's predisposition for playfulness, his or her readiness ludically (playfully) to accept "contrived" attractions as if they were real. This predisposition becomes culturally sanctioned by the post-modern ethos. "Contrived" reconstructions thus seem to entertain an interstitial location between "natural" attractions and completely imaginary "contrived" ones: they therefore appeal simultaneously to the culturally sanctioned modern as well as post-modern touristic motivations.

The proliferation and growing popularity of the last type of attractions which will be considered here, the imaginary "contrived" attraction, appears to be particularly well suited to the latter kind of motivations. Such attractions are usually high-technology simulations of either futuristic environments, such as the "Future Worlds" at the EPCOT Center in the Walt Disney World (EPCOT Center 1987), which enable the visitor to experience a projected or imagined future, or simulations of fantastic environments such as the Magic Kingdom (Magic Kingdom 1987) in the Walt Disney World, which may be based either on myths of the past or even completely invented. The latter enable the visitor to undertake a completely imaginary journey without any, even imputed, reference to the real world. Entertainment centers such as the Disneylands, theme parks, such as Sentosa Island, and similar commercial entertainment facilities often feature several kinds of such attractions, sometimes in conjunction with ethnic or historical reconstructions.

There is, in itself, nothing new in such facilities. Newfangled devices and fantasy rides have been common offerings at popular fairs for many years, although the technology was more primitive, and the experience perhaps less realistic. But the point to note is that those rather modest devices were located in the realm of the local entertainment business, and not of the tourism industry. Their catchment areas were local or at most regional: they usually did not attract a national or international touristic audience. In contrast, the large contemporary entertainment centers, such as the Disneylands in the United States, Japan and France, are complexes of huge proportions, involving investments of the order of hundreds of millions of dollars and the most modern technology and management techniques. The very scale of such enterprises necessarily limits their number, while the existence and profitability of each is dependent on a wide, preferably world-wide, touristic appeal. Indeed, not only the Disneylands, but many other similar complexes of less renown and of a more limited scale emerged in recent decades, and have been incorporated into the tourist itineraries of many countries, especially the industrial ones.

A variety of specific factors, related to changes in lifestyles, income distribution and mobility, could he invoked to account for the contemporary proliferation of these large-scale imaginary "contrived" attractions. But for present purposes it is important to note that this proliferation corresponds to an apparently pervasive shift in the dominant mode of experience desired by contemporary tourists, sightseers or vacationers. This mode, which is congruent with, and derives its legitimation from, the emerging "post-modern" ethos, is that of playfulness (Chapter 6). If the culturally sanctioned mode of travel of the modern tourist has been that of the serious quest for authenticity, the mode of the post-modern tourist is that of playful search for enjoyment. In the former, there is a cognitive preoccupation with the penetration of staged fronts into real backs (MacCannell 1973), in the latter there is an aesthetic enjoyment of surfaces, whatever their cognitive status may be. The ludic attitude to attractions is becoming culturally sanctioned, and may well in the future overshadow that of the serious quest for authenticity. Post-modern tourists are engaging in an "as if" game with the attraction (MacCannell 1989:1). In order to enjoy the experience they are prepared to accept, although not wholly seriously, an even totally fantastic "contrived" attraction as real. This concern with the enjoyability of the surface appearance of the attraction, rather than with its "reality" or "authenticity," makes it possible for the variety of imaginary "contrived" attractions to flourish.

One can, in fact, advance this argument, somewhat speculatively, one step further. It appears that post-modern tourists, owing to the nivellating tendency of the post-modern ethos and its stress on surfaces, evince a readiness to reduce or suspend the saliency of the boundaries between different "finite provinces of meaning" (Schuetz 1973: Vol. I:229ff.), between fact and fiction, reality, reconstruction and fantasy. This readiness makes it possible for different kinds of "contrived" attractions to co-exist within the same complex, as it were, on an equal standing. With the rapid contemporary development in simulation technology, those boundaries will become ever more reducible, and the suspension of their salience ever easier.

The most advanced of these developments are the various techniques of creating the impression of a "virtual reality" (Ernsberger 1990), an artificial environment which is so completely simulated that it resembles, for the observer or participant in the situation, the "paramount" reality (Schuetz 1973: Vol. I:229ff.). In principle, any environment, natural, historical or fantastic, could thus be almost perfectly realistically simulated in any location.

The combination between the lowered saliency of boundaries between provinces of meaning for post-modern tourists and the development of such advanced simulation technology poses an unexpected potential threat to contemporary tourism, namely, the progressive disappearance of "placeness" (Relph 1976). If any experience could he virtually had in every location, no experience will be place-bound any more: then why should one travel? The boundary between tourism and leisure seems thereby to be put into question.

Tourism and Leisure

The literature on tourism does not draw a clear distinction between tourism and ordinary leisure. Many students of tourism come from the field of leisure studies, and indeed, one of the proposed definitions of a tourist is "a person at leisure who also travels" (Nash 1981:462). The sociology of leisure has provided one of the major theoretical approaches to the study of tourism (Cohen 1984b:375). Nevertheless, modern tourism is not merely a leisure activity, it possesses some crucial characteristics which distinguish it from other kinds of leisure. Indeed, not all tourism can he seen merely as leisure, and some definitions of tourism include aspects such as business travel. Consequently, tourism research emerged in recent years as a fairly distinct field, separate from leisure studies (Butler 1989; Fedler 1987).

The crucial distinctive feature of tourism is that it involves travel; it is an activity carried out at some distance from home. The distance is of sociological as well as spatial significance, and it implies exposure to the strangeness of an unaccustomed environment, along with the experiences of novelty and change for the tourist. This distinguishing characteristic of tourism, which is not found in ordinary leisure, can he employed as a point of departure for a sociological approach to tourism (Chapter 3). It is the basis on which a distinct institutional nexus, the "tourism industry," has emerged. Tourism is based in part on the assumption that the experience offered by the destination is not available in the tourist's home environment. The distinctiveness of the destination could be termed its "placeness." The theory of intervening opportunities (Stouffer 1940) teaches us that, if the same experience were available it home, tourists would not have to take the trouble to travel.

It is this very distinctiveness of tourism, the "placeness" of the destinations, which is threatened by the deflection of much of modern tourism to "contrived" attractions and by the emergence of simulated environments which provide experiences approximating "reality." Some kinds of "contrived" attractions, especially entertainment complexes like the Disneylands or Sentosa Island can in principle be established anywhere: there is no intrinsic connection between them and the place in which they are located, as the examples of Disneylands near Paris (Privat and Gleizes 1992) or Tokyo demonstrate. However, these attractions do still have a fixed location; and, as they become part of the tourist system, they themselves may endow this location with an image and character which it had not earlier possessed; "placeness" is an emergent quality.

In contrast, the more advanced simulation techniques, conjuring up a "virtual reality," are in principle not at all place-bound: they can, or soon will, be enjoyable in the privacy of one's home. Hence, the distinction between the experience of an attraction in the real world and its simulation in one's home environment may be gradually disappearing. Under the assumptions of a post-modern ethos, which tends to reduce the salience of the authenticity or reality of the source of the experience, and is concerned, primarily, with its "surface" quality, the two kinds of experiences will tend to become asymptotically indistinguishable. The boundary between tourism and leisure may then become virtually erased and tourism, as an activity, lose much of its distinctiveness.

Hereby is reached a perhaps unsuspected, but certainly fundamental, challenge which tourism, as a distinct type of activity, will have to face and come to grips with in the foreseeable future. Tourists are being gradually deflected, for reasons elaborated above, from "natural" to "contrived" attractions. Such attractions, however, are increasingly less place-bound, and hence lack the distinction of "placeness" characteristic of "natural" attractions. As modern simulation techniques gradually erase the distinction between real and simulated experiences, and as the post-modern ethos endows this distinction with less and less saliency, experiences which could previously be attained only by traveling to attractions can now he increasingly approximated at home. This trend towards the "de-placement" of experiences which in the past were distinctly touristic thus poses a threat to the attractiveness of tourism in the future.

How realistic is this threat? It would he easy, but facile, to extrapolate from it a prediction that it spells the end of tourism. We can learn from past experience that historical trends rarely, if ever, lead to their ultimate consequences. It is, rather, more reasonable to predict that tourism will he reconstituted and given new, but as yet not clearly foreseeable, meaning, form and direction. The trend away from "natural" and towards "contrived" and increasingly home-bound attractions reflects, as we have seen, a more general trend of change in contemporary society and culture, expressed in the post-modern ethos. Post-modernism, however, as the term itself implies, is a transitional phenomenon, rather than a novel, well-integrated and permanent cultural system. It is, of course, difficult to foresee the defining traits of the cultural ethos which will supplant it, but one reasonable prediction is that, as a reaction to the nivellating tendency of post-modernism, a new hierarchy of phenomenological "realities" and corresponding experiences will emerge. In the process, some experiential shortcomings of displaced, "contrived" attractions and simulated environments will be discovered or rediscovered and gain increased salience — such as the loss of remoteness, of genuine placeness or of a sense of unprogrammed adventure. While, for reasons discussed above, there are few resources left on this globe which will satisfy those longings — the endless expanses of the universe still remain unexplored. While space-tourism in the foreseeable future will be the privilege of a small elite, it may well become the frontier of a reconstituted tourism of the coming centuries (Kaufmann 1983).

Conclusion

In order to put the preceding discussion in a wider perspective three observations are offered by way of conclusion. First, the post-modern touristic stance of nivellation of attractions, natural and contrived, of enjoyment of surfaces and simulations, and legitimation of ludic attitudes is not a naive, unwitting or unconscious one. Rather, it is a reflective stance, which could, paraphrasing Eisenstadt (1982), he called "post-axial." This stance is a consequence of the process of radical secularization (Cohen 1988) and of the breakthrough (or breakdown) of all absolute ("privileged") criteria of judgment and evaluation, on which the "post-modern" ethos is grounded. It is a studied stance, close to the post-modern equalization of high and low, elitist and popular art. Hence it is different from the allegedly undiscerning attitude of the mass- tourist as portrayed earlier, for example, by Boorstin (1964). Post-modern tourists are sophisticated individuals, who choose not to discern, though they are aware of the possibilities of distinction. The tourists' tendency not to discern is the consequence of rational penetration of all criteria as socially constructed, a kind of "*Aufhebung*" of modern distinctions, which endows them with a newly won freedom (though perhaps of the Sartrian kind).

Second, in the contemporary world there are, in fact, two trends at work: one, emphasized in this chapter, leads away from "natural" to "contrived" attractions and towards a fusion of tourism and leisure. But there is a contrary trend at work, indicated in the first section of this chapter — towards a more radical preservation of historic (heritage) monuments, ethnic culture and pristine nature. This indicates the continuing cultural importance of authenticity. However, such preservation is not necessarily intended to serve tourism but may be intended as a defence of such sites from tourism. In that sense this is a relatively recent trend.

Lastly, two contrasting processes of transformation can be discerned on the contemporary tourist scene. On the one hand, the very effort of preserving attractions, and their defence from touristic impact, often makes them more "contrived." Preservation often involves the need to create contrivances which at least change the outward appearance of authentic physical, historical or cultural attractions. On the other hand, a contrary process is at work. "Contrived" attractions originally created for tourist purposes, increasingly become part of the physical, historical or cultural environment — they become "naturulized." These contrasting processes eventually blur the distinction between "natural" and "contrived" attractions, making it ever harder to distinguish between "natural" attractions to which "contrived" elements have been progressively added, and initially "contrived" attractions which became progressively integrated into their natural surroundings. This process is likely to continue into the future.

Acknowledgment—Thanks are due to Zali Gurevitch and Boas Shamir for their useful comments on an earlier draft of this chapter.

Part Two

Interfaces

Chapter 10

Tourism and Religion: A Comparative Perspective

Introduction

The sociological analysis of the relationship between tourism and religion has focused primarily on the question of the similarity and difference between the tourist and the pilgrim (Cohen 1992b; MacCannell 1973; Smith (ed.) 1992). Although this is without doubt a major theoretical issue, it tended to overshadow other important aspects of the complex interface between these two domains. This interface remains largely unexplored.

Even the basic sociological issues involved have rarely been stated systematically, whereas empirical research on the topic is scarce and often incidental to wider concerns (Din 1989:542–543; see also Mathieson and Wall 1982:152–153). The purpose of this article is therefore programmatic: I shall merely outline an approach to the principal issues involved, illustrating it with some comparative material. Although much of my analysis is rather speculative, it raises some significant problems for further research.

Tourism and religion are both closely related and diametrically opposed modalities of social conduct. They are historically related through the institution of the pilgrimage from which — according to some authors — modern tourism developed (Sigaux 1966; Smith (ed.) 1992). Indeed, contemporary publications on "religious tourism" (Din 1993; Juiff 1990; Rinschede 1992) mostly refer to modern versions of the religious pilgrimage.

Some leading sociologists of tourism go beyond this historical relationship and claim that there exists a structural affinity between tourism and the pilgrimage; in particular, Dean MacCannell (1973) argued that the modern tourist is a secular pilgrim, paying respect to the diverse symbols of modernity embodied in tourist "attractions." According to some others, tourism is a form of implicit, personalized religion (Allcock 1988). However, religion and tourism are also mutually opposed — because tourism is often an inversion of ordinary life (Gottlieb 1982; Graburn

1977; Turner 1969), giving vent to the satisfaction of hedonistic drives contrary to religious precepts. Moreover, particularly in its more extreme manifestations, the tourist's goal tends to be the inverse of that of the pilgrim: whereas the pilgrim travels towards the sacred place symbolizing the Center of his or her religion (Eliade 1969a; Turner 1973), the tourist is often in quest of the Other (Cohen 1992b). According to MacCannell (1973), modern secular tourists, alienated from modernity, depart in quest of authentic, but vicarious, experiences, in other places, times, or cultures. It should be noted that both pilgrims and tourists may therefore visit the same sites but for very different reasons: the former to worship, the latter merely to observe and vicariously participate in the pilgrim's experience — but without the pilgrim's belief in the meaning and efficacy of his or her worship. Some authors sought to conceptualize a category of travelers that is intermediate between pilgrims and tourists — "religious tourists" — who both tour and worship on their journey. Some church authorities, particularly in the Catholic Church, turned the concept of "religious tourism" into a practical objective, namely, to turn the tourist's presence at religious sites and events into an occasion for a religious experience or act of worship. The tourist would thus become a pilgrim, at least for a brief moment.

Though most major religions articulated explicit theological positions towards the pilgrimage, they generally failed to do so with respect to tourism — probably because tourism was perceived as a secular activity, of little relevance to religion. In this article I shall therefore begin by exploring the possible points of departure for an analysis of the mostly implicit theological positions of various religions to tourism. I shall then explore the principal concrete issues in the interface of religion and tourism, and briefly discuss the practical activities of religions — particularly Christian churches — in the sphere of tourism.

Theology

Travel and tourism were not generally recognized as significant issues by theologians or students of religion. It is symptomatic that neither "travel" nor "tourism" are listed in the indexes of the two major encyclopedias of religions, Hastings' (1925) or Eliade's (1987). No major world religion seems to have formulated a systematic "theology of tourism," which would examine the religious meaning, justification, or legitimation of tourism and relate it to broader religious goals and aspirations. There exist only some very broad pronouncements by supreme religious authorities, like the Pope himself (John Paul II 1984), and discussions of specific problems regarding tourism by individual theologians (e.g. Amoa 1986; de Sousa 1988; Srisang 1985). However, there exist few, if any, systematic theological treatises that would relate tourism to the fundamental positions of a religion towards such issues as travel and attitude to strangers. Modern religious institutions and leaders have been concerned with tourism mainly on a practical level, rather than in abstract theological terms.

Although explicit theologies of tourism seem to be rare, it is still possible to extricate the implicit attitudes of the various religions to tourism on a number of relevant issues from their respective basic theological positions.

· Tourism can be seen as a modern secular leisure activity, involving travel away from the tourist's home in quest of some novelty and change in different, unfamiliar, and often remote and strange environments and cultures (cf. Chapter 2).

Four issues of theological relevance can be extricated from this definition:

(1) travel into unfamiliar or strange surroundings;
(2) contact with strangers and their cultures;
(3) leisure and leisure pursuits;
(4) secularity and secular modernity.

I argue that the attitude of a given religion to tourism, and its practical consequences, will depend on its position towards each of these four issues. Within the confines of the present article, however, it is impossible to deal exhaustively with each issue in a systematic comparative manner. Rather, I shall merely sketch out a general approach to these issues and illustrate it with a few examples.

Travel

Traditional religions often conceived of the world in mythological terms, with a sacred territory (Sopher 1967:147ff.), in the midst of which is located the Center of the World, and a "cosmicized" space, surrounded by chaos (Eliade 1969a). Travel to the Center is the prototypical pilgrimage. Travel in the opposite direction, beyond the boundaries of the cosmicized world — the prototypical "touristic" journey — was seen as dangerous and antinomian (Cohen 1992b). These ancient beliefs, however, have gradually faded with the demythologization of the planet Earth: but some religions, especially Judaism and to a lesser extent, Hinduism, retained a concept of a "sacred" homeland, namely, the Land of Israel or India. Rabbinic law prohibits Jews living in the Land from leaving it without a legitimate reason. Leaving India was in the past considered polluting for a Hindu, and high-caste Indians until recently performed penance after a journey across the ocean (Sopher 1967:48). Such strictures may act to restrict touristic trips abroad by the faithful, even though only few Jews and probably even fewer Indians at present adhere to them. Such strictures on tourism are absent in religions such as Christianity or Buddhism, which do not claim a sacred homeland.

Strangeness

The prevalent attitude of traditional religions, as of most pre-modern cultures, towards strangers is one of ambivalence: strangers are regarded with fear and animosity: but they are also often considered as sacred messengers of the divine, or god-like (Hocart 1952:78–86; Pitt-Rivers 1968:18–21; Yoshida 1981). This ambivalence is generally overcome by the religiously sanctioned rules of traditional hospitality (Greifer 1945:741; Pitt-Rivers 1968). Such deeply ingrained mores have disposed locals, especially during early stages of tourist development, to relate to tourists as "guests," even though the expansion of mass tourism, as a form of "commercialized hospitality" (Cohen 1984b:374–375), led to the virtual disappearance of the traditional, personalized guest-host relationship between tourists and locals.

The major world religions reflect to various degrees this archaic ambivalence towards strangers, even though they tend to discern between different kinds of strangers, according to their degree of affinity to themselves, which, in turn, may predispose their members to distinct attitudes towards tourists of different ethnic or religious backgrounds.

Ambivalence towards strangers is most clearly perceivable in Judaism and Islam, though its consequences for tourism are not the same. In ancient Judaism, during the prophetic era, the "ideal of the brotherhood of man" (Greifer 1945:743) evolved, but Jews throughout history remained acutely aware of the difference between themselves and the Gentiles (*goyim*), and suspicious of the latter. Islam sanctions hospitality and compassion to travelers (Din 1989:552), but many Moslem countries are not interested in having non-Islamic visitors (Ritter 1975:59). Although traditional Jewish attitudes to Gentiles do not seem to have had any impact on tourism to Israel, Islam has a significant impact on the scope and shape of tourism, even in those Islamic countries that actively seek to promote it (Din 1989; Poirier 1995).

In Christianity the problem of attitudes to strangers seems to have been less salient from the outset, perhaps because of a lesser overlap between ethnic origin and religious membership than in either Judaism or early Islam. In Buddhism, with its encompassing tolerance and fuzzy boundaries, ambivalence towards strangers seems to be comparatively least pronounced, a fact that helps to explain the ease with which outsiders integrated in Buddhist societies in the past and the facility with which tourism expanded rapidly in such Buddhist countries as Thailand.

Although some religions, such as Islam, encouraged the faithful, "to travel through the earth so that they appreciate the greatness of God through observing the 'signs' of beauty and bounty of His creation" (Din 1989:551), a positive attitude towards intercultural exchange in travel is a modern phenomenon, found especially in the liberal streams of contemporary Judaism, Catholicism, and Protestantism, which favor "dialogue" between the world's cultures and faiths (cf. Przeclawski 1994:82–89). Indeed, only in those streams can be found an explicitly positive theological attitude to tourism as a means towards the realization of such religious values as self-expression and a widening of the spirit through contact with other people or religions (e.g. Simon, Barral-Baron and Barbier 1985).

Leisure

The concept of "leisure" as free time, devoid of work and other obligations, is a modern temporal category. Religions that do not recognize the concept of "leisure," and do no consider leisure activities as a legitimate pursuit, will not encourage tourism or will even oppose it as a waste of time — in the sense of *bittul zeman* in orthodox Judaism. As "leisure" achieved religious recognition, as, for example, in Protestantism (Eisen 1991; cf. also Cosgrove and Jackson 1972:9ff.), an important precondition for the religious sanctioning of tourism has been attained, even though new issues arose, such as leisure pursuits that are "worthwhile," and how these could be realized through tourism.

Secularity

Religions differ considerably in the degree to which they recognize the separation of a "secular" from a "religious" sphere of human life, and in their attitudes to the former. The concept of secularity is most salient in Christianity — but there is a vast difference in attitude to it between Christian denominations. One could assume, in general, that Christian "sects" tend to reject the secular world, whereas "churches" are more concerned and involved with it. It follows that sects, particularly the more fundamentalist ones, will tend to reject tourism out of hand as a secular activity; churches will at least compromise with its existence and concern themselves with the improvement of its quality, in accordance with their goals and values.

Choices and Conduct

I have argued above that, though religions have not evolved express "theologies of tourism," their general attitudes to tourism can be gauged from their basic theological positions. I claim now that these attitudes, in turn, will have a significant impact on the specific motivations, attitudes and conduct of members of different religions in the sphere of tourism. Their impact will be the stronger, the more individual members adhere to the precepts and teachings of their respective religions — in other words, the more "religious" they are.

Religion influences the "sociography" of tourists — their demographic composition, itineraries, modes of travel, and choice of destinations. Observant Jews will engage in tourism less than members of most other religions, for both "theological" reasons and practical constraints: dietetic rules (*kashruth*), observance of the Sabbath and Jewish holidays will restrict their freedom of movement and choice of destinations. Similar but less rigorous religious constraints will also apply to observant Moslems and high-caste Hindus. Most religious Christians, however, will be free of religious injunctions against travel, or from practical constraints, and will therefore travel relatively more frequently and freely. Among religious Jewish and Moslem tourists, males will predominate; women will be accompanied by their spouses, but will generally not travel alone. The demographic composition of religious Christian tourists will be more balanced, with more women traveling by themselves.

In general, people adhering to a religious tradition will tend less than purely secular individuals to expose themselves to total strangeness and will tend to choose destinations with which they share a degree of affinity: religious, historical, or cultural sites related to their religion or countries, or communities, of co-religionists. Thus, many traditional Western and especially American Jews frequently visit Israel, not necessarily as "pilgrims" merely to visit and pray at the holy sites, but rather to see the country and immerse themselves in its Jewish atmosphere ("*Yiddishkeit*"), which they often miss in the diaspora. Catholics tend similarly to visit famous medieval cathedrals or Christian holy places, even if they are not "pilgrims" in a strict sense. The difference in the choice of destinations and itineraries between Christians and Moslems has been recently empirically demonstrated for Israeli Arabs (Mansfeld and Ya'acoub 1995).

Some religions, particularly Judaism and Islam, also interdict their adherents from visiting places of worship of other religions — thus imposing a limitation upon their choice of destinations.

In general, adherence to the prescriptions and proscriptions of a religion acts as a constraint to the exposure of the tourists to the Other, which is frequently the goal of the secular tourist, and directs them to their own cultural domain. Such constraints appear to be stronger in Judaism and Islam, and weaker in most Christian churches and probably also in Buddhism.

There is, however, another, and perhaps less manifest, relationship between religion and tourism relevant in the present context: tourism has a liminal, permissive, and hedonistic character. Released from normative strictures and social control and in a playful mood, many tourists tend to engage in activities and forms of conduct proscribed at home: scant or loud clothing, boisterous behavior, excessive drinking, promiscuity, prostitution and gambling. Religions generally seek to restrain their members and to enjoin them to adhere to the normative prescriptions of their faith and engage in "worthwhile" or "uplifting" activities. Although it could be routinely assumed that religious persons will tend less than secular ones to engage in excessive behavior on their trip, for some, however, the period of absence from home may be perceived, like carnivals and other religiously sanctioned and tolerated spells of permissiveness, as an opportunity to release tensions and fulfill otherwise suppressed or "sinful" desires, which they cannot fulfill at home. A somewhat extreme example is the conduct of Moslem tourists from some countries on the Arab peninsula, where Islamic law is strictly enforced, on their visits to India or Thailand, during which they often engage intensively in activities proscribed in their homeland. Moderately religious persons, such as traditional Israeli Jews, will also tend to be less observant regarding dietary and other religious prescriptions on their trip than they are at home; and secular Israeli Jews may use the opportunity of a trip abroad to enjoy foods prohibited or difficult to obtain at home, such as pork or sea-food.

Destinations and Attractions

I now turn to the consideration of the impact of religion upon countries and localities that serve as tourist destinations and attractions.

Religion may have a negative impact on the number of tourists visiting a destination, for two main reasons. The first is an explicit policy against visitors who do not adhere to the dominant religion of a country, as was the case in Saudi Arabia or in Iran after Khoumeni, at least until recently. Such countries do not have a tourist industry in the modern sense, though they may be important pilgrimage destinations.

Secondly, the dominant religion at a destination may influence negatively tourist decisions, even in the absence of an express anti-tourist policy. Thus, the Islamic character of Pakistan or Malaysia may deter prospective Christian tourists, who will prefer religiously more liberal Hindu India or Buddhist Thailand. Terrorist attacks by fundamentalist groups against tourists, such as occurred in recent years in Algeria, Egypt and Bali, are obviously an extremely powerful deterrent.

Religion may also influence the attractiveness of a destination in more practical ways; thus, the absence of public transportation on Sabbath in Israel, or the dietary strictures on the menus of most Jewish restaurants in the country, may be a source of annoyance to non-Jewish visitors, although their impact on the volume of tourism to Israel is probably negligible, especially because religious strictures are ameliorated in major destinations, such as the Red Sea resort of Eilat.

The principal impact of religion on tourist numbers however, is a positive one, owing to the importance and appeal of religious sites, rituals, and festivals as tourist attractions. This attractiveness however can also be a source of inconvenience and tension.

Many of the principal Christian religious sites of Europe, such as the great Gothic and Romanesque churches and cathedrals of Italy, France and Germany have been almost completely taken over by tourism; in some instances they have virtually ceased to serve as places of worship. Religious feasts and festivals, especially in Third World countries, are being advertised as major tourist attractions, and are increasingly dominated by touristic concerns: rituals and performances, and even timing, are frequently adapted to the visitors' interests and convenience. The ambience of festivals is often changed by the growing predominance of foreign visitors, who come to see, but fail to participate or worship. Tourists may also disturb local worshippers by their very presence or by often inadvertent disrespectful conduct at holy places and festivals.

In many instances, particularly in the Third World, religious rituals are taken out of context, and become "commoditized" (Greenwood 1977) shows for foreign visitors. Although in some instances such profanation may not have — at least in the short run — a significant effect on the local community of believers (cf. McKean 1976b), it has probably in most cases a secularizing impact, affecting the belief of worshippers in the sacredness or efficacy of the ritual.

Religious authorities are ambivalent towards the growing popularity of religious sites, rituals, and festivals as tourist attractions. On the one hand, most religious sites are open and even welcoming to visitors (Din 1989) and their personnel are, at least initially, proud to display their religious traditions and art. With time, they also develop an economic interest in tourism: they gain an income from the sale of souvenirs or voluntary contributions; on the more important sites they often charge an entrance fee. Indeed, the religious authorities in many countries are becoming increasingly aware of the economic importance of tourism, and seek to preserve religious sites for tourism, while the income from tourism often helps this preservation (Panfilis 1986; Vizjak 1993). On the other hand, however, as a site is turned into an "attraction" of mass tourism, the religious authorities may become alarmed lest the ambience of the site be compromised.

Tourism also has another ambivalent impact on religious attractions: it creates the motivation and also often supplies the means to add adornment and splendor to religious sites and festivals (Boorstin 1964), as it does, for instance on Bali (McKean 1976b); but it may also encourage spectacularity, extravagance, and exoticism — as, for example, in the self-immolating practices in the Hindu procession at the Thaipusam festival in Singapore or in the procession of Chinese spirit mediums during the Vegetarian Festival in Phuket in southern Thailand (Cohen 2001).

Because religious festivals attract tourists, new festivals of only marginal religious significance are sometimes created, for example, in Thailand, where many touristically marginal communities have in recent years invented new festivals in order to gain a place on the "tourist map." In many of these new festivals secular themes prevail, though they may be tenuously related to Buddhism.

Tourists purchase souvenirs and art or craft objects on their trip, some of which are of religious significance to locals, but at most of sentimental or aesthetic value for tourists; sometimes, indeed, they are acquired as mere curiosities. Religious objects may, in the eyes of believers, be debased in the process (e.g. the use some foreigners made of bronze Buddha heads from Thailand as lamps stands). Indeed, to prevent such sacrilege, the Thai authorities have some years ago prohibited the export of Buddha images.

In instances where art or craft objects are believed to possess magical or religious power, artisans sometimes differentiate between their production for religious and for secular commercial purposes. For example, Navaho sand painters make subtle changes in the symbolism of their gods on commercial paintings, thereby robbing them of their magical potency (Parezo 1983).

Although fundamentalist or sectarian communities are averse to tourism, they often become intensively attractive for secular tourists as one of the principal manifestations of the Other in the modern world. The reactions of such communities to the unwelcome intrusion of outsiders vary: inhabitants of ultra-orthodox Jewish neighborhoods in Jerusalem are passively resentful and generally ignore the intruders, merely requiring, on signs hung at the entrance to their neighborhoods, that they be modestly dressed. The Amish show a more active, though ambivalent, attitude: they seek to profit from tourism by carefully staging themselves for visitors, while barring them from penetrating beyond the boundaries of the "tourist space" (MacCannell 1973) into their private world (Buck 1978a).

Tourists ordinarily seek at most to experience the strangeness of other cultures and religions; these are in my terminology, "experiential" tourists (Chapter 5). However, there are some who do not seek to experience other religions merely vicariously, but in their quest for an alternative to secular modernity seek to "taste" them or immerse themselves in them, thus becoming "experimental" or "existential" tourists. Young seekers in Hindu ashrams in India or in Buddhist temples in Thailand exemplify these types of tourists. This new demand has in fact led to the emergence of Hindu or Buddhist religious establishments specifically oriented to the needs of the foreigners (e.g. Halpern 1986).

In conclusion, it could be asked, what is the impact of mass tourism on the religiosity of the people at the destinations? From the above it appears to follow that the impact is generally a secularizing one — a weakening of the local adherence to religion and of the belief in the sacredness and efficacy of holy places, rituals, and customs. But tourism may also engender a reaction to what is perceived as pernicious outside influences, and lead to a local religious revival, as it apparently did in a Moslem village in Kenya, after tourism had provoked there considerable social disintegration (Beckerleg 1995), or in Tunisia, where Moslem women returned to "the veil as a symbolic protest over increasing Western influence" (Poirier 1995:167).

Tourist Establishments

The institutions of modem mass tourism — hotels, resorts travel and tour companies, shopping, leisure and entertainment facilities — tend to be impersonal and "nivellating," providing standard services to customers of any nationality or religion. They do, however, recognize special requirement groups: many airlines and hotels will provide kosher meals to observant Jews or vegetarian ones to Hindus. Such establishments, however, are generally limited in the extent to which they can accommodate the requirements of strictly observant individuals. Airlines cannot set their schedules so that they do not infringe on the Jewish Sabbath, and Jewish bathers cannot insist upon the separation of the sexes on public beaches to satisfy demands of religious modesty. Small specialized agencies have therefore emerged, catering to the needs and demands of such specific groups, paralleling those of secular mass tourism. Thus, Tower Airlines catered to orthodox Jews, small travel and touring companies in Israel provide transportation, and small "*glatt-kosher*" hotels and hostels in orthodox communities provide accommodation for them; in some seaside communities segregated beaches have been set up, at a respectable distance from the public facility. In the United States, the Catskills provided a vacation playground for American Jews, with kosher food and liturgical services on Jewish Holidays (Brown 1996).

Religion can be a factor influencing the staffing of tourist establishments, and a source of psychological strain for personnel working with tourists. Jewish and Moslem women will tend to abstain from employment in jobs involving contact with male tourists. Jews and Moslems will also avoid employment in restaurants offering pork dishes, or will at least feel uncomfortable serving such dishes, even if they themselves are not strictly observant.

Strains can also appear in the tourist guide's role — for example, when Jewish guides have to present the events that have, according to Christian tradition, taken place on holy sites in Jerusalem to an audience of Christian pilgrims or religious tourists. However, their professional training usually enables them to evolve a mode of presentation that is acceptable to the audience without compromising their own convictions.

The obverse of religious constraints in the performance of touristic roles is that members of other religions may be called upon to perform proscribed tasks. Thus, Israeli hotels that observe the Jewish Sabbath employ Moslems or Christians to perform the necessary routine work — such as restaurant service — which Jews are prohibited from engaging in on their day of rest.

The various ways in which religion impinges upon the development, structure, and operation of tourist establishments have not yet been thoroughly studied. The few examples presented above indicate the significance of the problem and the need for its comparative investigation.

Tourism and Religious Action

As far as I know, only the Christian churches manifested an active, practical interest in tourism. Indeed, if for Islam, for example, tourism is more of a "theological" problem, in contemporary Christianity it is more of a "pastoral" one: there is less concern with the religious meaning or legitimacy of tourism, and more with the various moral, social, and cultural problems that it poses, for both the tourists and the tourist-receiving destinations. Even in this respect, there appears to exist a slight difference of emphasis between the churches, particularly between the Catholic Church and the established Protestant denominations. The Catholic Church has accepted tourism as a fact of modem life, but seeks mainly to improve the quality of the tourist experience (cf. Przeclawski 1994:89–91). In various meetings and publications of church-related organizations, such matters as the anonymity inherent in mass tourism and irresponsibility in the conduct of tourists are discussed, and novel ways are sought to enhance self-expression, contact with the natives, and intercultural communication and understanding in touristic situations (e.g. Poix 1985; Simon *et al.* 1985). The growing awareness of a need for a new style of pastoral service for tourists (Poix 1985) has recently disposed the relevant church authorities to encourage "religious tourism." The intent is to reach tourists, who do not travel for an express religious purpose, with a religious message on their tour, especially during visits at sites of worship, and transform them, as it were, from mere observers into participants; in my own terms — to turn them, at least temporarily, from mere "experiential" tourists who vicariously experience the life of others, into "existential" tourists, who have a religious experience during their visit. However, unlike tourists having an existential experience at the centers of the

Other (Chapter 5), "religious tourists" are induced to have such an experience of their own Center, of which they may have been estranged: they become momentary pilgrims.

In other societies tourism and worship are often integrated on the trip; for example, Buddhist tourists in Thailand often spontaneously worship Buddha images in museums or on archeological sites. In modern Western society tourism and religious worship have become largely disassociated. The Catholic Church seeks to reintegrate them, at least to some degree.

Protestant churches, especially those active in the Third World, appear to have taken a more critical stance to mass tourism than the Catholic Church. They seem to be less concerned with the quality of the tourist experience, and more with the consequences of tourism for the people at touristic destinations. This concern was expressed on the institutional level in the foundation, in 1982, of the Ecumenical Coalition on Third World Tourism, and of its mouthpiece, the journal *Contours*. The general tenor of the Council's consultations and publications is highly critical of tourism, which is usually pictured as a morally, socially, and culturally destructive force, even as its alleged economic benefits to Third World communities are much smaller than claimed by politicians and the tourist industry. However, while radically criticizing tourism, the Coalition and its various platforms have had little success in formulating applicable practical proposals for forms of tourism, which would safeguard the benefits of tourism for the Third World destinations, while substantially reducing its drawbacks.

Conclusion

Tourism is a complex phenomenon, and this complexity also marks the relationship between tourism and religion. This relationship is ambivalent both on the abstract and on the practical level. The world's religions find it, therefore, hard to formulate a principled theological position on the phenomenon, even if they recognize its religious potential and social and economic significance. Like other cultural institutions, religions also experience a contradiction between an often critical attitude to tourism and practical interests in the industry: many religious establishments and holy places flourish on income derived from tourist visits. The paradoxical consequence is that they often seek to preserve the religious sites, rituals, and festivals, not necessarily for purely religious reasons, but also in order to safeguard the stream of visitors, whom they may at the same time see as responsible for their desecration. Such ambivalences and contradictions could offer an incisive point of departure for systematic studies of the dynamics of the relationship between tourism and religion in concrete contexts and situations.

Chapter 11

The Tourist Guide: The Origins, Structure and Dynamics of a Role

Introduction

The role of the modern tourist guide has its direct historic origins in the Grand Tour of the 17th and 18th centuries (Brodsky-Porges 1981; Hilbert 1969; Lambert 1935) and in the beginnings of modern tourism which eventually superseded the Grand Tour in the 19th century. Its antecedents, however, are many and diverse and reach far back into mythology, allegoric literature, history, and geographic exploration. To understand the structure and dynamics of the role of the modern tourist guide, one has to examine these antecedents, because they set the cultural background against which the modern role developed.

For all its apparent simplicity, "guiding" is a complex concept; and while there are many different types of guiding, some of this complexity also marks the tourist guide. A good start to appreciate that complexity can be made by considering an authoritative dictionary definition of the term: the *Oxford English Dictionary* defines the concept "guide" as "One who leads or shows the way, especially to a traveller in a strange country: spec. one who is hired to conduct a traveller or tourist (e.g. over a mountain, through a forest or over a city or building) and to point out objects of interest" (*Oxford* 1933:IV/490). In another, but also relevant, sense, a guide is, according to the same source, "One who directs a person in his ways or conduct. . ." (ibid.:IV/491).

The two definitions obviously relate to very differently structured social roles. The role of the modern tourist guide, however, also developed from diverse antecedents: one, the *pathfinder*, which embodies primarily the first of these definitions; the other, the *mentor*, which embodies, essentially, elements of the second. Both these antecedents are, in a modified way, reflected in the role structure of the contemporary tourist guide.

The antecedent role of the pathfinder, or the geographical guide who leads the way through an environment in which his followers lack orientation or through a socially defined territory to which they have no access, is simpler and easier to document. In the absence of maps, guide-books, signposts, and other orientational devices, strangers entering an unknown territory were, in the past, dependent upon guides to lead the way and gain access in face of an often suspicious or hostile local populace. Guidance of this kind was especially in demand by armies who penetrated an unreconnoitred territory (*Oxford* 1933:IV/491) and travellers and explorers who dared to enter unknown lands (e.g. Roberts 1970:7–8).

Pathfinders were originally locals with a good native knowledge of their home environment, but with no specialized training. Such guides apparently existed already in Greco-Roman antiquity (Casson 1974) and re-emerged with the expansion of travel during the age of the Grand Tour (e.g. the Italian *vetturino*, see Brodsky-Porges 1981:180). As traveling conditions improved with the penetration of modern Western infrastructure into ever more outlying areas, and guide-books and maps facilitated orientation (Knebel 1960:28), pathfinders were ever more relegated to guiding special interest travellers in remote, uncharted areas. Local youths can still be hired as pathfinders by travellers in some remote areas of the world, such as in the hill tribe villages of Northern Thailand where local youths volunteer to lead the occasional visitor from one village to another, or on the Kiribati Islands in the Pacific (Cornell 1980). Pathfinding frequently becomes a specialized occupation, serving special interest travellers, e.g. as hunting guides (Story 1982), safari-guides (Almagor 1985) or fishing guides (LaFlamme 1979:143). The latter are found not only in sportive fishing, but also in commercial fishing, where specialized guides, such as the *pesca* (cf. Zulaika 1981:82–85) are depended upon to lead the fishermen to their bounty.

The most prominent form of pathfinding, however, is found in mountaineering. Specialized mountain guides lead climbers and trekkers in many formidable mountain areas around the world, such as the Alps (Faux 1981:14; Knebel 1960:27) the Andes and the Himalayas. Indeed, the local youths who guided the early mountaineers in the Alps were among the immediate predecessors of the modern tourist guide (Knebel 1960:27); while the Nepalese Sherpas in our day acquired world renown as mountain guides of the Himalayan expeditions and trekking parties (Baumgartner *et al.* 1978:21–22, 84–87, 217–218; Coppock 1978:63; Sacherer 1981).

The role of the mentor, or personal tutor or spiritual advisor, is much more complex in origin, heterogeneous in nature, and difficult to trace historically. The role is, of course, most fully developed and institutionalized in those religious settings in which a specialist serves as a "guru" to the novice, adept, or seeker, guiding him towards insight, enlightenment, or any other exalted spiritual state. This kind of guiding may appear of little relevance to our subject, were it not for the fact that the spiritual advance of the adept is frequently represented as an allegorical pilgrimage which takes the form of an imaginary geographic journey, in which the spiritual advisor plays a role analogous to that of the geographic guide. Indeed, some of the great allegoric journeys in Western literature are conducted by mentors who guide the hero in both a spiritual and a geographic sense: Virgil and Beatrice in Dante's *Divine Comedy*, the Interpreter in Bunyan's *Pilgrim's Progress*, and in an inverted sense, Mephisto in Goethe's *Faust*.

It is this double sense of guidance — geographical as well as spiritual — which marks the ideal leader of a religious pilgrimage, and which was subsequently transferred to the role of the tutor leading the young Englishman on the cultural pilgrimage of the Grand Tour to the centers of European learning or classic antiquity. The ideal tutor, according to Vicesimus Knox was conceived of as ". . . a grave, respectable man of mature age, who would, in addition to his duties as pedagogue and guide, 'watch over the morals and religion of his pupil. . .' " (Hibbert 1969:15–16). It is immaterial for this chapter that this ideal was but rarely realized in practice (Hibbert 1969:229). The role of the mentor, rather than of the geographic guide, was the dominant component in the role structure of the tutor on the Grand Tour. Indeed, even experienced tutors occasionally had to seek the assistance of local pathfinders such as *vetturinos* (Brodsky-Porges 1981:180–181) on particularly difficult or dangerous stretches of the journey, as had probably the leaders of religious pilgrimages before them.

The role of the modern tourist guide combines and expands elements from both antecedents, that of the pathfinder and that of the mentor. This confluence is neatly expressed in the Hebrew term for the role, *moreh-derech*, i.e. "teacher of the way." The two, however, do not necessarily merge harmoniously; rather there exist incongruencies and tensions between these two major components of the modern role, which at least partly account for its developmental dynamics as well as its further differentiation.

Structure

Holloway (1981:380) has pointed out that ". . . the occupation of leading groups of tourists carries a number of different titles (e.g. tourist guide, tour leader, courier, etc.) and there is as yet little consensus on their use . . ." Since career guiding is an occupation of recent origin, according to Holloway, it is ". . . not yet ritualized and institutionalized," and hence is still ". . . subject to interpretation by the passengers taking part in the excursion." Moreover, "the guiding role is composed of a number of subroles . . ." (ibid.:385, 398), the relative emphasis on each of which may vary from one type of guide to another (Cohen 1982a). This variation will be used as the basis for a systematic classification of the empirical variety of different kinds of guides observed by Holloway (1981:381).

The purpose of this section is to develop a composite analytical conceptualization of the tourist guide's role, which will integrate the principal existing approaches to the role and serve as a common frame of reference for the comparative study of concrete guiding roles in different touristic settings. The following analysis extends the earlier attempt of the author to distinguish four principal components in the guide's role (Cohen 1982a:236–239).

A review of the existing, rather meagre, literature reveals two principal conceptualizations of the role of the tourist guide: as a "leader" and as a "mediator." We shall integrate these in a more complex conceptual scheme.

The first principal conceptualization, that of "leader" is epitomized in the dictionary definition of the guide as one "who leads or shows the way" (*Oxford* 1933:IV/490); but, as discussed later, the leadership sphere of the role is much more complex than simply leading the way. This sphere is obviously an extension and elaboration of the "pathfinder" role of earlier times — although the spatial leadership of the guide in modern tourism may consist not so much of showing the way through a geographically little known or unmarked region, but primarily in providing priviledged access to an otherwise non-public territory (Schmidt 1979:450). This latter form of leadership indeed informs Schmidt's conception of the guide's role in her structural analysis of the "guided tour" — even if she also refers to other components of the role, such as his social leadership (ibid.:457).

The other principal conceptualization of the tourist guide's role in the literature sees him as a "mediator" (deKadt 1979; Nettekoven 1979:142; Pearce 1982:73), a "middleman" (van den Berghe 1980:381), or a "culture broker" (McKean 1976a). This, too, is epitomized in the dictionary definition of a guide as one who "points out objects of interest" (*Oxford* 1933:IV/490), but the mediatory sphere of the tourist guide's role, as noted later, is much wider and more complex than the simple direction of tourists' attention to such objects. The mediatory sphere is obviously an extension of the earlier role of the guide as "mentor" — McKean (1976a:13) indeed, calls the tourist guide "a teacher, a confidant and guru," and Schmidt (1979:458) compares him to a shaman. However, his mediation under modern conditions may consist not so much in edifying his party as in social mediation and cultural brokerage.

An analysis of these conceptualizations, as well as some wider theoretical considerations, plus much empirical evidence, indicate that each of these spheres of the guide's role consists, from the perspective of the guided tour, of an outer-directed and an inner-directed component (Cohen 1982a:236–237, 1996a). Therefore, the guide's role can be represented schematically as in Figure 11.1.

	Outer-Directed	Inner-Directed
(A) Leadership sphere	(1) Instrumental	(2) Social
(B) Mediatory sphere	(3) Interactional	(4) Communicative

Figure 11.1: Schematic Representation of the Principal Components of the Tourist Guide's Role

Virtually all of the concrete activities of the tourist guide, reported in diverse sources, can be subsumed under one of the principal analytic components in this scheme.

Leadership Sphere (A)

The distinction between instrumental and social leadership is well founded in general sociological theory (e.g. Bales and Slater 1955). Its utilization here is justified by empirical information on the guide's activities. The well-known tension between these two forms of leadership, indeed, occasionally engenders stresses in the guide's role and may well have contributed to its further differentiation.

(1) *The Instrumental Component*: This component of the guide's role relates to his responsibility for the smooth accomplishment of the tour as an ongoing social enterprise (Knebel 1960:120). While the kernel of this component consists of "leading the way," the modern guide's instrumental leadership task is more complex and consists of several interrelated elements:

(a) *Direction*: Assuming that the general route and ultimate destination of the tour are usually set in advance, the guide is responsible for the spatio-temporal direction of the trip: to find and sometimes also to choose the way, which under unsettled conditions may necessitate considerable orientational skills (Cohen 1982a:242) and "navigational expertise" (Holloway 1981:392). Even where the territory is well marked and the route a routine one, the guide has at least to make sure that it is properly followed. If the route is essentially open to choice, as in safari, fishing, and shopping trips, the guide has to possess considerable knowledge of available alternative locations and access routes and of the likelihood that his party will indeed encounter the desired "objects of interest" at a given location (cf. Almagor 1985).

(b) *Access*: The guide leads his tour not only through a geographical space, but also through a socially organized territory. One of the advantages of guided tours, as particularly Schmidt (1979:450) has pointed out, is that they grant the tourists access to non-public spaces, which they would not otherwise be able to enter — e.g. access to the "back regions" (MacCannell 1973:597–598) of educational, medical, governmental, and other institutions (Schmidt 1979:449–451). The guide provides access to these regions, and thereby also shoulders the responsibility for his party's behavior — e.g. that the visitors will not interfere with ongoing activities or cause damage.

(c) *Control*: The guide bears responsibility for the safe and efficient conduct of the party. Within limits, he is responsible for the security, safety (Schmidt 1979:457–458), and comfort of his party. This means not only that he should follow a reasonably safe and secure route, but also that he should exercise control over his party, prevent members from breaking away, collect stragglers and, generally, monitor the pace of movement of the party. This is sometimes referred to as the "shepherding and marshalling" (Holloway 1981:38; cf. also Buck 1978a) function of the guide. The problem of control is complicated by the fact that guides are normally responsible for keeping to the timetable of the tour, including the duration of the various stages of the trip, as well as the length of stay in the intermediate destinations. Where the guide is bound to a strict timetable, this aspect of keeping the itinerary may become an important source of strain between the guide and members of his party.

(2) *The Social Component*: This component of the guide's leadership role relates to his responsibility for the cohesion and morale of the touring party, and stands in some contrast to his role as an instrumental leader. This component also embraces several concrete elements:

(a) *Tension-Management*: The guide is expected to take steps to prevent the emergence of tensions between members of his party (Schmidt 1979:457) and intervene to smooth out relations once a conflict breaks out.

(b) *Integration*: Several authors see the guide as responsible for the social integration of his group. Thus, Holloway (1981:388) pointed out that he is the ". . . catalyst who encourages social cohesion in [his] group," and Schmidt (1979:457) claims that he is an "instigator of sociability" and "provides integration" (p. 454) to the group. It is questionable, however, how successful his integrative efforts will be in view of the demands which the performance of his instrumental functions put upon his party.

(c) *Morale*: The guide is supposed to keep his party in good humor and in high morale through pleasant demeanor and occasionally jocular behavior. The latter grows in importance in brief tours, when there is little time for the party to integrate (Schmidt 1979:457). It is a particularly important element in the role performance of not fully qualified guides, such as the British "driver-couriers" on excursions (Holloway 1981:390), or "couriers" accompanying a tour (Gorman 1979:480), who may compensate for their inferior competence as guides by playing the "good fellow" or clown.

(d) *Animation*: Finally, in some circumstances, the guide may try to "animate" members of his party, i.e. to induce them to undertake various activities offered by the touristic facilities encountered on the itinerary. This rather marginal element of the tourist guide's role when conducting a sightseeing tour, tends to become the kernel of a new role, that of the animator (e.g. *Animation* 1975) under the more stationary conditions of vacationing tourism.

Mediatory Sphere (B)

The distinction between the interactional and the communicative components of the mediatory sphere is well founded in the more general distinction between social and cultural mediation, a distinction expressed, in this context, in the difference, e.g. between van den Berghe's (1980:381) conception of the guide as a social "middleman" and McKean's (1976a) conception of him as a "culture broker."

(3) *The Interactional Component*: This component of the guide's role relates to his function as a middleman between his party and the local population, sites and institutions, as well as touristic facilities. It consists of two principal elements:

(a) *Representation*: As Schmidt (1979:454) has noted, the guide both integrates his party into the visited setting as well as insulates it from that setting. He does this by interposing himself between the party and the environment, thus making it non-threatening to the tourist. Thereby he comes to represent the party to the setting, as well as the setting to the party (Cohen 1982a:243–250), a position which, insofar as the demands made by the sides of the encounter are incongruent, may well put the guide under considerable strain. The fact, however, that he frequently functions as a "go-between" (Goffman 1959:149; cf. Cohen 1982a:246) — i.e. the only link in the encounter between complete strangers — may provide him with some maneuvering space and thereby reduce the strain of his task.

(b) *Organization*: The guide is frequently responsible for the provision of services and amenities to his party during the tour, such as refreshments, meals, and overnight stays, as well as medical care and other services in cases of emergency. This may involve him in dealings with the local population in remote, non-touristic areas and with various specific touristic facilities, such as restaurants and hotels in touristically well developed areas. This function may demand considerable skills to ensure supplies and hospitality under unsettled touristic conditions (e.g. Cohen 1982a:243–245); where a tourist system is well developed, however, arrangements are usually formally institutionalized, but demand some expertise in the proper procedures on the part of the guide.

(4) *The Communicative Component*: This is frequently considered to be the principal component of the guide's role (e.g. Holloway 1981:380–381; Pearce 1982:73). It is certainly the component given primacy in the formal training of guides (e.g. Smith 1961), even though some guides receive only superficial training and possess scanty knowledge of the area (Nieto Piñeroba 1977:163); even where guides receive thorough education, some aspects of their communicative role are, according to some authors, insufficiently emphasized (deKadt 1979:57). This component consists of four principal elements, which can be ranged by the extent to which the guide interposes himself between the tourist and the site as a "culture broker."

(a) *Selection*: For the guide to "point out objects of interest" as he conducts his tour, means, at a minimum, that he selects from the multifarious stream of impressions impinging upon his party those which he deems worthy of their attention (e.g. McKean 1976a:15; cf. also Buck 1978a:230–231; Schmidt 1979:442–443). The guide may select the "objects of interest" in accordance with his personal preferences and taste, his professional training, the directions received from his employer or from the tourist authorities, or the assumed interests of his party. In any case, his selection will, to a considerable extent, structure his party's attention during the trip: not only will they see what he wants them to see, but perhaps more importantly, they will not see what he does not want them to see (cf. Schmidt 1979:458–459). Even this apparently innocuous activity of the guide may thus have some manipulative significance; the import of this grows in the following forms of his communicative activity.

(b) *Information*: The dissemination of correct and precise information is by many considered to be the kernel of the guide's role (e.g. McKean 1976a:13; Nettekoven 1979:142). He is an "information giver and fount of knowledge" and a "teacher and instructor"; indeed, guides themselves tend to "... perceive their prime role to be that of information giver" (Holloway 1981:385–386). They often possess impressive knowledge about the sites on the tour and are eager to demonstrate their expertise (Holloway 1981:387). In advanced touristic countries, indeed, the dissemination of information takes on an almost academic character. Despite the academic veneer and the frequently dry presentation of the information such as the recitation of dates, numbers, and events connected with a given site — the information imparted is rarely purely neutral; rather it frequently reflects the information policy of the tourist establishment or of the official tourist authorities, intended either to impart or maintain a desired "touristic image" of the host setting, or to engender in the visitors some wider social and political impressions, as part of a national propaganda campaign. The latter is particularly, though not exclusively, the case in less democratic societies, such as the martial-law Philippines (cf. Richter 1980), or communist countries ". . . such as the USSR, [where] local tourist guides [gave] highly ritualized accounts of their environment" (Pearce 1982:74). What appears as "information" may thus be subtly transformed into an interpretation of the visited site intended to influence the tourists' impressions and attitudes.

(c) *Interpretation*: In my view, interpretation and not the mere dissemination of information, is the distinguishing communicative function of the trained tourist guide. In transcultural tourism, a cultural gap ordinarily exists between the visitors and the locals. The guides play a prominent role in mediating the encounter between cultures (Nettekoven 1979:142) — and they do this by an act of "interpretation." In its general form, transcultural interpretation takes the form of translation of the strangeness of a foreign culture into a cultural idiom familiar to the visitors. Schmidt (1979:458) expresses this point most poignantly be comparing the guide to a shaman who ". . . must translate the unfamiliar." Guides are therefore supposed not only to know well the culture they intrepret, but also to ". . . understand the tourists visiting from another culture." They thus play a ". . . Janus-faced role . . . as they look simultaneously toward their foreign clients and their ancestral tradition" (McKean 1976a:1, 12). Interpretation is the essence of the role of the "culture-broker."

The tourist, and especially the mass tourist, however, does not arrive at the foreign destination a *tabula rasa*, completely open to whatever strangeness he may encounter. His choice of the tour has been, at least partly, conditioned by preconceptions and expectations (McKean 1976a:14), and it is the guide's task, through interpretation, to relate to these the visited sites (deKadt 1979:57; McKean 1976a:14). Such interpretation does not necessitate particular skills on the part of the guide where attractions are "authentic" and easily recognizable. But the challenge to those skills grows the more heavily "staged" (MacCannell 1973) the attractions. Under such conditions, the interpretative skills of the guide will express themselves in his capacity for "keying" (Goffman 1974:45ff) — i.e. the representation through the use of appropriate language and dramaturgic effects of often blatantly staged attractions as if they were authentic. "Keying" as such is ordinarily considered a legitimate device in the professional ethics of guides, and is often one of the most important informally acquired skills (McKean 1976a:10–11); however, brought to an extreme it may turn into outright "fabrication" (Goffman

1974:83ff), a type of activity which does not meet with general approval in the occupation.

(d) *Fabrication*: While "keying" is still based on at least some vestiges of truthfulness, as understood by the guides themselves, "fabrication" consists of outright invention or deception. The most prominent example are guides who present fake antiques, encountered in shops on the tour, as if they were genuine, with the intent of deceiving the tourist and receiving a cut from the shopkeeper's profits; or guides who bring their party surreptitiously to a false destination on the tour, but present it in a manner intended to convince its members that it is the one promised in the program. Such practices may eventually induce the authorities to intervene and regulate the guiding occupation.

Dynamics

The various components of the modern tourist guide's role can, to some degree, be found in the role performance of most guides; however, the importance of and emphasis upon the major components, as well as upon the constituent elements of each of them, varies considerably between different kinds of guides (e.g. Halloway 1981:389–390). It is beyond the scope of this chapter to list all the empirically detectable constellations of the guide's role. Rather the focus is on the general trend in the dynamics of that role: i.e. the transition from the role of the *Original Guide*, concerned mainly with *instrumental* activities, to that of the *Professional Guide*, which focuses primarily on the *communicative* ones. This process is accompanied, in the most highly developed tourist systems, by the further differentiation of the guide's role and the separation from it of two new touristic occupations: the *Tour-leader*, who is concerned primarily with *interactionary* activities and the *Animator*, who focuses upon the *social* ones. The two processes can be represented on the basis of the previous scheme as in Figure 11.2.

The process of transition from the Original to the Professional Guide's role has been extensively discussed in an earlier article (Cohen 1982a). This process is closely related to two major sets of variables: the emergence and development of a tourist system and the often concomitant arrival of institutionalized types of tourists on the tour (Cohen 1972:168ff).

The role of the Original Guide, which developed from the antecedent role of the pathfinder, as described in the introductory section, is characteristic for tours composed of non-institutionalized tourists, such as "explorers" or drifters (Chapter 3), into areas not yet much penetrated by the tourist system, such as jungles, mountain areas, and deserts (Almagor 1985; Cohen 1982a). The principal reason for such

	Outer-Directed	Inner-Directed
(A) Leadership sphere	(1) Original Guide (instrumental primacy)	(2) Animator (social primacy)
(B) Mediatory sphere	(3) Tour-leader (interactional primacy)	(4) Professional Guide (communicative primacy)

Figure 11.2: The Dynamics of the Tourist Guide's Role

tourists to join a tour or hire a guide is their need for someone who would "lead the way" into an unknown and potentially dangerous area. Secondly, since such areas do not offer standard touristic facilities, the tourists need someone who would deal with the natives and be able to ascertain some basic hospitality services. The outward-oriented components — primarily the instrumental, and secondarily, the interactional — are thus the principal components of the Original Guide's role.

Persons performing the Original Guide's role are typically "marginal natives," locals who are thoroughly familiar with the environment, but who have at least a smattering of a foreign language and a basic notion of the tourists' culture and needs (Pearce 1982:73; Smith 1977b:68–69), even though these may be deemed insufficient as more demanding tourists enter the area (van den Berghe 1980:381). Such guides acquired their knowledge of the region from personal experience, e.g. through work, military or police duty in the area, or through apprenticeship and informal learning from more experienced guides. They usually have little formal education and no formal training in guiding (Cohen 1982a:242). They are either self-employed "free lancers," catching the tourists at their points of arrival or sojourn in the region, e.g. train and bus stations or hostels (cf. Noronha 1979:188), or work for small touring agencies, specializing in "unconventional" trekking, motoring, riding, or canoeing tours to remote areas (Cohen 1982a:241). They are typically not permanently employed as regular guides by large touristic enterprises, and are not licensed.

Though even non-institutionalized tourists on tours in remote areas may desire information and need some social support, these inner-directed activities are of distinctly minor importance compared to the outer-directed ones. The kind of tourists taking such excursions typically strive for direct experiences; if they could find their way by themselves, they would dispense with the guide altogether (cf. Pearce 1982:75). Insofar as they do use a guide's service, they will primarily seek basic information, rather than elaborate interpretations of the sights and will be much more suspicious of falsification than the sedate tourists on more routine tours (Cohen 1982a:252).

The Original Guide thrives in the early stage of touristic development in a newly penetrated area. At that stage, he often still possesses a naive enthusiasm for his job, reciprocated and reinforced by the enthusiasm of the visitors, who frequently befriend him and help to build up his reputation by word of mouth among their friends and acquaintances (Cohen 1982a:253).

Tourism, however, is a process. With its growth, initial conditions rarely, if ever, remain unchanged. After the early stage in which tourists are welcomed in an area as "paying guests" within the confines of traditional hospitality (Cohen 1982a:146), a period of relative anomie often sets in as the number of tourists increases and less interested, less friendly, and more demanding individuals replace the pioneering early visitors. Tours become routinized, advertised in travel brochures and listed in guidebooks; and commercial catering facilities are established in strategic locations along the routes. Under these conditions, the informally acquired, but often impressive, skills of the Original Guide are less needed, while their bigger, but less select, clientele is also less eager for exceptional experiences. As this author's study in the hill tribe area of northern Thailand has shown (Cohen 1982a:249–250), with the routinization of the guide's job, ever fewer skills are needed to lead tourists on the increasingly standardized treks in the jungle. As the older Original Guides leave the occupation for more attractive jobs, many new, less experienced and less qualified individuals enter the field, riding the tide of growing demand. Without much external control, the quality and reliability of their services decline sharply, causing a loss of prestige and morale — which in turn accelerates the negative selection into the occupation. In this anomic stage of tourism development, the guides, like other locals dealing with tourists, frequently approach their clients with an attitude of predatory exploitation (Cohen 1984b:380), seeking to squeeze the maximum out of them as long as they are around, with little thought of the impact of their conduct on the long range touristic reputation of the guiding occupation and the region as a whole. At the same time, tourists become more demanding towards the guides, asking for improved service and fuller information and interpretation of the sights; they express dissatisfaction ". . . with run of the mill tourist guides who speak a broken version of their language and whose knowledge of tourees (i.e. the locals visited on the tour) is often superficial" (van den Berghe 1980:381; cf. also Almagor 1985).

The complaints and the implied threat to the general reputation of the region eventually move the touristic authorities to intervene and attempt to regulate non-conventional tourism — in the process attempting to professionalize the guides (Cohen 1982a:254–257). This intervention, in turn, is usually also a step in the process of the incorporation of a new touristic area into the national or even international tourist system (Cohen 1984b:382–383). It should be noted, however, that this system rarely, if ever, embraces all tourism in a country — and that some Original Guides, as well as many of their less qualified imitators, may continue to operate in marginal regions even of touristically well developed countries.

The role of the Professional Guide developed from the antecedent role of the "mentor" as described in the introductory section; it is characteristic for tours composed of institutionalized types of tourists, especially organized mass tourists (Chapter 3), on routine tours in the central sectors of well developed tourist systems (Nettekoven 1979:142). Professional guides operate mainly in urban areas, museums, and institutions (Fine and Speer 1985; Schmidt 1979) and historically, ethnically or culturally important regions (e.g. Buck 1978a).

The emphasis in the Professional Guide's role is on the inner-directed sphere, in comparison with which the outer-directed sphere is distinctly peripheral (cf. Nettekoven 1979:142). Professional Guides usually work for big bureaucratized travel agencies and tour operators, where they are but one kind of tourist-oriented service personnel. The breadth of functions performed by the Professional Guide depends on the division of labor between the guide and other functionaries serving the tourists. The more advanced the division of labor, the narrower will be the definition of the Professional Guide's role. The scope of the Professional Guide's role will be considerably narrowed if a Tour-leader accompanies the party — taking care of the program (Knebel 1960:120) and making arrangements with tourist facilities on the route. In such a role-constellation, the guide will be able to concentrate exclusively on the inner-directed sphere of his role, and particularly its communicative component. Indeed, the principal expectation of mass tourists from Professional Guides is that they provide information and interpretation of the sites visited (Nettekoven 1979:142); while the guides themselves derive their professional pride principally from the demonstration of their communicative competence (e.g. Fine and Speer 1985; Holloway 1981:386–387). The communicative component is the kernel of the Professional Guide's role.

The social component of the role of the Professional Guide also increases in importance in comparison with its place in the Original Guide's role, although it normally does not become the dominant function in the role-performance of well-trained guides. It might, however, become highly prominent in the conduct of guides with deficient training, such as the driver-couriers in Britain (Holloway 1981:382, 390). Some couriers, acting as Tour-leaders, apparently also take upon themselves some element of the social component of the guide's role — such as care for the party's morale (Gorman 1979:482). The social component tends to crystallize into a separate role, that of the Animator, insofar as the emphasis in tourism moves from rather passive sightseeing to group activities (*Animation* 1975); but the role of the Animator is more characteristic of vacationing, rather than sightseeing situations, especially in active group vacations such as those offered by the Club Med (Finger and Gayler 1975:19).

To conclude, the principal dynamics in the transition from the Original to the Professional Guide's role is thus away from leadership and towards mediating, and away from the outer- and towards the inner-directed sphere, with the communicative component becoming the kernel of the professional role. Moreover, with the changed conditions on the tour, a change of emphasis takes place within most components insofar as they are still performed by the Professional Guide, and not taken over by another specialized role. In the instrumental component, with the routinization of the itinerary, emphasis changes from path-finding, to the gaining of access to non-public space, and to control over the group; in the interactional component, with the emergence of commercialized tourist facilities, emphasis shifts from representation to the making of routine arrangements; in the social sphere, from integration to the active care for group morale, and eventually, animation. But the most important change takes place in the communicative component: from mere selection of sights and information to more sophisticated interpretation. The importance of the interpretative element increases with the growing artificiality of "staged" tourist attractions: in the extreme, it may turn into fabrication. The major professional dilemma of the Professional Guide, indeed, is that while he takes pride in his interpretative skills, through which he dramatizes the presentation of the attractions, thereby enhancing their impact on his party (Fine and Speer 1985), he should not willfully slip into fabrication. He thus frequently finds himself treading the narrow path between refined interpretative keying and outright fabrication.

Incumbents of the Professional Guide's role are ordinarily outsiders rather than natives to the areas visited (cf. van den Berghe 1980:381). They typically acquired their expertise in some form of formal education rather than merely through prior experience and informal, on the job training. Even so, many of the finer points and "tricks of the trade" making for a successful performance of the role are acquired by informal socialization into the occupation and contact with more experienced colleagues. While the nature and scope of formal education of guides varies from country to country (Smith 1961), a tendency towards increased formalization and professionalization of guides is found in most advanced tourist countries; this is expressed in the establishment of special courses or schools for guides, which grant diplomas; the regulation of entrance into the profession through the licensing of guides (e.g. deKadt 1979:56–57); and the complementary establishment of professional associations of guides. However, in comparison with well established professions, such as physicians, dentists, or lawyers, the guiding profession is, at best, semi-professionalized, even in the most advanced tourist countries. Indeed, it is not wholly clear which is the professional role-model, towards which its professionalization aspires — though it is probably that of the teacher (Pearce 1981:74; cf. also Buck 1978a:230) or even more, the academic lecturer.

Like many other not wholly professionalized "service roles" (Shamir 1980), the role of the tourist guide suffers from internal and external role-strains (Holloway 1981:385–386), which are not readily resolvable within its existent normative structure. Indeed, the various attempts to resolve these conflicts have significantly influenced the process of change of the guide's role.

The principal intra-role strain is that between the outer-directed and inner-directed components of the guide's role. Each of these make different demands on the guide's conduct. These necessitate very different skills, not all of which an incumbent may possess to the same degree. Moreover, under some conditions these demands may become incompatible and provoke an intra-role conflict. Such a conflict typically emerges in the leadership sphere — between its instrumental and its social components. A person who has to shepherd his party and urge it on in order to keep to a timetable may find it hard to create, at the same time, a pleasant and relaxed atmosphere or otherwise contribute much towards the integration of the group (Holloway 1981:386). Indeed, tensions between the guide and his party may, in extreme cases, contribute in an unintended way towards the integration of the latter — the guide's conduct, deriving probably from his instrumental function, may well ". . . unite the group against him" (Schmidt 1979:457).

Such intra-role conflicts may well have contributed to the further differentiation of the guide's role — e.g. the emergence of the Tour-leader — and have certainly been an important factor in the dynamics of the role, especially in generating pressure towards its professionalization. However, since professionalization remains incomplete, even in the most advanced touristic countries, intra-role conflicts continue to plague even the incumbents of the Professional Guide's role.

In addition to the endemic intra-role strain, tourist guides also suffer from different kinds of external role-strain. The tourist guide's is a boundary role — he occupies an intermediary position between the employer, usually a travel company and the tourists in his party (Nieto Piñeroba 1977:161–162); and between the latter and the natives of the sites visited. Incongruent demands emanating from his role partners may well become a strain on the performance of the guide's role. This, however, is attenuated by the particular conditions of his work: the fact that he works in isolation, remote from the employer's inspecting eye (Gorman

1969:482), and that he is usually the sole "go-between" between the tourists and the natives (Cohen 1982a:246), who lack the means of direct communication, makes it easier for the guide than for incumbents of other "boundary roles" to maneuver between conflicting demands.

A more important source of external role strain is contained in the relationship between the guide and members of his party. This focuses primarily on the problem of the relative authority of the guide and his clients (cf. Almagor 1985) — a conflict which he shares with incumbents of other service roles (cf. Shamir 1980:744). As in the case of these latter, the guide is hired to render a specific service (McKean 1976a:13) and from this perspective, as one Balinese guide put it, *"The client is king"* (McKean 1976a:10, emphasis in original). The client ordinarily, but by no means always, also enjoys a higher social status than the guide (Pearce 1982:74), which may be expressed not merely in socioeconomic but also in ethnic or racial terms (Almagor 1985). The competent performance of the guide's role, however, demands that he have jurisdiction, i.e. temporary authority, over his clients for the length of the tour, in a manner similar to that enjoyed by most professionals, such as physicians or lawyers. But owing to the semi-professional character of the role, such jurisdiction is far from unequivocally defined or institutionalized. Hence, conflicts between guides and their clients may well turn into personal power contests, with no clear guidelines for their resolution.

The crisis of the guide's authority may become particularly acute if members of his party express doubts concerning his competence — particularly his credibility as a source of information and interpretation of the sites visited. Such a situation may emerge when poorly trained guides lead demanding tourists (cf. van den Berghe 1980:381), but also when relatively competent guides face a party of exceptionally knowledgeable amateurs, as in the case reported by Almagor (1985).

Another source of stress derives from the relationship between the incumbent's self and his role (Holloway 1981:390). The successful performance of any kind of service role including that of the guide, involves a degree of acting (Shamir 1980:752), which sometimes finds expression in insincerely subservient conduct or even in the outright deception of clients through "fabrication." As yet there exists no well-developed professional ethic, like that found in full-fledged professions, which would provide firm guidelines on the appropriate conduct of guides. Incumbents may thus develop considerable alienation from their role, being aware of the unethical character of their conduct, even as they are unable, due to the existing conditions of competition in the occupation, to desist from it.

This situation is aggravated by the fact that the boundaries of the occupation are, in most countries, only vaguely defined, another consequence of its incomplete professionalization. Side by side with diplomed or licensed Professional Guides, other less qualified individuals such as couriers (Gorman 1979:480; Holloway

1981; Noronha 1979:187), also engage in guiding tourists. Since such individuals are less bound to whatever professional ethic has developed in the occupation, they represent a threat to the fully qualified guides. Considerable tensions may thus build up between the occupational sub-groups, with the more professionalized ones putting pressure upon the more marginal ones, attempting to regulate or even to professionalize them (Cohen 1982a:254–257).

Conclusion

In this chapter, a general analytical approach to the role of the tourist guide has been proposed; this was founded upon some wider sociological premises and tested against the available, admittedly meagre, empirical information on the guiding occupation. It remains to link the analysis to some wider concerns in the sociological study of tourism.

A tourist system can be conceived as having a touristically well-developed central region, surrounded by touristically poorly developed peripheral areas. The central region possesses a developed infrastructure, with good and well-marked roads and touristic facilities, which the marginal areas lack. But the difference is not purely ecological. Using a modified version of MacCannell's approach (1973, 1976), one can argue that the central region consists, to a considerable extent, of "tourist space": in it are located clearly defined "sacralized" (MacCannell 1976:44–45) attractions, the authenticity of which is "staged" to various degrees (MacCannell 1973; Schudson 1969:1251–1252). The degree of staging, however, is not random, but is distributed through the system in a typical manner. The most important attractions, such as major natural sights and the most renowned historical monuments and greatest works of art are rarely in need of staging. They attain the quality of a Center (Cohen 1992b; Turner 1973), and visits to them are, in many respects, analogous to a pilgrimage.

In contrast, in the periphery of the system, attractions are as yet not well defined. The further one advances into these margins, the stranger and more chaotic one's surroundings are perceived; they eventually attain the character of the undifferentiated, dangerous, but fascinating, Other (Cohen 1992b) and their penetration is, in many respects, analogous to mythical or adventurous travel. Here no distinct attractions have yet appeared, and hence no staging can take place; indeed, staging here is well-nigh impossible. It follows that the section of the tourist system which lends itself best to staging is that of the minor attractions in the central region of the system, which have to compete on the one hand with the attractive power of the major attractions, and on the other, with the fascination of the undifferentiated periphery. The expansion of the tourist system into the periphery constitutes, in this perspective, the formation of new attractions. This typically also signifies the beginnings of the progressive staging of their authenticity in an effort to enhance their attractiveness and competetiveness with the better-known, major attractions of the central region of the tourist system. Staging, however, is the more effective, the less it is noticed by the tourists, thus posing new problems of interpretation for the guides.

One can now turn to the problem of the place and function of different types of guides in this rather schematic outline of the structure of the tourist system. It was argued that the Original Guide typically operates on the periphery of the tourist system, and the Professional Guide in its central region. These locations in the system endow each with his distinguishing role-profile. We now argue, borrowing a pair of terms from A. Giddens (1976:353–354) that the former's role in the tourist system is primarily "productive" — he contributes to its growth and expansion; while the role of the latter is primarily "reproductive" — he contributes primarily to maintenance and perpetuation of the already existing system.

The Original Guide, although he may be "outside" the tourist system in a strict sense, by his very activity of leading tourists into its less well-known periphery helps the expansion of the system. By leading tourists into new areas and selecting specific sites within them to show to tourists, the Original Guide is, initially, not only a "pathfinder" but also a "pathbreaker." Insofar as an initial tour has been successful, others will follow, and soon the new area will be mapped out by a number of more or less fixed, but expanding, routes. Concomitantly, select sites along these routes gradually coagulate into distinct new "attractions," while others are passed by as of little touristic interest. By selecting the route and the sites to be shown to the tourists, the Original Guide thus contributes to the production of attractions. As the routes and their adjunct attractions become easier to find and more accessible, they increasingly become part of more routinized itineraries, visited by growing numbers of mass tourists, led by Professional Guides (cf. Cohen 1982a:254). These guides receive, so to speak, "ready-made" attractions and do not have to produce new ones. Rather, their job is to maintain and strengthen the attractiveness of the existing ones, in face of their increasingly staged authenticity, accompanying their transformation (Chapter 3) under the impact of mass tourism. The reproduction of the attractions is performed by Professional Guides through the communicative component of their role: in particular, through interpretative "keying" of the tourist's perceptions, which induce them to accept a staged attraction as authentic. These interpretative activities, in turn, contribute to the gradual "sacralization" of the attractions (MacCannell 1976:44–45), a process impressively described by Fine and Speer (1985).

The process of sacralization may eventuate in the physical "enshrinement" of the attraction, through which it becomes set apart and forbidden like any other sacred object. This effect will be achieved through the spatial separation of the attraction from its surroundings (MacCannell 1976:45), the establishment of barriers controlling or preventing access, the display of the attraction through the establishment of viewing points or striking illumination, etc. Enshrinement, in turn, will have an ambivalent impact on the task of the Professional Guide. On the one hand, it may facilitate it, by providing a suitable backdrop for a dramatized interpretation; on the other hand, however, it will make it more difficult for the guide to convince his audience of the attraction's authenticity. The guide's problem will increase in reverse proportion to the importance of the attraction: the better known and established an attraction, the more its enshrinement will be taken for granted by the visitors and the less it will impair its perception as authentic. In such cases, exemplified by visits to, for example, Leonardo's "Mona Lisa" in the Louvre, or to the Niagara Falls, the guide may be spared his efforts to explain or interpret. In the case of minor attractions, however, an elaborate enshrinement may be incongruent with the importance of the attraction, and hence impair its perceived authenticity. In cases like this, well exemplified by the Lindheimer home in Fine & Speer's article (1985), the very minor status of the attraction may well prompt the guide to an elaborate display of his communicative abilities in an attempt to maintain (i.e. "reproduce" in Giddens' terminology) the credibility of the attraction. One thus finds that, for opposite reasons, there is relatively little need for the tourist guide's interpretative activity at the very center of the tourist system and in its remote periphery; the need for this activity grows in the in-between section; and it is here that one should commonly expect the Professional Guide to give the most impressive and convincing display of his interpretative competence.

Acknowledgment—Thanks are due to Glenn Bowman and Boaz Shamir for their useful comments on an earlier draft of this chapter.

Chapter 12

The Tourist as Victim and Protégé of Law Enforcing Agencies

Introduction

Mister X, a Scandinavian TV producer, spent a few days in Yaoundé, the capital of Cameroon. On the penultimate day of his stay, having to visit several offices, he hired a taxi; however, since he was not satisfied with the driver, he paid him off and dismissed him. On leaving, the driver offered to take him to the airport the next morning, but Mr. X decidedly refused the offer. Next morning, Mr. X indeed left for the airport in another taxi. However, when he was in the departure lounge, the driver of the previous day arrived, forcefully demanding "his" money; he claimed that Mr. X had broken his promise to hire him for the trip to the airport and wanted to be reimbursed for his loss. When Mr. X refused to pay him, arguing that he had dismissed him the day before and refused his offer to take him to the airport, the driver brought a couple of policemen, who dragged Mr. X away into an interrogation cell at the airport police station. There he was threatened with physical violence and told that he would be kept until he paid up. Scared, alone, defenceless, and with a few minutes left before the departure of his flight, Mr. X decided that he had no choice but to capitulate to the demand. Having to pay off not only the driver but also the policemen, his release cost him a few hundred dollars. Nevertheless, he felt relieved once his plane took off. (Reported to the author by Mr. X.)

The Problem

This personal account, though perhaps extreme, will remind many readers of similar stories from their own or other people's experiences during travel abroad. Surprisingly, however, the sociological and anthropological literature is silent on the problem of the relationship between tourism and the law enforcing agencies.

Insofar as the problem of deviance and crime in tourism has been touched upon, it has mostly been by "hard-nosed" criminologists who examined the question of the statistical relationship between tourism and criminal activities (Farrell 1982:157–160; Fujii *et al.* 1978; Jud 1975; Loeb and Lin 1981; for a summary of the literature, see Mathieson and Wall 1982:149–151). The principal problem addressed by such studies is whether crime rates tend to grow in touristic areas or during the tourist season. In the literature on victimology, brief references to the vulnerability of tourists can be found (e.g. Karmen 1984:66), but I am unaware of any systematic victimological study on the subject. Little attention, indeed, was devoted even to the formulation of the problems of investigation in this area. Approaching the matter systematically, three interrelated issues can be distinguished in this area:

(1) The tourist's vulnerability to criminal offences by hosts (the tourist as an offended party);
(2) The tourist's proclivity to engage in criminal or other illegal activities in the host setting (the tourist as an offender);
(3) The attitude and actions of the host legal institutions towards tourists (the tourist as potential victim or protégé of the law and its enforcing agencies).

The main interest of this chapter is the last of these issues, though the preceding two will also have to be touched upon. But even the third issue is too broad: the relationship between tourists and host legal institutions can be treated on three distinct levels.

The law: Here, the principal question is whether the host country has laws relating specifically to tourists, or more general ones relating to aliens, which under certain circumstances may become applicable to foreign tourists. If such laws exist, do they stipulate or imply preferential or discriminatory treatment of tourists in comparison with citizens of the host country?

The legal process: Do the legal institutions of the host country, in particular the courts, apply the law equally to citizens and foreign tourists, or do they extend discriminatory or preferential treatment to the latter, by, for example, paying more or less credence to them as witnesses, meting out more lenient or more rigorous punishments to them, etc?

The conduct of law enforcing agencies: Are the law enforcing agencies of the host country, especially the police, stricter or more lenient with foreign tourists than with citizens? Are they, in cases of conflict, extending protection to the tourists or supporting the locals? Do they tend to misuse their authority for personal advantage when dealing with tourists? And if they do, do they misuse it more or less frequently or seriously than when dealing with locals?

On the first level, the questions relate in the present context primarily to background information, though they might be of sociological interest in a different context, for instance in studies of comparative legal institutions. This is, however, a matter beyond the scope of the present chapter. On the second level, the questions are of concern to both legalists and sociologists of law, but, to the best of my knowledge, no studies have yet been conducted which would examine it systematically; neither have I done any work on it. We are thus left with the questions on the third level, to which, indeed, this chapter will be primarily devoted. However, any systematic treatment of these questions would necessitate a comparative study of the conduct of law enforcing agencies towards tourists as against their conduct towards citizens, since only such a comparison will make it possible to determine whether the tourists are victimized, or, on the other hand, enjoy special protection. Since such comparative work does not exist, I will rely in the following mainly on illustrative case material which will furnish some plausible, but by no means definitive, answers to our questions.

The Tourist in the Host Setting

The foreign tourist in the host country is in an ambiguous position, which makes it plausible that he may become both a victim of the law enforcing agencies as well as their protégé. This ambiguity derives from the fact that the tourist's role embodies several structural contradictions.

The tourist is first of all a stranger, and as such is marked by many of the ambiguities implicit in the contradiction between nearness and remoteness, which served as the basis of Simmel's (1950) pioneering analysis of the stranger's role. The tourist, however, is usually a highly temporary stranger, who, while physically present in the host society, typically remains socially and culturally tangential to it, to a much higher degree than the permanent stranger discussed by Simmel. The tourist is, thirdly, a more or less welcome guest, and as such is also marked by the ambiguities in his hosts' attitudes and actions, which typically reflect a mixture of friendliness and hostility, curiosity and suspicion, generosity and avarice. In traditional society, these contradictions are largely mediated by elaborate rituals of greeting and hospitality (cf. Pitt-Rivers 1968). The tourist, however, is an impersonal paying guest, making use of the services of commercialized hospitality; hence there emerges a contradiction, in the hosts' relationships with him, between two types of exchange: economic and social (Blau 1967; cf. Cohen 1982d:414–416). This contradiction creates strains which are often only lightly covered up by the professional veneer of "staged" (MacCannell 1973) friendliness on part of the touristic service personnel.

The structural contradictions in the tourist's role may induce a variety of attitudes and reactions in the locals, ranging from extreme solicitude to extreme predatoriness. Depending on a variety of factors, such as the stage of development of tourism in the destination, the type of hosts, the type of visitors and their own conduct (Doxey 1975; Knox 1978; Pi-Sunyer 1977:154–155), the tourists may thus be either solicitously protected, or viciously victimized by the locals. However, while the literature indicates a connection between the growth of tourism and tourism-related crimes, it also shows that tourists, being temporarily liberated of the constraining forces of social control in their home environment, themselves tend to more non-conventional, risqué or even deviant behaviour when abroad (e.g. Lett 1983:54–55). These indications are very general and do not answer specific questions, such as which types of tourists are victimized (or protected) by which kinds of hosts, or what is the relationship between the tourists' own conduct and their victimization (or protection) by the locals.

Here, these specific questions shall be dealt with in terms of only two principal variables: namely, the victimization (or protection) which various types of tourists experience at the hands of two major categories of hosts: the locals with whom they come in contact, and the representatives of the law enforcing agencies. Some general propositions on this subject shall be developed, illustrated mainly with case material which came to the author's attention in the course of several studies of tourism in Thailand.

Types of Tourists and the Law Enforcing Agencies

The structural contradictions marking the tourist's role in the host setting lend plausibility to a pair of contrasting assumptions, namely that the tourist will primarily be victimized by the hosts or the law enforcing agencies of the host country; or, on the contrary, that he will generally enjoy their protection. There are good grounds to assume that he will be victimized: as a temporary and highly visible stranger, ignorant of the customs and laws of the host country and socially isolated, he may easily become a victim. Local offenders may not only find it easier, safer and more profitable to rob a tourist than a local, they may also find it less reprehensible. Particularly in traditional settings where moral obligations are often restricted to the in-group, outsiders, such as tourists, may be considered fair game for local offenders — especially if their behaviour is reprehensible by local standards. Local offenders may in fact justify their conduct in terms of some of the well-known techniques of "neutralization of delinquency" (Sykes and Matza 1957), such as "denial of the victim" — claiming that the victim is the aggressor — or "appeal to higher loyalties" to the in-group, accompanied by a denial of any moral obligation toward foreigners. Representatives of the law enforcing agencies may similarly feel less obligation to deal fairly with the tourists, especially if the latter have a reputation of being unruly or deviant, or alternatively, of being naive or innocuous, so that they can be safely extorted or otherwise victimized.

However, there are also grounds to assume that the tourist will be given preferential treatment and enjoy the protection of the locals or the representatives of the law. Being a stranger, he may be pardoned for small infringements of custom or law, his ignorance being an extenuating circumstance. As a guest, he may enjoy the benevolence of the locals, who protect him in order to preserve their honour and reputation as hosts. His temporariness may also serve him well if he commits a more serious offence: the law enforcing agencies may prefer to expel him rather than prosecute him, or let him leave the country with a light punishment. Once tourism becomes an important branch of the local economy, governments frequently initiate a policy of extending to tourists special protection and privileges, not enjoyed by the locals, such as exemption from strict law enforcement when they engage in some technically illegal activities such as gambling. Some countries even established a special "tourist police" whose primary task is to assist and protect the foreign visitors.

Since, in principle, the tourist may plausibly become both a victim and a protégé of the locals or of the law enforcing agencies, the analytically important question becomes: which type of tourists will become primarily victims and which protégés? This question helps to integrate the problematics of this chapter within a wider sociological approach to tourism.

In earlier work, I developed a typology of tourist roles (Chapter 3), which appears prima facie to be suitable for the present purpose. The typology is based on the extent of institutionalization of tourist roles, which is, in turn, related to the extent to which the tourist tends to expose himself to the strangeness of the host environment, rather than to encapsulate himself within the familiarity of the "environmental bubble" of his home environment, provided by the tourist establishment through its hotels, restaurants, touring companies and other facilities. Institutionalized, or as I shall here call them, "conventional" tourists, experience little direct exposure to strangeness, and travel primarily within the familiarity of their environmental bubble. The bubble provides them with security and protection: hotels have safes and security officers, tourist shops guarantee the genuineness of their wares. Conventional tourists are thus little exposed to danger. This is particularly so in the case of the "organized mass tourist," who travels in a group. It is somewhat less so in the case of the "individual mass tourist," whose trip is largely confined to the facilities of the tourist establishment, but who, travelling alone or with his family, frequently leaves the confines of his environmental bubble and penetrates into the fringes of the tourist establishment or even beyond them.

Non-institutionalized, or "non-conventional" tourists experience considerable direct exposure to the strangeness of the host environment and take little, if any, recourse to the services of the tourist establishment and its "environmental bubble." This is somewhat less so in the case of the "explorer" tourist, who travels on his own, often in remote areas, but still makes use of some basic tourist facilities wherever these are available; it is particularly so in the case of the "drifter," who, in the extreme case, shuns any tourist facilities, and, avoiding contact with conventional tourists, tends to travel completely on his own in as yet touristically little-frequented areas. However, with the popularization of this type of travelling among the younger generation of Western youth, the phenomenon of "mass drifting" appeared, served by specialized facilities catering to this type of tourist (Chapter 4). This and kindred phenomena may be referred to as "youth tourism."

Non-conventional tourists, and particularly drifters, tend to have more frequent and more intense contact with members of the local society than conventional tourists, even though such contacts are usually limited to the lower local social strata. In this chapter reference is made primarily to the extremes of the typology, the organized mass tourists on the one hand, and the drifters, or more broadly the youth tourists, on the other. My principal hypothesis can be formulated as follows: drifters, while more exposed to local criminals, will often enjoy the friendship and protection of the host population, but be victimized by the law enforcing agencies; organized mass tourists, on the other hand, while less exposed to local criminals, will be coveted victims of avaricious hosts, but enjoy the protection of the tourist establishment and the law enforcing agencies. The other two types of tourists fall between these extremes.

Law and Tourism in Thailand

Contemporary Thailand possesses a modern legal system, with laws and regulations covering virtually every aspect of social and economic life, a developed judiciary (Darling 1970:208–217; Lyman 1955) and complex legal procedures, backed by a huge law enforcement apparatus, of which a powerful police force is the principal component. In general, Thai civil and criminal law applies equally to citizens and aliens sojourning in Thailand. There are, however, some specific laws relating to aliens. Thus, laws like the Aliens' Business Registration Law and the Law on Occupation of Aliens, impose occupational restrictions on foreigners; they reserve certain types of occupations to Thai citizens, impose some restrictions on alien business activities, and demand that all aliens who desire to work in the country apply for a work permit (Atkinson 1973; Roisarn 1973; Vichaidist 1973). While these laws are not primarily intended for tourists, they may impinge upon some long-term drifters and other youth tourists who finance their trip by working in the countries of their sojourn.

Long-term, non-conventional tourists may also be affected by some clauses of the Thai immigration laws. In the 1980s these stipulated that foreigners overstaying their visas are liable to a fine of 100 baht (about US$4.00) per day, up to a total of 5,000 baht; if they were unable to pay, the fine could be commuted to imprisonment at the rate of 20 baht a day. The laws also stipulated that a foreigner staying in the country for 90 days or more had to obtain a tax clearance before departure. If assessed, the foreigner was not permitted to leave the country until he settled his debt to the tax office. Tax assessments were not convertible into prison terms, since the refusal or inability to pay taxes is a civil, not a criminal, offence. Hence, a "Catch-22" situation was created for impecunious foreigners, including long-term, non-conventional tourists. Unable to leave the country unless they paid their debts, and not granted a visa to stay on, they could in principle be kept indefinitely in the Thai "immigration jail."

The formal comprehensiveness of the Thai law, and the complex bureaucratic and police apparatus supporting it, should not, however, lead one to believe that contemporary Thailand is a *Rechtsstaat* in the Western sense of that term. Western legal concepts were implanted upon vastly different traditional ideas of law and justice (Engel 1975, 1978; Viraphol 1975), and the principles of abstract impersonal justice, equality before the law and due process are by no means always upheld in practice. Law enforcing agencies, particularly the police, often act arbitrarily and high-handedly, using existing laws and regulations as they suit their ulterior purposes (cf. "Dark Society" 1984). Corruption, extortion and bribery are rife in the police force, and only part of the offences discovered by the police are brought before the courts, while others are settled between the policemen and the offenders. Many of these offences are relatively minor, such as traffic transgressions or engagement in prostitution, but even serious crimes, such as murder, can be informally settled by bribes well placed by knowledgeable intermediaries.

Such informal settlements are common in the case of both locals and aliens. Anyone who seeks to investigate whether tourists are in any way discriminated against — or favoured by — the law enforcing agencies would therefore have to determine whether the law enforcing agencies behave more or less arbitrarily towards the tourists than they do towards the locals, demand bigger bribes from them or extort them more severely.

Non-Conventional Tourists and Law Enforcement

Non-conventional tourists, especially drifters and other youth tourists, are more likely to become involved in conflict with the law of the host country than their more conventional counterparts owing to their life-style, travelling-style and personal conduct (cf. Karmen 1984:67). They generally stay in the country longer; they do not enjoy the protection of the environmental bubble provided by the tourist establishment; they often seek work or some other source of income to finance their sojourn. Some of their pursuits are shady or illegal. Many use at least light drugs, such as marijuana; a minority are heavy drug users. They tend to associate with the local population, but owing to their style of travelling and interests, they often encounter marginal members of the local society. This generalization holds for Thailand, as it does for other Third World countries preferred by this type of tourists.

In outlying areas, locals often show a personal interest in the few non-conventional tourists who reach them, and develop personal friendships with them; thus, in Thailand, the young tourists who came first to the beaches of the southern islands established close friendships with villagers with whom they stayed (Cohen 1982b:200) and later with the owners of the small bungalow resorts which were established on the beaches. Between the early trekkers in the hill tribe area of northern Thailand and local "jungle guides" (Cohen 1982a) many personal friendships also emerged; indeed, the reputations of these guides were made by word of mouth, spread by the young tourists whom they befriended. The foreign dropouts in the *soi* (lane) in Bangkok, which I studied, are more isolated, living in the interstices of the local society (Cohen 1984a). However, they also tend to establish personal ties with locals, particularly those with whom they have some illicit dealings — whether in drugs or in sundry forms of fraud.

Drifters and other young tourists usually dispose of little money and carry few valuables. Hence, they are not coveted targets of exploitation and fraud by locals. However, since they do not enjoy the protection of the environmental bubble of conventional tourism, and are often prepared to engage in interaction with locals of whose background and intentions they are ignorant, they are more exposed than conventional tourists to acts of theft and robbery perpetrated by local criminals. Their particular life-style makes them a highly exposed and hence vulnerable group. My studies of youth tourism in Thailand furnish ample evidence on this point. On the beaches of the southern Thai islands, theft and robbery of young tourists was a common ocurrence. In the early stages of touristic development, delinquents from the surrounding area justified their offences against tourists by the "immoral" behaviour of the latter, particularly nude bathing (Cohen 1982b:219–220). Such conduct was resented by the locals engaged in touristic enterprises. On one beach, indeed, the local owners of tourist establishments were able to retrieve the stolen goods and return them to their owners (1982b:220). Young tourists on trekking tours in the hill tribe area of northern Thailand were frequently robbed of their money and cameras in the mountains; the trekkers and their guides were virtually defenceless against the armed bandits roaming the area. In one rather exceptional case, the guide acted in collusion with the robbers (Cohen 1982a:255).

A good example of the differential exposure of non-conventional and conventional tourists to the risk of theft is the public transportation in Bangkok. Conventional tourists, though they may carry more valuables on their person and hence be more coveted targets, travel mostly by tourist bus or taxi, and are hence less accessible to delinquents. Youth tourists, however, usually travel in crowded public buses where they are easily robbed by local Thai youths, who simply slit their bags open with sharp knives and avail themselves of their contents.

In the slum in the Bangkok *soi* which I studied, electrical appliances such as stereo equipment were quite frequently stolen from the rooms of the foreign dropouts who lived there. It is easy for a local well acquainted with the area to break into a slum-dwelling; it is much more difficult to break into a hotel safe and empty it of the much more valuable contents deposited by conventional tourists. However, the safe in a simple bungalow resort on one of the southern islands has indeed been carried away by thieves, with all the money, travellers cheques and passports deposited by its non-conventional guests.

Against this background we may now ask: what do these non-conventional tourists do when they are robbed, and how do the law enforcing agencies relate to them?

Shoe-string travellers are generally not particularly welcomed by the authorities of host countries; so-called "hippie" tourists have been persecuted by the authorities in several localities (Chapter 4), and denied entry to others, particularly to Singapore. In more tolerant Thailand, no positive steps to ban youth tourists have been taken by the authorities; however, they are suffered rather than encouraged to stay in the country. Little, if anything, is done for their security and protection in the localities and regions which they frequent and which usually lie outside established tourist areas. Thus, the police did practically nothing to protect the trekkers in the hill tribe area from robbery or to apprehend the bandits who robbed tourists. Their principal action was to increase the surveillance over the entrance routes to the hill tribe trekking areas; but even this action was undertaken more in order to prevent foreigners from buying drugs or to apprehend those carrying them, than to extend protection to the trekkers. It can be said, therefore, that the police encourage by default the victimization of the young trekkers. It should be added, however, that it is doubtful whether the inhabitants of the region enjoy any more police protection than do the tourists.

A similar situation prevails on the beaches of the southern islands; here, the local population is generally reluctant to deal with the police and deeply distrustful of it. Lack of cooperation on the part of the locals precludes the solution of even serious crimes, such as murder. The attitude that the police are inefficient, corrupt and dangerous has been imparted to the tourists; the latter, hence, usually omit to report to the police on the many petty thefts which occur on the beaches; and the police can consequently boast that there is no significant tourist-oriented crime on the islands (Cohen 1982b:220–221).

The dropouts in the Bangkok *soi* who had their stereos stolen likewise never complained to the police, but tried to find out, through informal local networks, who had stolen their equipment. Their reluctance to contact the police may have derived not only from their lack of faith in police efficiency, but also from the fact that they did not want to draw the attention of the police to themselves. Such dropouts — half tourists and half expatriates — often engage in activities that are at least technically illegal (Cohen 1984a).

Most of the dropouts are on extended sojourns in Thailand, which may last from several months to several years. While some finance their stay by brief periods of intensive work abroad, others strive to make a living in Thailand. However, owing to the legal restriction on employment of foreigners and the difficulties of obtaining a work permit, they are technically breaking the law even if they work in legitimate occupations. Many, indeed, find work as teachers in the innumerable small language schools found all over Bangkok. Since the occupation laws are only loosely applied, these foreigners are only rarely molested by the police; and the employers, in case the police inspect their premises, are usually able to protect the teachers.

Some dropouts, however, make a living in a variety of other activities, ranging from the shady to the criminal: illegal dispatch of labourers to the Middle East; purchase and sale of travellers cheques (declared as lost by their owner, himself usually a young tourist or dropout); purchase of valuables with stolen credit cards; the distribution of drugs. Most such activities are undertaken in collaboration with Thais, who themselves usually enjoy some sort of police protection, and may, in turn, protect the foreigners to some extent.

The dropouts engaging in illegal activities may operate undisturbed for considerable periods of time. However, such activities make them vulnerable, and can be used against them whenever it suits the law enforcing agencies. The point here is not that the dropouts are necessarily victimized by the police, but that the selective and arbitrary use of the law against them, even if they are guilty of an offence, may come close to victimization.

Finally, many drifters, youth tourists, and dropouts use at least some light drugs, especially marijuana, while a small but important minority use heavy drugs, particularly heroin. Again, the Thai law enforcing agencies do not pursue drug abusers rigorously and systematically, though they occasionally carry out searches in cheap hotels frequented by this type of foreigner. But the very fact that drug abuse is widespread among them marks them as a category, and exposes them to potential police harassment and extortion. Indeed, the most common ground for arrest of non-conventional tourists in Thailand is the alleged possession of drugs.

It is extraordinarily difficult to establish the truth of allegations of drug possession, since most tourists so arrested proclaim their innocence and claim that they have been framed. But cases came to my attention which appear to show that at least some non-conventional tourists are harassed and victimized by the police.

In one such case, reported by a reliable witness, a young foreigner was sitting in a small open restaurant in the *soi* in which I conducted my study. Suddenly several policemen appeared, throwing him to the floor and handcuffing him, while reportedly inserting several "Buddha sticks" (sticks of marijuana) into his back pocket. The location of the restaurant in one of the more ignominious *sois* in Bangkok and the kind of tourist attacked made a charge of illicit possession of drugs highly plausible. The foreigner was indeed taken to the police station, but got away after paying a bribe of 5,000 baht (approximately US$200) to the policemen.

This case serves our purpose well, because it shows one manner in which the tourist can be discriminated against in comparison with the local offender: even if the tourist were not set up by the police, and were not innocent, the bribe he was asked to pay was disproportionate in comparison with the bribe usually paid by locals for a similar offence who get off with a mere 300 baht (approximately US$12.00). Judging from other cases which came to my attention, this case is not exceptional: foreigners are generally asked for amounts varying between 5,000 and 10,000 baht for the possession of drugs, about 20–30 times more than local offenders. The foreigner is considered pecunious; he is also defenceless and scared of Thai jails, and hence a suitable victim of police cupidity.

To sum up: the non-conventional tourists in Thailand, while not expressly persecuted as they have been in some other countries, are vulnerable to police harassment and extortion. Their vulnerability is caused by their exposure, and the fact that many engage in some kind of at least technically illegal activities. It is only slightly tempered by whatever ties such tourists may have established with the locals. Not only are such ties usually limited in scope and intensity — particularly in the urban slum studied — but also, because the degree of commitment to others is usually limited and conditioned by the individual's other considerations, interests and opportunities in Thai society (cf. ten Brummelhuis 1984), foreigners cannot depend too much on protection by locals.

The non-conventional tourist in Thailand is thus a potential victim of the law enforcing agencies, but, interestingly enough, he is typically a victim of police extortion rather than of orderly prosecution.

Conventional Tourists and Law Enforcement

The bulk of conventional tourists who visit Thailand on brief vacations or sight-seeing tours have no dealings whatsoever with the law enforcing agencies; they rarely encounter the kind of problems experienced by their less conventional co-travellers. Thailand differs somewhat from some other popular tourist destinations in that there is no widespread overt animosity against tourists of the kind found, for instance, in some Caribbean destinations (cf. Lowenthal 1972:13); there is also no blatant tendency among locals to accost or molest tourists. Most conventional tourists leave Thailand enchanted by the "friendliness of the people," and have no inkling of the resentment which sometimes lurks behind the famous Siamese smile. They often pass smoothly through the heavily staged "tourist space" (MacCannell 1973) without noticing that they are deftly manipulated or cheated by the obliging natives: tourists are commonly overcharged (Jasvinder 1981) or sold fake or shabby products, a practice which is currently widespread throughout Southeast Asia (Brown 1985). The fact that conventional tourists spend most of their sojourn within the confines of the environmental bubble in fact facilitates their subtle exploitation once they leave it and enter the fringe region surrounding the tourist establishments, in which operate tourist-oriented shops, bars, night-clubs, massage parlours and similar businesses, and where they may encounter hustlers, prostitutes and various "professional natives." The fact that these tourists are usually not "street-wise" makes them gullible and relatively easy to mislead. However, in Thailand, at least, they are rarely victims of more serious offences. Conventional tourists are rarely bodily harmed; theft, especially bag-snatching, is the most common criminal offence committed against them. Such tourists, once they leave the protective shelter of their environmental bubble, are convenient victims of this kind of offence: they are easy to spot, ignorant of dangers and pitfalls, and frequently carry a great deal of value on their person. However, they are less easily accessible to local criminals than are non-conventional tourists; and if they are careful they are better able to protect their valuables, by depositing them, for instance, in the hotel safe.

Theft or robbery of conventional tourists is relatively safe; even if apprehended, the offender has a good chance of getting away scot-free. Most tourists, if robbed, forego to notify the police, and even when they do so, they usually hand in a complaint merely in order to be eligible for reimbursement by the insurance company. Since their sojourn in Thailand is limited in time, they would in most cases have left the country before their case reached the courts, and few would return just to serve as witnesses in a trial. To ameliorate that situation, the Thai government simplified procedures in cases involving foreign witnesses so that they may be more speedily brought to conclusion.

This problem is, of course, not specific to Thailand, but appears to be a widespread one. Thus Karmen (1984:66) notes that "a tourist's average length of stay of a few days to a few weeks is invariably too brief to see a case through to a conclusion. As a result, charges against defendants are usually dropped or drastically reduced because of the absence of the key witness or the complainant [victim]." Indeed, in order to fight tourist-oriented crime, the Hawaii tourist industry has recently introduced a "tourist return project," which provides free transportation and accommodation to tourists who are willing to press charges and testify at trials against local offenders (Farrell 1982:257; Karmen 1984:66).

In Thailand, the tourist police is also, among other things, intended to protect tourists from local offenders. Thailand, however, is not an extreme case in comparison with some other countries, since there is no widespread or severe victimization of tourists by the local population; hence tourist protection is in Thailand by no means such a serious problem as it is, for instance, in Honolulu in Hawaii, where tourists are frequently attacked and mugged by criminals and more than a hundred police officers a night have to be on duty for their protection (Farrell 1982:258). Tourist police, however, may also be intended by the authorities to protect the visitors from extortion and other kinds of misuse of power by the ordinary police (of the kind illustrated by the case introducing this chapter). The various ways in which the authorities of the host country seek to improve the protection of tourists are, in principle, intended for all kinds of tourists; it appears, however, that the principal beneficiaries are the conventional, rather than the non-conventional tourists.

While outside his environmental bubble the conventional tourist risks exposure to local offenders and is dependent, to a degree, upon police protection, the bubble itself shields from the eye of the law whatever shady or illicit activities in which he himself may engage. The police rarely interferes with such activities and is thus, in fact, proffering passive protection to the conventional tourist offender. Thus, in Bangkok, guests in luxury hotels are rarely, if ever, searched for drugs by the police; this practice is limited to the cheap hotels frequented by non-conventional tourists. It could, hence, be quite safe to use drugs in the privacy of a luxury hotel. In their own interest, hotels may also use their connections and influence to cover up some serious offences committed by tourists on their premises. For example, a Thai woman engaging in tourist-oriented prostitution was stabbed to death by an Arab tourist in a room of one of these hotels; however, after both the hotel and the tourist paid a considerable bribe to the police, the affair was apparently quietly suppressed and the tourist permitted to leave the country without being charged. The hotel, in collusion with the police, can thus under certain conditions become a sanctuary protecting the tourist, even if he has committed a most serious crime.

Conclusion

My exposition clearly supports the claim that the ambivalences in the tourist's role may make him either a potential victim or a potential protégé of the locals, as well as of the law enforcing agencies of the host destination. However, it has been argued that who will be victimized — or protected — by whom, will depend on the degree of institutionalization — or conventionality — of the tourist's role. Less conventional tourists, since they travel outside the environmental bubble provided by the tourist establishment, will be more exposed to criminals; they will tend to establish social ties with locals (who may or may not give their protection), but will be harassed by the law enforcing agencies. On the other hand, more conventional mass tourists will be less directly exposed to criminals, since they tend to travel within the protective confines of their environmental bubble; they do not establish personal ties with locals, who may find them convenient and coveted victims; however, they will enjoy the protection of the tourist establishment and the local law enforcing agencies.

This hypothesis is, on the whole, supported by the data at my disposal. In Thailand, drifters, dropouts and other youth tourists are clearly more exposed than conventional tourists to the danger of being robbed or injured by criminals, whether in remote outlying areas or in the public transport facilities and the urban slums of Bangkok. Conventional tourists do not frequent such remote places and are generally less exposed to the risks of robbery and injury. Conventional tourists, however, are more frequently cheated and exploited by the locals, particularly those operating on the fringes of the tourist establishment, frequented by this type of tourist. Moreover, once they leave the protective shelter of their environmental bubble, they may also be robbed — though less frequently in Thailand than in some other popular tourist destinations, such as Hawaii.

There is some evidence that drifters and dropouts, insofar as they stay for a long time in a locality, befriend the locals or even collude with them, and may thereby gain some protection either from criminals or the police. However, at least in the case of Thailand, such protection does not seem to be very strong and reliable. On the whole, drifters and young tourists are thus left very much to their own devices on their travels, and have little to fall back upon once they are robbed or in trouble with the authorities. It was with respect to the relationship with the authorities, indeed, that major differences were found between the non-conventional and conventional tourists. The former are generally looked upon by the law enforcing agencies with disfavour, if not outright hostility. In their dealings with the police, they usually appear as the offending party. Non-conventional tourists thus provide the law enforcement agencies with better opportunities, and a greater plausibility to use — and misuse — the law against them than do the conventional tourists. On the other hand, conventional tourists, if they have any dealings at all with the law enforcing agencies, usually appear as the offended party, cheated or otherwise exploited by the locals. This circumstance, coupled with the fact that they (rather than the non-conventional tourists) are the principal source of income from tourism to the host country, prompts the authorities to extend to foreign tourists special protection and consideration, for instance by the founding, in Thailand as well as elsewhere, of a special tourist police, or by the increased policing of touristic areas (cf. Mathieson and Wall 1982:151). Both these forms of protection are intended to benefit principally the conventional, rather than the non-conventional tourists.

Acknowledgment—The case material in this chapter derives from data incidentally collected in the course of several studies of tourism in Thailand, conducted by the author between 1977 and 1985, with the support of the Harry S. Truman Research Institute for the Advancement of Peace at the Hebrew University of Jerusalem, which is hereby gratefully acknowledged. Thanks are also due to L. Sebba and S. Goldstein for their comments on an earlier draft of this chapter.

Chapter 13

Tourism-Related Crime: Towards a Sociology of Crime and Tourism

Introduction

Tourism-related crime is a moot topic with an ill-defined field. "Crime" is a difficult term to define sociologically, while legal definitions, such as "events and actions that are prescribed by the criminal code of a particular county" (Cressey 1968), do not lead to theoretically significant insights and are not always helpful for the sociological study of crime, particularly in the Third World countries. Customary rules entertained by specific groups, such as tribes or ethnic and religious minorities, may define certain actions as "crime," even if these are not legally encoded in the wider society.

The definitional problem is further aggravated in the case of international tourism, because locals and foreigners may entertain very different notions as to what constitutes "crime" or "criminal conduct," since the legal or customary definitions of "crime" in their respective societies may differ substantially.

The scope of "tourism-related crime" remains undefined in the literature. Sociologists of deviance and criminologists, as well as students of tourism have been concerned merely with crimes against tourists and paid very little attention to the broader field of tourism-related crime as a theoretical issue. Empirical studies on the interface of crime and tourism are rare and offer few cues for possible theory-informed generalizations. The first volume of articles solely devoted to the topic was published only in 1996 (Pizam and Mansfeld (eds.) 1996). In this work, an initial attempt has been made towards the formulation of a theoretical approach to tourism-related crime (Tarlow and Muehsam 1996). However, although that article contains some important insights and leads for an understanding of changing social conditions impinging upon tourism-related crime, it does not attempt to relate contemporary criminological theory to the sociology of tourism in order to create a theoretical basis for a genuinely inter-disciplinary approach to the interface of tourism and crime. This is the principal intention of the present chapter.

We begin with a clarification regarding different categories of tourism-related crime:

(1) Crimes of locals against tourists, or tourist-oriented crime; this is the category most frequently dealt with in both quantitative (Jud 1975; Pizam 1982) as well as qualitative studies of tourism and crime. It is, for practical reasons, the category of greatest concern to developers of tourist projects and to the authorities concerned with tourism: growth in tourist-oriented crime has a significant negative impact on tourist arrivals in the countries of destination and provokes concern for the safety of their citizens in the countries of origin.

(2) Crimes of tourists against locals; this category of "tourists as offenders" has until recently received very little attention in the literature. However, there exist good theoretical reasons, such as the allegedly "liberating," "liminal" or "ludic" (Chapter 6) nature of tourism, the increased sense of permissiveness of individuals outside the constraints of their home environment, as well as their ignorance regarding local laws and custom, to assume that tourists fairly frequently engage in criminal, illegal or at least deviant behavior at their destination (LeBruto 1996; Ryan and Kinder 1996).

To this should be added that in recent years a new phenomenon became widespread, which significantly increased the frequency of technically legal offenses committed by foreigners traveling on tourist visas: many arrivals from the Third World and ex-communist countries to developed Western states on such visas, are not in fact *bona fide* tourists, but illegal immigrants (Spencer 1991), and, in some cases, small time criminals or even members of international crime syndicates, looking for shelter or new fields of activity. While these are important phenomena, they could more appropriately be dealt with under the rubric of migration and crime (Schmid 1995), rather than in the present context.

(3) Crimes of tourists and other foreigners against tourists; this category has not received any attention in the professional literature. However, touristic situations in which large numbers of strangers come together in relatively informal unstructured situations invite "crimes of opportunity" (Tarlow and Muehsam 1996), such as small scale larceny; moreover, there are foreigners who enter another country as tourists, in order to prey on other tourists — like for example, foreign — mostly Filipino — card swindlers in Thailand, who seek out wealthy tourists, involve them in gambling and fleece them (Corben 1990).

(4) Crimes by locals against other locals on tourism-related matters; this category should be included in the field of crime and tourism, even though such crimes do not directly involve tourists: tourism creates new economic opportunities,

generates new interests and provokes new kinds of conflict; this may therefore lead to offenses of locals against other locals on such matters as control over access to tourists for business or fraud, control over tourist-oriented supply of prostitutes, or over casinos and gambling dens; conflicts over ownership or possession of land suitable for the location of tourist facilities may also lead to violent crime between locals.

The field of tourism-related crime is thus more complex and much wider than usually assumed; it is also only vaguely bounded, flowing almost imperceptibly into other fields. Our categorization indicates that the official statistics on crime and tourism underestimate the frequency of the phenomenon, since they ordinarily relate only to one category, tourist-oriented crime, while disregarding the others. It should be especially noted that crimes of locals against other locals on tourism-related matters appear to involve more serious and organized criminal activity in some Third World countries than the other categories, including tourist-oriented crime. However this aspect of the interface of crime and tourism remains wholly unexplored.

Since tourist-oriented crime is the best explored of the four categories, it lends itself better than the others for the development of a theoretical approach to the interface of crime and tourism. In this chapter we shall restrict ourselves to this category; if successful, my approach can then be extended to the other categories. I intend to relate current theories in criminology to some insights of the sociology of tourism, and to adapt those theories to the distinguishing characteristics of touristic phenomena. The focus of my analysis will be the touristic situation, an approach which is well attuned to the current criminological interest in situational analysis (Bierbeck and LaFree 1993).

However, I shall develop a model integrating the micro-social situation into the wider, macrosocial context of the society of origin of the tourist, the tourist system and the host society.

Crime and the Touristic Situation

An implication of all the major theories of victimization, such as that of techniques of neutralization (Sykes and Matza 1957), opportunity theory (Bierbeck and LaFree 1993) and routine activities theory (Newman 1973) is that tourists are relatively easy and attractive victims of crime and particularly of predatory criminal activity (Messner and Blau 1987; Schiebler *et al.* 1996). In their early article on techniques of neutralization, Sykes and Matza (1957) claim that the delinquents' awareness of their victim is weakened if the latter is an unknown, vague abstraction. While criminals do not necessarily lack moral restraints (Bierbeck and LaFree 1993), such restraints appear to be less effective if the victim is depersonalized. Depersonalization typically accompanies the development of mass tourism (Tarlow and Muehsam 1996). Locals tend to entertain personalized relations with "paying guests" at the early stages of touristic penetration of a locality. However, according to Pi-Sunyer (1977:154), as increased numbers of foreigners visit a locality, "it becomes progressively harder for residents to differentiate between them on personalistic criteria." Hence, with "the growth of mass tourism, traditional stereotypes are applied to all foreigners"; the tourist is then perceived as "a stranger . . . devoid of his essential individuality and human qualities. He or she is faceless" (ibid.:155). Under such circumstances, locals appear to have few qualms when they over-charge or deceive tourists (ibid.:155), or even when they rob them.

Another factor which may help to neutralize the locals' attitude to tourists as potential victims, is the nature of the stereotype of "the tourist" frequently entertained by locals in developed touristic destinations and particularly in countries of the Third World "pleasure periphery" (Turner and Ash 1975). Tourists are usually seen as immensely rich, but also stingy and exploitative; hence in the locals' view, cheating or robbing them will not seriously hurt them; and if it does, this may be perceived more as a rightful retribution than a wrongful act.

The last point links up with the principal argument of opportunity theorists regarding potential victims of crime: according to those opportunity theorists who emphasize the situational selection of victims by offenders, ease of access, risk of being caught, and expected reward are the principal factors influencing the selection of victims (Bierbeck and LaFree 1993). To this should be added a factor emphasized by routine activity theorists, namely, exposure of the victims, particularly their physical visibility to potential offenders (ibid.).

In all these respects, mass tourists appear to be potentially the most suitable victims. Though they may be "faceless," they are far from imperceptible; rather, they are usually highly conspicuous and easily recognizable even in a crowd, by their bearing, attire and conduct. They are also relatively easy of access: most tourists frequent well-known, often crowded destinations, by well-defined routes. Alternatively, some risk-taking tourists wander into "hot spots" (Schiebler *et al.* 1996; Sherman *et al.* 1989) of criminal activity, such as risqué entertainment areas, illegal casinos and brothels (Ryan and Kinder 1996) in quest of "experiences"; by thus exposing themselves they become easy targets for local offenders.

It should be noted that local offenders can expect relatively high rewards from robbing tourists since they usually carry on their person cash, foreign currency, travelers checks, jewelry or other valuables to a much grater extent than most locals. Moreover, local offenders run little risk of being apprehended or punished for their deeds. While victims are generally reluctant to report crimes committed against them (Kidd and Chayet 1984), tourists are even more reluctant than locals to do so: they have little time, scant knowledge of local legal procedures and are often wary of being exploited or further victimized by the local police (Chapter 12). However, even if apprehended, offenders run a low risk of being brought to trial, because their victims, the tourists, are usually not available to witness against them in court, having left the country a long time ago. Most tourists are reluctant to spend the time and effort to return to the host county merely for the trial of their offenders.

Routine activity theory is another important current criminological theory, which can be adapted to the study of touristic situations. Routine activity theory is based on a premise which makes it particularly relevant, albeit with a peculiar twist, to the study of crime and tourism, and helps to link contemporary victimological theory with the sociology of tourism: according to this theory, victimization rates are a function of risk factors inherent in the situations entered by potential victims in the course of their everyday, routine activities, such as work and leisure (Bierbeck and LaFree 1996). Tourism is a paradoxical phenomenon in this respect: from the perspective of the individual tourist it is a non-routine activity (Chapter 2), a break-away from everyday, ordinary life (Graburn 1977). At first glance, therefore, routine activity theory does not appear applicable to tourists. The twist, however, is that although most tourists might perceive and experience their trip as a non-routine and unique one, tourism is a mass phenomenon: in terms of routes, activities, use of accommodations and other facilities, tourist flows are highly routinized and the behavior of mass tourists is fairly predictable. It is important to note that the very fact that tourists frequently fail to perceive the routinized character of their apparently unique experiences, exposes them to risks of which they remain unaware to a much greater extent than they would under comparable circumstances at home. The often ludic or playful attitude (Chapter 6) which many tourists entertain towards their surroundings during "vacations," and the eagerness of some to engage playfully in risqué behavior, increases the chance that they may fall victim to a criminal act. Owing to the relative naivity of many mass tourists abroad they offer more convenient opportunities for offense by local — and even foreign — criminals, than do locals under the same circumstances.

Routine activity theory postulates that the exposure of attractive victims to risk is countervailed by "guardianship," which is defined, rather broadly, as "the effectiveness of persons and objects in preventing violations [offenses] from occurring" (L.E. Cohen *et al.* 1981).

The concept of "guardianship" is a vague one and in need of further specification. In the domain of tourism, two principal kinds of guardianship can be distinguished: those provided by the host society and those provided by the tourist system.

For the present purposes both types of "guardianship" can be usefully further divided into three main types: directives, protective agencies and barriers: "Directives" consist of warnings and advice given to tourists with regard to temptations and dangers in the host society.

"Protective agencies" are the "guardians" in the narrow sense of the term: rules, institutions and roles intended to protect the tourists.

"Barriers" are institutional and physical arrangements intended to reduce access to tourists by potential offenders or reduce the attractiveness of tourists as victims.

Safety is one of the principal considerations in the choice of destinations by tourists. Local unrest, terrorism and crime are significant deterrents of tourism (Hall *et al.* 1996). Host countries therefore seek to project a safe and secure image, and to take measures to provide tourists with protection against potential offenders.

The host society's guardianship of tourists consists primarily of "directives" and "protective agencies." The authorities of tourist destinations advice tourists on "proper" or inoffensive conduct, and warn them of potential safety threats. In Thailand, for example, the authorities produced posters, warning tourists of the gems confidence game (Cohen 1996b), or advised vacationers on islands on proper attire outside bathing areas, in order not to provoke the hostility of the local population. Local tourist authorities may also warn visitors that some local merchants tend to overcharge them, and advise them to patronize "safe" businesses — especially those which have received the official tag of approval; however, such tags can sometimes also be surreptitiously misused to cheat tourists (ibid.).

The "protective agencies" providing guardianship to tourists consist of laws and regulations, and the institutions charged with their enforcement. Most of these are general in nature and apply only incidentally to tourists. Thus, the police, the principal law enforcement agency in most countries, is supposed to provide protection and assistance to all individuals under its jurisdiction. However, since tourists often encounter different problems than the locals and may be exposed to other — and more serious — threats, special agencies have been created in some countries for their protection, especially a "tourist police." This force is supposed to be better able than the local police to communicate with the tourists in their own or in an international language, and to be trained to assist them with their particular problems. Nevertheless, police protection provided to tourists is often deficient, particularly in many Third World countries. Extortion of tourists by local police is not uncommon, as is collusion between policemen and offenders in cheating or robbing tourists (Chapter 12).

The tourist system tends to reinforce, complement or even substitute for the "guardianship" of the host country. It disseminates directives in various ways: guide books often contain some directives as to the "dos and don'ts" at the destination. Travel and tourist agencies provide brochures, and other printed and oral information intended to help visitors gain some initial orientation at the destination regarding threats and pitfalls. This is sometimes complemented at the destination itself by warnings regarding specific dangers and "hot spots" of tourist-oriented crime, provided by the local personnel of touristic establishments and services.

However, the principal types of guardianship by the tourist system are the "protective agencies" and "barriers," which provide and secure the "environmental bubble" enveloping the tourists, and particularly the mass tourists, in their host setting (Chapter 3). The main "protective agents" are security personnel in tourist hotels and resorts, and a variety of tourist-oriented roles, such as tour-leaders and guides, who accompany and shepherd tourists and are responsible for their safety. "Barriers," intended to hinder offenders from access to the tourists and their valuables, range from "defensive" building of hotels and resorts (Newman 1973), to a variety of "physical security devices" (Bach 1996), such as sophisticated locks, surveillance systems and safes for the guests' valuables.

The extent of guardianship provided by both the host society and the tourist system differs according to the tourists' mode of travel, that is, the type of tourists: it appears to be densest and least penetrable in the case of conventional mass tourists, and sparsest in the case of non-conventional tourists such as drifters or "back-packers"; the latter also appear to be less protected and sometimes even persecuted, by the local law-enforcing agencies, which seem to care more for the security and well-being of the former (Chapter 12). However, the conventional, better protected tourists are also the wealthier ones, and hence more desirable objects of predatory crime. This opens an intriguing possibility: namely, that the very guardians of these tourists, the law enforcing agencies, ostensibly appointed to protect those tourists, may overtly use their position and power to victimize them, or to extend protection or assistance to offenders, while sharing part of the proceeds (Cohen 1996b). The extent to which representatives of these agencies, such as the police, who come into direct contact with tourists, are able to exploit their position is a function of the degree of connivance between them and their superiors — i.e. the extent to which corruption is common in the higher echelons of the force. Insofar as corruption is limited only to the lower echelons, it will be difficult for them to attempt to victimize the well-to-do conventional tourists with impunity; hence victimization by the police will be limited to the more marginal, less protected, but also relatively impecunious, drifters and other non-conventional youth tourists. Insofar as corruption permeates the police force as a whole, wealthy conventional tourists may well become victimized with the connivance of the police.

A General Model of Tourist-Oriented Crime

Our preceding discussion has dealt with crime in the touristic situation and with the boundary factors — the two kinds of guardianship intended to curb access of criminals to tourists and their valuables, and to protect tourists against criminals. However, although in the spirit of much recent criminology the touristic situation is the focus of our approach, it does not stand by itself. It has to be related to its broader social context. I therefore propose a general model (Figure 13.1) for the study of tourist-oriented crime, which specifies systematically the principal macro-social factors impinging upon the micro-social situations of potential encounters between tourists and criminals. The model lays out the string of mutually related factors, emanating from the society of origin on the one hand, and from the host society on the other, which impinge upon the touristic situation. I assume that these factors will determine the probability of certain kinds of attempted offenses against different types of tourists in various touristic situations, and that the relative success of such attempts will depend upon the effectiveness of the two types of guardianship.

The model proposes that some broad background factors — here subsumed under the rubric of "economic and socio-cultural characteristics" — of both, the host society (A1) and of the society of origin (B1), significantly influence, respectively, the crimogenic culture of the hosts (A2) and the nature of the potential tourist population in the country of origin (B2). The crimogenic culture, in turn, influences the principal kinds of local criminality and thereby constitutes the immediate

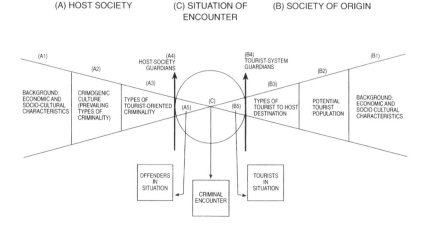

Figure 13.1: General Model for the Study of Tourist-Oriented Crime

context from which emerge the various types of tourist-oriented criminality (A3); while from among the potential tourist population will emerge the specific types of tourists travelling to a particular destination (B3). Finally, from among the tourist-oriented criminals will emerge the specific offenders seeking to enter the touristic situation under consideration (A5); while from among the tourists at the destination will emerge the particular individuals who enter that touristic situation (B5), and who become potential victims of criminal encounters (C). The background factors, in my view, thus determine the probability of certain kinds of attempted criminal offenses against particular types of tourists in different touristic situations. The actual frequency of attempted offenses and the rate of their success, however, will be mitigated by the effectiveness of the two kinds of guardianship: that of the host society (A4) on the one hand and that of the tourist system (B4) on the other. The touristic situation (C) thus remains at the focus of my approach, but the other components of the model stipulate the series of factors which filter access to that situation of both, potential offenders and potential victims, and determine the probability of offenses and of their rate of success.

Conclusion

In this article I pursued three principal aims: (1) To distinguish several categories of tourist-related crime; (2) to relate one of these categories, tourist-oriented crime, to current criminological theories; and (3) to place the touristic situation — which constitutes the focus of most of these theories — within a broader social context. This led me to the formulation of a general model for the study of tourist-oriented crime.

It must be stressed that this is a conceptual model and not a generative one: it does not seek to explain how tourism-oriented crime is generated, but only specifies the factors determining the probabilities, and the potential rates of success, of certain kinds of offenders against different types of tourists in various situations.

The principal contribution of the model is in its clarification of the relationship between stuctural, macro- and situational micro- factors in the study of tourist-oriented crime; it thereby helps to lift the study of the situation from its isolation. A host of specific theoretical and comparative problems can be raised with regard to this relationship, and with regard to the role played by the two kinds of guardianship in controlling crime in touristic situations: for example, problems regarding differences in the kind and rate of offenses against tourists in comparable situations in host countries differing in their basic characteristics (A1) or in their crimogenic cultures (A2); problems regarding such differences with respect to tourists hailing from different social backgrounds (B1), or with respect to different types of tourists coming from the same backgrounds (B3); or problems regarding the relative effectiveness of different kinds of guardianship with respect to particular kinds of offenses against different types of tourists in various situations.

Particularly significant problems can be raised with regard to the relationship between the two kinds of guardianship: for example, do they generally tend to supplement each other or to overlap — so that some kinds of tourists, particularly wealthy mass tourists tend to be over-protected while other, less conventional or less affluent tourists tend to be under-protected.

Finally, the proposed model could also serve as a proto-type for similar models for the study of the other categories of tourism-related crime listed above. This would facilitate the integration of the investigation of these neglected phenomena into the conceptual and theoretical framework for the study of the interface of crime and tourism, as well as help to expand the scope of comparative research in this increasingly important field.

Chapter 14

Language and Tourism [*]

Introduction

Language barriers are, as everyone knows, an important obstacle to transcultural communication. Tourists are strongly aware of this difficulty, which has important effects on their choice of prospective destinations, their preparations for a trip, the scope and content of their interaction with the locals, and the quality of their experience. However, despite the obvious importance of language in tourism, the problem has been given surprisingly little attention in both the sociological and the sociolinguistic literature.

Sociolinguistics has seen a considerable emphasis on the study of transcultural linguistic phenomena, such as pidginization and creolization (Corder and Roulet 1977; Hymes 1971; Muhlhausler 1974; Valdman 1977) and particularly foreigner talk (Clyne 1981; Ferguson 1971, 1975, 1981) used in the linguistic interaction between locals and various kinds of foreigners. Thus, the study of encounters between tourists and members of the host population would constitute a natural extension of traditional sociolinguistic concerns.

There are numerous sociolinguistic studies of groups who come to a society from outside without knowing the local language or the rules for its use. Studies have focused on ethnic groups (e.g. Fishman *et al.* 1966; Haugen 1953; Seckbach and Cooper 1977), immigrants (Cooper and Horvath 1973; Fishman *et al.* 1975), guestworkers (e.g. Snow *et al.* 1981), colonials (e.g. Muhlhausler 1981), and residents of locales with two or more coterritorial ethnolinguistic groups (e.g. Gal 1978; Lambert and Tucker 1972; Lieberson 1970; Rubin 1968). While the study of the social context of languages in contact has a long and rich tradition, it has disregarded the extensive sociological literature on strangers (e.g. McLemore 1970;

---

[*] Co-authored with Robert L. Cooper.

Schuetz 1944; Simmel 1950) and especially one crucial variable, temporality (e.g. Cohen 1977:17–19).

Though sociolinguists are obviously aware of the temporal nature of the processes of second or foreign language acquisition and of language spread, the temporal status of the foreigner learning the host language (HL) has not been given theoretical significance in their studies. Thus while groups which vary in their temporal status have been the subject of individual sociolinguistic researchers, temporality is not a variable in these studies. The authors know of no sociolinguistic comparisons of groups which vary in their temporal perspective, for example guestworkers and immigrants. Sociolinguists hence disregarded such problems as the differences in the patterns of language accommodation between locals and foreigners with a more extended vs. a more limited time perspective: e.g. sojourners, expatriates (cf. Cohen 1987b) and the most temporary category of foreigner, tourists. Whatever sociological attention has been paid to tourists seems to have been incidental, as in Hall's (1962:152) argument that "casual, short-term contact between groups which do not have a language in common" is the matrix from which pidgins arise, using as one of several examples interaction between sightseer and guide, as in a Florentine or Roman *cicerone*'s simplification of Italian. Sociolinguists may well have considered that the briefness of the tourists stay and the marginality of tourists to host societies make their interaction with the locals linguistically uninteresting.

This was, however, an oversight. Language in touristic situations is not only an important practical problem, it is also of theoretical interest precisely because such situations are marked by different parameters than other forms of transcultural communication studied by sociolinguists. This chapter is primarily intended to draw the attention of both sociologists and sociolinguists to the problem of language in tourism, and to develop and illustrate an approach to it. It does not, however, report systematic findings of well-planned research. Rather, it is primarily based on materials collected incidentally in several anthropological studies of tourism in Thailand, conducted by Cohen between 1977 and 1984 (Cohen 1979a, 1982a b, c, 1983b, 1985a, 1987b) and supplemented by whatever information could be culled from the sociological literature on tourism.

Sociolinguistic Characteristics of Touristic Situations

Touristic situations represent a reversal of the local-foreigner situations usually studied in foreigner talk (FT) research. FT is a simplified register which the members of a speech community consider appropriate for use with outsiders who have imperfect mastery of the community's language. This kind of speech is termed a *register* because it is a language variety associated with a particular use (Halliday *et al.* 1964). It is called *simplified* because members of the community view it as a more basic version of the normal adult vernacular. Although FT may contain features which are more complex than those found in the ordinary vernacular, it is reduced in both lexical variability and syntactic complexity. In addition, it is likely to have distinctive intonation contours and to be spoken more slowly and enunciated more carefully than is the ordinary adult vernacular.

As Ferguson (1981) points out, one advantage of naming registers such as FT is that attention is focused on phenomena which might otherwise be ignored. By the same token, he further notes, such names may obscure systematic differences among varieties of the same register. FT includes talk by locals to guestworkers, migrants, and immigrants. If the relationships inherent in these interactions are considered, one notes that in each case there is typically an asymmetry of power or status; it is the more powerful or the incumbents of higher status who use FT and the less powerful or those of lower status who receive it. While guestworkers, migrants, and immigrants are not necessarily of inferior power or status vis-à-vis locals, they typically are so. But note that even if interlocutors are of equivalent power or status, the use of FT implies a superiority, a talking down on the part of the user (as a hypothetical example one might take a monolingual French engineer speaking to an American expatriate colleague, recently arrived in France, whose school-boy French, which at its best was poor, is now deplorably rusty). Perhaps the condescension stems from each speaker's first experience with a simplified register, as the addressee of baby talk, where the power and status differentials between infant and adult are indubitable. Perhaps the condescension derives from the FT user's demonstration of superior competence. In any case, when real power and socioeconomic status differentials are added to a symbolic or metaphorical differential, one sees a clear asymmetrical relationship between interlocutors in FT interactions.

Touristic situations, like the other local-foreigner situations which have received sociolinguistic attention, are asymmetrical. But, in touristic situations, it is the foreigner rather than the local who is usually of higher status. The dominant trend of tourism is for members of richer, highly developed societies to travel to poorer, less developed ones. Moreover, the wealthier, higher status individuals in the former are more likely to travel abroad than the poorer, lower-status ones. Finally, in the encounter between tourists and local service personnel, the tourist is assigned a high situational status, even if he might otherwise be of a lower status than those who serve him.

Whereas in most local-foreigner situations subjected to sociolinguistic analysis it is the foreigner who tries to learn the locals' language, in touristic situations this rarely takes place. Instead, at least some locals learn the foreigner's language.

As Nuñez (1977:206) notes, "Perhaps the most striking example or asymmetry in host-guest [i.e. local-tourist] relationships is to be found in linguistic acculturation in which the usually less literate host population produces numbers of bilingual individuals, while the tourist population generally refrains from learning the host's language." Nuñez, however, fails to explore further the implications of this statement, since it only served him to illustrate one aspect of the general host-guest asymmetry in which he was interested.

One can now formulate the differences between FT generally studied by sociolinguists, and tourist talk (TT) in the following manner: In FT *higher* status locals typically talk *down* to lower status foreigners in the *host* language (HL). In TT lower status locals typically talk *up* to *higher* status tourists in the tourists' language (TL), (where by TL is meant either the tourists' first language or a *lingua franca* assumed to be generally spoken by the tourists). TT is thus the counterpart of host talk (HT), the variety of HL typically spoken by lower status foreigners to higher status locals.

Several general characteristics of touristic situations, in addition to the status differential, may help to explain the remarkable linguistic reversal common to touristic situations:

(1) Tourists are *temporary visitors*, whose penetration of the host society is ordinarily superficial and whose contacts with the locals are fleeting: they have neither the time nor the opportunity to learn the HL during their stay: nor are they expected by the locals to acquire the HL as a preparation for their visit. There is thus no normative injunction for tourists to acquire and use the HL, as there is towards most other, less temporary strangers. Locals working in the tourist industry, however, are normally in permanent contact with a flow of such temporary visitors: this indeed is one aspect of the asymmetry of tourist encounters (Sutton 1967:221). Locals hence have a greater opportunity to acquire the TL, and, as discussed below, are more motivated than the tourists to do so.

(2) Tourists are *travelers for pleasure*, at leisure rather than at work in the host society; hence they have only a limited need for instrumental communication with the locals, in comparison with other temporary foreigners who come to the host society to work as laborers, technical specialists, or on professional assignments or official missions.

(3) Tourism is a *service industry*: the institutional structure of tourism allocates to the tourists a higher status in comparison with the locals working in the industry, most of whom are engaged in service roles (Shamir 1978).

(4) Tourism is *commercialized hospitality*; locals, especially those engaged in the tourist industry, have an economic interest in the tourists' visit. Hence they tend

to accommodate to the tourists needs and preferences, rather than demand that the tourists accommodate to the local situation (as other kinds of foreigners might be asked to do). Such accommodation includes, among other things, the acquisition by locals of the TL.

It follows from a commonsense consideration of language spread that when two language groups are in contact, the group with the greater incentive (often but not necessarily the lower power or status group) will learn the other group's language. Cooper and Carpenter (1969) and van den Berg (1985), for example, have demonstrated that in linguistically diverse markets, the multilingualism of sellers rather than of buyers facilitates trade. Sellers learn buyers' languages rather than the reverse. As Whiteley (1969:13) observed, "It is worth remembering that the desire to learn an other's language springs only very rarely from a disinterested wish to communicate with one's fellow humans"; rather, it is normally related to some specific interest. This is true for individuals engaged in the tourist business, as it is for people engaged in other types of cross-cultural interaction.

The TL most likely to be learned by locals engaged in the tourist industry is English, in part because native speakers of English constitute a substantial portion of international tourists, and, more importantly, because English is the foreign language most widely taught throughout the world due primarily to economic incentives (Cooper 1982; Lieberson 1982).

The general distinguishing characteristics explain the general reversal in language use in such situations noted above. But tourists and touristic situations vary widely, and so do the specifics of linguistic interaction between tourists and locals. While various criteria could be proposed to explore systematically these variations, the approach which appears most promising for this preliminary analysis is one which has already proved its usefulness in other areas in the comparative study of tourism: the typology of touristic roles. Several such typologies have been proposed (e.g. Chapter 3; Smith 1977a). Cohen's typology is followed here. The principal criterion of this typology is the degree to which a tourist exposes himself to the strangeness of the host society or, contrariwise, encloses himself within the familiarity of the "environmental bubble" of his home society provided by the tourist establishment. This approach is germane to the purposes of this chapter, since the more the tourist exposes himself to the strangeness of the host surroundings, the greater will be the linguistic demands upon him; while the more he encloses himself within the "environmental bubble," the greater will be the linguistic demands put upon his local interlocutors. Therefore, the linguistic practice in touristic situations will largely covary with this typology or tourists.

The types of tourists who tend to be more strongly ensconced within the environmental bubble provided by the tourist establishment are called "institutionalized."

Within this category two specific types are distinguished, the organized mass tourist, and the individual mass tourist. They differ in that the former, traveling in a group, is more fully enveloped by the tourist establishment than the latter (Chapter 3). The types of tourists, who tend to expose themselves more strongly to the strangeness of the host environment, are called "noninstitutionalized." Within this category, two specific types are again distinguished, the explorer and the drifter. They differ in that the former makes some limited use of the tourist establishment while the latter does not (Chapter 3). However, a separate tourist establishment catering to drifters and youth tourists emerges where mass-drifting becomes a widespread phenomenon (Chapter 4). While the hosts tend to accommodate linguistically to all these types of tourists, there are marked differences in the degree, level, and manner of their accommodation and acquisition of the TL.

Language in Situations of Institutionalized Tourism

The organized and individual mass tourists are typically ensconced within an environmental bubble of their home society, from the security of which they observe and experience the strangeness of the host environment. This bubble includes, besides familiar surroundings, foods and other services, also a linguistic component. A relatively high competence in the TL is here expected on the part of most or all employees of the tourist establishment who come in contact with the tourists. Indeed, such competence is normally a precondition of employment in standard tourist establishments such as hotels, restaurants, souvenir shops, tour agencies, and car-rental agencies. The hosts staffing the environmental bubble are expected to accommodate linguistically virtually completely to the tourists, whereas the tourists are not expected to accommodate at all. Ideally, they should not encounter situations, within the bubble, in which they would have language difficulties in their own or in a normally used *lingua franca*, when trying to communicate with waiters, deskmen, chambermaids, guides, or drivers, at least on topics relating to their respective roles. In the most developed touristic countries at least some personnel, such as deskmen and guides, would be multilingual, and thus able to communicate with tourists from each of the principal countries of origin in their own languages. Similarly, guided tours of important attractions are organized by language groups so that each tourist can receive guidance in his own tongue.

In touristically less developed countries, especially in many Third World countries, local personnel would at best speak only one foreign language, nowadays mostly English, which, as mentioned above, is the most widespread *lingua franca* in the realm of tourism. Tourists who do not possess a competence in English may here encounter serious communication barriers even within the environmental bubble provided by the local tourist establishment. Under such circumstances, foreign tourist companies will tend to bring in their own personnel to serve as intermediaries between the tourists and the local situation. Thus, for example, the Neckerman Company found, for their hill tribe excursions into northern Thailand, a German-speaking Thai guide who conducted the tour in impeccable German, whereas most of the jungle guides (Cohen 1982a) who worked for small local trekking companies spoke only a rudimentary English. In other situations, the tour leader may double as interpreter between the non-English speaking tourists in his group and English-speaking local personnel, or even hire a local guide who would serve him as a translator (cf. Adler 1980:35).

Owing to the relatively high linguistic requirements of personnel in facilities serving institutionalized mass tourism, the penetration of such tourism into a new destination often engenders a formalization of TL acquisition. No longer does a smattering of English, acquired at school or in practical work with other foreigners, suffice to get a job at a five-star hotel. Rather, specialized language training is introduced by the management of tourist establishments to teach the personnel correct, formal, and polite speech, related to their respective jobs. Thus, for example, in Bangkok, several new hotels hired English-language teachers or approached a language school to provide an English-language course adapted to the particular needs of their personnel. Such courses are usually brief affairs, extending for several weeks, and assume some basic school English on the part of the participants. In addition to an improvement of the personnel's general competence in English, they include specific lessons in which expressions related to the participants' work are taught, as well as polite speech (i.e. set phrases which underline the service role of the personnel and which may well be learned by heart, rather than fully understood by the speakers). Other employees of tourist establishments may take private tuition in the TL. Hassan (1974:19), in a paper on Japanese group-tours in Singapore, reports that in shops specifically catering to such groups "a working knowledge of the [Japanese] language is imperative," according to the saleswomen. One employee reported taking tuition, every evening at 6, in Japanese.

One may thus conclude that, within the environmental bubble of the standard tourist facilities provided by the tourist establishment, the personnel is typically characterized by a relatively high competence in formally acquired, specialized and polite speech in the TL. In this it is distinct from its counterparts outside the bubble.

Organized mass tourists rarely venture outside their environmental bubble and if they do, they are accompanied by a tour leader. Typically, therefore, they do virtually not encounter problems of communication with locals which would pose even a minimal need for linguistic accommodation. Individual mass tourists tend to break out into the zone surrounding the bubble, though they do not seek total strangeness. They thus typically enter the wide fringe of non-standard establishments, located within or close to major tourist centers, which cater in various degrees to mass tourism, such as local shops and stalls selling souvenirs and other goods attractive to tourists, local restaurants, bars, and other services. It is in this zone that a special form of TT develops in the host population. It resembles the attempts by immigrants, migrants, and guestworkers to speak the imperfectly learned language, but, of course, instead of being addressed to locals, it is addressed to foreigners. It is here, too, that individual mass tourists are faced by at least a minimal need for linguistic accommodation as well as given an opportunity to exhibit or practice their knowledge of the HL.

Some competence in the TL on the part of locals engaged in the enterprises at the fringe of the tourist establishment is a precondition of their doing successful business with the tourists. Indeed, such enterprises may seek to attract the attention and confidence of mass tourists, by advertising their competence in the TL. The simplest form of such an advertisement is a sign "English spoken" (or French or German, etc.) in a shop window; an extreme example of this kind is a sign hovering over the stalls of the Istanbul Bazaar "We speak your language!" In Bangkok, and probably also everywhere else, taxi drivers and other individuals who hover around hotels and hustle tourists, similarly advertise themselves by accosting the tourists in the TL. In Baja California (Mexico), ". . . storekeepers and employees in the stores which wish to attract tourists try to greet each *americano* in English as he enters" (Brewer 1978:88).

However, the level of TL competence of individuals engaged in the fringe is generally lower than that demanded of the personnel in the tourist establishment, and the further away they are on the fringe, the lesser their competence. Competence in the TL is here not normally acquired in specialized courses or classes: rather it either derives from previous, general study (mostly in school) supplemented by experience, or merely from interaction with tourists. Individuals working in the fringe, typically acquire rudiments of several languages, but their level of competence in each is limited to those linguistic resources needed to carry on their business dealings with tourists. Thus, Arab stall keepers in the market of the Old City of Jerusalem switch easily from one language to another when talking to tourists from various countries, yet in each language possess primarily the repertoire needed to sell their goods.

How close the TT of such local individuals is to the HT spoken by low-status strangers is a problem for detailed comparative investigation, which has not as yet been conducted. One factor which may make a difference is a certain dissimilarity in the mechanisms of TL as against HL acquisition. HL is acquired in relatively stable, though restricted, intercourse between locals and strangers; while TL is acquired in the asymmetric encounters between stable locals and a flow of tourists, with each of whom only a fleeting and highly limited contact is made. This may well make local-tourist encounters less conducive to the acquisition of TL, than, e.g. employer-employee situations are for the acquisition of HL; hence TT would appear to be typically characterized by an even simpler structure than HL particularly at the outer fringes of the mass tourist system.

On the other hand, TT heard in this fringe may give an appearance of greater fluency than HT. In the case of TT a relatively small number of routines may become well practiced through repeated, essentially similar encounters with numerous tourists whose similarities, like those of the waves of the sea on a calm day, are much greater than their differences. Within this limited range of interaction with tourists, locals often develop a pseudo-personalized style of speech, less restricted by formal demands of politeness than that common within the confines of the tourist establishment; it is intended to derive an advantage from the passing tourist by staged friendliness and intimacy. Speakers of HT, in contrast, usually require a wider repertoire than speakers of TT, because it is used for a greater variety of role relationships but they have less opportunity for practicing the individual elements of their repertoire. Thus one would expect that the repertoire of TT, as heard in the tourist fringe, is narrower but more fluent than the repertoire of HT.

There are, however, some tourist-oriented service occupations, notably barbers, coiffeurs, taxi-drivers, barmen and bargirls, in which a somewhat wider competence in the TL than strictly necessary for the job performance enhances success. Thus, the bargirls working in a major tourist entertainment area, investigated in Cohen's study of a *soi* (lane) in Bangkok (Cohen 1982d and 1985), claimed that some ability to converse in English is an essential precondition for success at work. Those who had recently arrived in Bangkok from far-off provinces, and did not speak any English, felt handicapped: they would have fewer customers than those bargirls who could engage a tourist in conversation. They claimed to be wary of leaving the bar with a non-Thai speaking customer, since they do not speak "*farang*" (i.e. the language of white foreigners; this is a common collective term used by lower-class Thais for *all* languages spoken by foreigners). After some time in the bar, most bargirls would acquire a smattering of English, from interaction with tourists. The very absence of a common language in fact gives rise to one of the major themes of conversation in the bars: the half-playful teaching of each other's language. The range of conversation, however, being limited, the women's competence in the TL remains very low. Since the number of women working in that particular tourist area is fairly large, on the order of several hundred, some enterprising individuals opened small and low-standard language schools catering to the rather particular needs of these bargirls. To illustrate the flavor of language instruction in such schools, a few examples are selected from the mimeographed textbooks prepared by the owner of one of these schools. One textbook called

Tenses, renders 48 possible conjugations of a single verb, to love: from "*I* love, *you* love . . .," through "*Do* I love? *do* you love? . . ." all the way to a concluding "*Shan't* I have been loving? *Won't* you have been loving?" Another textbook, called *Conversation*, gives snippets of small talk useful to the women, not always in fully grammatical English; a few passages taken from one such conversational exercise may serve as illustrations:

(1) Do you like Thailand?
(2) Yes, of course, I do.
(3) Do you like Thai girls?
(4) Yes of course I like very much.
(5) Where do you want to visit?
(6) I want to visit . . . Chiengmai, Phuket, Pattaya . . . .
(7) Do you want me to go with you?
(8) Yes, of course. I want you to go with me.

The kind of English taught in such schools is thus the substandard fringe equivalent of the formal English taught in specialized courses to the personnel of enterprises within the confines of the tourist establishment.

On the extreme end of the fringe of the mass tourist system are those individuals who seek to make a living by leeching on the mass tourist. The most prominent category among these are beggars, and particularly children pestering the passing tourists. These individuals also need a minimal language competence, to get their supplication through. This frequently consists of only a single standard TL word or phase. Thus, children in touristic hill tribe villages in northern Thailand cry for "one baht," often accompanied by the sign of a circle made by the thumb and middle finger. A three-year old toddler in a bungalow resort in southern Thailand, ran happily through the restaurant full of tourists, shouting "number one!" "farang!" and "hello!" Elsewhere children adopted more complex exclamations, ranging from "School-pen, rupies, bonbons!" of Sri Lankan children (Karasek 1980) up to the ingenious "No mama, no papa, no whisky soda!," latter transformed into "No mama, no papa, no air-conditioning!" emitted by young beggars in Katmandu (Tichy 1978:19–20).

Individual mass tourists, on entering the fringe, are thus faced with the problem of minimal linguistic accommodation, with which their organized counterparts are not: to communicate with locals who possess only a limited competence in the TL. Observation suggests that many such tourists, not used to speaking with individuals lacking competence in their language, fail to cope with the situation. They fail to simplify their speech, thus becoming incomprehensible to the locals. In extreme cases, they speak to the locals in a language in which the locals have no competence at all. German tourists have been observed speaking in fluent German to tactfully silent but bewildered, uncomprehending Thais.

Few individual mass tourists make any effort to learn the HL prior to departure on their trip. But some have a previous knowledge of the HL from school or earlier sojourns in an HL-speaking country. Others acquire phrase books or simplified dictionaries as auxiliaries on their excursions. For many tourists the acquisition of a few words or phrases in the HL is the linguistic equivalent of a souvenir which they bring home from their trip. To assert that one speaks the HL is a status badge, but competence is often markedly lower than the claim made. Thus, Brewer (1978:94) reports that in Baja California (Mexico) "some [Americans] assert that they speak enough Spanish to 'get along.' This competency is generally limited to a few words and questions; this is not enough to carry on even a limited conversation." However, "All tourists play down communication difficulties" partly "because of this assumed competency in Spanish."

It could be argued, however, that the use of the HL by individual mass tourists has not merely an instrumental function: it is also often a half-playful display of competence, the linguistic component of the generally playful attitude to tourism common among this type of tourist (Chapter 6). Locals, indeed, often play the game of opening a conversation in the HL, but tend to switch to the TL when serious business is discussed. Owing to the asymmetry of the touristic encounter they will generally be more competent in the TL in matters relating to their job, than the tourists are in the HL.

In short, the major sociolinguistic characteristics of mass touristic situations can be summarized as follows: mass tourists generally expect that their interlocutors speak a TL — their own language or a *lingua franca* in which the tourists are competent. They normally communicate only with locals who are in some way related to the tourist industry. However, it is suggested here that, from both a sociological and a sociolinguistic perspective, a distinction should be made between locals engaged in the central tourist establishment and those who are located on its fringe. The linguistic competence of the personnel of the central tourist establishment can be characterized by the following principal traits:

(1) The personnel are expected to accommodate wholly to the tourist's needs and demands; here, the client is king. Linguistically, this means that the local staff is expected fully to accommodate to the tourists' linguistic capabilities and limitations, while no such accommodation is expected on the part of the tourists. The ability of the staff to speak the TL is an essential part of the familiarity of the environmental bubble provided by the tourist establishment. Competence in the TL is thus a precondition of employment in mass touristic enterprises.

(2) The TL is formally studied by the personnel; they typically have some general background in the language from school. This is amplified through additional formal training, in specific language courses, with a limited practical intent: to endow the employee with a role-specific competence in the TL.

(3) The TL spoken by the personnel is instrumental rather than personal in orientation (Gumperz 1964): the tourist-employee encounter being formal and bounded by their respective roles, employees are obliged to use standard formal phrases and polite expressions, in which they may have been drilled in language courses. It should be noted, however, that the touristic encounter being essentially asymmetric, the tourists are under less obligation to use standard formal language and might more easily slip into informal personalized usage, sometimes to the embarrassment of their local interlocutors.

(4) Within their specific sphere of activities, local personnel usually possess a fairly rich verbal repertoire and employ complex grammatical structures, even though their usage is marked by set phrases and their ability to generate new ways of expressing themselves is limited. Outside the sphere of their occupational role, their repertoire is typically much more limited, and their speech is simpler. These inconsistencies in the personnel's language competence present their tourist interlocutors with some difficulties: particularly, to find the right level which would not be too simplified (and thereby insult the local staff) or too complicated (and thereby embarrass the listener and produce misunderstandings). This problem is exacerbated by the fact that tourist-local encounters are asymmetric and fleeting — there is little time available for a mutual accommodation between unequal interacting individuals. The misunderstandings and confusions caused by this situation and the mechanisms of their resolution harbor a rich potential for sociolinguistic study.

In the fringe of the central tourist establishments, these characteristics do not prevail. Rather, locals working in the fringe are marked by a much lower linguistic competence, which is, moreover, generally acquired through practical interaction with tourists, rather than by formal training. Locals in the fringe are less restrained by formal role demands; they tend more towards a pseudo-personal rather than a strictly instrumental orientation in their TL usage. They pay less attention to correct, polite speech and more to the creation of an apparently friendly and intimate relationship with the tourists, which is generally motivated by ulterior predatory interests. Their linguistic repertoire is typically limited, and their register simpler, putting upon the tourists a demand for a minimal linguistic accommodation, at least to simplify their own register and to make an effort to understand the simpler register of their interlocutors. It is in the fringe, too, that tourists may venture to use their mostly very limited knowledge of the HL, often in a playful manner, intended to gain status or achieve solidarity, rather than to conduct serious business.

Language in Situations of Noninstitutionalized Tourism

Noninstitutionalized tourists make at most only a limited use of the services provided by the tourist establishment, or virtually none. The former is typical of the mode of travel of the explorer tourist, the latter of the drifter. It should be pointed out that, as various modes of alternative tourism become popular, a separate type of services catering to the needs of these noninstitutionalized tourists come into being in many destinations. Especially common are services oriented to the needs of mass-drifters, mostly youth tourists on long vacations who roam remote areas but are less enterprising than the self-reliant original drifters of the past (Chapter 4). Both explorers and drifters, however, tend to be much more exposed to the strangeness of the host environment than the typical mass tourist discussed above. They do not seek the protection of the bubble of the tourist establishment, and they venture far beyond the fringes of the tourist system, patronized by the individual mass tourist.

It would be analytically correct to expect that the linguistic situation at the extreme pole of noninstitutionalized tourism, the drifter, would be the reverse of that of the organized mass-tourist. In other words, while in the latter case no linguistic accommodation on the part of the tourist is demanded, in the former he or she could be asked to accommodate fully (i.e. to learn the HL in order to cope with the strangeness of the host environment). This, indeed, is the ideology of the original drifter. This ideology is clearly formulated in a culture-critical tract on tourism, by the German traveler and ethnographer Adler (1980). The following is an account of his purported linguistic accommodation during his travel in New Guinea:

> There exist there alone [in New Guinea] 700 language areas. During my trip I crossed only three language boundaries, and each time I had to start anew. I had my already existing vocabulary translated by the natives into the new dialect on each boundary. The vocabulary notebook is always a permanent component of my equipment. It is of course not necessary to master a language perfectly; for daily communication the knowledge of guest-workers [i.e. such knowledge of German as foreign workers in Germany possess] is absolutely sufficient. In my experience, round 200 words and concepts should be appropriated by a tourist (Adler 1980:35, authors' translations).

Adler, however, is aware of the fact that not everybody possesses his linguistic prowess and energy, and he concedes that tourists would generally not make the effort to learn a foreign language just for a three to four week long trip (ibid.:35). But the same appears to be true not only for mass tourists who are the butt of Adler's criticism, but also for the great majority of explorer and drifter tourists. Sure enough, such travelers do not expect that the locals will as a matter of course understand and speak TL. But it is only the really exceptional original drifter and hardy traveler on untrodden paths who will make an effort at learning the natives' language in order to be able to communicate with them. The great majority of such tourists try to cope with their environment despite linguistic strangeness in ways yet to be discussed. Even long-term drifters after some time give up the intention to learn the HL. Thus a widely traveled German drifter on an island in Thailand, on which he was staying for many months, reasoned that he had already traveled through more than a dozen countries and he could not possibly make the effort to each time learn a new language. His case is typical of most long-term tourists and drop-out expatriates in Thailand, who, though they may live among Thais, only rarely make an effort to learn the language.

Moreover, even the locals who work or otherwise interact with these types of tourists do not usually expect them to learn or speak the HL. Hence, establishments catering to them seek employees who will have at least some competence in the TL. Smith (1977a:4) argues that, in developing countries, ". . . potential employees [of tourist establishments] discover that only a limited segment of their population — either already established leaders or bilingual, bicultural marginal men — can truly profit in their new roles. Hiring policies are often discriminatory favoring those who have the linguistic skills to cater to tourists." This is true not only of luxury hotels, but also of the simplest enterprises catering to youth tourists. Thus, bungalow resorts on southern Thai islands, one of the simplest and cheapest forms of accommodation, could be run successfully only if there were one or several local staff who spoke some English and were hence able to hustle tourists in the port and understand their orders in the restaurants. If the local owner could not speak English he would bring in a bilingual Thai youth, sometimes from the mainland, or even engage a foreigner, to communicate with the tourists. All owners emphasized the importance of TL for running their business.

TL is thus the dominant language in both institutionalized and non-institutionalized tourism. However, there are marked differences between them in terms of the locals' competence in the TL, the manner of its acquisition, the demands for linguistic accommodation made upon the tourists, and their manner of coping with them.

The language competence of locals working with non-institutionalized tourists is generally similarly acquired and similar in scope to that of locals working on the fringe of the mass-tourist system or even more limited. The basics of TL are usually acquired at school, but the competence is increased through interaction with tourists. Though here too TT with a highly simplified register is common, it appears that this TT is more personal than instrumental in orientation owing to the less specific and more personalized interaction between locals and these types of tourists. The further away one moves from the beaten track, the more limited local TL competence becomes. One young local Thai in a small bungalow resort on a beach in southern Thailand, who spoke virtually no English, would address newcomers almost ritually with a sentence he apparently learned by heart: "Come, I will show you your room!" But the low language competence of locals often aggravates communication problems for less experienced tourists. A good example is a conversation between a young German tourist and the waiter in another small bungalow resort: the young woman asked the waiter for fish:

Waiter: Oh, no fish!
Tourist: You have no fish?
Waiter: Yes!
Tourist: You have fish?
Waiter: No.

The tourist, confused shook her head and discontinued the conversation.

This example illustrates the impact of temporariness on linguistic interaction between locals and tourists: the young woman in the bungalow restaurant was not acquainted with the manner the Thai TT is formed through interference from the Thai language (in which a confirmation of a negative question constitutes, in fact, a negation).

In contrast, foreign residents who continuously interact with locals should become aware of the peculiarity of the latters' TT; thus expatriates living in Thailand become familiar with the way their Thai acquaintances speak their peculiar variant of English, and in fact learn to converse with them in that variant.

In the most remote destinations, reached by the more adventurous explorers or drifters, only a negligible knowledge of TL, if any at all, will be found. Thus, in a remote Lisu tribal village in northern Thailand, Cohen encountered a local youth who was obviously used to dealing with occasional visitors and catering to their needs. Though by then it was taken for granted that visitors pay for hospitality received (Cohen 1982a:248−249) he motioned him into his house with the remarkable exclamation: "I pay for you!" This was later repeated on various occasions (e.g. when food, drink or opium were offered). Eventually it turned out to be apparently the only English expression the youth knew, and used indiscriminately as an all-purpose linguistic device. Even such a knowledge of a simple TL phrase is often exceptional in remote destinations, reached by explorer and drifter tourists. These, then, are tourist encounters characterized by total linguistic strangeness.

Such situations may be taken as a point of departure for the discussion of linguistic accommodation of non-institutionalized tourists. Assuming that no interpreter mediated the interaction between locals and tourists (discussed later), what kind of communication emerges in such situations? Since no reports exist in the literature on this question, the authors can only speculate on the basis of limited observations in the hill tribe area of northern Thailand.

The most extreme outcome of such an encounter would be a complete breakdown of communication, in which no messages are meaningfully exchanged between the mutually uncomprehending parties. In tourism, however, such situations appear to be rare, although they might have been typical of first encounters between Europeans and the natives of Oceania and Africa in the past. Less experienced travelers may indeed get confused in such situations, but well-traveled explorers and drifters (and these would be the ones who most frequently dare to expose themselves to complete strangeness) tend to develop coping mechanisms, based primarily on nonverbal communication. These mechanisms presumably include the focusing of attention on the locals' facial expressions and perhaps an exaggeration by the traveler of his own, inasmuch as certain expressions have a universal meaning (Zajonc 1985). Rather than collecting a basic vocabulary, as suggested by Adler, such travelers resort to gestures and sign language to communicate simple messages, and, perhaps more importantly, to create rapport with the often suspicious or slightly frightened locals. Some such travelers become through prolonged practice highly adept at this kind of communication: even if they occasionally learn a few words of HL, these serve primarily to punctuate the gestures in their nonverbal communication, rather than represent an attempt to switch to verbal interaction.

Sign-language, however, is ill-suited for abstraction: non-verbal communication between hosts and tourists, as observed in northern Thailand, is thus necessarily reduced to the immediate givens of the situation. The very attempt to communicate across apparently insuperable boundaries, however, usually initiated by the tourists rather than the locals, is an enjoyable game in itself and certainly serves to ease the tension of the encounter between complete strangers. While some basic instrumental purpose may be accomplished by such attempts at communication (e.g. the purchase of food or souvenirs, or the demonstration of the way tourist gadgets such as the camera work), much of it serves to create and express a mutual interest and sympathy. Some tourists use a kind of opening gambit to break the ice: one Australian used to take out a flute upon entering a hill tribe village and play it while walking around, thus attracting a huge crowd of children; another pulled out a frisbee and started throwing it, thereby inducing the locals to try their hand. Apparently pointless fooling around and laughing are very common in such a situation and serve the same function.

Some non-institutionalized tourists, particularly those who intend to stay for a longer period in the host country, do acquire some competence in the HL, whether just by picking up the language through interaction with natives or through a more systematic effort (cf. Cohen 1987b). This may include self-instruction through textbooks and dictionaries, courses, and language schools; it is difficult to judge, on a worldwide scale, how widespread such HL acquisition by long-term tourists actually is. Data from Thailand indicate that it is rather exceptional and that the majority of such tourists acquire only the barest rudiments of the Thai language; but then Thai is considered by native speakers of European languages a very difficult language to acquire. In Spain and the Latin American countries, which are popular destinations of long-term tourists, the linguistic situation may be quite different.

The display of some competence in HL may serve explorers and long term drifters to impress their interlocutors. But its use appears to be for this type of tourist less playful and more a consequence of real communication needs than it is for individual mass tourists, since the former are in more direct and closer contact with the local population than the latter. This need becomes particularly marked when such individuals enter into a more intimate relationship with a local who does not speak, or possesses only a limited competence, in their language (in particular, if they acquire a local girl friend or boy friend). Under such conditions a process of privatization appears to be taking place, both sides to the relationship learning some elements of each other's language and mixing them up in the conversation. The impression gained from such cases observed in Bangkok is that, rather than a common Thai-English patois developing from such interaction, each mixed couple or small group develops a private patois of its own, moulded by the particular linguistic competence of its members. The temporariness of such relationships may well preclude the development of an institutionalized patois as found in situations of more permanent cross-cultural interaction. In addition, if the private patois serves as a marker of intimacy between its speakers, its function as a barrier between them and the outgroup which does not share their special relationship would also preclude its institutionalization. That the generation of such spontaneous pidgins, if pidgins they are, may not be confined to touristic contexts can be seen from Gilmore (1979). He described the private language created by two children, five and six years old, who were neighbors and friends in an isolated Kenyan community. Their private language which initially had all the structural earmarks of a pidgin, was created from elements of English and a somewhat pidginized Swahili but was distinct from both and intelligible only to them. Gilmore suggests that their continued use of this private code after they learned other languages, which they could have used with one another, demonstrates that the private code served as a marker of intimacy. It would be of interest to determine whether the private codes which appear to develop among cross-cultural couples in Thailand (or for that matter, anywhere) are further used or elaborated by their speakers, as was the case with the code described by Gilmore, even after they have acquired a common standard language.

Private patois between English, the *lingua franca*, and the mother languages spoken by the tourist may develop in cases where the tourist's competence in English is low. Some excellent examples can be found in the correspondence between foreign men and Thai women. A letter written by a German in a mixture of German and English may be quoted as an illustration:

> Wie geht you hoffe good? You glaubst garnicht wie schwer mir the Abschied von [Dir] gefallen ist . . . [Ich] bin und had my in you verliebt.
> [Translation: How are you, I hope well? You would not at all believe how difficult the parting from you was for me . . . [I] am and have fallen in love with you.]

The writer has essentially substituted those English words which he knew for the German ones; but, at least in one case, the introductory sentence, he has also simplified the German, omitting the auxiliary verb and the personal pronoun (in standard German the sentence would be "Wie geht es Dir, Ich hoffe gut"). Letters could furnish particularly salient examples of private patois, since almost by definition, they are not shared by a community of speakers, and hence cannot contribute to the development of a common patois.

As the discussion indicates, a further more systematic examination of the verbal innovations created for use in temporary, touristic interactions would be worthwhile for at least two reasons. First, it would help one to understand better the creation of pidgins, languages which are drastically reduced in syntactic and lexical variability and which no one speaks as a mother tongue. Are all pidgins the descendants of a proto-pidgin, from which they have diverged under the influence of the languages with which they are in contact? Or do some pidgins arise spontaneously, their similarities to other pidgins explained not by diffusion from a common ancestor but by universal processes of simplification? While Gilmore's (1979) documentation of the private language created by two boys suggests that the theory that all pidgins derive from a single source is wrong, such documentation is quite rare. If it could be demonstrated that the verbal innovations developed for use in temporary touristic interactions show a structure similar to that of pidgins, one then had stronger support for the argument that at least some pidgins result from spontaneous generation.

The second reason that an examination of verbal interactions between tourists and locals in non-institutionalized settings would be useful stems from sociolinguists' interest in social evaluation as a factor in language change. When tourists speak to locals who are unaccustomed to interacting with foreigners, the dialect characteristics which in the tourists' home community immediately stamp their geographical, ethnic, or social-class origin no longer serve to do so. Thus neither speakers of high-prestige dialects, nor speakers of low-prestige dialects, can signal their social status by means of speech cues. Kroch (1978) hypothesizes that speakers of high prestige dialects resist the normal processes of phonetic conditioning (processes which lead to language change), in order to distance themselves from the masses and as a symbolic assertion of their conservative ideology. If the hypothesis is correct, one would expect to find that higher class individuals or elites are less careful in touristic situations to use prestige speech forms when interacting with those who cannot make social evaluations of their speech. Similarly, one would expect speakers of low-prestige dialects to make less effort to avoid stigmatized forms of speech.

The sociolinguistic characteristics in situations of encounter between locals and non-institutionalized tourists may now be summarized:

(1) TL remains the dominant means of communication in various situations, but its form becomes less standard. Locals who interact with such tourists normally speak some TL. This is usually not acquired through specialized training channels and derives to a considerable degree from experience of talking to foreigners. Here the speech which locals address to tourists is typically encoded in a simple variety which was called TT. It may well be close to the HT spoken by low-status foreigners to high status locals. The degree of similarity between TT and HT and the mechanisms of its acquisition, however, are topics deserving more careful comparative research.

(2) The further the context of tourism from the beaten path, the further from the standard TL is TT. Just as regional dialects of standard European languages are more dissimilar to one another the lower the social status of their speakers, so are varieties of TT further from the standard TL, the further their speakers from institutionalized tourism. The contrast between center and periphery has linguistic correlates, in both tourist and non-tourist social encounters.

(3) Though TL remains dominant, a higher degree of linguistic accommodation is demanded of non-institutionalized tourists. This finds expression first and foremost in efforts to adapt to the nonstandard TT spoken by local interlocutors and, at the extreme, to develop a dexterity in non-verbal communication. Only secondarily does such accommodation involve even an elementary

acquisition of the HL, the romantic ideology surrounding this kind of tourist notwithstanding.

(4) The variety of TL spoken by the local interlocutors of non-institutionalized tourists tends to be — owing to the less formalized nature of their encounters — more personal than instrumental in orientation. Only more systematic comparative research will determine how this influences the respective shape of language competence of locals working with institutionalized tourists within and on the fringe of the tourist establishment as compared with those interacting with noninstitutionalized tourists.

"Language Brokerage" in Touristic Situations

The presentation until now has dealt exclusively with situations in which tourists communicate directly with locals. Tourists, especially mass tourists, are frequently not directly exposed to the locals. Rather, their interaction is mediated by a variety of bilingual individuals such as guides, tour leaders, professional natives (Forster 1964:226), hustlers, etc. They collectively may be called language brokers. Their role in the linguistic mediation between locals and different types of tourists may now be described. The principal aim in this section is to show that language brokers are a sociolinguistically important type, distinct in outlook and function from translators and interpreters. The latter are concerned exclusively with linguistic exactitude. Their function (their primary professional concern and value) is to reproduce the communication value of the source text (Schmitt 1982); they are professionals of understanding (García-Landa 1981/1982). In contrast, in the language broker's role, linguistic interpretation is only incidental to a wider range of tasks. Therefore, for example, the role of the guide includes, among other things, social mediation with the local population and the dissemination of information, explanation and interpretation of the sites visited (cf. Chapter 11). Competence in the TL is a valuable asset for the performance of such roles, and becomes of particular importance in mass tourism, where much of the guide's success depends on his competence in the TL. Van den Berghe (1980:381) thus points out, with respect to tourism to the ancient city of Cuzco in Peru, that "More and more demanding tourists are no longer satisfied with run-of-the-mill tourist guides, who speak a broken version of the language . . ." and demand a higher level of linguistic competence. Indeed, proficiency in the TL is a major asset to guides and an important precondition for becoming a professional guide (cf. Chapter 11) in the mass tourist business. However, such proficiency is valued as a means to perform the guide's communicative functions. Even professional guides do not normally consider the ability for correct simultaneous translation of conversations between tourists and locals an important professional skill. Though a communicator, the guide is not, strictly speaking, an interpreter. But he may become one by default like Mr. K in Hassan's study of Japanese tourists in Singapore who was "... really a translator, more than a guide ..." (1974:8). Mr. K was an untrained guide and probably strove to make up for his professional deficiency by making himself useful to the Japanese tourists, whose competence in English was negligible.

Even more important, guides and other language brokers do not feel under obligation to faithfully translate the tourists' indirect conversations with locals. Rather, they are in the position of go-betweens (Shanklin 1980). They often have other than purely linguistic considerations in mind when they find themselves in situations of mediation. These may be of two major kinds: self-interest and concern for frictionless interaction between tourists and locals. Thus, guides are often asked to help with the negotiation in the purchase of souvenirs and other goods by tourists in local shops and stalls. As go-betweens they may well use their ability to monopolize communication between the sides to their advantage, for example, to get a cut of the price paid by the tourist (cf. Cohen 1982a). But where ignorant or insensitive tourists visit far-off localities unused to tourism, the function of the guide as go-between may well be to interpret the sides to one another rather than to translate literally, thereby reducing the chances for the emergence of conflict or tensions between them. Other types of language brokers, such as professional natives, taxi-drivers, and other individuals lurking around hotels and offering their services may, if at all, be even more unscrupulous go-betweens than professional guides, in mediating communication between tourists and locals.

Non-institutionalized tourists are less likely than institutionalized ones to make use of professional tourist guides. Insofar as they do depart on guided trips, such as on trekking tours and similar expeditions into otherwise inaccessible areas, they will normally be led by "original guides" (Ch. 11). In other words they are guided by locals who derive their expertise from familiarity with an area or its inhabitants and not from formal professional training. The competence of such individuals in the TL is frequently rudimentary, as the study of jungle guides in northern Thailand (Cohen 1982a) illustrates. The principal function of original guides is to lead the way. Hence their low communicative competence, at least at the early stages of touristic development in an area, may not be a serious disadvantage in their work (even if it is an impediment to their professional advance). However, the limited linguistic competence of such guides may seriously hamper their ability to explain the sites visited on such trips and lead to misrepresentations of the culture of the local groups. Such problems are multiplied in situations of ethnic tourism (Keyes and van den Berghe 1984) where three or more languages may be involved: that of the minority group visited, that of the guide, and that of the tourists. Under such conditions complicated multilingual chains may develop;

insofar as each link in the chain only partly understands the language of the one next to it, insuperable problems of communication emerge. For example, on one of the trekking expeditions in the hill-tribe area of northern Thailand, a group of French-speaking tourists was observed on a visit to an Akha village. They were led by a Karen guide. The guide spoke northern Thai, in which he was not very fluent, to the Akha people, who had only a very limited competence in that language. He attempted to translate in a rather broken English, what the Akhas told him, to the French youths whose grasp of English was far from perfect. The probability that any accurate reproduction of communication value took place in this chain, which resembled the children's game of a broken telephone, was obviously very low. A more detailed study of such multi-lingual chains of linguistic communication would be a fascinating subject for systematic sociolinguistic inquiry.

Conclusion

The sociolinguistic study of language in touristic situations provides an opportunity to examine communication between different linguistic groups under unusual circumstances. Of significance is the high temporariness of the foreigners on the one hand and the high degree of linguistic accommodation of the locals to them — which stands in marked contrast to the prevailing tendency of less temporary and lower status foreigners to accommodate linguistically to the locals. Though such accommodation by the locals is common to virtually all touristic situations, the degree of proficiency of locals in the TL varies considerably and hence also the extent to which tourists are forced to accommodate linguistically. In an effort to integrate the sociological and sociolinguistic analysis of tourism, a typology of tourist roles was used as the principal variable to organize the linguistic variation in touristic situations. This effort was admittedly impressionistic. Due to the absence of systematic research, the authors could only illustrate their exposition by incidental data from the literature on tourism and Cohen's fieldwork in Thailand. But it is hoped that a case has been made for this line of analysis and that other researchers will find it rewarding to pick up some of the problems raised here. Several such problems deserve particular attention:

(1) Is tourist talk (TT), linguistically different from host talk (HT) in its form or mechanisms of acquisition?

(2) What is the extent of formalization and specialization in TL acquisition on the part of the locals? How do different mechanisms of TL acquisition influence the degree and shape of TL competence among locals? When do specialized frameworks of TL instruction emerge, oriented to the particular needs of the

tourist industry? What are the sociolinguistic properties of the language taught and what are the methods of instruction?

(3) What is the role of text books, phrase books, and dictionaries in both HL and TL acquisition? Does a specialized body of such literature emerge, serving the specific needs of tourists or locals engaged in the tourist industry? What are its distinguishing sociolinguistic characteristics? What are its uses in tourist-local communication?

(4) How do tourists cope with situations of linguistic strangeness? What strategies do they employ to overcome noncomprehension and to resolve misunderstandings? What is the purpose of their attempts to use the HL? What is the role of nonverbal communication in such situations?

(5) Does tourism lead to the emergence of private pidgins? What are the conditions of their emergence? What are their distinctive sociolinguistic characteristics? Do they become institutionalized?

(6) Do tourists pay less attention to prestige forms or to stigmatized forms in their speech when they interact with locals who are unable to evaluate the formers' social position on the basis of speech cues?

(7) What is the role of language brokers in communication between tourists and locals? What are the distinctive characteristics of language brokerage vs. translation?

Many of these problems have been touched upon in this article. But much systematic empirical work is needed to find reliable answers and thereby bring touristic phenomena within the confines of mainstream sociolinguistic research.

Part Three

Case Studies

Chapter 15

Arab Boys and Tourist Girls in a Mixed Jewish-Arab Community

Introduction

In this chapter I shall try to gain some insight into the manifold problems of Arab predicaments in a Jewish state (encapsulated, on its part in an Arab world), by focusing on one very specific, but concrete and symptomatic issue: the rather surprising significance which relations with foreign tourist girls acquire for Arab youths in a mixed, Jewish-Arab Israeli city.[56] I will have to sketch, briefly, the most important stresses and problems implicit in the life-situation of these youths. I will then proceed to show how the tourist girls seem to offer a way out of this situation, a possibility, though a fickle and elusive one, of a solution to the dilemmas which life in Israel in general and in a mixed Jewish-Arab city in particular poses for Arab youths.

The theoretical purpose of this paper is to illustrate the latent functions of tourism as a mechanism for the alleviation of system-generated tensions; it thus touches upon the wider theoretical issue of the impact of inter-societal interaction on local communities.

The Life-Situation of Arab Youths in Israel

The data presented in this chapter derive from a six-month anthropological field-study of Jewish-Arab relations in a mixed city in 1966. The city had at the time approximately 34,000 inhabitants, about a fourth of whom were Arabs, the rest Jews. The material here presented thus relates to a period of relative relaxation and general easing-up of tensions between Jews and Arabs within Israel, preceding the Six Day War of 1967. It was a period of hope, overshadowed only occasionally by sporadic outbreaks of hostilities on the borders. However, though relations were relaxed and no serious outbreaks of violence occurred during the period of my stay in the city, the underlying uneasiness in Jewish-Arab relations was not removed. The basic problems which troubled these relations for years were never near to a real solution; and these problems affected no one more than the Arab youths. These youths, ill-educated and of very restricted life-experience, found themselves caught in the cross-currents of not only two, but three worlds, to neither of which they fully belonged or into which they would be fully accepted: the small, quiet and rather traditional world of their parents; the new Arab world around Israel, on which they kept informed as best they could through radio and television, and which was epitomized by Egypt and personified by its leader at that time, President Nasser; and the modern Jewish world around them, represented by the European immigrants and particularly by their descendants, the Sabre — the Israeli-born second generation youth, generally typified as unbridled, irreverent and purposeful. The world of the parents had lost its appeal and meaning for these youths. It is the backward world against whom the new Arab nationalism rebelled, the world which permitted the disaster of 1948 to happen. But neither did they really belong to the new, revolutionary Arab world — not only because they did not have any direct contact with it, but also because this world actually rejected them as quislings, traitors to the Arab cause.[57] Obviously, they also did not belong to the surrounding Jewish world, though they live in closed proximity to the Jews. Not only were they prevented, as Arabs, from symbolic participation in a state based on purely Jewish national symbols, but their very existence was deeply affected by the unchanging hostility between Israel and the Arab countries; and they were sometimes held responsible by some of the Jews for the behaviour of the leaders of those countries. This can be best related by an actual event: when the Syrians executed an alleged Israeli spy, Eli Cohen, in Damascus, a Jewish girl said to a local Arab youth whom she approached in the main street of the Jewish part of the city: "What are you doing here, after you [plural] have killed Eli Cohen?" Whenever hostilities broke out on the borders, the Arabs tended to disappear from the Jewish part of the city and shut themselves up in their quarters. The Arab youths thus faced a hopeless situation: they are a minority within a majority of Jews who, on their part, are a minority, threatened by a large Arab majority in this area of the world. The Arab youths were thus caught up in a major historical upheaval, over which they are powerless, but which profoundly affects their fate.

Thus, the fundamental problem of the new generation of Arab youth in the community was one of identity, not only in the sense of "Who am I?" but also in the sense of the purpose and meaning of their existence in a Jewish state.[58] There are no readymade, easy answers to these problems. Some of the youths were driven by the circumstances to extreme nationalism, coupled with a rather nominal attachment to communism, and found their peace of mind and security in the Arab Communist Party (Rakach). But such extreme nationalism was mainly negativistic and largely barren, since it drove the individual into extreme isolation and broke all possibilities of accommodation with the Jews, whilst it was unable to cause any real change in the predicament of the Arabs themselves. The majority lingered on passively, vaguely accepting the nationalist cause, but not really embracing it whole-heartedly, ready to face all the consequences. They would prefer to "opt out," to escape the dilemma of their situation and not to face it squarely. Some, indeed, took refuge in drugs — drug taking, mostly hashish, among Arab youths was very widespread indeed. Still others would like to emigrate — but not to an Arab country. After living in Israel, the Arab countries seemed to Israeli Arab youths backward and unattractive. During my stay in the city one family got special permission to emigrate to Jordan. Their decision was almost unexceptionally questioned and derided by the local Arab youth. The two youths of the family said before leaving that they are going there only in order to help topple the reactionary regime in power in Jordan. On the other hand, many of the youths would like to emigrate to the West, particularly to Canada and to Scandinavia. Their problem of identity here ties up with two related but more concrete and practical problems which deeply affect the life of the Arab youths in Israel in general and in the city in particular: the problem of a satisfying occupational career and the problem of sexual gratification.

The large majority of the Arab youths in the city had only a very limited preparation for an occupational career of any kind; some had none at all. Their education has been generally deficient, even by standards of some other Arab communities in Israel: they attended school irregularly, the majority dropped out before completing secondary education and many did not get beyond elementary education. The quality of their education was low, the teachers often incompetent and their methods archaic. Only very few of those who finished secondary school succeeded to matriculate in state-wide examinations, where the standards of evaluation for Jew and Arab are identical. Moreover, successful matriculation did not necessarily open the doors of social and economic advance; owning to the low quality of their preparation, many Arabs who attend the universities found it hard to compete with the Jewish students. Those who did not go for higher learning found it difficult to obtain suitable jobs: there were very few openings for white-collar jobs for Arabs, such as clerical or governmental jobs. Many of the youths who have completed secondary education were therefore forced to work at menial jobs. Secondary education lend the youths some prestige in their peer-group, but unsuitable employment after matriculation caused shame and discontent.

The vocational training provided in the city to those who did not go for a complete secondary education was highly deficient; the technical facilities were inadequate, and the training insufficient to enable the youngster to obtain grading as a skilled worker.

As a consequence, most Arab youths in the city were forced, upon leaving school, to work as unskilled or semi-skilled laborers in industry, agriculture (including fishing) and particularly in construction. Some of them learned new skills at work and qualified as skilled workers. But their employment patterns were highly irregular and even haphazard: most of the youths I knew were constantly on and off employment, shifting from one temporary employer to another, and from one occupation to another. Many of them have worked in different and sometimes highly dissimilar occupations: some moved from one locality to another and would even follow employment to far-away sites if none had been available in the town or the surrounding area. A typical case in point would be the occupational career pattern of a 24-year-old youth, one of my chief informants: he had not completed secondary schooling but in his teens started as a construction worker and obtained a grade as a skilled builder; however, he did not persist in this line, but started to work in a formica shop in the nearby large city. He was discharged when a recession began in 1966; for some time he did not work. Then he got a temporary job as an usher during a local festival; afterwards he toured the surrounding Arab villages with a jeep, selling clothing. Finally, he returned to the building industry, working in the city for an Arab contractor.

This career pattern was by no means exceptional. It was influenced on the one hand by objective factors, such as the fact that the youths lacked real skills as well as by the exploitative attitude of the employers, who preferred to hire and fire these youths frequently, instead of being burdened by the various social-benefit payments which accrued to permanent employees. There were also some subjective factors at work; the youths were not deeply committed to any occupation; they had little stamina and often drifted along aimlessly, taking and leaving jobs as they came, living-off the moment. Many were idle for considerable periods of time, either because they were unable to find employment, or because they were not looking for it energetically enough.

This pattern is, of course, familiar from similar situations in which youths are caught between two worlds to neither of which they really belong. The same problems could be found, to an extent, among Jewish immigrant youths in Israel, particularly among those of Oriental origin. However, the Arab youths showed some peculiarities which were closely associated with their crisis of identity: their relative lack of concern with the future largely reflected their feeling of lack of meaning and purpose in their life situation. They envied and admired the purposeful Jewish youth who strove to get on in life. Very few of them felt that they had something to strive for, or that there were opportunities offered to Arabs in Israeli society. Whatever their objective opportunities might have been, they were discouraged from trying too hard by a number of barriers for advancement or disabilities imposed on them by the state; these were generally justified by the Jews as "security measures"; obviously, it is almost impossible to determine whether such measures were really warranted and it was even more difficult to convince the Arab youths of their necessity under prevailing conditions. One of the chief problems in this respect in the city under study was that two of the largest heavy industrial plants employed only very few Arabs, "for security reasons." The Israeli Technion, located in the near-by large city, did not accept Arabs to some departments, such as electronic engineering, for the same reason. The actual impingement of such restrictions on the life-chances of the youths is difficult to assess; but even if it was negligible, its symbolic significance was considerable: they felt that they were excluded from society-wide participation, discriminated against by the institutions, and that even if they had tried hard they would not be given a fair chance. Therefore they were often ready to forego even those employment-services which were actually made available to them. A case in point is that very few Arab youths in the city made use of the governmental labor exchange, officially the only legal way through which employment could be obtained. They explained to me that the office of the labor exchange was situated at a great distance from the Old Town where they live; it was inconvenient to drag one's feet daily all the way to the office, when in any case they would have to wait for months before getting a chance at employment. (The study was undertaken in a period of economic recession, when jobs were scarce, particularly for unskilled laborers.) Many of these youths preferred therefore to look on their own for occasional employment, touring work-places and building sites; they would accept any kind of temporary work offered them by exploitative employers at reduced rates of pay and without social benefits. In this manner they effectively barred themselves from achieving anything like permanence and security at work. They thus tended to maneuver themselves out of the official employment market and to perpetuate the pattern of erratic employment and sporadic jobs.

In addition to the occupational problem there was the sexual dilemma which an Arab youth faced. The traditional Arab family provided but few opportunities for an unhindered, informal meeting between young members of the sexes before marriage. Very little sexual guidance was provided by the parents or by any other socializing agent. However, underlying and complementing the overt austerity of Arab sexual life there were covert patterns of gaining sexual release; institutionalized prostitution in the red-light districts of the larger Arab towns was one and probably the most important of these.

This traditional pattern was gradually breaking down in Israel in general and in the mixed city, with its manifold contacts between the Arab and the modern Jewish society, in particular. However, it was breaking down at unequal rates for males and for females. The girls were still kept under the watchful eyes of their mothers and, however strong their resentment, they are effectively prevented from breaking away from home or from rejecting parental authority. Strong social sanctions accompanied the slightest misdemeanor on their part. A few of the girls in the city dared to meet Arab youths occasionally, when on errands during the day, but they were not able to date regularly on evenings. They were forced to display much shyness — they would not even greet an Arab youth they knew when meeting him in the streets of the Old Town. Most of the girls get married very early, mostly in their teens. Paradoxically, some gain a degree of freedom after marriage — a few cases were related to me of young married women who have had extra-marital affairs with local youths. Infidelity seems to be more common when young girls are married to elderly men, often against their wishes.

Male youths got married much later than the girls, partly because they encountered difficulties in paying the relatively high bride-price, still common among local Muslims, and partly because they are generally slow in getting settled in life, particularly economically. Their period of adolescence was often prolonged into the late twenties. They had mostly shed the sexual mores of their parental home as well as parental authority on sexual matters. However, being essentially inexperienced in these matters and having nobody to consult with, they often roamed wide and wild in their search of sexual adventures. They not only insisted upon choosing their own spouses, but eagerly looked for as much sexual experiences as possible. They were, indeed, enormously preoccupied with sex, and this preoccupation is possibly one of the reasons for their relative lack of concern with other, particularly occupational matters. The matter of sex invariably came up in talks with the youths and often provided the chief subject of discussion. The youths were very proud of their sexual exploits and usually boasted of their achievements. They eagerly interpret any clue from a girl as an invitation, often on rather flimsy grounds.

The important point to note is that this enlarged sexual freedom and exploration has not been accompanied by increased sexual education. A thoughtful member of a high-status Moslem family expressed to me his concern about lack of sexual education among Arab youths. He related that a Jewish teacher at a Catholic Arab school once merely explained the terms for sexual organs to his class; there was an uproar and the teacher was fired. The youths were perplexed by sexual matters and had really nobody to talk to. We ourselves felt their concern very much, since some of our young Arab friends would discuss their problems with my wife, who was one of the few women they felt free to talk to frankly.

The physical propinquity of the Jewish community complicated the problem for the Arabs. The Jewish youths generally had free and informal relationships with Jewish girls. This was often falsely interpreted by the Arab youths as utter sexual freedom or promiscuity. They would feel that the Jewish girls are sexually uninhibited and that they had sexual relations with Jewish youths as a matter of course. They believed that their own approaches, however, would be rejected by these same girls, because they were Arabs. Such fantasies generated jealousy, as well as a strong desire to imitate the Jewish sexual practices, as these were understood by the Arab youths.

The sexual sphere loomed large as one of the chief points of friction between Jewish and Arab youths in the city.[59] There was very little informal contact, on an equal basis, between the two groups of youths. Jewish youths would not accept Arabs to their clubs and gatherings, claiming almost invariably that "the Arabs would take our girls." The Jewish youths complained that the Arabs would not bring along Arab girls, but would make approaches to the Jewish girls; on the other hand, they claimed, these same Arabs would deeply resent it if a Jewish youth made such approaches to their own sisters. The Jewish youths were intent to protect the Jewish girls from intimidation by Arabs and to prevent any competition for Jewish girls on part of the Arabs. Their anxiety was probably strengthened by the widespread tendency to impute extraordinary sexual prowess to Arabs.[60]

The Arab youths thus had to look for sexual gratification outside the one sphere in the city in which it seemed, but was actually not, easily available — the local Jewish community. Within the Israeli society they had two other potential sources of gratification: Jewish girls out of town, and particularly in the nearby large city; and prostitution, both local and in the nearby large city. However, both these sources had some serious drawbacks: it was true that it is easier for an Arab youth to take a Jewish girl out in the large city than it was in his own community. The large city is anonymous, and the Arab would be less likely to suffer public censure for his behavior on part of the Jews; he would also be less affected by any hostility on their part than he would be in his hometown. Moreover, being a stranger, he might as well attempt to feign a false identity. Cases were known in which Arab youths adopted Hebrew names and pretended to be Oriental Jews when going out with Jewish girls. However, it is difficult to conceal one's identity, and the concealment cannot go on when the relationship with the girl becomes steady; and even in the large city Jewish girls are usually reluctant to go out with Arabs.

Prostitution, too, was not a satisfactory solution. Several prostitutes, Jewish and Arab, lived in the Old Town. They did not, however, ply their trade in the community but in surrounding localities and in the large city. I was told that they avoided having relations with local youths, even if they happened to meet them in the large city. Obviously, other prostitutes existed in the large city, and Arab youths occasionally made use of their services; though I had difficulties to establish the frequency of visits to prostitutes, it seems that many of the Arab youths had some experience with them. The point, however, is that prostitutes did not provide that kind of gratification which the youths were really after: they did not constitute a challenge to their manliness and could not be wooed and conquered. The problem of manliness, of proving one's mettle, is an important one for Israeli Arab youths; it became even more salient in a mixed city, where the Arabs felt particularly keenly the want of a central symbol of masculinity of which the Jewish youths were so proud: the Arabs did not serve in the army. Sexual exploits, then, played an important compensatory role with these youths, and prostitution could not satisfy this kind of desire.

Cultural change, coupled with the peculiar and uneasy position in which the Arab youths found themselves in a mixed city in Israel, had generated in them a new type of longing for sexual gratification and at the same time denied the means to achieve it.

The Tourist Girl in Town

My analysis of the life situation of the Arab youths pointed out a number of serious stresses which, under the circumstances, were not readily resolvable. Consequently the youths were generally tense; many searched desperately for a way out of their predicament. In their search they were prone to adopt most far-fetched schemes or to delude themselves with unrealistic hopes. It is in this context that the tourist girls who visited the town gained an unexpected significance.

The mixed city which I studied is an old historic city, well-known for its antiquities, as well as for its beaches. Hence, it is a point of attraction for tourists. When I started my study, I looked upon the tourists — as many anthropologists would — as a nuisance "contaminating my community." Gradually, through my young Arab informants, I became aware of the fact that the tourists play a role in local life. The first point I noticed was that they provided the young Arabs with a "window to the wide world" outside their small community. The Arab youths, cut off as they were from outside contact, have been eager to learn about life in other countries. Here were people who are not involved in the Jewish-Arab dispute, strangers from interesting countries of which the local youths knew little. They would hang around public places in the hope of encountering tourists, show them around the city and pick up a conversation with them.

Many kinds of tourists came to the city. Not all were of equal interest for the Arabs, nor equally approachable for them. One group of tourists stood out particularly and as my research proceeded I started to realize that this group had more than casual importance for the youths: the young, unattached drifters, often penniless, wandering around without a clear aim or a definite itinerary, looking for a good time, a meal, a place to sleep, or an adventure. Many such tourists were attracted to the town, for various reasons: its exotic appeal, its beaches, and, sometimes, its renown as a place where hashish could be obtained.

The Arab youths were much attracted to these young drifters. They would pick them up in the streets, take them to their houses, provide them with food and shelter. One youth related a typical instance in which he met ten foreign tourists working in a kibbutz as volunteers; they had nowhere to sleep, so he took them to the house of his maternal aunt, where they spent the night. Another youth, who was living alone, kept an "open house," where, he said, tourists were always welcome. This fellow, who was ekeing out a narrow living as a fisherman, seems, however, to have had other dealings with the tourists: he would buy foreign currency from them (he said he needed it for his own travels abroad) and he was reportedly selling hashish to some of them. Many of these tourists, being penniless, gladly accepted the traditional Arab hospitality when proposed; others would seek out Arab company in a quest for hashish. Still others would go around the Old Town, asking unabashedly where hashish is sold, to the embarrassment of the local population (sale of hashish is illegal in Israel).

However, the main attraction for the Arab youths were the tourist girls. Cut off as they were from both local Arab and Jewish girls, these youths unexpectedly found in the foreign girls an almost perfect object for their emotional needs: these girls were emancipated and free in their behavior, fairly approachable and not part of the Israeli setting with is manifold problems. The Gentile girls, at least, were not prejudiced against the Arabs; this could not always be said of the Jewish foreign girls; at least in one instance which I recorded a foreign Jewish girl refused to continue to walk on the street with an Arab youth, when his nationality became known to her.

All foreign girls were sought after by the Arab youths, but there was one kind of girls they were particularly keen on: the fair-haired girls from Scandinavian countries. I was told endless stories about these girls, the adventures the youths had with them, and the more or less permanent relationships they had established or hoped to establish with them.

On the face of it, this infatuation is readily explainable by the usually held stereotype of the mutual attraction of the dark Orientals and the fair Northerners. Indeed, one of my informants once told me that "in Scandinavia the youths are not hot enough, are not good, and therefore the girls come over here, since they like Sephardis (sic)" (this term actually denotes Jews of Spanish [Sepharad in Hebrew], or more broadly Oriental descent, but does not apply to Arabs). I was told that there were different kinds of tourist girls, such who would not allow anyone to touch them and such who were looking for sexual adventures. The Scandinavian girls were often said to be of the latter type. Though one of the reasons that the Arab youths were infatuated with the Scandinavian girls was undoubtedly the prospect of easy conquest, I doubt whether actual sexual relations took place very often. The youths, though superficially emancipated from traditional mores, were still pretty much inhibited. Some of them explained to me that they do not touch the girls when they take them to their homes, where they are received with great honor by their parents. Another youth said that when he took a girl home, he treated her "like my sister." One of the reasons of their success with the foreign girls seems to have been their rather diffident, gentlemanly manner, which contrasted so sharply with the uninhibited straightforwardness of some modern youths. Generally, the girls seem to had liked their company, but they did not necessarily attach to the relationship that fateful importance which it had for the Arab youths.

Intimate relations between Western European and Scandinavian tourist girls and local youths can be found in the sea-resorts all around the Mediterranean, in Spain, Italy, Yugoslavia, and Greece. Most of these are short-lived, intensive but shallow adventures, often seemingly initiated by the girls, mostly for kicks. The local youths, though they probably enjoy it, take the flow of foreign temptresses rather nonchalantly in their stride.

The situation with respect to the Arab youths in the mixed Israeli town is somewhat different. For one, the flow of girls is not that steady and strong as in other Mediterranean resorts. Real success is difficult to come by and much looked for. For another, the youths attach to the relationship with foreign girls much more than casual importance. Indeed, as my study progressed, I became more and more impressed by the intensity of preoccupation of the youths with the occasional tourist girl whom they met in the town. Gradually I came to realize that the importance of the relationship with the foreign girls was for the youths much more than purely sexual: it impinged, rather, on some of those basic problems in their life-situation which I have discussed above.

Though sex might have been important to the youths in their relationship with the girls, they also attached considerable importance to other aspects of the relationship. Here, for the first time in their lives, they encountered nice, open-minded and modern girls who would gladly accept their hospitality and like their company, an attitude which was not shared by the neighboring Jewish girls. Such acceptance by a foreign girl would endow the Arab youth with status in his peer group. Living as they did rather pitiful and eventless lives, there were only few status symbols by which they could bolster their ego and show their mettle. The acquisition of the friendship of a foreign girl was one of the few ways by which status in the peer group could be obtained. Hence the boastfulness of the youths with their conquest: a reputation for success with foreign girls was much sought after. It is characteristic that the other important status symbol was a reputation for the use of drugs. My informants would point out a particular youth and say with awe that "he is a great hashish user." But they were ambivalent towards the drug-users; they were less ambivalent towards the tourist-chasers.

When asked for the reasons for their interest in foreign girls, the youths would start by saying that these contacts enabled them to learn foreign languages and to gain interesting information on foreign countries. They claimed that they did not have the opportunity to learn these languages at school, but had to pick them up from the tourists. Some would boast that through their contact with the tourists they learned to speak English, French and German and even possessed a smattering of other languages.

Obviously, it could be argued that the youths' alleged interest in the language and country of origin of the foreigner was only a pretext for some ulterior motive. But the point is that it was not. The youths were really and seriously interested in these matters, though for very practical reasons and not for abstract ones. This brings us to the most interesting and, for our purposes, most important motive behind their infatuation with the tourists: the intention or fantasy many of them harbored to get away from their predicament, and from Israel, to visit a foreign country, stay on indefinitely and, if possible, settle there; any foreign country would do (except Arab countries) but Canada, and of course, Scandinavia, are the preferred ones. For almost all of these youths this was a far-off, probably unrealizable dream. However, their contact with the tourists, and the information they got on the latter's language and country of origin, at least created the illusion that they are doing something by way of preparation for this future enterprise. These preparations also often took a more concrete form: after making the acquaintance of the tourists, and especially of tourist girls, the youths exchanged addresses. They attempted to keep the friendship going by exchanging letters with the girls when these returned home. Addresses of tourists were avidly collected and represented cherished treasures. The youths would boast of the number of addresses they had got. They would relate that the girls had invited them to visit with them in their home country. Many of the youths intended to make use of these addresses and invitations when they would finally go abroad, and some said that they had been promised a travel-ticket by the girls. Many youths even extended their hospitality with a view to future reciprocity. Some hoped that they will be helped by the girls or their families in obtaining work abroad, some that they will ultimately marry one of the tourists; or, alternatively, they hope to meet a suitable girl abroad, marry her and settle in a foreign country. It was difficult to establish how serious and lasting the relationships had actually been; in any case, few youths ever got abroad or actually emigrated. Even fewer of these got there through their connections with tourists. Those who did, however, are kept in lively memory. Three such cases came to my attention: in one case a local youth married a Canadian girl whom he previously met in Israel. The youth had some difficulties with the authorities in obtaining a permit to leave the country; his girl friend was said to have helped him to get out of the country, through her lawyer. The youth is a Canadian citizen now and recently came to visit the city, with his wife and child. In another case a youth met a Danish girl in the city, fell in love, married her and emigrated to Denmark, where — as the youths related — he got settled in a steady job after some initial difficulties; they had a child; however, later they parted, though the youth remained in Denmark. In the last case, a local youth went abroad to follow another Danish girl, but they ultimately decided not to marry, since as it was related "she could not bear life in Israel, and he could not bear to live in Denmark"; however, he was still in Denmark at the time of the study, working. In the two latter cases a friend, respectively a brother of the emigrants intended to join them abroad. One of them started already to learn Danish from tourists and intended to visit Denmark in 1967 and, if possible, stay there. However, when I met him again in 1968 he was still talking about going there "next year."

In addition to the youths who married foreigners and left the country, there were a few others who emigrated on their own, mostly to Canada. During my stay in the town one such case of emigration occurred. The friends of the emigrant were deeply affected by his departure, but sympathized with his motives. Most of the youths kept a lively interest in the fate of those who left, discussed the pros and cons of emigration and were much impressed by the money the emigrants made abroad, which indeed was a lot by Israeli standards.

The problem of emigration of Arab youths disturbed some local Arab leaders. One of the younger ones, who strove hard to find some accommodation between the Jews and the Arabs in the city, proclaimed the tendency to emigrate as an "awful cross" and was thoroughly opposed to it, in the same manner in which some Zionists are opposed to the emigration of Jews. But he was exceptional in that he saw a place for the Arabs in Israeli society, which the other Arabs usually did not see.

Though relatively few youths had actually emigrated from Israel, many played with the idea of emigration as a way out of their predicament. Some took it seriously; others took it fancifully, as a daydream or a fantasy, rather than as a realistic possibility. Both embraced the "dream of the tourist girl," who appeared to them as perfect vehicle for the resolution of their manifold problems. In order to evaluate properly the significance of the dream for the Arab youths, we have to analyze the manner in which the relationship with the tourist girl seemed to resolve these problems.

We discussed above three types of problems which the Arab youths face: the problem of identity, of an occupational career and of gratifying sexual relationships. Most obviously, the tourist girls provide the youths with the opportunity for open and gratifying relationships with members of the other sex, which they were longing for but could not achieve within the confines of Israeli society. They not only gain some sexual gratification, but are also able to establish a meaningful personal relationship with the girls, of a type they were not accustomed to in their own society and unable to achieve with Jewish girls. Such relationships, in turn, raise their status in their peer-group, reinforce their self-reliance and flatter their vanity.

However, the tourist girl also seems to hold out a promise to solve the other two problems, by facilitating emigration to and absorption in a foreign country. Many of the youths would like to change their identity through emigration. Such a transition, however, is not easily achievable; it is not easier for an Arab to become a Dane or a Swede than it is to assimilate to the Jews. Attachment and marriage to a girl from one of these countries, however, would greatly simplify their problem. It would enable them, so to speak, to marry into the host society; many also believe that their future parents-in-law will facilitate their economic absorption abroad, by helping them to attain steady and remunerative employment. Several of the youths related how rich and important the father of some girl who "invited them" to come to visit her abroad, really was. Obviously, many of these hopes were pure fantasies. But, objective probability is one thing; the subjective belief of a youth rather desperately holding on to a fantasy, quite another. It would seem that for many of the youths the very existence of such a chance, however remote it may be, is inherently significant, and enables them to cope with their bleak predicament. This is rather similar to the poor man's hope that he will one day win the big prize in the national lottery, and thus become rich overnight. The few cases of the youths "who made it" support the fantasy in the same way in which the pictures and life-histories of those who won the big prize do for the lottery-gamblers.

The unsuspecting tourist girl thus suddenly acquired an unthought of potential for the solution of the problems of the local Arab youth. I assume, however, for the girls, the local youths did not have such a fateful significance. Though they might have flirted with the youths and occasionally had affairs with them, they were probably far from ever giving a thought to the idea that one of these youths may become their permanent companion or even husband. Their attitude to and interpretation of the situation seems to be similar to those which characterize the relationship between tourist girls and local youths along the beaches of Italy or Yugoslavia. They might been attracted to the dark, strange and rather gentle youths, but might not have attached that importance to the relationship which the youths, in their relative lack of experience and under the pressure of their own circumstances, tended to attach to it. The solution of the problem of the Arab youths through attachment to tourist girls was thus largely imaginary; in the main the tourists helped to create new and essentially false hopes for these youths who were trapped in a situation from which, under the prevailing circumstances, there was no way out.

Arabs, Tourists and the Jewish Community

The local Jewish youths showed relatively little interest in the tourist girls. No particular need of theirs, sexual or other, would be served by an attachment to such a girl. Thus, the Jews in the community did not generally object to the Arabs' interest in the tourists. As one Jewish youth told me: "We have our girls, the Arabs have the tourists." If anyone had personal complaints, then these came from the all-but-forgotten Arab girls, who were locked up at home while their male contemporaries and future husbands ran around with shapely and well-dressed European girls. No wonder one of them inquired of an Arab youth: "Are Arab girls no good any more?"

However, if Jews at large did not care, there are some institutions which did, and first and foremost among these, the police. People with varied interests in the town considered the Arab youths a nuisance to the tourists: they claimed that the youths intimidated the tourists who visited the town, and that they represented a danger for their safety. They complained that the youths did not work but hung out in the town, spied for tourists, and molested the girls with unseemly proposals. The youths must, indeed, have made quite a name for themselves, since one day I met a German girl who asked whether it was safe for her to walk alone into the Old Town; she had been told that foreign girls used to be raped there by the local Arab youths. Actually, during my whole stay in the city no case of rape of a tourist by an Arab had been recorded; the only case of the kind occurred some time before my arrival: two Moroccan Jews and an Arab drugged a couple and raped the girl; the couple was looking for hashish and thereby met the youths. The case was wholly exceptional.

As a matter of fact the tourists were often attracted to the Arabs and sought them out or at least willingly accept their hospitality. However, even in such cases there was police interference. In several instances the Arab youths have been molested by police without any provocation while they entertained tourist girls. The policemen demanded emphatically that the youths stop seeing tourist girls. I witnessed an incident in which a youth from a respected Arab family was dragged from a taxi in which he was about to leave for the nearby large city with a tourist girl. He was arrested on the spot as suspect of selling drugs to some tourist girls; immediately afterwards he was released; he never had any dealings with drugs. He claimed that the purpose of the arrest was actually to prevent him from going to the city with the girl; the police, in his opinion, knew well enough that he was not peddling drugs. He complained that one of the policemen told him: "How do you, a youth from a good family, go around with a tourist whore?" The youths were extremely bitter about such interference of the police with their activities, but would not complain formally since they were afraid of police retaliation. The point of view of the police was simple: they had to protect the tourists from any possible danger to their safety on part of the youths — such as rape, temptation of drugs which the tourists might be offered, etc. The police were also concerned by the fact that some tourists actually sought contact with the youths in order to get or buy drugs. As one policeman explained to me: "I am taking extreme steps to prevent contact [of Arab youths] with the tourists; there is no other choice; we have to prevent the emergence of problems [by the youths]." In fairness it must be added that he considered the penniless tourists drifting into the town as much of a nuisance as the Arab youths who ran after them.

The youths, however, suspected some ulterior motives on part of the police: they asserted that the police were in fact bent to prevent the Arab youths, known for their nationalistic opinions, from talking politics to the tourists and explaining their lot to them. In their eyes, this was another trick played by the governmental institutions to keep the Arabs isolated from the outside world and encapsuled in their own society. Police interference with contact between Arabs and tourists was thus viewed by the Arab youths within the context of the general situation of the Arabs in Israel and acquired for them a political significance. The youths related gleefully how the girls would not let them down and did not comply with the policemen's request to stop meeting the youths. The outsiders, as it were, would in this case become their only support.

It is hard to establish the real motives behind the behavior of the police in respect to contacts between the tourists and the Arab youths. I tend to view them within the general context of the police's attitude towards the Arabs: the police were extremely suspicious and assumed as a matter of course that the Arabs are treacherous and prone to become spies. The general policy was therefore to contain them, and, as much as possible, to isolate them from strangers. The interference with the youths' romantic contacts with the tourist girls was thus only a special case within this general policy. I tend, thus, generally to agree with the view of the Arab youths, though the chief motive of the policy of isolation, to my mind, was not political — the prevention of free speech and venting of complaints — but rested with considerations of national security. Whether such suspicions are justified is a matter which I cannot judge.

Conclusion

In this chapter I attempted to point out some of the major stresses in the "life situation" of Arab youths in a mixed city in Israel and the rather unexpected manner in which the tourist girls seemed to hold out a promise for the resolution of these problems. In this concluding section I would like to take up two interconnected theoretical problems raised by my discussion and suggest some questions and hypotheses for future analysis.

My exposition could be stated in terms of interaction between two social systems: that of the Israeli society and that of the Arab Middle Eastern society; the Israeli Arabs were a sub-system of both of these systems. The clash between these two systems was, thus, acutely felt by the Israeli Arabs and particularly so by the as yet unsettled Arab youths. The clash created a number of severe stresses in the life situation of the youths; I have discussed these as the triple problems of identity, occupational career and sexuality. Looked upon from the point of view of the Israeli social system, these were integrative problems: the system had generated stresses for the resolution of which it did not provide any adequate mechanisms, and was thus faced with the threat that a major part of the Arabs will become alienated from it. Under the exigencies of the political and ideological situation — Israel being threatened by the surrounding Arab countries and intent to remain a Zionist state, closely identified with Jewish national symbols — these stresses were actually irresolvable. The Arab youths felt the stresses more acutely than the rest of the Arab population and were consequently most alienated. Their alienation took various modes: some took to drugs, others to extreme nationalism; still others wanted to emigrate from Israel into a Western country. Obviously, these were three modes of reaction to the strains the system imposed upon these youths, three types of "deviation" from the point of view of the dominant Israeli social system: regression from the system (drug-taking), rebellion against the system in an attempt to change it radically (extreme nationalism) and opting out of the system (emigration). The tourist girl provided a potential vehicle for the realization of the last mentioned option. An interesting theoretical question in this respect would be: which kind of other social traits characterized the youths who react in each of these ways? My information is not detailed and systematic enough to be able to explore this problem, but I would suggest the hypothesis that the least educated youths, those who have the least chances in Israel or abroad, would tend to take to drugs more than the more educated ones; the latter would take either to nationalism or to emigration. I would not venture a hypothesis as to the variable which differentiates between the youths who tend to nationalism as against those who tend to emigrate. But the two modes of behavior tend to be mutually exclusive, since I encountered only few extreme nationalists among the girl-chasers and prospective emigrants.

My other theoretical point relates to the broader implications of the finding on the unexpected role tourist girls play in the city. I mentioned above, that the plight of the Arab youths was generated by the system but was under the prevailing conditions irresolvable within the system. In this respect, the tourist girls, by the very fact that they derived from *outside the system*, performed an ameliorating role *within* the system: they provided these youths with a hope of escape from their situation, a strongly felt opportunity to flee from their present reality and to resolve miraculously their manifold problems. By clutching to the hope that one day, somehow, they will find a foreign girl and get away from all this, the Arab youths gathered strength to continue to cope as best they could with their predicament and not to succumb to either of two extremes: extreme activism (found in nationalism) or extreme passivity (found in drugs). In the strict sense of the term the innocent tourist girl, out for a good time and some exotic adventure, was thus performing a latent function in the community. It is to be noted, however, that this function was not generated by the system, it was not a response of the system to a "need." There is a function here, but no self-regulating mechanism in the functionalist sense. Indeed, if the system responded at all, it rather tended to interfere with the Arab-tourist relationship (e.g. police interference); in this context, such interference must be seen as a "latent dysfunction."

The serendipitous impact of the tourist girls upon the Arab youths — the fact that it was a chance occurrence that tourists tended to visit this particular city, since it is an old and interesting place, and thus come to meet these Arab youths raises a more general theoretical issue: the manner in which modern communities become intertwined not only in the national but also in international social systems.[61] We have learned long ago that, under modern conditions, local social structure could not be analyzed except in terms of its interrelationships with the national structure. But we do not generally go beyond that in our sociological analyses of community structure, except in those rather special cases in which we study the impact of immigrants on a community. The example discussed in this chapter, however, points out the importance of international factors in the analysis of local processes: the life-situation of the Arab youths was largely affected by the prevailing relations between Israel and its Arab neighbors; and they strove to resolve their difficulties, partly, by getting involved with strangers, who were of interest for them precisely because they hailed from outside the Middle Eastern context and hence did not partake of its tensions and prejudices. The arrival of a particular tourist girl into the city is a chance occurrence. But the flow of tourists in the host country seems to be patterned to a degree; through the operation of the institution of tourism, members of different and far-away societies regularly meet and influence each other's lives. Tourism is thus a mechanism through which localities and nations become intertwined into a huge, super-national system of social interaction, from which even the most remote island can nowadays scarcely escape. However, we know relatively little on the impacts of the more ephemeral forms of inter-societal contact, such as youth tourism, upon the structure and way of life of local communities. I hope to have demonstrated in this chapter that such contacts merit more attention on the part of anthropologists and sociologists conducting community studies.

Acknowledgment—The study on which this paper is based has been supported by a grant from the Eliezer Kaplan School of Economics and Social Sciences at the Hebrew University of Jerusalem. Thanks are due to Yohanan Peres for his useful comments.

Chapter 16

The Pacific Islands from Utopian Myth to Consumer Product: The Disenchantment of Paradise

'We Know Paradise Best'

(Air New Zealand Advertisement)

Introduction

The quest for an Earthly Paradise is a widespread and perhaps universal theme in the history of man's longings (Eliade 1969a; Manuel and Manuel 1972; Niederland 1957). According to the eminent historian of religion, M. Eliade there is "...something in the human condition that we may call *nostalgia for paradise*" (Eliade 1969a:55; italics in original).[62] From ancient times and up to the dawn of modernity, whatever the immediate practical purposes of man's journeys into distant parts, they were frequently motivated by a deeper, more pervasive paradisiac quest. Mythology, anthropology and history abound in examples of journeys in quest of paradise. Legendary culture heroes, like Jason (Appollonius of Rhodes 1959) traveled to the enchanted site of Paradise and returned from there with wondrous prizes. Whole tribes wandered for enormous distances in search of the Earthly Paradise (Eliade 1969a); the paradisiac quest was one of the most potent themes of the voyages of discovery up to the treshold of the modern era.[63]

In its original, mythical setting, Paradise is a multivocal symbol (Turner 1969:52). To appreciate the extent to which the paradisiac imagery current in modern tourism is rooted in the ancient symbol, as well as the manner in which the original symbol has been transformed by tourism, a short discussion of the traditional meanings of Paradise is necessary.

Turner (1969:52) argues that the referents of multivocal symbols "...tend to cluster around opposite semantic poles"; hence "Such symbols ...unite the organic with the sociomoral order, proclaiming their ultimate religious unity, over and above conflicts between and within these orders."

I suggest that the sustained attraction of the paradisiac symbol consists in its "dense multivocality"; it is a multivocal symbol of multivocal symbols: it blends two basic, deep-structural themes in the human consciousness, the Center and the Other, each of which is a multivocal symbol in its own right. The Center is the source of the hallowed order of the cosmos, the point at which creation began, where the primaeval force broke into differentiated Being. The Other is that unformed, primordial and undifferentiated unknown, lurking in the chaos surrounding the cosmos.[64] The Center is the source of the sociomoral order (Shils 1975), the Other the embodiment of the primordial state of nature. Both these symbols are, however, themselves multivocal, each comprising, as it were, some of the traits of the other: behind the Center, as the source of the cosmic order stands the undifferentiated, charismatic creative force, unknown and unknowable, Otto's (1959:39–44) numinous "Wholly Other." The Other, in turn, is a dark but powerful force, awesome but enticing — a potential Center. Both symbols signify life, though in different senses: the Center is the source of all created, differentiated existence. Contact with it is, hence, contact with the source of creation; as such it exerts a powerful attraction on the Pilgrim, the seeker of recreation, rejuvenation and healing (Cohen 1992b). The Other is a more ambiguous symbol than the Center: it symbolizes life, not in its differentiations, but in its primordial, chaotic and changing unity. In its benign aspect the Other holds forth the promise of return to a "natural" state, in which there is no distance between the self and its surroundings, and no tension of "need": every desire is immediately and effortlessly satisfied, unimpeded by any moral restrictions. In its dark, malignant aspect, however, the chaotic Other is also dangerous and repellant — in the extreme, hellish. But even in its malignant aspect, the Other exerts a unique fascination on man and lures the intrepid, adventurous Traveller (Cohen 1992b).

Both, the Center and the Other fired man's imagination throughout history. I suggest that the pervasive power of the symbol of an Earthly Paradise consists precisely in that it overcomes the tension between the Center and the Other, the created and the pre-created, the sociomoral and the organic, or natural, spheres. It represents a strategic point of integration in man's mythical thought, and as such holds forth, as it were, a promise of the "best of both worlds." In the symbol of paradise, the sociomoral and the organic spheres are not in a state of tension; rather, they are fused. This is perhaps most poignantly expressed in the Biblical image of Paradise as the ideal garden, where perfect, divine order and harmony prevail, but each creature's needs are fully and effortlessly provided for.

If this interpretation is correct, then the myth of the loss of Paradise symbolizes the separation and the consequent persistent tension between the "sociomoral" and the "organic" spheres in human life; while the paradisiac quest expresses man's desire to regain their unity: to achieve both, the perfect order as well as the happiness of an undifferentiated, primordial state.

Paradise, as the symbol of the Center, is the point at which Creation begins; as such it represents the Center of the World (Eliade 1969b:43), the point of contact between the world and ultimate reality. While in itself the prototype of perfect Creation, it is also the point at which divine charisma enters the world, and as such life-endowing and re-creative. The paradisiac quest is, hence, one version of the ubiquitous religious "Quest for the Center" (Eliade 1971:17; Sanford 1961:32), prototypical of all pilgrimage (Cohen 1982a; Turner 1973). Paradise entices the seeker with the promise of immortality and eternal bliss. The visitor to the Earthly Paradise will experience re-creation and self-renewal; he will be rejuvenated or healed and his powers will be replenished. Sojourn in Paradise signifies the highest state of individual consciousness, the existential experience *par excellence*. As the symbol of the Other, however, paradise also holds forward the image of the land where man's creaturely cravings, whether oral or sexual, are fulfilled without sin, guilt or shame; it is the place of plenty, abandon and self-indulgence. While one facet of paradise offers men the prospect "to. . . transcend the human condition and to recover the divine condition . . ." (Eliade 1969b:55), the other facet entices him by playing upon his desire to shed all responsibility and to retreat into a pristine, primordial state in which all needs are effortlessly fulfilled, a desire which was psycho-analytically interpreted as a wish to re-enter the motherly womb (Manuel and Manuel 1972:87, 106; Niederland 1957:71−72). While such a state has been caricaturized, e.g. in the mediaeval German story of the Schlarafenland, it also expresses a deeper search for forgetful happiness, a primordial unity. Insofar as the symbol of Paradise preserves its multivocal character it will attract both, the seeker of the Center and the seeker of the Other, though their respective quests may differ in their particular motives.[65]

The religious traditions of the past have altogether preserved the multivocal quality of the paradisiac symbol, though in the course of its long "natural history" (Bloch 1959:Vol. 2, 873−929; Manuel and Manuel 1972) each of its facets has been emphasized to differing degrees; moreover, within any given tradition, the religious specialists probably tended to stress the sublime facet, while the laity emphasized the creaturely one.

Indeed, the ancient and mediaeval times left us a rich legacy of images of animalistic, orgiastic paradises (e.g. Manuel and Manuel 1972:88–89), located predominantly in the southern hemisphere (Bloch 1959:Vol. 2, 911), in which the themes of sexual pleasure, merriment and feasting predominate. However, the crea- turely theme is ultimately embedded in and redeemed by the sublime, sociomoral one. Thus, e.g. Giamatti (1966:52), discussing the poet Claudian's description of a lush paradise of erotic passion, points out that nevertheless "Claudian's spot is sanctified . . . by the presence of Venus." The basic harmony of the sublime and the creaturely is thus preserved: according to Giamatti, in the Renaissance epic ". . . the idea [of] bliss consisted precisely of comfort, repose and pleasure in beautiful surroundings" (ibid.:358). The state of physical bliss here symbolizes spiritual redemption.

The Touristic Experience

With the coming of modernity the paradisiac symbol came gradually to play a diminishing role in the domain of formal religion. The paradisiac longings of modern man found expression in other directions, particularly in various utopian and revolutionary movements, while the religious pilgrimage has given way to "secular" travel, whose most common expression is modern tourism.[66] Recent theoretical work suggests a closer connection between tourism and pilgrimage than was generally assumed. Reacting against the common-sense view of the tourist as a superficial half-wit, as protrayed, e.g. by Boorstin (1964), MacCannell (1973:589–590), argued that tourism is a search for authenticity, and as such a substitute for religion; the tourist's trip thus becomes analogous to the traditional pilgrimage, as a "Quest for the Center." Graburn (1977), in an article significantly entitled "Tourism: the Sacred Journey," argues on similar lines. If we accepted this view, the modern tourist's trip to a touristic "paradise" would then become analogous to the traditional religious paradisiac quest.

While this approach is promising, it needs further elaboration and qualification. In one sense the modern tourist embodies the traditional Pilgrim, but in another he is the modern version of the mythical Traveller (Cohen 1992b). In other words, it seems useful to distinguish between the pilgrim-tourist, who visits the attractions which symbolize the authentic Center of his own culture and the traveler-tourist, who is in search of the Other, beyond the boundaries of his "world" and who, in the more extreme cases, may transform that Other into his own, new "elective Center" (Chapter 5; Cohen 1992b). Modern tourism is in many respects a search for the Other, rather than a quest for the Center of the Judeo-Christian tradition; it is a search for the primaeval unity and simple naturalness, to be found in the remote recesses of the world, far beyond the boundaries of civilization. It is a search for the Other, in its benign, rather than fascinating but malignant, aspect. The image of the commercial touristic paradise, as we shall see below, was evolved to correspond to this variety of the modern paradisiac quest.

A further qualification concerns the level of analysis at which MacCannell's and Graburn's approach is applicable; it relates to the deep-structural, rather than to the phenomenological, perceptual level of the tourist's experience. Their approach, indeed, receives indirect support from Leymore's (1975) pioneering work on the deep structure of modern advertisements, in which she claims to have discovered a "hidden myth," encoding the same general cultural themes as are contained in traditional mythology. In Leymore's view, "Advertising is . . . a mediator . . . between the abstract and the concrete" (Leymore 1975:34), through which fundamental cultural values are translated into consumer preferences (ibid.:124). One could then argue that the tourist industry, with the help of its advertising media, is able to attract tourists to a locality by advertising it as a "paradise" and thus invoking deeply set, unconscious cultural motives in the prospective visitor. His trip to the touristic paradise offered by the industry would then have a cultural meaning analogous to the traditional paradisiac quest.

This should not, however, be construed as meaning that every tourist consciously seeks authenticity or "paradise" in that deep structural sense. The actual mood and motivation of his trip may well be, in terms of the phenomenology of traveling experiences, as far removed from the mood and motivation characteristic of the religious experience, as is the modern housewife who, by buying baby foods, re-enacts on a deep structural level the mythical victory of life over death (Leymore 1975:47–50).

While on a deep structural level the similarities between the cultural themes expressed by the traditional and the touristic quest for paradise may be striking, one should not overlook the important phenomenological differences on the surface, perceptual level. Structuralists like Leymore disregard the perceptual quality of the concrete experiences of people when confronted by deep cultural themes, whether in myths or in advertisements. MacCannell does not distinguish between the deep-structural and the conscious, perceptual levels of analysis; hence he makes it appear that, since tourism is structurally equivalent to the pilgrimage, each individual tourist also actively or consciously seeks authenticity. In the light of the manifest inauthenticity of much of what is consumed by contemporary tourists, such a conclusion is unwarranted. For an understanding of the far-reaching changes which the ancient paradisiac symbol underwent as paradise was turned into a consumer product for mass tourism, one has to take account of the quality of experiences which most tourists desire on the conscious, perceptual level.

I have dealt elsewhere extensively with the problem of the relationship between the deep-structural and perceptual levels of touristic experiences (Chapter 5) and shall here only recapitulate the principal points of my argument. The modes of experiences sought by tourists can be ranged from deep to superficial ones — according to the degree to which they reflect the deep-structural themes. The depth of the desired experience, in turn, will be related to the depth of their alienation from their own society and culture and to their desire to overcome it. Accordingly,

I distinguish five basic modes of touristic experiences. The deepest modes are the "existential" and "experimental" ones, namely those in which the tourist either expressly adopts an "elective center" beyond the boundaries of his "world," or alternatively, experiments with various potential "elective centers." Intermediate is the "experiential" mode of the tourist who, alienated from his own society, actively seeks vicarious participation in the "real" or authentic life of others. This type comes closest to MacCannell's (1973) conception of "the tourist." Most superficial are the "recreational" and "diversionary" modes — the modes of experience sought by tourists who, while not alienated from their society, desire to recuperate in their trip from the tensions which it generates, rather than seek any deeper, authentic experiences; or by those who, while alienated, merely seek in travelling some entertainment and diversion from the tedium of their meaningless lives. Such tourists do not, at least not consciously, seek authenticity, and hence accept as enjoyable situations of "staged authenticity," even if they are aware of their inauthentic nature.

"Existential" and "experimental" tourists are few in number; they tend to be found primarily among the younger set of self-styled "Travellers" and are embodied in the type of the original drifter (Chapter 4). They may very well engage in a paradisiac quests, but in localities far remote from the commercialized touristic paradises which are our principal concern here (e.g. Blakeway 1980).

The bulk of modern mass tourism consists of the experiential, recreational and diversionary tourists. They constitute the principal clients of the "tourist establishment," the commercialized facilities and services especially created for tourism. They are the main users of the tourist ecological system — the system of attractions and connecting routes within which most mass tourists circulate. They constitute the bulk of visitors of the commercialized "touristic paradises" which are the central theme of this study.

The Touristic Paradise

In its endeavor to create appealing images of its destinations in the travelling public, the tourist establishment makes ample use of religious symbolism — and perhaps most of all of the paradisiac symbol (Turner and Ash 1975:149ff.). Under the impact of the tourist industry and the advertising media, however, the original religious symbol of paradise has been considerably transformed, in response to the vastly different moods and motivations of the public whom the industry serves: the mass tourist, travelling primarily in the experiential, recreational or diversionary moods. For a comprehension of the image and reality of the contemporary touristic paradise, it is necessary to understand both its roots in religion as well as the nature of the transformation. Following Leymore one could argue that the advertising media used the powerful paradisiac theme, which has still preserved its vitality at a deep-structural level, to enhance the attractiveness of a mass product — vacation destinations. I argue that, precisely because paradise no longer plays an important role in the consciousness and life plan of modern mass consumers, the industry could indeed succeed in selling its "paradisiac" product. Only those tourists, who are in serious quest of paradise as an "elective center" will reject the alluring advertisements of the tourist industry as phoney and inauthentic and strive to reach such remote and unspoilt "paradisiac" locations which have not yet been penetrated by the industry.

Through the use of the traditional paradisiac symbolism, the industry strives to endow the touristic paradise with the appealing mystique of the more popular paradisiac images common in religions. Indeed, the literature abounds with rich images, in word and picture, of pristine nature and "magic" or "enchanted" islands. In a deeper sense, however, in the image of the contemporary "touristic paradise" the traditional paradisiac symbol is throughly "flattened": its originally rich multivocality tends to become thinned down to univocality, as its character as sociomoral Center is separated from its natural, creaturely aspect, and abandoned, even as the latter becomes only an expurgated, toned-down version of the Other; its "enchantment" becomes charm without a deeper spiritual significance; but even its natural aspect becomes domesticated; touristic paradises are not the animalistic, orgiastic centers of creaturely pleasure, but mild resorts of simplicity and repose in beautiful surroundings. They are "marginal paradises" (Cohen 1982b) in more than one sense: they are not only geographically, but also culturally remote — they do not symbolize the sociomoral Center of modern Western society, whatever deep-structural human themes they might express; neither are they central to the life plan of the modern mass tourist. Rather, they constitute a part of the wider "Pleasure Periphery" (Turner and Ash, 1975), emerging in the less developed countries surrounding the modern, industrial West.

The touristic paradise is in many respects an inversion of the intensive, complex, highly differentiated, "unnatural" modern life: it is a far-off place where life is simple and toilless, nature unspoilt, the natives happy and their women free and lovely. For most mass tourists, however, it is not a serious alternative to modernity; rather, it either complements modernity by offering a glimpse of allegedly "authentic" life, assuages the strains and stresses created by modernity or, at least, provides a temporary refuge from its turmoil.

The change in meaning of "paradise" in its touristic variety, is accompanied by a corresponding change in the quality of experience offered the visitor to the touristic paradise. These represent a secularized or disenchanted version of the experience which the visitor to the traditional paradise was led to expect by the religious imagination: in the touristic paradise, spiritual or physical rejuvenation (re-creation) becomes recreation, self-renewal becomes relaxation and refreshment; self-fulfillment — the satisfaction of consumer desires. Whereas man-in-Paradise was portrayed as leading a pristine and blissful existence in complete harmony and unity with nature, tourist-in-paradise is portrayed as enjoying the "unspoilt" scenery and the hospitality and services of the naive and friendly natives, the actual inhabitants of his "paradise." The experience offered by the touristic paradise is thus devoid of the deeper spiritual quality of the experience of the traditional religious paradise.

Closely related to these changes is the accessibility of the touristic paradise. The Center of the religious imagination is located on a mythical plane; it is not physically accessible. Paradise, located at the Center, may be reached in dreams, imaginary, mythical and magical voyages, but not by "normal," mundane travelling. It is Utopia, an ideal place, approximated by but ever beyond the reach of the explorer (Bloch 1959:Vol. 2, 873–929). The touristic paradise, however, though it may appear remote and isolated to the mass tourist, is a concrete locality, to which one can travel by the modern means of transportation. Instead of Utopia, a place beyond reach of ordinary experience, the touristic paradise is a palpable place, a "last resort," located ". . . not merely outside the physical borders of urban industrial society, but just beyond the border of peasant and plantation society as well" (MacCannell 1976:183).

Abetted by the industry, the modern man's quest for paradise was transposed from the realm of religion to that of mass consumerism. The industry's main achievement in this respect consists in its success in creating the impression that the once unattainable delights of paradise are actually procurable at a price well worth paying. If the oldest tenet of marketing is, as Glasser (1975:23) claims, that "You don't sell a product; you sell a dream" in the case of paradise a dream was actually turned into a product, but is advertised as a dream come true. Hence "paradise" became a concrete place, which, though remote and located beyond the limits of modern civilization, can be actually reached by taking a fast and comfortable trip; the provision of access to paradise, previously a matter of spiritual ascent, now became the preserve of travel agencies. The tourist industry thus took the place of priests, as the chief gatekeepers of paradise. To satisfy the demand so generated, the industry set out to select and promote destinations with natural "paradise-like" qualities or to create contrived "touristic paradises"[67] when the natural variety was in short supply. The "touristic paradise" thus becomes a supreme "pseudo-event" (Boorstin 1964:77–117) a place moulded so that it would correspond to the image disseminated among the mass travelling public and promoted by the travel industry.

Historically, the persistent attractiveness of Utopia has been at least partly con-tingent upon its unrealizability: a realized Utopia ceases to be Utopia in the same sense in which a fully comprehended God is no God any more.[68] The historical attractiveness of Utopia lies in its transcending quality, in the fact that it is always beyond the horizon, titillating in its promise, but ultimately beyond reach. It can be approached only asymptotically, a quality which, of all modern thinkers, was perhaps most clearly grasped by E. Bloch, who used it as a prime example to illustrate his philosophy of hope (Bloch 1959).[69] Nevertheless, extravagant claims that Utopia has actually been achieved or that its realization is imminent and can be realistically expected are by no means rare. Such claims have, for example, been put forward by some enthusiasts of the Israeli kibbutz or by some of the more vulgar communist ideologues, such as Khrushchev. The important point to note about "realized utopia" is that its "realization" is made possible not only, and sometimes not at all, by an approximation of social reality to the ideal; but also, and often primarily, by a vulgarization of that ideal, through which its lofty and exacting injunctions to perfection are lowered, and the ideal made closer to reality, as happened, e.g. in the case of Khrushchev's "goulash communism."[70] The process by which Utopia is adapted to reality and conceived of in concrete, usually material terms, robs it of its mythical, enchanted quality; it is a process of disenchantment of an ideal. Paradise, the ultimate Utopia, has been similarly disenchanted in modern tourism as it was transformed into a consumer product.

With the rising popularity of the paradisiac image in modern mass tourism, there was a proliferation of touristic "paradises"; the term became a catch-word, a trademark to advertise the superlative qualities of almost any tourist destination; any natural attraction or remnant of "untouched nature," may be transformed into a "paradise" at the hands of the tourist advertisement agencies; the word may be even utilized in a more remote sense to advertise such contrived attractions as "shopping paradises" (like, e.g. in the tourist advertisements of Singapore) (Cohen 1978:216).[71] Giesz (1968:163) may indeed be right in saying that tourist "paradises" are "the most exploited commonplace in international advertising . . . ." However, more than to any other kinds of touristic destination, the paradisiac label is applied to islands (e.g. Friedel 1978). The association is not fortuitous: there is a link in traditional Western paradisiac symbolism between the idea of Paradise and islands; the site of the original Earthly Paradise has often been imagined to be located on an island (Niederland 1957:56ff.). The modern touristic imagery of paradise has adopted this theme: touristic "paradises" are frequently located on islands.[72] Turner and Ash, discussing the paradisiac motive in modern mass tourism point out that "The most potent images of man's former-idyllic-natural state are located in islands: the homelands of the noble savage, the original sites of the Garden of Eden" (Turner and Ash 1975:151). And they continue: ". . . the image with the widest appeal is the simplest. This is still . . . the ideal of an isolated island life — that is, free from want . . . and free from sexual guilt. This is prelapsarian tourism. The people are innocent, uninhibited, ignorant of sexual vices, ignorant of money and politics: they are Rousseau's 'noble savages' " (ibid.:152). The paradisiac label has indeed been attached to a wide variety of island destinations — from the Seychelles and Bali to the Caribbean and the South Pacific (ibid.:151). The tourist industry both exploits and promotes the "paradisiac" appeal of these island destinations and directs to them a growing flow of paradise-seeking tourists. Remote and unknown destinations gain instant appeal by the evocation of the deep-seated, archetypal image of an "island paradise." The Pacific islands are one of the most outstanding examples of such an evocation and exploitation of an ancient theme for the development of modern tourist destinations; therefore they are eminently suited for a study of the transformation of the paradisiac theme in modern mass tourism.

The Pacific Islands as the Seat of Paradise — The History of a Mythical Image

The indigeneous cultures of the Pacific possess a rich paradisiac tradition of their own. The best known paradisiac myth belongs to Polynesia: it is the myth of Hawaiki, ". . . the source and origin of food, the paradisial land where food is abundantly available without labor . . ." (Orbell 1974:5). However, the paradisiac image which has been operative in the development of Pacific islands tourism was not the one indigenous to the region; neither did the islands consciously seek to project a paradisiac image upon the world. Rather, it is an image which, rooted in the Western imagination, has been projected upon them from afar.

It was the peculiar predicament of the Pacific islands that, long before the emergence of modern tourism — indeed even long before they had ever been uncovered to the eye of a Western traveller — they were already endowed in the Western imagination by the glamour and fascination of the site of the Earthly Paradise. When tourism to the Pacific islands region became a practical possibility in modern times, the alluring myth has thus already existed. It was only necessary to revive it, embellish it, and adapt it to modern needs by selecting, changing and even distorting the symbolic motives in the original image of paradise, and the ancient myth was adapted to the needs of modern tourism. The myth thus provided a connecting link between an ancient human theme and the modern touristic exploitation of the islands. In turn, the rapid growth of Pacific tourism, the patterns of touristic activities and behavior, and the changes which tourism wrought in the appearance of the Pacific islands and in the roles of their inhabitants vis-à-vis the tourists, have been profoundly influenced by that myth.

In order to understand the profound attraction of the Pacific islands for the modern consciousness, we shall review briefly the process through which they came to be endowed with the paradisiac image, and the changes which that image subsequently underwent.

In the long history of Western man's preoccupation with the paradisiac quest, the site of the Earthly Paradise was placed by imagination in a wide variety of locations, e.g. Mesopotamia, Palestine, India, Africa, etc. (Bloch 1959:Vol. 2, 873−929; Manuel and Manuel 1972; Sanford 1961). In the mediaeval Christian world, its site was most often deemed to be Jerusalem; but "Dante, assuming a spherical form of the earth, even relegated it to the *antipodes* of Jerusalem, into the South Sea" (Bloch 1959:Vol. 2, 890; my translation, author's emphasis). Thereby the paradisiac myth was linked to the myth of a South Continent, the Terra Australia Incognita, based on the speculation of ancient Greek geographers, the search for which provided such an important motive power for Pacific exploration up to Cook's days (see e.g. Day 1966, passim). Indeed, as discovery followed discovery and much of the geography of the globe became secularized, the alleged site of the Earthly Paradise was pushed into ever farther regions, until eventually the South Seas remained one of the last possible — because as yet unexplored — sites for its location. But even after the myth of a rich and fabulous South Continent was finally disproved, the paradisiac image continued to linger on, attaching itself henceforth to the Pacific islands world, this region of "unspoilt" nature where the "Noble Savage" continued to lead a pristine, edenic life, untouched by civilisation.[73] The conjunction of circumstances, by which Rousseau's idealistic view of the "Noble Savage" happened to find its apparent empirical counterpart in the Polynesian race discovered at about the same time (Wettlaufer 1973:2−3), probably contributed much to the perseverance of the myth. And thus it happened, in Eliade's words, that ". . . the myth of the Earthly Paradise has survived until today, in adopted form as an 'Oceanic paradise'; for the last hundred and fifty years all the great European literatures have vied with each other in exalting the paradisiac islands of the Pacific Ocean, havens of all happiness, although the reality was very different — 'flat and monotonous landscapes, unhealthy climates, ugly and obese women' etc . . . But the image of this 'Oceanic paradise' remained proof against geographical or any other realities. What had objective realities to do with the 'Oceanic paradise?' This was something of a theological order: it had received, assimilated and re-adapted all the paradisiac images repressed by positivism and scientism. The earthly Paradise still believed in by Christopher Columbus . . . turned into a South Sea island in the nineteenth century, but its function in the economy of the human psyche remained the same: over there, in the 'islands' in that 'paradise,' existence unfolded itself outside Time and History; man was happy, free and unconditioned; he did not have to work for his living; the women were young, eternally beautiful, and no 'law' hung heavily over their loves. Even nudity, in that distant isle, recovered its metaphysical meaning — that of perfect humanity, of Adam before the Fall. Geographical 'reality' might give the lie to that paradisiac landscape, ugly and corpulent women might confront the travellers' eyes; but, these they did not see; each one saw only the image he had brought with him" (Eliade 1969a:11–12). The Western image of a South Seas paradise apparently drew heavily upon an early pagan tradition rather than the mainstream Christian one: as Bloch has pointed out, it had a pronounced orgiastic character; it is a prime example of what he called the "animalistic paradise" (Bloch 1959:Vol. 2:911). In the image of the South Seas paradise, the natural, creaturely, rather than the sublime, facet of the original paradisiac symbol predominated: it is the alluring Other, rather than the august Center.

Historically, the image of the Pacific islands in Western eyes went through a series of modifications from the period of exploration up to the era of modern tourism; these were primarily a result of the interplay between the reports of explorers, travellers and writers and the changing ideas on primitive man in Western thought (Wettlaufer 1973). Toward the end of the 19th century, life on the Pacific islands was popularised through the work of artists and writers such as Robert Louis Stevenson, Herman Melville, Paul Gaugin, Pierre Loti, Mark Twain and Jack London (Doumenge 1966:561). Though most of these went to the Pacific in search of paradise, they soon became acutely aware of the changes which swept through the region in the wake of colonialism and which threatened, damaged or, in some cases, even utterly destroyed its "paradisiac" qualities. The net effect of their work, however, has been to revive or awaken the awareness of and longing for the Pacific islands among ever broader social strata, whose romantic impulses to visit the islands were given added urgency by the fear lest their paradisiac qualities disappear completely before they have succeeded to realize their desire. The work of these writers and artists served to popularize the Pacific islands among the modern reading public, and thus to provide a bridge between the paradisiac imagery of the Pacific islands as derived from mediaeval mythology and the image of the South Seas paradise as advertised in the modern mass media. Though many of them were "existential" tourists, for whom the Pacific islands were an "elective Center" (Chapter 5), their work served to spur the less lofty desire for "diversionary" and "recreational" tourism among the modern Western mass travelling public. Twain's and London's influence was probably directly responsible for the opening up of Hawaii as a tourist destination (Day 1965:15; Lind 1969:35–36).[74] But the influence of the other writers and artists, particularly Gaugin, is undoubtable. The popularisation of the Pacific in the literature and the arts, moreover, continued well into the 20th century.[75] Popular works, and particularly Michener's *Tales of the South Pacific*, which was made by Rogers and Hammerstein into the hit musical *South Pacific* in the early 1950s, helped both to acquaint large numbers of people with the paradisiac image of the Pacific, as well as to vulgarize it. An even more simplistic image of the Pacific islands was disseminated by the modern mass media in innumerable travel books, articles in travel magazines, newspapers and TV features and took hold of the popular consciousness. This image of the region is the one which most rank-and-file members of modern Western societies entertain. It may well be the case that even in this image there are hidden, on a deep-structural level, general human mythic themes; but in its overt manifestations the prevalent image of the Pacific islands is an impoverished, univocal version of the traditional paradisiac myth.

As the tourist industry penetrated the Pacific islands, it was able to build its advertisement campaign on the image, widespread among its potential customers, of the Pacific islands ". . . as a paradise of flowers and beautiful girls. These destinations, potential visitors believe, are lands of perpetual sunshine and cool ocean breezes, where work is unnecessary, and where smiling natives pass their time singing and dancing" (Crampon *et al.* 1972:23).

But while this image spread into ever broader social strata, the region itself underwent further important changes. The distance between image and reality grew progressively more and more acute. Hence, as it was building upon and further disseminating that image, the tourist industry was also forced to readapt reality to that image and thus insure that the product it advertises be actually identifiable by and available to its consumers.

The paradisiac image is the most prevalent and popular, but not the only image of the Pacific islands in the modern Western imagination. Shading off from it, and, in the extreme, contrasting it, is the less widespread but powerful image of uncouth, primitive wilderness. Against the paradisiac image of the innocent primitive, leading a careless, leisurely life on lush, palmy islands under an eternal sun, feasting and love-making, the image of wilderness conjures up the themes of primaeval savagery and cannibalism, of uncivilized man and untamed nature, of mysterious dangers lurking in dark jungle forests. The "heaven" of a pagan, sensual paradise is contrasted by a savage, chaotic "hell."[76] It reflects the malignant, threatening but fascinating aspect of the Other. This image of Pacific islands, like its paradisiac counterpart, is also deeply rooted in the Western imagination. The actual experiences of the early travellers in the region often contradicted whatever preconceived paradisiac ideas they might have arrived with. The severe hardships which most of them suffered through, and the dire end some found in fierce encounters with "savage" natives, most prominently one of the earliest explorers of the Pacific, Mendana, the discoverer of the "Isles of Solomon" (Beaglehole 1966:57) and the most famous Pacific explorer, Captain Cook (Beaglehole 1974:648−672) — well illustrate this contradiction. Attempting to accommodate the contradiction between the paradisiac image and harsh reality, European thinkers later proposed a distinction along geographical and cultural lines: "soft" primitivism was distinguished from the "harder" variety, and the balmness vs. harshness of climate was made responsible for the difference (Wettlaufter 1973:5, 7). While the paradisiac image stuck to northern Polynesia, the image of natural and human savagery was associated especially with Melanesia, and within that area particularly with Papua-New Guinea, a land characterized by a modern author as "... a jungled, mountainous nightmare ..." (Ryan 1969:3). The image of Melanesia as a green hell was considerably reinforced by the experience of the American forces during the Second World War in the Solomons; savage fighting combined with a difficult climate cast upon these islands a hellish image of untamable wilderness, "... a vision of wet, unhealthy unplacably savage jungles" (Brockfield and Hart 1971:LVIII), contrasting sharply with the paradisiac image of Polynesia. The writings of war-authors, particularly Normal Mailer, served to reinforce and popularize that image. Indeed, the changes which the war had brought were so pernicious, that a commentator claimed, immediately after it ended, that as a result of its impact, "The South Sea paradise of the nineteenth-century romanticists, much changed in the past three or four decades, is now gone forever" (Coulter 1946:419). Nevertheless, the war also popularized the Pacific region among the troops. And as the horror of the war experiences gradually faded away,[77] the reconstruction of the area combined with insiduous touristic advertisement, soon enough revived the paradisiac image.

While it may be granted that the paradisiac image possesses considerable powers of attraction for tourism, the image of wilderness and savagery apparently repulses, rather than attracts. It turns out, however, that this is not always the case. Wilderness, dark, chaotic and dangerous, may also be fascinating and challenging to the adventurous traveller. Adroitly manipulated by the tourist industry and its advertising agencies, the image of wilderness and savagery can be exploited to generate tourism, though its attractiveness is much more limited than that of "paradise" and bespeaks only a small public of adventure-seeking tourists. Thus, a report on the development of tourism in the region states that "... many potential pleasure visitors in America believe New Guinea to be a land of wild head-hunters. It makes absolutely no difference whether or not this is an accurate description of New Guinea; that it is believed will produce the image. While this image may frighten many into avoiding this island, there exist others who would visit New Guinea in hopes of seeing and photographing a 'stone-age man' " (Crampon *et al.* 1972:22). The area can thus be made attractive as offering the unique opportunity of seeing exotic "picturesque savages" (Tudor 1966:125), which cannot be found anymore anywhere else in the contemporary world: "It is ... one of the last frontiers of primitive man. It is still possible to take a plane journey of one or two hours from a coastal point and to travel back thousands of years in time to see Stone Age man living in the same fashion as our own remote ancestors probably once did" (Tudor (ed.) 1966:206). Such an image attracts "ethnic tourism," which is ". . . marketed to the public in terms of the 'quaint' customs of indigenous and often exotic peoples" (Smith 1977:2). While such tourism may be sometimes motivated by popular scientific interests, found, e.g. among teachers and students, it also relates to one aspect of the "paradisiac" image — namely that of "natural" man, living in the wilderness, untinged by "civilization."

While the two images of the Pacific islands as paradise and as wilderness or even hell stand in sharp contrast, they are also complementary. Turner and Ash pointed out, perhaps somewhat simplistically, that "The trouble with paradise is that it soon becomes boring . . . The human mind seems unable to conceive of any purely pleasurable activity (or blissful inactivity) that would not eventually pale. We should not expect the tourist industry to have solved the problem that has defeated the world's theologians — even if it does claim to offer us a variety of paradises to suit every pocket" (Turner and Ash 1975:167–168). To get away from the boredom, some tourists seek action — and they may find it in the challenges of wilderness. According to Turner and Ash, in contrast to the ordinary paradise-seeking mass tourist, "Perhaps the real avantgarde of 1970s tourism are those who seek the genuine primitive — who seek barbarity and, in Barthe's phrase, 'everything that is contrary to the bliss of travel' " (ibid.:170). To illustrate this type of tourism, they report that Cook's in 1972 organized ". . . a 'tribal tour' of New Guinea. In this tour the tourist has arrogated the role of the explorer and the anthropologist. The discomforts of tropical exploration are deliberately sought out. The tour involved walking for 100 miles through difficult terrain, including dense jungle *in the rainy season*. Also included were visits to tribes who have had little or no previous contact with white people — among them the Biami, a cannibal tribe with a war-like reputation"(ibid.:170, italics in the original). Summing up, the authors point out the contrast between this kind of tour and the quest for paradise and dwell upon the type of motives which possibly impel the hell-seeking tourist: "Instead of the conventional idyll with charming and friendly natives Cook's have offered a return to a violent and barbaric Stone Age and found a ready market. This would suggest a decadent and voyeuristic attitude on the part of their clients, recalling the Roman fascination with Barbarians and violence; it is, perhaps, a case of the bourgeoisie in search of 'The Other' " (ibid.:170–171).

Whatever its motives may be, however, this type of tourism is limited in scope — it is certainly not attractive to the mass-travelling public looking for a comfortable, enjoyable holiday. Hence, those Pacific island territories which approximate the image of wilderness and savagery most closely, encounter a problem: discussing tourism in East New Guinea, Brookfield and Hart (1971:379) remark that

"Presenting East New Guinea as a harsh, primitive country . . . government and publicists find it hard also to present the country as having the charm, sophisticated facilities and ease of circulation beloved of a majority of tourists." The tourist industry found it much easier to exploit the ready-made myth of the "South Seas Paradise," attaching primarily to Polynesia, than the image of untamable wilderness associated with Melanesia. The paradisiac image appeals to the majority of tourists and is hence emphasized by the industry for the area as a whole and tends to overshadow that of savage wilderness. The industry is helped by the fact that the sub-regions of Polynesia and Melanesia are not sharply distinguished in the mind of the average potential tourist; as Brookfield and Hart (1971:LVIII) remark: "The myth of the 'island paradise' belongs to Polynesia rather than Melanesia, but it tends to waft over the ethnic border, eagerly fanned along by tourist publicity in recent years." Indeed, in Fiji one of the consequences of the domination of the paradisiac image is a gradual "pseudo-Polynesation of Melanesian-Fijian culture" (ibid.:378).

Though the paradisiac image is not the only one employed by the tourist industry to propagate the Pacific islands, it is certainly the dominant one; and as Brookfield and Hart have pointed out, it encroaches even upon those areas which are in reality closer to a green hell than to paradise. The standardization of this image by the industry and the transformation of Pacific island reality in its terms is hence the major theme of our analysis.

The Touristic Paradise in the Pacific Islands: The Standardization of the Image and the Transformation of Reality

The Pacific island "paradise" exerts a powerful attraction for many Westerners, particularly members of the younger generation, who, alienated from the modern industrial world, depart in search of an "elective center" in the islands. As in other parts of the less developed world, "experimental" and "existential" tourists can be found on many remote islands, living in native villages or in simple resorts. Indeed, in the Pacific, like elsewhere (cf. Cohen 1982b), simple, small-scale "bungalow" resorts proliferated to attract this type of tourists, and its fellow-travellers, the "mass-drifters" (Chapter 4). Our concern here, however, is with the older, middle-class mass tourists, who, following in the wake of the drifters, are often less discriminating and less "authenticity-seeking," demand greater comfort and are able to pay for it. For many of these ". . . the ideal earthly paradise may combine natural or rural charm with urban convenience" (Lewis and Brissett 1981:87); hence, they have a profound transformational impact on touristic localities on the islands.[78] It is this kind of tourist which most Pacific island governments wish to attract to strengthen their economy.

As the "paradisiac" image of the Pacific islands gained widespread popularity and became a trade-mark of Pacific tourism, there was a rush by most territories in the region into the paradisiac bandwagon. As more and more remote islands were drawn into the tourist orbit by their desire for new sources of income and foreign currency and by the prodding of outside entrepreneurs, there is hardly an island left which has not been advertised as a "paradise" in the media. Special efforts are made to nurture and disseminate the paradisiac image of late arrivals at the tourist scene. Thus, it was reported that, with the opening of the Cook Islands to tourism "Air New Zealand is . . . flying in as guests tour-promoters and journalists, who are now prepared to write up the Cooks as the last Paradise in the Pacific" (Carter 1974:117).

The attractiveness of a destination depends, to an extent, on its real or imagined distinctiveness. But once a group of destinations is perceived as offering a certain type of attractions, competition between them works not to diversify, but to standardize their particular images, as they vie with each other to approximate most closely the general image of the attraction prevalent in the popular mind. Modern advertising media greatly assist this process of standardization, by creating a widely-disseminated, popular and often product-like image of the attraction. They provide, as it were, the guide-lines which have then to be followed by particular potential destinations if they want to partake in the benefits generated by the general image popularized in the media. Advertising also tends to simplify the image; a product is most effectively marketed if its image is reduced to a few easily recognizable, basic traits. Tourist destinations are, in this respect, similar to any other product. And when the product happens to be "paradise," the original multivocal symbol is simplified, often to the point of caricature, into a univocal product-like image. It is transformed into a stereotype with fixed and concrete traits. This stereotype in turn becomes the criterion by which the "paradisiac" qualities of any particular location will be judged, and which aspiring "paradisiac" destinations will strive to reproduce. This product-like image is almost schematically outlined in an Air New Zealand report on tourist development in Rarotonga (the Cook Islands): "The stereotype consists of a vision of a small island; palm trees waving in trade wind, with white coral, sandy beaches, a quiet island-studded lagoon and the surf pounding against the off-shore coral reef . . . Hills clothed in green vegetation rise to a deep blue sky. Inside the reef there is light green water and outside it the deepest blue imaginable. Friendly people, who welcome strangers with dancing, singing and leis, complete the picture" (Air New Zealand 1968:13).

Those islands which happen to possess the qualities advertised in the stereo-typical image are lucky in that they are able to cash in on it directly. Those islands, in which reality differs markedly from the image, are forced to replicate "paradise" artificially. As a consequence, the touristic areas of the islands come more and more to resemble one another. The process of "transformation of attractions" (Chapter 3) sets in: the touristic areas on the islands take on a standard appearance, corresponding to the standardized image of "paradise" and thus become a recognizable, interchangeable, easily marketable touristic commodity.

Generally speaking, those Pacific islands which are less developed, small and remote from the major Pacific communication routes, have usually preserved their "unspoilt" appearance, and thus most closely approximate the stereotype. Thus, the report on Rarotonga quoted above states that "Rarotonga measures up very well indeed to tourist expectations for it meets exactly the things people will expect of it. This can be capitalized on in both publicity and visitor satisfaction" (Air New Zealand 1968:14). And the first mass tourists who reached the Cooks are said to have confirmed ". . . that it is (sic!) indeed a miniature Tahiti-before-tourism, an island world that gives fresh meaning to such old cliches as beautiful, unspoiled and Eden-like" (PTN 1974:54). Similarly, the remote Yap islands in Micronesia, are said to ". . . exhibit almost all the elements which combine in the minds of most people to form a picture of a typical south seas island . . ." (Econ. Dev. Plan for Micronesia 1966:386). Even southern Viti Levu, in much more developed Fiji, in 1966 still presented "A real landscape of the South Seas as expected by the tourist" (Doumenge 1966:664; my translation); while "Fiji's Lau Islands . . . could be called the ultimate in a getting-away-from-it-all. Each is a Garden of Eden" (Barker 1970:33).

Turner and Ash (1975:164) relate that "In a recent series of articles in The Sunday Mirror the Marquesas Islands were described as 'paradises of sex' "; and the authors point out that "In this case it would seem that the conventionalized image promoted by the tourist industry is reasonably close to truth . . ." (ibid.:164), contrary to what seems generally to be the case with travel features or tourist advertisements.

In cases such as these not much prevarication is needed to meet tourist expec-tations; at most some selectivity might be practiced in the choice of tourist routes and sites so that the tourist will not become aware of the less "paradisiac" aspects and areas of the contemporary reality of these islands. Paradoxically, however, touristic development of an island necessarily reduces its "paradisiac" qualities. This reduction is effected by the logistics of mass tourism as well as the desires of the mass tourists themselves. Thus, a report on Tahiti by a consulting firm states ex-pressly: "The future of tourism in French Polynesia depends upon the continuation of the 'image,' but the 'island paradise' must provide the amenities and comforts that today's traveler has come to expect" (Harris *et al.* 1970:11−26). Though a minority of tourists may prefer the studied primitivism of the Club Méditerranée or similar resorts whose major attraction is a simple life close to nature and resembling that of the natives,[79] the enjoyability of paradise for the great majority of mass tourists is contingent upon the existence of such amenities, which provide them with an "environmental bubble" (Chapter 3), which partially replicates the amenities of their home environment and from the comforts of which they are able to enjoy the "paradise" around: "Many foreign tourists are usually more than willing to do some things 'Fa'a Samoa' (The Samoan way) but where this personal cost extends to staying in a true Samoa fale, lacking the privacy and comforts to which he is accustomed . . . the tourist would probably rebel" (Crampon *et al.* 1972:28). While the "paradisiac" qualities of simplicity and "naturalness" may be symbolized in the style of tourist facilities and in the costumes of the service personnel, they are meant mainly to flavor the tourists' experience, but are not intended seriously to interfere with the mass tourists' accustomed way of life.

Insofar as the tourist industry equips its "paradisiac" resorts with modern amenities, makes them accessible and well-serviced through a modern infrastructure and employs locals in service jobs, it is essentially transformational in character. Directly or indirectly, it helps to develop the area and despoil pristine nature and simple lifeways, thus contributing in fact to the gradual removal of island reality from the idyllic image projected upon it. However, in order to safeguard their tourist industry, the islands have to live up to the image they project. This becomes the more difficult, the greater the gap between the image and reality. Thus some ". . . destinations are having a problem producing the promised 'happy lazy natives,' if they ever existed at all" (Crampon *et al.* 1972:112). Where it does not exist any more, paradise has to be deliberately contrived. As a consequence, the more touristically developed an island, and the larger the number of mass tourists visiting it, the less authentic the "paradise" which it offers. "Tourist space" (MacCannell 1973) is constructed and inserted between the tourist and the real, daily life of the local population. This is particularly the case in the touristically most developed Pacific territories, which enjoy the greatest reputation as veritable "South Seas Paradises": Hawaii, Tahiti and even Fiji. Here, the paradisiac image is often not born out any more by undoctored nature and by the ordinary daily life of the local people. Though "to those who dwell in the darker cities of the North, Hawaii beckons as the lost Eden of innocence and freedom, at the edge of the horizon, only a plane ride away" (Kent 1975:169), the reality of contemporary Hawaii is far removed from that image, as Kent amply documents in his article. The same conflict between image and reality was pointed out even earlier by Huetz de Lemps, who talks about an unreal ". . . touristic image of Hawaii, 'islands of the South Seas,' which is, however, today quite removed from geographical reality" (Huetz de Lemps 1964:29;

my translation). Names like Honolulu and Waikiki Beach may call forth images of ". . . an insular paradise lost in the Pacific, whereas the waterfront of Waikiki singularly resembles, with its big buildings, that of Miami Beach" (ibid.:24; my translation); to this should be added that ". . . a dense cloud of Los Angeles-style smog frequently shrouds the sunshine resort" and ". . . the polluted coastal waters display a whole spectrum of colors other than azure" (Turner and Ash 1975:161). The irony is that, though some authentic Old Hawaiian landscapes and localities still exist, e.g. fishing villages populated only by Hawaiians, these are not readily accessible to the ordinary tourist, transportation being so difficult, that ". . . you have to have a four-wheel drive, know somebody, and borrow a couple of gate keys to get to any of them"(Simpich 1971:100−101).[80] Lacking access to such places, the contemporary mass tourists are made to do with experiences and views of "paradise" contrived and staged especially for them, on a huge industrialized scale. In the most extreme cases, the tourists are processed through a series of non-authentic experiences, starting with a contrived "Hawaiian" welcome, their fake "transformation" into "Hawaiians" (Huetz de Lemps 1964:23), the performance of specially staged Hawaiian dances such as the "Kodak hula show" (ibid.:23), and visits to the Ulu Mau Hawala Village (ibid.:24), especially constructed for the benefit of tourists, as well as to a variety of festivals invented for their enjoyment (ibid.:53). Hence the visit of the mass tourist to the paradise of Hawaii actually takes on the form of "entertainment," more akin in nature to other forms of mass-recreation, like film or TV, than of a visit to a "real" place.[81]

The case of Tahiti is similar to that of Hawaii though somewhat less extreme: Tahiti is still one of the most highly reputed Pacific "paradises," the marketing program for which could be easily based on the image of an "unspoilt, tropical paradise" (Harris *et al.* 1970:X-2); however, it is also a territory whose "paradisiac" qualities were the earliest to be discovered and exploited by Western travellers. Its long and intense contact with the modern world and especially with French culture, has almost completely transformed it. Contemporary Tahiti is immensely more developed and sophisticated than most of the remoter, smaller and lesser known Pacific islands; hence, it is suffering from an acute discrepancy between its well-known "paradisiac" image and its present-day reality. Thomson and Adloff discuss this state of affairs at length: "[The] insouciant and pleasure-loving attitude [of the Tahitian natives] has been one of the islanders' main attractions for foreigners, and therein lies the crux of the problem. The development of tourism . . . depends largely on maintaining the traditional Polynesian ambience . . . Yet the Polynesians are now succumbing to some of the material aspects of that civilization which they have come to enjoy as a by-product of the activity of the C. E. P. (Centre d'Expérimentation du Pacifique). After years of being forced on the road of modernization . . . the Polynesians are now moving voluntarily in that direction. It is ironic that in so doing they are jeopardizing the very asset that had drawn tourists to the islands, and thus risk drying up the source of funds most likely to provide them with the means of acquiring the material things that they have come to want" (Thompson and Adloff 1971:87). Other authors concur with this analysis. Thus, Donehower points out the discrepancy between the touristic image of Tahiti and reality: "Most Frenchmen dream of visiting Tahiti . . . yet as the legend of Hawaii is lost in the cement jungle of Waikiki, so falls *le mythe Tahitian* with the unpleasant welcome accorded to French sailors and the sorry state of 'romantic Papeete' " (Donehower 1969:72). In a similar vein, a report prepared by a planning and consulting agency warns that, "Even the mere mention of the names of Tahiti, Moorea and Bora Bora is enough to conjure up in most of us exotic images of a tropical paradise as depicted by such earlier travellers as Stevenson, Loti and Gauguin. The arriving tourist, therefore, has a preconceived notion of this tropical paradise, and although willing to find himself mistaken in certain aspects of this romanticised image, the tourist is not so forgiving where he is wrong in his image of the islands and their people. There is apparent initial lack of 'product identification' " (Harris *et al.* 1970:II–25). The problem is particularly acute at the early stages of the tourists' arrival, before the tourist is safely ensconced in one of the segregated paradisiac resorts. The authors therefore go on to make concrete suggestions as to how such a "product identification" could be accomplished: "Many areas with distinctive cultural patterns receive their arriving tourists in a manner typical to the culture of the country. If such a cultural pattern is lacking, one is created. This may appear to many purists to be influenced too much by Hollywood; however, it is just such procedures that build a country's reputation for friendly hospitality" (ibid.:X-20). In this manner a paradise once lost will be artificially reproduced for tourist consumption.

A similar tendency to contrive "paradise" can be observed in Fiji: "Prospective tourists are introduced to the 'sun-drenched' South Pacific where man's (sic!) longing for a Paradise, where nature and man are in harmony and where peace comes true. They are told that in Fiji they can see the Fijian natives dressed in their grass-skirts and performing their war dances, both of which they in fact abandoned generations ago" (Fong 1973:27). But the skirts are worn and the dances are danced in performances staged for the tourists, often in hotel lobbies or on the decks of visiting luxury cruisers.

The most developed touristic "paradises" in the Pacific islands are thus also those which demonstrate most clearly the ultimate disenchantment of paradise and its transformation from utopian myth into a consumer product: when Pacific realities cease to correspond to the standardized image, they have to be artificially adapted to that image, so as not to disappoint the tourist, since the continued flow of tourists depends on the availability of attractions which correspond to the preconceived image. Tourism in the Pacific islands hence closely approximates to what Boorstin (1964) so aptly called a "pseudo-event": first, an image, made ever more unrealistic as the development of tourism progresses, is projected upon the islands; then, selected aspects of island life and appearance are transformed in accordance with the image, while the natives, whose life has often been substantially changed through contact with the tourist industry, learn to play the role of "happy natives," in order to conform to tourist expectations. Crocombe is hence not far from the mark when he proclaims that ". . . the current trend in the tourist industry is to turn the Pacific islands into a great Disneyland and the islanders into well-trained puppets where life and behavior are to be fashioned to fulfill the dream expectations of the travelling public from the richest nations" (Crocombe 1973:94).

Conclusion

In this chapter I explored the processes through which the ancient paradisiac symbol has been transformed and, as it were, disenchanted, in the course of its application for the enhancement of the attractiveness of touristic destinations on the Pacific islands.

The existence of potential touristic attractions and even the provision of adequate touristic facilities in a region which has not yet been opened to mass tourism do not in themselves guarantee its attractiveness for tourists. As any expert in marketing knows, a new product has to penetrate into the consciousness, and even the sub-conscious, of potential buyers in order to "sell." In tourism, a region is "sold" through the creation of a magnetic and powerful image,[82] compelling enough to fire the imagination and awaken the desire of people to travel to a new, remote and hitherto unfashionable tourist destination. The ancient myth of the Earthly Paradise has endowed the Pacific islands even before the advent of modern tourism with an enchanting mystique which has assisted the tourist industry in its endeavor to promote them as one of the last surviving "paradises" on earth and to introduce them thereby into the mainstream of international tourism. The islands were thus made into the refuge of the unfulfilled desires and fantasies of modern man. In an act of "cultural imperialism," they were incorporated into what Turner and Ash aptly termed the "pleasure periphery" of the modern, industrialized world (Turner and Ash 1975:160). In the process, both the symbol and the island destinations themselves were transformed. The complex symbol of paradise lost much of its multivocality and became essentially univocal: while the significance of "paradise" as a sublime socio-moral Center was largely discarded, its other major facet, that of the Other, in its benevolent aspect, gained emphasis; even here, however, the themes of naturalness and the unmitigated fulfillment of creaturely pleasures are emphasized, rather than that of primordial unity. Moreover, unlike in the paradise of religion, this naturalness and creatureliness remain unredeemed by any emphasis on a divine presence. The connection to the Center has been undone; the touristic paradise is a marginal paradise.

It will be remembered that the Other has another, malignant but fascinating aspect, finding its fullest expression in the symbol of Hell. While some earlier travellers in the Pacific and soldiers in the Second World War tended to see the region as hell rather than as paradise, this image had only a minor impact upon tourism; it is used mainly to attract more adventurous travellers to a limited number of destinations. The vast majority are presented as inviting touristic "paradises." Indeed, the paradisiac image of the Pacific islands is assiduously nurtured and promoted by the tourist industry. It has been concretized and standardized by the industry, and imposed as a trade mark on the Pacific Islands and its often unsuspecting native population. Having so transformed the image, the industry moved to seek out ever remoter, as yet "unspoilt" islands, which could be trumped-up in well-conducted advertisement campaigns as newly discovered paradises.

Ironically, the reality of the Pacific islands changed rapidly, even as they were proclaimed by the industry as the last paradisiac refuges: the forces of modernity, sometimes introduced by the tourist industry itself, penetrated ever deeper the more mature Pacific destinations and thus progressively removed their reality from the paradisiac image. The industry hence set out to remake these destinations artificially, so that they will anew correspond to the image. This produced a paradoxical situation: while the initial attractiveness of the Pacific islands consisted precisely in their pristine, unspoilt "naturalness," at present such naturalness has often to be contrived artificially to maintain their attractiveness. Through such efforts, isolated, tightly bounded "tourist paradises" were created, remote from the contemporary reality of life in the islands (Turner and Ash 1975:153). "Paradise" thus becomes a consumer product, compactly produced to the specifications of the tourist industry to correspond to the current consumer demand. A corollary of this development is that the "paradisiac" localities, the Pacific tourist destinations, become physically and socially segregated from the actual life and problems of the islands in the contemporary world.

Even as efforts are made to adapt Pacific destinations to the paradisiac image, forces are at work which again undo the correspondence. The more commercialized a destination becomes, the more the "naturalness" and "pristinity" of its appearance is infringed by the establishment of facilities serving the tourists. Such facilities usuallly create an "environmental bubble" (Chapter 3) of the tourists' home environment — a chunk, as it were, of their own, familiar world, intended to mitigate, and make more enjoyable, the unaccustomed "paradisiac" surroundings. A developed touristic paradise is a paradise with all modern comforts.

A considerable gap thus emerges between the image of enchanted, magical islands conjured up in the touristic advertisements and the actual reality of commercialized "paradisiac" resorts. How could the industry get away with this discrepancy and continue to attract customers despite the growing gap between image and reality?

This brings us back to the problem of the extent to which the modern mass tourist seeks "authenticity." I have claimed above that most of these tourists travel in either the "experiential" mode — seeking to experience the authentic life of others — or in the "recreational" or "diversionary" modes — seeking pleasurable experiences, without, at least on the conscious level, caring much about the authenticity of the "paradisiac" destination. Accordingly, two approaches to the above problem can be formulated, depending on one's view as to which of these modes of de-sired experience prevails in the mass traveling public. The first approach, assuming with MacCannell that the majority of mass tourists travels in the experiential mode, would claim that the whole enterprise of Pacific tourism is in fact a colossal exercise in "staged authenticity," a tremendous deceit, in which otherwise easily recogniz-able fabrications are held forth, and are accepted in good faith, as the "real thing." A superficial, credulous public is tricked into accepting a contraption as reality.

The second approach, assuming that the majority of mass tourists travel in the recreational or diversionary mode would claim that the whole enterprise of Pacific tourism is nothing but "the greatest show on earth," pleasurable to the tourist who in fact connives with the tourist establishment in the creation of the "paradisiac" illusion. According to this view, the approach of the mass tourist to the paradisiac destinations in the Pacific, is akin to his approach to any other form of mass entertainment: it is a make-believe, enjoyable, but manifestly not part of reality.

In the absence of any reliable empirical data, no definite decision can be made between these contrasting interpretations of the nature of Pacific tourism. Indeed, if anything, our study indicates the need for in-depth investigations of the moods and motivations underlying tourism and their significance within the context of the tourists' life-situation.

I myself tend towards the second view, agreeing wit Huetz de Lemps (1964:28) that ". . . the [mass] tourist is not an ethnologist or historian infatuated by authentic-ity" (my translation). Indeed, it is difficult to imagine, MacCannell notwithstand-ing, that millions of tourists would, e.g. visit Hawaii and be processed through the tourist system unaware of the fact that they are participating in a show. It seems to me that mass tourism of the Hawaiian type can flourish only when there exists a tacit connivance between the visitor and the tourist industry. To argue otherwise, we would have to assume, in view of the manifest inauthenticity of the most highly frequented — and hence most commercialized — touristic paradise in the Pacific, that the modern mass tourist is stupid or gullible to an unbelievable degree. One may agree with Crocombe, who has claimed, regarding tourism in the Pacific, that "... most tourists are prepared to pay to have the images that the travel industry has trained them to expect, revealed to them and their cameras — even though double deception is necessary to artificially satisfy the artificial demand" (Crocombe 1973:80). But, in order to understand the mass tourist phenomenon, one has to realize that most tourists are rather willingly deceived, in the same sense in which a degree of self-deception has to be half-consciously induced for the reader or the viewer to enjoy a thriller or a show. The tourist's self-deception is not fully serious; rather, he is aware of the fact that he participates in a game, for the success of which it is imperative that the illusion be accepted as if it were the reality.

Owing to this circumstance, the task of contriving "paradise," facing the tourist industry, is much facilitated — since it is not dealing with a suspicious, questioning public, but with an acquiescent one, willing, even eager, to participate in the tourist game; there is no need for elaborate, costly deceptions. Like in a theater, a few props will suffice to create the illusion. Since few care to leave the touristic "paradises" during their sojourn, they will savour the contraption while remaining unaware or oblivious to the reality beyond (Cohen 1982b). Some tourists may even consciously avoid it, so as not to dispel the paradisiac illusion. A minority of mass tourists, desirous of a more "authentic" experience of primitiveness, will be dissatisfied or repelled by the "touristic paradises" with all the modern amenities and depart on a quest further afield. Even here, however, there are gradations. Some may find their happiness in the staged simplicity of "primitive resorts" of the Club Méditerranée type, where instead of observing the natives they themselves playfully "go native" (Turner and Ash 1975:108–109). The more adventurous or enterprising seekers, finally, may penetrate beyond the limits of the tourist sphere, to the as yet touristically unpenetrated islands. Particularly the "experimental" or "existential" tourists may venture far afield, to the remote, smaller islands, peripheral to the centers of the Pacific island groups (e.g. Blakeway 1980). The impecunious travellers may seek to live the simple life of the natives, while the well-to-do may carve out for themselves a little "paradise" of their own, as did Marlon Brando on Tetiaroa in French Polynesia (*Time Magazine* 1976b).

To sum up, the tourist industry plays upon and exploits the hidden desires of modern man, by tantalizing his imagination with the prospect of the realization of his paradisiac dreams; but it is precisely because in the modern consciousness the quest for paradise ceased to be a pursuit of a Center, that the paradisiac quest of most mass tourists is relatively easily satisfied with the commercialized "paradises" he is offered.

The very success of the tourist industry depends upon the willing participation of the tourists in the game of delusion; most tourists are, in a sense, "accomplices" of the tourist industry in their own half-serious deception. While the minority, those who more seriously seek authenticity, are either duped by the staged version of paradise or try to escape the tourist system altogether to become "counter-cultural" tourists.

It was John Guise who "...has pointed out that the tourist industry invests vast sums on the planned creation of largely spurious images of primitive men, condescending notions of simplicity and the exaggeration of differences. *The foreign visitors are seduced into becoming a participant in the myth so created*" (Crocombe 1973:92, my italics). The projection and maintenance of the South Seas "paradise" image is, hence, a three way game, played between the tourist industry, the islanders and the tourists themselves. But it is a game whose rules are largely set by the industry, since it is the industry which avails itself of the image, propagates and exploits it, bending it to its own purposes; it is the industry which fosters tourist demand for Pacific islands "paradises" and which, when conveniently located "paradises" are in short supply, contrives artificial ones to satisfy consumer demand.

Acknowledgment—The data for this chapter have been collected in 1974 and 1975, during two single-term guest-appointments at the School of Social and Economic Development, The University of the South Pacific in Suva, Fiji. Thanks are due to E. Ben Ari, J. Ben-David, J. Dolgin, S.N. Eisenstadt, N.H.H. Graburn and D. Handelman for their useful comments on an earlier draft of this chapter.

Chapter 17

Hunter-gatherer Tourism in Thailand

Introduction

'Unknown Thailand'
Discover it with us!
'Phi Thong Luang'
... or 'Forest people' is the name of a tribal folk,
inhabiting the jungle of Nan province ...
Five times a week from Bangkok
You can visit this tribe in the North of Thailand!
(From an advertisement in: *Reisen in Thailand* 1988, translated by
the author.)

Legalized murder
Taking only what they need to survive, the Mlabris have been roaming through northern Thailand for centuries. They still survive, no thanks to modern day man, living from day to day, place to place.

They live in harmony with nature, taking only what they need. They do not slash or burn, nor do they deplete wildlife to the point of extinction. When it becomes difficult to find food in the area they live, they move on ... allowing nature to regenerate itself and allowing the wild life levels to be replenished for future use ...

These people of the forest survived for centuries in this manner, but now only a few remain. Hunted down and murdered by other people, thinking they are animals, chased from their environment to make place for plantations, or as forests are cut down for their precious wood. They have nowhere to go as their natural domain is being depleted in search of profit. The Mlabris believe that they will die before the forest, and that death is now coming close as unscrupulous businessmen seek to increase their profits to the detriment of a people who have learned to live with nature.

(From an advertisement sponsored by Grey Thailand as part of an environmental awareness campaign, *Bangkok Post* 1992.)

Hunter-gatherers and Tourism

The nostalgic yearning for our beginnings, for the roots or origins of our modern human existence is, according to some authors (Eliade 1963) a powerful mythical and religious motif; it is also a potent touristic motivation of moderns, expressed in the quest for the primitive and more extremely, the primitive savage.

The fulfilment of this quest consists in meeting people who, while they represent the inversion of modern man, the "Other," also facilitate the realization by moderns of their own original nature. The quest, once it becomes institutionalized in organized "Cannibal Tours" (Bruner 1989; MacCannell 1992) may take on banal or even grotesque traits, but these do not necessarily deny the nature of the participants' quest.

In Thailand, the touristic quest for the primitive and its extension, the exotic, has been oriented primarily to the so-called "hill tribes" (Cohen 1996a; Dearden 1991, 1994; Michaud 1993). The number of these has been formally fixed at six (Lewis and Lewis 1984; Manndorf 1962) for many years, but was recently expanded to nine (Thaitawat 1990b). However, all of these groups, though often labelled "primitive," possess a complex culture and history: they are dressed in colourful and richly ornamented costumes and engage in agricultural pursuits. Though they were in the past shifting mountain rice cultivators (Kunstadter and Chapman 1978), most are by now settled in permanent villages. Hence they do not fully correspond to the general stereotype of the "primitive savage" and are hardly representative of that "Other" in whom the tourist could recognize his own original roots.

However, there are in Thailand some other small groups which come closer than the hill tribes to the image of the primitive savage. These are the small remnants of what could be broadly defined as hunter-gatherer people, of which there are three different groups in Thailand, each consisting of several bands. These groups were popularly considered savages, even animals, by the Thai people themselves. The image of these people in the popular literature and touristic promotional publications tends to be based upon and to expand this indigenous Thai image. While they are not explicitly presented as savages, they are promoted as the "real" primitives, simpler and more primitive than the hill tribes.

This image fits well the anthropological evolutionary model of human society, according to which hunter-gatherer bonds are considered to be the earliest and simplest form of social organization (Lee and DeVore 1968; see also Bird-David 1988). Hence one could safely assume that these groups, rather than the hill tribes, provide the modern visitor with the experience of that "Other" which also points to his own roots.

The irony, however, is that in Thailand this apparent encounter with primitive savages takes place under circumstances in which the life of the people visited has already been fundamentally transformed, under the impact of broader environmental, economic and political factors. The "growing gap" (Cohen 1992a) between image and reality in hill tribe tourism, has here become a chasm.

The three small groups in Thailand which can be classified as "hunter-gatherers" are the Mlabri of the northern forests, the Semang of the southern forests, and the Moken of the islands and beaches of southern Thailand. These groups range at present between a few hundred and a few thousand members. All of them are remnants of larger groups which roamed wider areas in the past, beyond the borders of contemporary Thailand. None plays any significant role in Thai society, nor has the government devoted to any of them, in contrast to the hill tribes, much attention. Many members of these groups are not yet Thai citizens, and even those who are, have only recently received their citizenship.

In contrast to the hill tribes, the hunter-gatherer groups in Thailand are not a particularly popular or much advertised attraction. Rather, they are minor attractions, which usually merit only a brief stop on a tour. Their relatively low popularity can be gauged from several indicators, for example, by the number of photo postcards featuring these groups in comparison with those featuring the hill tribes: there are about 250 postcards of the most commonly shown hill tribe, the Hmong (or Meo) in my possession, and about 200 of the second hill tribe most common on postcards, the Akha. In comparison, I possess merely ten postcards featuring the Moken, four featuring the Mlabri and none featuring the Semang. The situation is similar in the popular and touristic publications: while hundreds of popular articles in several languages, as well as a dozen lavishly illustrated books, have been published on the hill tribes during the last thirty years, in the same period only one book and a handful of articles in popular publications were published on each of the hunter-gatherer groups.

The sociological interest in studying hunter-gatherer tourism in Thailand therefore lies, not in their popularity as attractions, or in the number of tourists who visit them, but in their particularity as the potential "Other," at least as the image of that "Other" is constructed by the promotional literature and the touring agencies.

In the following I shall present case studies of tourism in each of the three Thai hunter-gatherer groups. Each case study is preceded by an outline of the past lifeways and present situation of the group, as a context for the description of its touristic penetration. The case studies are based on visits to two of the three groups, and on my extensive collection of published materials on each of them.

The naming of the three groups, like that of the hill tribes (Bradley 1983; Cohen 1992d) is problematic. I have here used the groups' ethnonyms, i.e. the name by which the group calls itself, in two cases (Mlabri and Moken) and the generic name for the group in the third case (Semang). However, I shall also list some of the other names by which the group is known to the Thais or in the touristic publications oriented to a foreign audience. As we shall see, these other names are often significant for an understanding of the perception of these groups by the Thais as well as of their touristic image.

The Mlabri

The term Mlabri (or Mrabri in an earlier spelling, as in Young (1974:69)) consists of two words in the language of the group, *mla bri*, meaning "people of the forest," or "forest people" (Pookajorn *et al.* 1992:43). Bernatzik (1951 [1938]), the first ethnographer who studied the group, referred to it as Yumbri: however, this may have been a misnomer, a name for a sub-group (Young 1974), or the name of another, kindred group of hunter-gatherers (Pookajorn *et al.* 1992). For present purposes it is important to stress that the term under which the group is generally known is *phi thong luang* (ibid.; Nimmahaemindra and Hartland-Swan 1962), a Thai term meaning "The Spirits of the Yellow Leaves," the actual name of Bernatzik's (1951 [1938]) book. However, the Thais also used to relate to them in other terms, which may throw some light on their attitude towards the group. One term by which they were often referred to is *khon pa* (Boeles 1963; Nimmahaemindra and Hartland-Swan 1962; Young 1974), a term which can be translated as "forest people" (Pookajorn *et al.* 1992:43), but also means "wild people" or "savages." Another term, by which they were more rarely referred to, is *kha thong luang* which means "The Slaves (or Servants) of the Yellow Leaves," a significant appellation in view of their present social position (Seidenfaden 1926; Young 1974).

The Mlabri are a small, originally nomadic hunter-gatherer people, living in remote parts of the northern Thai provinces of Nan and Phrae; their number is estimated at about 140–150 (Thaitawat and Thepthong 1991; Young 1974). Their women tended to forage for wild plants, roots and fruits in the forest, to a distance of up to one kilometer from their temporary shelters; the men foraged and hunted a variety of mostly small animals (Pookajorn *et al.* 1992) at greater distances. Their technology was simple and their material culture sparse. However, from the perspective of our present interest, their most important trait is their mystical elusiveness. The group was first discovered in Thailand, into which it has probably entered from Laos, only early in the twentieth century (Thaitawat 1993). Living deep in impenetrable forest, it shunned contact with outsiders; the published reports about the Mlabri were hence often derived from second-hand information, mainly collected from hill tribe people (Young 1974). Even the Thais had only rarely an opportunity to observe these people directly, since "whenever they come in contract with any outsider they feel untrustworthy, they will break camp immediately" (Pookajorn *et al.* 1992:66). Their camps consisted of temporary simple shelters, built from bamboo poles and covered by banana leaves; they were believed to abandon them once the leaves turned yellow. Hence the source of their appellation: "Because of [their] spiritlike behaviour and their breaking camp as the leaves turn yellow, they have earned themselves the name 'Phi Tong Luang' " (ibid.:66). This, indeed, is the term under which they are best known in the popular and touristic publications.

The nomadic lifeways of the Mlabri were dictated by the availability of foraging resources in their habitat. According to Pookajorn *et al.* (1992:1): "Each family moves or migrates with a different pattern depending upon the size of their group and usually they stay for 5–10 days at each place. The migration is usually within a radius of 30 square kilometers." This pattern was buttressed by their beliefs: the spirits of their religion are said to force them to migrate and to prevent them from settling down permanently, from owning land or from engaging in agriculture for their own use; however, they may work the land for others (Thaitawat 1993).

The Mlabri were able to maintain their isolated foraging and hunting life-style for as long as their population was sparcely dispersed in small groups, on a large area of primary forest. With the penetration of their forest area by lumbers and Hmong tribal settlers, and the eventual destruction of much of the forest itself in the last thirty years (Pookajorn *et al.* 1992), the lifeways and, indeed, the very existence of the Mlabri were threatened (Thaitawat and Thepthong 1991). Forced to leave the forest which could not nourish them anymore, they gradually established contact with outsiders, and particularly with the Hmong, one of the most economically enterprising tribal groups in northern Thailand. The Hmong employed the Mlabri on their fields, remunerating them in kind — mostly with rice and pigs, which are their favourite food (Pookajorn *et al.* 1992; Thaitawat 1990b; Thaitawat and Thepthong 1991), rather than money. Several critics described the emergent relationship between the Mlabri and the Hmong as "peonage" (Thaitawat 1993:34) or even "slavery" (Storey 1988). Even discounting such claims as too extreme, it appears that some kind of dependence relationship did develop, mainly due to the growing indebtedness of the Mlabri to the Hmong, who demand the performance of considerable amounts of hard work on the fields for the pigs and rice which they have provided to the Mlabri. The Mlabri, unable to return to the forest, and lacking other means of subsistence, are forced to stay close to the Hmong, even if they are exploited by them.

As they emerged from the forest, the Mlabri gradually discarded the sparse *G*-strings which were their only attire, and began to dress in handed-down or discarded Thai and Western clothing. However, they did not give up their beliefs and the fear of their spirits.

The Mlabri have not been included among the nine "hill tribes" who came under the official auspices of the Hill Tribe Division of the Thai Department of Public Welfare; they were considered too small and too insignificant a group for that (Thaitawat 1993). However, several governmental programmes were recently instituted in order to assist the Mlabri to adapt to changing circumstances (Thaitawat and Thepthong 1991) and to integrate gradually into Thai society.

The Mlabri also attracted the attention of Christian missionaries. In 1979, an American missionary and his family belonging to the New Tribes Mission, settled in an outlying district of Phrae province, and invited the Mlabri to come and live with them. About forty Mlabri responded to the invitation (Thaitawat and Thepthong 1991). The family taught the Mlabri agriculture, trade and the Thai language, developed programmes in hygiene and child care for them and provided them with occasional employment, in such areas as reforestation (Thepthong 1990). However, after a few years the Mlabri left, for unclear reasons (Thaitawat 1993); only a few returned later on. While the Mlabri stayed at the missionary compound, tourists occasionally visited them there (Thaitawat 1990c). Since the Mlabri departed, the only ones accessible to tourists are those living in the vicinity of the Hmong. Forced to abandon their self-sufficient life in the forest, pauperized, facing deculturation, or even extinction (Storey 1988; Thaitawat 1990a), and prey to economic, and possibly also sexual exploitation (Thaitawat 1990b), the Mlabri entered the wider society at its lowest rung. Under these circumstances the Mlabri became exposed to organized tourist visits as a novel and exotic attraction.

The Thai public entertained an ambiguous view of the Mlabri: while some may have seriously believed that they were mysterious spirits (cf. Pookajorn *et al.* 1992; Thaitawat 1990b), inviting apprehension or fear, even those who did not, tended to consider them as not wholly human creatures; they seem to have been generally seen as wild (*pa*) people (or savages) or as slaves (*kha*), devoid of human dignity. Indeed, as such they could be exposed, like animals in a zoo, in "a Bangkok department store, for people to gape at" (Thaitawat 1990a), "as if they were circus animals" (Thaitawat 1990b:28).

The touristic image of the Mlabri reflects, in a modified way, the Thai stereotype of these people: they were described as the "most primitive" among the tribes in

Thailand, exotic forest dwellers without a sense of time or numbers, and without an understanding of the value of money (Panyacheewin 1990; Thaitawat 1990b). In touristic materials, such as postcards, they are represented almost naked, wearing only a *G*-string, deep in the jungle. In contrast, in critical newspaper reports, they can he seen wearing Thai or Western clothing (Thaitawat 1990a, b, 1993).

Paradoxically, only with their exit from the forest have these "forest people" become available to touristic visitations. Even so, they are not usually met by the tourists at their contemporary place of abode, but rather at a location chosen by the touristic entrepreneurs for the encounter. Mlabri tourism, similarly to the visitations to the phoney Philippine "stone age" people, the Tasaday (Nance 1975), takes a good deal of stage-management, though for different reasons: the Tasaday did not exist (Berreman 1991); the Mlabri do, but their lifeways have changed radically, so that the entrepreneurs have to re-enact the savagery and exoticism expected by the tourists (Panyacheewin 1990).

Tourists cannot ordinarily visit the Mlabri by themselves, but have to use the services of Thai tour companies, selling "exotic jungle tours to Thailand's last primitive tribe" (Thaitawat 1993:25). However, the tour companies are unable to organize the visits by themselves and need the mediation of additional middlemen. Thus a chain of mediation emerges. In one instance, the tour company first approaches a Thai police sergeant working in the area; according to the sergeant's account, he "started befriending the tribespeople some five years ago by collecting food and clothes to take to them as New Year gifts" (Panyacheewin 1990:31). He claims that: "When people think of coming to visit the *Phi Tong Lueang*, they think of me, and they come to ask for help. Even now, I don't get paid for doing this. It's my duty as a police officer to provide convenience and protection to tourists." However, the sergeant himself also has no direct access to the Mlabri. Hence, when "a tour group is scheduled to come . . . he will pass on the news through Hmong and Lua hill tribe villagers who the *Phi Tong Lueang* usually work for in the fields" (ibid.:31). After making the contact, the sergeant sets up the encounter: "I set the time and place and they'll come. They always show up." Some of the Mlabri appear in their *G*-strings for such an encounter; others wear ordinary clothes (ibid.:31). As a reward for their appearance, they receive a pig (since they are believed not to know the value of money). "As part of the exoticness and excitement of the tour, the *Phi Tong Lueang* will kill and prepare the pig, then share and eat it among themselves" (ibid.:33). According to one account, the tourists watching such a show "held their breath as the moment of death [of the pig] arrived. Some turned their backs, but most had their cameras ready to record every move" (Thaitawat 1990c:29). In addition to the pig-killing, "a tree-climbing show act is always included" on such visits (Panyacheewin 1990:33).

During the period some of the Mlabri stayed with the missionary working with them, the missionary — who was not opposed to tourist visits — served as the intermediary between them and the tourists (Thaitawat 1990c). On such occasions, the Mlabri also tried to sell their handicrafts to the tourists: these were mostly "pipes carved from bamboo roots, simply decorated with straight-line patterns; bags intricately woven from tree fibers and dyed with natural colours" (ibid.:29, see also Kanomi 1991:346). However, in comparison with the rich crafts tradition of the hill tribes (Kanomi 1991; Lewis and Lewis 1984), those of the Mlabri appear crude and unspectacular; hence they are "valueless to most tourists . . . some buy [them] seemingly out of pity . . . give the money and leave them" with the missionary (Thaitawat 1990c:29). It is interesting to note that, while the Mlabri are generally supposed not to know the value of money, and are rewarded by the guides for their performance only with pigs or cigarettes, blankets and rice (Storey 1988), the Mlabri are in fact quite eager to sell their crafts to the tourists for money (Thaitawat 1990c; Thaitawat and Thepthong 1991).

Opinions regarding the touristic penetration of the Mlabri differ. Some, like Professor Kwangsuan Atipote of Chulalongkorn University in Bangkok, condemn it as "inhuman" and as creating a "human zoo" (Panyacheewin 1990:33), claiming that commercialization of culture destroys its meaning for the group, as well as its economic self-sufficiency (ibid.:33). Others, including the missionary and the representative of the Tourism Authority of Thailand (TAT) in Chiang Mai stress the positive role tourism can play in introducing the Mlabri to the wider world and in bringing economic benefits to this remote area (Thaitawat 1990c; Panyacheewin 1990). These opposing evaluations derive from contrary attitudes toward the group, particularly with respect to the question, whether its lifeways and isolation should be preserved from external impacts, or whether it should be introduced into the modern world? However, even if the latter is, under the circumstances, considered preferable or inevitable, there still remains the question of whether tourism is the optimal way for such an introduction, particularly in view of the problematic consequences which the meeting of extremes in such encounters (Panyacheewin 1990) had upon similar groups, in other remote areas of the world. Still, one has to consider the alternatives. With regard to the Mlabri, the principal alternative is work for the Hmong, and if it is true that they receive from the Hmong a pig and some rice as reward for clearing a whole field for their employers (Thaitawat 1990b), then it becomes apparent that, whatever their exploitation by tourism in absolute terms, its relative reward for the group is enormous: in return for a pig they are merely asked to kill and eat it under the eyes — and the lenses — of their visitors. How this relative ease to come by much coveted rewards will impinge upon the Mlabri's view of the "outside" world, and upon their attitudes to their inherited lifeways, is an as yet unexplored question.

The Semang

The Semang in Thailand call themselves *munni* (Phanchan 1992; Suwanich 1988), meaning "human beings" in their language. They are part of the aboriginal population of the Malay peninsula, and have therefore been designated by the Malaysian authorities as *orang asli* ("original people" or "aborigines" in the Malay language). Whereas their number in Malaysia reaches about 70,000 (Suwanich 1988), in Thailand they are a small, residual group of about 200 individuals (Charernwat 1980). The Thai used to call them *ngo pa* (wild rambutan), allegedly because of their curly hair. The term under which they are presently best known is Sakai (Suwanich 1988), a derogative Malay word meaning "savage" (Phanchan 1992). However, Thais who do not speak the Malay language, seem to be unaware of the derogative nature of the term; indeed, the change from *ngo pa* to Sakai seems to have been made in order to neutralize the apparently derogative implications of the former term. The term Semang itself is not commonly used in Thai, although it appears to be the most neutral designation for the group.

The Semang are a Negrito group (Brandt 1961; Schebesta 1929) of great antiquity in the South-East Asian region. They have probably been driven deeper and deeper into the forests as a consequence of the invasion of the area by other groups. In Thailand they are found only in the southernmost provinces adjacent to the Malaysian border. In the past, their habitat was the deep mountainous forest, where they existed on foraging and hunting. They were divided into four small groups each numbering several tens of individuals (Suwanich 1988). Not unlike the Mlabri, the Semang lived in simple temporary lean-tos usually for not longer than a few days at a time (Charernwat 1980). They are best known in Thailand for their hunting method — the use of poisoned arrows shot from blowpipes (Boonthanom 1988; Kaje 1991). Their original clothing was made of woven algae leaves or tree bark, but at a later stage with the availability of cloth women wore skirts, with their breasts covered with cloth, while men wore shorts (Charernwat 1980).

In contrast to the relatively recently discovered Mlabri, the wider Thai society was aware of the Semang for a long time. In fact, King Chulalongkorn (Rama V, reigned 1868–1910) encountered the Semang on one of his journeys, ordered a Semang boy to be brought to Bangkok and educated there, and wrote a play called "Ngo Pa" in which this boy acted (cf. Phanchan 1992).

Though the Semang became known to the Thai public at an early stage, until the 1970s there was little contact between them and the national society. As in the case of the Mlabri, by that time their isolated forest existence began to he threatened by accelerated deforestation, which was continually reducing their traditional habitat. In the 1970s an additional factor dramatically impinged upon the lives of some of the Semangs: their location in the communist insurgent area along the

Thai-Malaysian border. Some Semang were accidentally killed by the Thai army in pursuit of the insurgents (Suwanich 1988) or by the insurgents themselves (Kaje 1991). Consequently, one group of the Semang, presently numbering about forty individuals, has been relocated by the authorities and settled in the Thanto district of the southern Yala province. The authorities have built bamboo shacks for their use and given them land for a rubber plantation. A member of the Thai royal family visited the settlement, and endowed the inhabitants with a family name, Srithanto (ibid.).

The destruction of forests, the gradual disappearance of wildlife, and their eventual settlement disrupted the accustomed lifeway of the Semang (Phanchan 1992). Like the Mlabri, they were forced to enter the wider society on its lowest rung. Also like the Mlabri, the Semang were "hired to clear the land at the villagers" plantations' for a minimal remuneration (Suwanich 1988:44). The Semang in the Thanto settlement underwent considerable deculturation, losing some of their traditional skills, which they could not practise any more under the new circumstances. Unlike the Mlabri, they became fairly quickly, but superficially, acculturated to the local Thai culture. They dressed in discarded Thai clothes, learned to communicate in the southern Thai dialect and sent their children to Thai schools. There is also some intermarriage between them and the Thais (Kaje 1991).

The Semang settlement in Thanto district became known as the "Sakai village" (Boonthanom 1988; Kaje 1991), and is the principal — and perhaps only — site of touristic visitations of the Semang. Tourism to this group is less complicated than that to the Mlabri. Located in the vicinity of the road between Yala city and the border town of Betong, the village can he reached by organized tours, as well as by individual visitors. Indeed, both domestic and foreign tourists visit the village, although for different reasons. Domestic visitors are not so much interested in the exotic aborigines, as in their medicines. The Semang have developed a complex system of folk medicine, based on forest products, mainly various roots, which they claim to be effective for many illnesses, for birth control (Suwanich 1988), as well as for the enhancement of male potency (Charernwat 1980). Thai visitors are much attracted to these medicines, and especially to those enhancing potency. Coming from those "savage" forest people, the medicines appear to possess a particular power. The sale of the medicines, collected by the Semang women in the remnants of the surrounding forests, is an important source of income for the group. However, with the dwindling of the forest, even this resource is gradually disappearing (Kaje 1991).

As in the case of the Mlabri, the Thai public tended to deny the Semang full human status: they were considered as wild or savage creatures (*pa*) or even as animals (Phanchan 1992). In the past the Semang were frequently put on show in cages during local festivals. Their settlement and their royal endowment with a

Thai name may have helped to modify that image, at least among those living in their vicinity, if not necessarily among the Thai population at large.

The touristic image of the Semang is not as well developed as that of the Mlabri; there exists little promotional material on the group, and no postcards or brochures depicting or describing them. In one of the few advertisements in which they are explicitly mentioned, the Semang are rather factually described as aboriginal, forest dwelling Negritos (*The Nation* 1992). They are not a touristically especially "marked" group.

However, since the Semang are the only "tribal" group in lower southern Thailand, the tourist authorities seek to exploit their presence to bolster tourism to the area. The TAT therefore decided some years ago to feature their "lifestyle and characteristics in souvenirs for tourists"; such souvenirs could then "be regarded as symbols of Yala," the province in which the "Sakai village" is located (*Bangkok Post* 1989). It is unclear what role the Semang themselves were supposed to play in the production of these souvenirs. In any case, not much seems to have come of the scheme. The Semang remained a minor touristic attraction.

Tourist visits to the Semang are typically a stop on an organized tour: "strangers in tourist buses often stop to see the . . . aborigines in flesh and watch them display their sharpshooting and cheerful music-making in amazement, in exchange for some money" (Suwanich 1988:31). Blowpipe shooting seems to be the main attraction of such visits. Indeed, the picture of a Semang man, clad only in a red loincloth, shooting arrows from his blowpipe, commonly illustrates articles on the Semang (e.g. Charernwat 1980; Kaje 1991; Suwanich 1988). The Semang have few if any crafts to sell to the visiting foreigners, not even the blowpipes or arrows, which are their touristic "trademark." According to one inhabitant of the village:

> No quiver or arrow is left in anybody's house. Whenever a bigwig [Thai official] comes, he will always take one with him. The other day we were left one set, but finally we sold it to a bigwig at a price of 250 baht [10.00$]. The simple reason is we have no money to buy rice. On the other hand, we haven't used them for a long time, as there is a ban from bigwigs on hunting in this village (Kaje 1991:114).

Whatever the credibility of this version of the disappearance of their traditional weapons, it seems that the number of Semang who are still able to shoot the blowpipe — and even more to manufacture it — is rapidly diminishing through lack of opportunity for its use, while the raw material of which they used to be made, a particular variety of bamboo, is becoming very hard to find. Extracted from their habitat and unable to roam and hunt in the forest, the Semang of "Sakai village" are gradually losing that part of their culture which is the basis of whatever attractiveness they may have for foreign tourists.

The Moken

The Moken (also spelled Mawken) are a nomadic coastal hunter-gatherer people, living on the islands and the coasts of the Andaman Sea; they belong to a wider category of "sea nomads" (Sopher 1977), who inhabit, or have inhabited, the coasts and islands of much of South-East Asia. The Moken are found in the coastal areas of three countries: Burma, Thailand and Malaysia. The Malays call them *orang laut* (i.e. "sea people" or "sea folk" (ibid.:47; Hogan 1972:206). In Thailand, they are known as *chao lay* (also spelled *chao lae*), a southern Thai version of the standard Thai *chao talay* (also spelled *chao talae*), namely "sea people" (Court 1971:84). They are also referred to as *chao naam*, i.e. "water people" (Hogan 1972), and some other synonymous terms. However, in popular Western usage, they are commonly known as "sea gypsies," a term coined by Thompson as early as 1851 (Sopher 1977; cf. White 1922).

The total number of the Moken has been estimated at about 5,000 (Ivanoff 1991); of this number there are about 3,000 in Thailand (Ekachai 1991). The largest concentration of Moken is found on the island of Phuket (Kajanavanit 1992; Kanwerayotin 1987; Phatkul 1992), its satellite island of Koh Sireh (Fang 1992; Photikij *et al.* 1993), on the Surin Islands group (Ekachai 1991; Ivanoff 1986; Kanwanich 1993; Rojanaphruk 1993; Tangwisuttijit 1990), and the islands of Phi Phi (Jivananthapravat 1990) and Li Pae (Jinakul 1987).

Traditionally, the Moken's "way of life [was] characterized by families living in boats, and moving about the sea coasts in nomad fashion" (Sopher 1977:47). They lived in their boats close to the shore or in huts on the shore itself. They derived their livelihood from the sea and the coasts. Their culture was based "on the gathering of sea produce, tripang [sea cucumber], shellfish, fish, lobster, coral and shells of different types. The only shore produce they normally gather is Pandannus leaves, which they use to make sleeping-mats and . . . [a] type of matting . . . which is used as tenting on their boats . . . and was formerly used as a sail" (Hogan 1972:213). Though they also engaged in fishing, they were fish-hunters rather than net-using fishermen (Ekachai 1991). Their material culture was simple: they had few hand-icrafts, but were skilled boat builders (Hogan 1972).

The simple life of the Moken in Thailand came under pressure in recent decades: as many observers pointed out, their culture is threatened with disappearance (Ekachai 1991; Jinakul 1987; Jivananthapravat 1990; Phatkul 1992; Rojanaphruk

1993; Tangwisuttijit 1990). However, while all Moken are exposed to forces of change, the degree and pervasiveness of these forces varies with their distance from major Thai population concentrations; they are lowest at the remote islands, and highest on Phuket.

On the most remote islands, traditional lifeways are still preserved to a considerable degree; thus, "The Moken of the Surin Islands, according to French anthropologist Dr Jacques Ivanoff, are among the country's last traditional sea gypsies" (Ekachai 1991:23). However, even here, the establishment of a National Park (Prang-riew 1992) has put limitations on their hunting and gathering activities and thereby induced changes in their way of life (Ekachai 1991).

On Phuket and Koh Sireh, where the Moken lived in close proximity to a large Thai population, they abandoned their dwelling boats many years ago and established permanent settlements on the beaches. The Thais refer to these settled Moken as "*Thai mai*" (new Thais), a generic term used for all newly Thaified groups (Hogan 1972:206). In fact, on the entrance to the biggest of their settlements, that on Rawai Beach on Phuket, there is a sign proclaiming it to be "The Village of the *Thai mai*."

The Thai people tend generally to look down upon the unsettled Moken, considering their life "primitive" (Kanwerayotin 1987) and referring to them in derogatory terms, such as "barbarians" (Rojanaphruk 1993). As in the case of the Semang, settlement and Thaification is considered as "progress" for these people. In fact, however, their settlements, and particularly that on Rawai Beach, are run-down, slum-like conglomerates of shacks built from various materials. No dwelling boats are seen anymore on the shore, and the one in the Rawai settlement itself is a slum-like habitation. The inhabitants are employed in a variety of jobs on the island; some have even worked in tin-mines (Hogan 1972). Those who engage in fishing, are commercial fishermen, rather than fish-hunters; they sell their catch, often for meagre rewards, to local fishmongers and middlemen, most of whom do not belong to the group (Ekachai 1991; Phatkul 1992).

Its slum-like quality notwithstanding, the Rawai settlement became the Moken site most frequently visited by foreign tourists, owing to its accessibility to the vast number of tourists vacationing on Phuket island: "Every day, a train of tour buses stops at Rawai Beach, bringing tourists from Hong Kong, Korea, Japan and western countries, to look at the Chao Lay as if they are something strange" (Phatkul 1992:24). However, the encounter between the tourists and the Moken on Rawai Beach occurs in a situation in which the Moken have already lost most of the distinctive characteristics of sea-roaming nomads, by which they are touristically marked. This transpires well from an, admittedly engaged, description of such an encounter:

Every day at about 9 am, the gleaming tour buses start to arrive at the sea gypsy village on Rawai beach. From the road, the village does not look much different from a Bombay slum, providing a perfect Third World photo opportunity: well-heeled tourists gingerly traipsing around patched-up huts and mounds of garbage, and in their wake some grubby children, begging for money. As recommended by a tourist publication, some tourists throw coins into the sea for children to dive after (Kajanavanit 1992:6).

Tourists entering the village are typically met by the indifferent gaze of the inhabitants, bored by the recurrent visits of strangers, with whom they have no communication; the similarity with the visit to a zoo struck one commentator:

Scenes of tourists peeking into Chao Lay huts are little difference [sic!] from those of visitors peeking into cages at a zoo. People from civilized lands are looking at the uncivilized with curious but suspicious eyes (Phatkul 1992:24).

The tourists are often taken aback during such visits by the unexpected squalor and poverty of these people, who are pictured in the touristic periodicals, the promotional literature and on postcards, as free-roaming, primitive boatdwellers. The children, particularly, arouse the sympathy of some visitors: "Unable to communicate [their sympathy], the best [the tourists] can do is to throw [the children] a few coins; some even throw them on the ground, for the children to pick up" (ibid.:24). Making money from tourists became a relatively lucrative source of income for the children, some earning up to 50 baht ($2.00 a day), whether by begging or by diving for coins (ibid.).

Begging, however, is almost the only manner by which the Moken can extricate some benefit from the tourist visits, for tourism has not significantly benefited the inhabitants of the Moken settlements in any other way. An editorial note, attached to a popular article on Moken culture sums up the situation:

The sight of Sea Gypsy children waiting to beg from tourists is a daily one on Rawai. Turning Phuket's two Sea Gypsy villages into tourist attractions has done little for these people's economic status and less for their self esteem.

Bus-loads of varied intruders tramp among their pathetically poor shanties, sticking cameras into what little is left of their traditional way of life .... Turning [the Sea Gypsies] into a tourist attraction [by the tourist industry], then leaving them to beg for a tiny share of the passing wealth, is not the right answer (Fang 1992:20).

Since the Moken settlement on Rawai Beach attracts tourists in significant numbers, a row of shops catering to the visitors, selling souvenirs, tourist art and shells has sprung up on the road leading to the settlement. While the shells may be collected by the Moken, the shops are owned exclusively by Thais or Chinese, who derive the principal benefits from their sale. The fact that others profit from the touristic attractiveness of the Moken, while the Moken themselves do not derive any meaningful benefit from it, further aggravates their sense of deprivation.

Paradoxically, however, the opportunities of employment on the island, generated by the tourist boom, attract growing numbers of Moken to Rawai Beach, especially those who were removed from other islands in the wake of the takeover of their settlement sites by tourist developers ("Normita" 1991).

However, Moken on the Rawai Beach settlement are also not immune from similar pressures for removal, as their land becomes increasingly valuable and coveted by developers. As is the case with Moken settlements everywhere, the Moken on Rawai Beach, though occupying the site for many years, have no legal ownership rights to it (ibid.). The landowners of the Rawai Beach site, as of other beachland on which the Moken are settled, have the legal right to remove them from the land. As the value of beachland, owing to its suitability for tourist development, has increased steeply, pressure grew to resettle the Moken from the beach to a less valuable inland site.

However, here tourism comes to their assistance: Their very attractiveness to tourists has become an important safeguard for their continual possession of the beachland on which they live:

> With the booming of tourism every beautiful beach has become an investment target.... As a result, the land which once belonged to native people has been changing hands. This is the most serious problem threatening the survival of Chao Lay society, especially in their four villages on Phuket....
> Changing of land ownership could mean death to the Chao Lay. Legally they wouldn't probably stand a chance to win. Ironically, the boom in tourism, which has made the Chao Lay at Rawai Beach a new product in popular demand, proves their biggest hope in this fight (Phatkul 1992:24).

The Moken, though generally timid, began to show signs of resistance to threats to remove them from their land, most conspicuously in their protest, in 1993, against attempts of developers to push them out of their settlement on Koh Sireh, by causing the destruction of the mangrove forest which shelters their boats and in which they forage for food (Photikij *et al.* 1993). Whether and for how long the Phuket and Koh Sireh Moken will be able to withstand such growing pressures remains to be seen.

In contrast to the mass tourism to which the Moken of Phuket, and to a lesser extent those on Koh Sireh, have been exposed for many years, tourism to the more remote islands is more recent and more limited in scope.

Until a few years ago, only a handful of tourists were able to reach these islands, owing to the difficulties and the costs of access. Even now, regular cruises are restricted to the period between November and April. Recently, however, with the growing popularity of cruise and nature tourism in the Andaman Sea, the volume of tourism even to remote islands has increased, and so have visits to the Moken sites, which are often included in the tours. Of special interest to tourists are "the once isolated Surin Islands [which] have become the latest hot spot in tourism" (Ekachai 1991:23). The islands, which were proclaimed a National Park in 1981 (Rojanaphruk 1993), attract up to 300 visitors on some days; their total number reaches between 3,000 and 4,000 a year.

About forty Moken families inhabit the Surin Islands; they are one of the principal attractions of the islands tours (Ekachai 1991). Here, tourists are able to observe the Moken in their natural habitat. The Moken derive some income from the visitors from the sale of garuda shells. These are big shells which the Moken collect from a depth of up to ten feet and sell for 10 baht apiece to the visitors (Rojanaphruk 1993). While it is prohibited to tourists to collect shells on the islands, the Moken are permitted to lift them out of the sea. This permission was granted in order to enable them to earn some income, and compensate them for other restrictions in the use of natural resources which were imposed upon them within the confines of the Surin Islands National Park (Ekachai 1991; Kanwanich 1993).

The Moken are generally happy about tourist visits, which are a new source of livelihood for them, but tourist visits, even at this early stage of touristic penetration of the islands, have already had an impact upon their cultural traditions. The Moken celebrate a major festival, called *loy reua* (Setting the Boat Adrift). The best known venue for this festival is the Moken settlement on Koh Sireh (Fang 1992), where it became a tourist attraction. However, tourism led to adaptation and embellishments of the festival, even on such a remote location as the Surin islands:

> In the name of tourism, the miniature boat floating ceremony of
> the Moken, which takes place on the moon rising days of the fifth

month in the lunar calendar, is being used as an annual festival to attract tourists from afar.

As part of the fun and games, the *chao lay* take part in the boat racing, diving, parties, and dances with the townspeople. Dr. Ivanoff [the French anthropologist] says the event dealt a big blow to the Mokens' culture.

'To suit the tourists, the event is set on weekends instead of according to their traditional calendar.
    Their customs also prohibit the Mokens from entering into the sea or going into the jungles during the ceremonies . . . But they have to violate their traditions' (Ekachai 1991:40).

The chief of the National Park on the Surin Islands is also worried by the impact of tourism on the Moken; he says that,

Like it or not, the *chao lay* have changed. They now like to dress like the tourists. They start to beg, look for sympathy, or charge too much [for shells].
    Before, when there was . . . food left over from the tourist parties, the food would be given to the *chao lay*. Now they come and wait for the food. I don't like this at all. It's losing your dignity (Ekachai 1991:40).

However, the park staff also has some positive ideas as to the possible tourism-related employment of the Moken as maintenance personnel during the off season, and as guides during the tourist season: "They have the boats equipped to take tourists safely around the islands to see the marine resources or the tropical forests in the hills above beaches and mangroves" (Kanwanich 1993). A problem is that, since they are not yet Thai citizens (ibid., Rojanaphruk 1993), the Moken cannot work as tourist guides, which is a protected occupation in Thailand.

Tourism has gradually penetrated even to the most remote Thai islands — such as the small Li Pae Island, which lies 80 kilometres off the shores of Tarutao Island in Satun Province, and where several hundred *chao lay* people live on a semi-permanent basis (Jinakul 1987). As on the Surins, restrictions have been imposed upon the Moken on this remote island regarding the use of the natural resources of their marine habitat — which has become part of a marine park, reserved for tourists by the government (ibid.). Consequently, because of the lack of alternative forms of income, the *chao lay* have turned to tourism as a last resort. The traditional fishing methods and primitive tools, normally honoured as family secrets and heirlooms, can now be seen on display. Tourists gladly photograph these once mysterious people, now performing their skills for foreigners to see (ibid.).

Tourism thus becomes a major factor of social and cultural change precisely in those locations where the Moken way of life, though under growing pressure, is still maintained to a significant degree. According to a Thai anthropologist, Narumon Hinshiranan, working on the Moken on the Surin Islands, the threat of tourism is augmented by a lack of comprehension of its impact; in her view, "many tour guides just sold the 'sensational' side of the Moken culture without understanding how intrusion from outsiders affects the villagers." She fears "that in the near future the Moken islanders will become a human zoo" (Rojanaphruk 1993:C2), as, according to some observers, they have already become in their settlements on and around Phuket Island.

Conclusion

The encounter between well-to-do Western tourists and hunter-gatherers in Thailand — particularly if the latter still inhabit their traditional habitat — is an encounter between extremes; the parties to the encounter are at the outset complete "Others" to each other. Despite that, the encounter is asymmetrical: not only are the Westerners often uninvited visitors, and the hunter-gatherers involuntary "tourees"; but there seems to exist a deeper discrepancy between the parties in the meaning of their encounters: the tourists seek the experience of primitive savagery, of the exotic "otherness," ultimately perhaps of their own roots.

The tourees, if they are at all interested in the encounter, primarily seek some material benefits, even though the strangers may become a source of information and even a model of imitation. Basically, however, from the point of view of the hunter-gatherers, the tourist is a novel potential resource in their changing environment, an extension of the field of opportunities, the exploitation of which helps them to muddle through and make a living. Relations with tourists are thus just an extension of the hunter-gatherers' relations with "other people" (Bird-David 1988), which they seek opportunistically to use for their immediate, though often meagre, benefit. Hence, what from the perspective of the outside may appear as exploitation of the hunter-gatherers, from their own perspective may well appear as a windfall opportunity, not to be missed. The example of the pig, given to the Mlabri by tourists merely to be eaten by them, can serve as an extreme example of this claim. It may not be too far-fetched to argue that these people "gather" the benefits from tourists, like the foodstuffs from the forest or from the beach. "Begging" under the circumstances, becomes a "gathering" strategy.

However, the great majority of encounters between tourists and hunter-gatherers in Thailand do not take place in the latter's natural habitat. Except for tourism to the Moken on the remoter islands, all other situations of hunter-gatherer tourism take place under conditions in which the tourees' ways of life had already been seriously disturbed, and even destroyed, by societal forces which had little to do with tourism. All the hunter-gatherer groups in Thailand with the partial exception of the Moken on remoter islands have undergone processes of acculturation or deculturation, social marginalization in the wider society, and acute pauperization. Indeed, as is particularly the case with the Mlabri and the Semang, only the removal from their natural habitat has made them at all accessible to tourists.

The changed circumstances under which the hunter-gatherers are exposed to tourists, modify, to some extent, the strangeness of the encounter for the tourists. However, these circumstances pose new problems for the tourist entrepreneurs who initiate and facilitate the encounter. The image of the hunter-gatherers, as presented in the touristic media, creates expectations as to the encounter which are radically at variance with the reality of the hunter-gatherers' contemporary existence. In order to relate the tourists' image to the actual encounter, the encounter has to be staged (MacCannell 1973); but the variance appears to be so great that the entrepreneurs are usually unable to stage the encounter covertly, thus creating the illusion of (staged) authenticity in the tourists; most encounters tend to be overtly staged (Cohen 1979b), with the tourists generally aware of their, at least in part, staged nature. The entrepreneurs typically make the group, or its representatives, perform some elements of their traditional culture; these are mostly related to their traditional ways of making a living — tree-climbing, diving, blowpipe shooting. These activities become accessible to tourists only once they become "performances"; and they become "performances" only after they have ceased to be "work" in the people's daily existence.

In contrast, the actual contemporary work of these people, tilling fields, fishing or performing unskilled jobs, is of no touristic interest. In some cases, a certain confusion of "frames" (Goffman 1974) takes place: thus the encounter of the tourists with the Mlabri is, from one perspective, an almost completely "staged" activity, with the actors, the Mlabri, coming appropriately dressed to the "stage," a previously agreed place, at an appointed time. From another perspective, however, it is a "real" activity: the Mlabri actually kill the pig donated by the tourists, and have a feast of eating it, even though the killing and the feast is a show for the tourists.

The Mlabri feast is in fact the closest that tourists ever come to experiencing the authentic otherness of hunter-gatherers in Thailand — and probably the furthest ordinary tourists are capable of exposure to the "real" life of "savages." Most tourists are probably capable of exposure to "savagery" only after it has been modified for touristic consumption; and such modification becomes practically possible, in the case of hunter-gatherers, only after they have left their accustomed environment and given up a good deal of their traditional ways of life.

To put this discussion into a comparative framework, the question can be raised, how far and in what respects does hunter-gatherer tourism in Thailand differ from hill tribe tourism?

There is no clear-cut division between these two kinds of tourism; hill tribe tourism has a broad range, and some of its manifestations come quite close to those of hunter-gatherer tourism, as described here. Specifically, tourist visits to the poorest, most deculturated and marginalized tribal groups, particularly the Akha (Cohen 1979a), resemble those to the various hunter-gatherer locations. The Akha, like the hunter-gatherers, are passively exposed to tourists, from whom they derive few, if any, benefits. Hence they tend to hawk cheap trinkets, such as tobacco pipes and bracelets, made by themselves; and those who are not able to extract any other benefit from the tourists, are reduced to begging.

Beyond this, however, there are some major differences between the two kinds of tourism. Although the hill tribes are often described as "primitive" (Cohen 1989), they are never presented as barbarian, savage or non-human. In fact, their rich material culture, particularly their "colorful costumes" are a major component in their attractiveness. On the other hand, their mode of production, beyond opium growing, is not of much touristic interest. Hence, hill tribes are not asked, as hunter-gatherers are, to perform their work activities for the tourists.

One could attempt to summarize the difference by saying that the hunter-gatherers are presented and viewed by tourists more as "nature people" in the sense of the German term *Naturvoelker* than the hill tribes, whose culture, especially crafts, endow them with a place among the "culture people" (in the sense of *Kulturvoelker*), even though their life is perceived as more "natural" than that of the modern Western city dwellers. The metaphor of the "human zoo" for the tourists' encounter is thus in a profound sense more appropriate for hunter-gatherer tourism than for hill-tribe tourism since it touches upon a deep-set general human theme: the desire to see man as he was before "civilization" or even "culture." The zoo-like touristic display of hunter-gatherers can therefore be seen as a modified version of the display of these people, in cages at festivals or in department stores, for the Thai public, whose motivation to gawk at these "savages" was probably not much different from that of contemporary foreign tourists.

Chapter 18

Thailand in "Touristic Transition"

Introduction

Tourism raises complex ecological, social and cultural issues, in part because its development, particularly in Third World destinations, faces a fundamental paradox. Their initial attractiveness to foreign tourists is based on an inventory of what I call natural attractions (Chapter 9) — pre-existing environmental, cultural and historical sites and events, which appear, or are promoted in the language of tourism (Dann 1996), as "authentic," "pristine" or "untouched," in alleged sharp contrast to the prevailing state-of-affairs in the contemporary West.[83] However, once tourism takes off and increasing numbers of mass tourists visit those destinations, a ubiquitous process takes place. As the once "untouched" attractions come under growing pressure of sheer numbers of tourists, they become gradually transformed in order either to adapt them to tourist demand or to prevent their progressive destruction. Simultaneously new, contrived attractions are created to enhance the attractiveness of the destination and to deflect tourists from the declining natural attractions, or even to substitute for the latter. The principal thesis of this chapter is that there exists a close interconnection between the decline in the attractiveness of natural attractions and the emergence of new, contrived ones. This interconnection enroutes countries whose tourism has initially been based on a variety of natural attractions, on a process of "touristic transition" with far-reaching consequences for their tourist image and the composition and motivations of their tourist clientele.

The Process of "Touristic Transition"

While initially the charm of many new destinations is that their natural, environmental and cultural attractions are "unmarked" (Chapter 9) and integral to the habitat and flow of life of the local society, with the growth of tourism a segregated tourist sphere gradually emerges. As tourism expands, these attractions become marked and gradually transformed and degraded. A growing gap (Cohen 1996a:145–148) emerges between the tourist image of the destination (based on the attractiveness of its natural attractions) and reality. The newly emergent contrived attractions at first often tend to simulate, in a staged manner (MacCannell 1973), the increasingly less attractive natural attractions: clear, blue swimming pools substitute for polluted beaches, gardens for destroyed nature, cultural shows for live ethnic customs. However, as the destination matures, such contrived attractions are increasingly implanted into the local environment, without being related to it.[84]

The boundary between the local society and the tourist sphere is, however, not fixed but permeable. Some of the initially contrived attractions become, in the course of time, "naturalised" and incorporated into the local "tradition" and way of life, especially if locals tend to patronise them as venues of domestic tourism or leisure activities (Chapter 9). Older contrived attractions frequently undergo a process of "emergent authenticity" (Chapter 7), even as new ones are added to the tourist sphere. In the most developed destinations, the boundary between the tourist sphere and the rest of society may become blurred (Cohen 2001b; Picard 1992).

The general process described, which I call the "process of touristic transition," raises important issues and dilemmas in countries in which tourism plays an important role in development. I shall describe, in some detail, this process as it has evolved in Thailand. Since Thailand's transition is more advanced than in most Southeast Asian countries (excepting the city-state of Singapore), the study of this transition may indicate incipient trends in those countries, and hence draw attention to problems and dilemmas of their future tourism development.

Recent Developments in Thai Tourism

The general outlines of the development of tourism in Thailand are well known and fairly well documented (see Cohen 1996a; Meyer 1988) and need to detain us here only briefly. Thailand has enjoyed, in the West, the image of an enchanted Oriental kingdom throughout much of modern history. This image was probably the source of the prevailing favourable attitude toward the country and it people in the contemporary Western world. However, until the 1960s, Thailand was also a remote country visited by relatively few, elite tourists. The rapid development of foreign tourism to Thailand began only in the late 1960s and reached massive proportions during the 1980s and the 1990s (Figure 18.1).

Year	Number of arrivals	Average length of stay (days)
1960	81,340	3.00
1965	225,025	4.80
1970	628,671	4.80
1975	1,180,075	5.00
1980	1,858,801	4.90
1985	2,438,270	5.58
1990	5,298,860	7.06
1993	5,760,533	6.94
1996	7,192,145	NA
1999 (target)	8,280,000	NA

Figure 18.1: Number of Foreign Tourist Arrivals and their Average Length of Stay 1960–1999 (Selected Years). *Source:* Tourism Authority of Thailand

In the last 40 years, foreign tourism to Thailand expanded a hundred-fold and the tourists' average length of stay more than doubled. Tourist expenditure in 1997 was estimated at 120 billion baht (about US$3.24 billion at the April 2000 rate of about 37 baht to the dollar), and probably amounted to even more in 1999 when tourism picked up again after a slowdown during the 1997–1998 Asian financial crisis.

The popularity of Thailand at the outset of its tourism boom has been largely based on its "hedonistic appeal" (Peleggi 1996:433), particularly the easy availability of various sexual services. Partly to overcome its image as the "brothel of Asia" and to broaden its appeal to a wider spectrum of prospective visitors, the Tourism Authority of Thailand (TAT) sought from the 1980s onward to promote the country as a destination for cultural tourism (Peleggi 1996:433) and seaside vacationing. The TAT initiated a series of promotional campaigns such as the "Visit Thailand Year" (1987) (*Business Review* 1986), the "Thailand Arts and Crafts Year" (1988–1989) (*Holiday Time in Thailand* 1988), and the recent "Amazing Thailand 1998–1999" (*Thaiways* 1997). The authorities attached great importance to the latter campaign, since in a period of deep economic crisis, tourism was one of the few bright spots contributing significantly to employment and foreign exchange. The government initiated an ambitious plan to attract 17 million tourists to Thailand during the two years of the campaign. The actual effectiveness of these promotional campaigns, however, has never been reliably established.

Following the example of Thailand, other mainland Southeast Asian countries have instituted their own promotional campaigns, such as "Visit Myanmar Year 1996" (*Bangkok Post* 26 November 1996; *Die Zeitung* 1995) and "*Visit Laos Year 1999*" (Tourism Authority of Lao People's Democratic Republic circa 1998).

The sheer growth in the number of tourists is an important precondition for the process of touristic transition. Equally important are more specific trends in the composition, motivation and distribution of tourists. In the case of Thailand, several significant trends could be observed in recent years.

First, while the authorities seem to have targeted mainly affluent Western and Japanese tourists in their promotional campaigns, it is noticeable that close to half of foreign tourism to Thailand originated in Asian countries (excluding Japan), especially neighbouring Malaysia. More recently, two new major sources of tourists have opened up: mainland China (*International Herald Tribune* 6 April 1998) and Russia (*Bangkok Post* 21 May 1998). Though there are differences between the principal concerns of the Asian and Russian tourists, it appears that sightseeing of natural attractions is relatively low on the list of priorities of both, a fact which facilitates the process of touristic transition in Thailand.

Second, even among tourists from the West, a change of relative emphasis from sightseeing to vacationing, particularly in the seaside resorts of central and southern Thailand, appears to have taken place. This trend seems to be in tune with similar developments in other maturing tourist destinations. As once remote exotic destinations become more accessible, especially through an expanding network of cheap air links, they cease to be the preserve of elite sight-seeing visitors and become affordable to mass tourists who are more interested in vacationing than their predecessors. Moreover, first-time visitors tend to engage more in sightseeing than return visitors. Such a re-orientation also facilitates the process of touristic transition.

Third, tourism in Thailand is concentrated mainly along a north-to-south axis (Cohen 1996a:6–8) with three major nodes: Bangkok in the centre, Chiang Mai in the north and Phuket island in the south. The axis has been gradually extended further into the north and south towards the boundaries of the country and broadened to include adjoining peripheral areas. New, "unspoilt" destinations are thus penetrated by tourism even as the natural attractions along the axis gradually decline. However, the basic geographic pattern of tourism has not changed over the period of its expansion. Outside the central axis foreign tourism is scarce, as indicated by the fact that the huge Northeast of the country known as Isan, the home of 20 million inhabitants, attracted a mere 200,000 foreign tourists in 1997 (*Bangkok Post* 10 August 1998). The recent trend to regionalisation of Southeast Asian tourism, as we shall see, encourages the further expansion of tourism into ever more peripheral areas of the country, including into Isan, while also intensifying the touristic transition of the mature tourist areas along the central axis.

Finally, during the period of rapid growth of foreign tourism, there was a parallel, though little noticed, growth in domestic tourism. Domestic tourism constitutes a significant component of tourism to some of the most popular destinations of foreign tourism, such as Phuket. It also dominates tourism to more remote, little known areas such as Isan which, according to one estimate, was visited by about 10 million domestic tourists in 1997. More important, domestic tourists and locals are the principal clientele of the large-scale amusement centres and other contrived attractions which have mushroomed in recent decades in the vicinity of the major cities, particularly around Bangkok.

The Thai authorities have until recently sought to attract foreign tourists to the country by emphasising its exoticism — "Exotic Thailand" was the name of a news-sheet distributed by TAT, while "Thailand — the Most Exotic Country in Asia" was one of its principal promotional slogans. However, as Thailand underwent a process of rapid economic development in the decade preceding the economic crisis of 1997, with often disastrous consequences for its environment (*Bangkok Post* 24 December 1997) and the cultural traditions of its people, the emphasis upon the exotic character of the country was attenuated. This can be seen in the substitution of the vaguer and broader term "amazing" for the former "exotic," as in the later slogan "Amazing Thailand." In spite of the change, the emphasis remained on Thailand's natural environmental, cultural and archaeological attractions. However, with the decline of many of these attractions, the gap between the image of the more mature attractions promoted by the tourism authority and the reality encountered by the visitors has widened. As if to make up for the discrepancy, increased stress has been put on eco-tourism (*Bangkok Post* 20 December 1997), a slogan which in many instances serves as a convenient cover for the exploitation of locations such as natural parks, from which tourism was heretofore excluded (*Bangkok Post* 1 August 1998). The contemporary promotional material reflects to a much smaller degree one of the principal current trends in Thai tourism — the emergence of a great number of often large-scale contrived attractions, besides, and often as substitutes for, the declining and transformed principal natural attractions. Thailand's touristic transition was, perhaps intentionally, largely disregarded in the promotional media and possibly also overlooked by the tourist authority itself.

The process of touristic transition in Thailand can be observed on several levels: the local, the national, and even the regional or international. I shall deal with each of these levels in some detail.

The Touristic Transition at the Local Level

The touristic transition is most advanced in the mature tourist destinations of Thailand, especially in major seaside resorts which have experienced the most intensive tourism exploitation. I shall therefore deal more extensively with one of these resorts, and then briefly describe the process in two other kinds of destination.

Seaside Resorts

Though my own fieldwork took place primarily on the islands of Phuket and Koh Samui (Cohen 1996a:151–246), I chose the case study of Pattaya as the most extreme example of the touristic transition of a seaside resort. Patong on Phuket and the Chaweng and Lamai beaches on Koh Samui follow a similar trajectory, though the transition in these resorts has not yet reached the stage which has been attained by Pattaya.

Pattaya is the biggest, and in the language of its promoters, the foremost seaside resort of Southeast Asia. The resort has experienced a phenomenal growth in its relatively short history. "Discovered" only in 1961 by American GIs stationed in Thailand (*The Nation Review* 31 December 1978; Vielhaber 1984), the small fishing village in the Gulf of Thailand rapidly became a center of international vacationing due to its favourable natural endowments and convenient location in the proximity of Bangkok. Initially a popular destination of rest and recreation (R&R) trips of American GIs, Pattaya boomed in the course of the late 1970s and the 1980s into a popular destination for foreign, especially German and Arab, vacationers (Montague 1989; Vielhaber 1984) who were attracted by its beaches and burgeoning nightlife. However, the rapid, uncontrolled and speculative growth which transformed the little village into an expanding city (*Bangkok Post* 25 July 1989; Vielhaber 1984) soon provoked environmental degradation, even as the growth of tourist-oriented prostitution, drugs and crime spoilt the initially favourable image of the resort (*Bangkok Post* 4 July 1978, 25 July 1989; *Far Eastern Economic Review* 28 November 1991). The pollution of the sea, which made it unfit for bathing; the destruction of marine life; the degradation of the beach environment; the rapid and mostly uncontrolled construction of hotels, shophouses, "beer-bar" complexes and similar commercial projects, accompanied by growing tourism-related crime, engendered a deepening crisis by the mid-1990s. The authorities and the private sector sought to rehabilitate the resort and to enhance its attractiveness for wider segments of the tourist public (*Asia Magazine* 20 March 1988: *Bangkok Post* 26 November 1993; *The Nation* 12 September 1993), but despite their efforts, Pattaya has not yet fully recovered from the crisis. Significantly, as efforts at environmental rehabilitation have met at best with moderate success, the private sector stepped in to enhance Pattaya's attractiveness by creating a broad spectrum of new, contrived attractions in the city and its surroundings. Often constructed on a grand scale, these attractions served to some extent to broaden the image of Pattaya as a place offering natural amenities and sexual attractions, to a multi-purpose resort with attractive offerings for all kinds of tourists. Rather than as a beach resort, the place is now conceived of and promoted as a resort city, replete with a variety of different (mainly contrived) attractions (*Bangkok Post* 9 January 1997).

The contrived attractions of Pattaya fall into two major categories: establishments and events. The number of establishments is very large indeed, but here I shall briefly review only a few outstanding examples. The older establishments are often tenuously related in some way to the natural characteristics or the cultural or historical endowments of Pattaya or of Thailand, while the newer ones tend to be extraneous "implants," devoid of any connection to the place or the country. The latter were brought to Pattaya or its vicinity primarily because the entrepreneurs expected that most of the visitors would come from the resort.

Probably most closely related to the local context is the Khao Khiew Open Zoo, established in 1978 in the vicinity of the main road leading from Bangkok to Pattaya and easily accessible from the resort. Covering about 1,200 acres, it houses about 200 animal species, "grouped in spacious compounds in the park which, except for the wire fences, are exact replicas of the jungles of Thailand. Perhaps . . . even more so than the original habitat, little of which is left due to exploitation of the forest" (*Explore Pattaya* 1993:14).

Some of the other major older contrived attractions emphasise Thai environmental and cultural themes even though many are presented in an overtly "staged" (MacCannell 1973) form. Their spectacular shows are intended for the amusement of tourists and some of the items on their programmes are only tenuously, if at all, related to Thai culture. Nevertheless, they contain few, if any, purely implanted features. The Nong Nooch Orchid Wonderland, a park located on 500 acres on the road from Pattaya to Sathahip, advertises itself as "a fine example of Thai culture and hospitality set in a paradise of flourishing gardens" (*Nong Nooch Orchid Wonderland* brochure circa 1993:n.p.). The park features a variety of differently styled gardens, a cultural spectacular as well as various hospitality and leisure services. Though the emphasis is on the Thai character of its shows, the popular elephant show includes many spectacular features which have little to do with Thai culture.

The Million Years Stone Park and Pattaya Crocodile Farm, located in the vicinity of Pattaya, is another contrived attraction, which seeks to present itself as a natural one. Thus, the somewhat garbled language of its brochure claims that its rock garden was "genuinely created in a natural way" as a "splendid combination of science and nature. Virtually [sic] for this creation proves perseverance and quest for a perfectly natural wonder" (*Million Years Stone Park and Pattaya Crocodile Farm* brochure circa 1994:n.p.). The garden is said to consist of a "selection of stones [from] many places" and is thus, in a sense, similar to a zoo or botanical garden. But the park is intended more to entertain than to edify. Its logo is a crocodile fully dressed in a Western outfit. The park offers a variety of entertainment and "exciting shows featuring wild animals including tigers and bears . . . sword fighting, Thai games and magic shows." As in the preceding case, some of these shows have little to do with Thai culture.

Mini Siam, a theme park on the outskirts of Pattaya, is a particularly interesting case. It was initially intended, in the language of its brochure, to be "Thailand's first wonder displaying Thai heritage on a miniature scale [which] brings together more than 100 models of important art objects and historical sites throughout the Kingdom" (*Mini Siam* brochure circa 1994:n.p.). Mini Siam was meant to serve "those [tourists] who cannot afford to visit and admire all the real beautiful ancient objects and ancient remains." A visit to the park will thus enable "the visitors [to] boast of a trip throughout the country" (*Hotel Information News* 1990). At a later stage, however, new, implanted components were added to Mini Siam — Mini Europe and Mini World — probably to serve the growing number of domestic and Asian tourists who may not have a chance to travel around the world.

In contrast to the preceding examples, most of the more recently established major contrived attractions in Pattaya and its vicinity had from the outset a markedly implanted character, unrelated to the local or national environment or culture. Most prominent among such recently established attractions are the Paintball game range (*Bangkok Post* 19 May 1994; *The Nation* 7 August 1994), the World Dogs Centre featuring, among other things, a show which includes "dogs-boxing [sic], doing by order, protecting dogs, [dogs] jumping fire's loop, [and] jumping knife's loop [sic]" (*World of Dogs* brochure circa 1998:n.p.) and a branch, established in 1995, of *Ripley's Believe It or Not*! museum (*Bangkok Post* 13 January 1995).

Pattaya is also the venue of some major tourism events, especially festivals, all of which are contrived attractions. Unlike other tourism locations, no "traditional" temple festival from the period prior to the arrival of tourism has survived to the present, if any had been celebrated at all in the little fishing village. However, while the tourist-oriented festivals created at an earlier stage resemble "traditional" Thai festivals, the more recent ones are implanted affairs, unrelated to local or Thai culture. I shall illustrate this difference using the Pattaya Festival and the Pattaya Carnival.

The Pattaya Festival, the older of the two, replicates many of the features found in other Thai festivals. It is celebrated on, or close to, the traditional Thai New Year — the Songkran festival — and it includes a floral float parade, dragon dancers, *bong fai* (rocket) contests and a handicraft fair, all elements found in various other festivals around the country (*Bangkok Post* 21 April 1990, 17 April 1994). The organisers of these events were able to draw upon the cultural resources of the employees of various tourist establishments in Pattaya who had migrated to the city from different regions of the country, especially from the northeast (Isan), a region rich in festival traditions.

The Pattaya Festival, however, also features some events which are extraneous to Thai culture, such as the Pattaya Midnight run, female parachute jumpers, a beach buffet and an international food festival. It is important to note that though the festival is tourist-oriented, the local Thai population takes part in it, both as performers as well as spectators. Like many other newly instituted festivals in Thailand (to be discussed below), the Pattaya Festival, though initially created for foreign tourists, is becoming incorporated as an emergent local tradition.

In contrast to the Pattaya Festival, the Pattaya Carnival is primarily an implanted event unrelated to Thai culture. It is a replication of a Western, basically Christian custom for the pleasure of foreign tourists (*Thailand Traveller* 1995). It should be noted, however, that other Christian festivals, like Christmas and Silvester, though also alien to Thai culture, are becoming popular — in a commercialised form — with the Thai public. Therefore it is possible that carnival may also find positive resonance among the fun-loving local public.

In the 40 years since its "discovery," the fishing village of Pattaya, whose original assets were its striking natural amenities, has become a resort city whose attractions are not only increasingly contrived but also implanted, with features unrelated to the local or even the national environmental or cultural setting. Pattaya is thus suffering a loss of "placeness" (Chapter 9), since many of its more recently established implanted attractions could be located elsewhere, and have been brought to the resort only owing to the presence of a large number of foreign tourists. In that respect Pattaya suffers a similar fate as some other large, mature resorts elsewhere in the world (cf. Butler 1980) and like many of these, it faces an uncertain future. An analogous process of touristic transition can also be discerned in some other tourism locations in Thailand, even though they may differ in their concrete manifestations from Pattaya. I shall illustrate this process in two other kinds of local situations, namely the craft villages and the hill tribes.

Craft Villages

Thai handicrafts have undergone considerable transformation and a significant degree of "heterogeneization" (Cohen 1993a, 2000) as they became re-oriented from their traditional clientele to an external audience (Graburn 1976) of domestic and foreign tourists and exporters who sell to Western countries. The marketing of tourist crafts is a form of "indirect tourism" (Aspelin 1977) because only few consumers of such crafts come into direct contact with their producers. In Thailand, only a few craft villages have become tourist attractions in their own right, and even those are not visited by many foreign tourists. Most tourists still make their purchases in the principal craft markets, especially in the Weekend Market of Bangkok and the Night Bazaar of Chiang Mai. The process of commercialization of their crafts has therefore not imparted major changes to the appearance of the craft villages except that in some of the more important ones, like the carvers' village of Ban Thawai (Cohen 1998) and the potters' village of Dan Kwien (Cohen 1993a), big markets selling local and other craft products have emerged. An analogy to the transformation of natural attractions, and to the emergence of contrived and implanted ones in the tourist resorts, is therefore found primarily in the changes undergone by the commercialised craft objects themselves: their origins, materials, methods of production, forms, functions and styles (Cohen 2000).

Tourists are often enthusiastic about "authentic" ethnic arts and crafts, but few actually purchase them in their "unadulterated" form. In Thailand, like elsewhere in the developing world (Cohen (ed.) 1993), the commercialization of crafts usually necessitates their adaptation to the tastes and preferences of the external public. In its early stages, such adaptation usually remains limited to "orthogenetic" changes. This means that although materials, forms and functions of the objects may undergo change, their style continues to resemble, or constitutes merely a variation or a development, of the current style during the period preceding commercialization. This is analogous to the transformation which natural attractions undergo in resorts and other tourism locations. In some craft villages, however, especially those which produce large quantities of crafts not only for the tourist market but also for export, the link to the "traditional" local products and styles has been gradually severed and a growing number of products presently undergo "heterogenetic" changes (Cohen 1993a). This means they absorb external, often foreign, influences, or are based on models or photographs of foreign craft products. Such heterogeneization may proceed spontaneously as artisans respond to market demand, but frequently it is a result of orders placed by local businessman and foreign importers, who supply specifications, models or photos. The heterogeneization of craft products, a trend prominent in the two above-mentioned craft villages of Ban Thawai and Dan Kwien, can be seen as analogous to the implantation of contrived attractions, unrelated to the local environment or culture, into mature tourist resorts. While the specific indicators of the process of touristic transition are different in craft villages from those in seaside resorts, the process is analytically similar in both kinds of attractions.

Hill Tribes

The process of touristic transition is, in general, less advanced in hill tribe settlements, even in those most commonly frequented by tourists, than in the other kinds of tourist localities dealt with above. Few, if any, contrived attractions have been established in the tribal settlements themselves. The commercialized hill tribe crafts, though they have also been adapted to tourist tastes and preferences (Cohen 1983a, 2000), have remained on the whole within the scope of the various tribes' orthogenetic traditions. They have been transformed, but not heterogeneized like those of some of the principal Thai craft villages.

In the process of their incorporation into Thai society, the more accessible tribal villages often suffered extreme de-culturation. Consequently, a growing gap has emerged between the exotic image and the everyday reality of hill tribe people (Cohen 1996a:145–148). In many of the tribal villages visited by tourists, the inhabitants have had to stage themselves in order to preserve their attractiveness. Tribal members, especially women and children, seeking to derive some income from tourists, either by selling their crafts or other souvenirs, or by posing for photos, tend to dress in conspicuous tribal costume to attract the attention of potential clients. This is particularly the case in tribal settlements popular with tourists, such as Meo Doi Pui in the vicinity of Chiang Mai, a village which began to attract tourists as early as the 1970s. The Hmong and the Akha tribal women hawking their crafts in the Night Bazaar of Chiang Mai also don spectacular costumes in order to attract the attention of visitors to this large and diversified market.

The case of the peculiar attire of the women of the Padaung people, a Karen sub-group in Burma (Bernard and Huteau 1988; Diran 1997; *Sawaddi* 1993), illustrates how a natural, though spectacular, hill tribe attraction can be turned into a contrived one, merely by change of context. The Padaung women customarily adorn their necks and knees with brass coils, which has earned them the appellation "long neck Karen" (*Lookeast* 1993; Zaw 1996) or "giraffe women" (*Bangkok Post* 6 April 1998). Initially brought to the vicinity of the Thai border by an enterprising Padaung man in 1985 to be viewed by trekking excursions from Thailand (Mirante 1990:36), the Padaung later fled together with Karenni rebels and refugees into Thailand, and were placed into refugee camps along the Thai-Myanmar border. Here the women became a standard attraction of tourist excursions. Their attractiveness hindered their repatriation (Mirante 1990:37) and so they have remained in Thailand up to the present, despite periodic decisions by the authorities to send them back. In the course of the 1990s, as the Padaung women became the most popular hill tribe attraction in northern Thailand, a Thai businessman attempted to lure some of them into a compound close to a tourist location, where they could be shown to passing tourists. Here the Padaung women were virtually imprisoned in a kind of "human zoo" until the establishment was eventually raided by the Thai police and the women returned to the refugee camps (*Bangkok Post* 6 April 1998).

By virtue of their relocation into a "human zoo," and exposure to the tourists' gaze, the Padaung women have become a contrived attraction or, in Mirante's phase, "hostages to tourism" (Mirante 1990), shown to tourists against their will. But their attire did not have to be spectacularized or changed — their ordinary, natural attire was spectacular enough. The case of the tribal girls who make a living by taking photos with tourists at the northernmost point of Thailand, in the vicinity of the bridge leading from the town of Mae Sai in Thailand to Kachilek in Myanmar, differs significantly from that of the Padaung women. These girls willingly don a contrived tribal costume, which, while comprising some elements from various tribal attires, is altogether a free invention. Despite that, it is often featured in tourism publications as a "traditional" tribal costume (e.g. *Saen Sanuk* 1989). It is ironic that the author of an article in a tourist-oriented periodical chose a picture of some girls dressed in that costume for a caption stating that "Each hill tribe has its own language and culture" (*Thailand Traveller* 1996:28–29). However, like in other cases of "invented traditions" (Hobsbawm and Ranger 1983), this costume may well eventually become incorporated into the evolving tribal culture of Thailand and be, for example, exhibited in a tribal museum, though it did not originate in any specific tribal group.

While hill tribe people may stage themselves for tourists, and transform their crafts to catch the tourists' eye, they normally lack the financial and managerial resources to establish sustainable contrived attractions in their villages. All contrived attractions featuring Thai hill tribes have been established in non-tribal locations and initiated and owned by non-tribal entrepreneurs. The biggest and most popular of such attractions are the so-called "tribal villages" and tribal performances staged in theme parks and similar tourism establishments in or close to urban areas in northern and even central Thailand. The process of touristic transition of the hill tribes is thus in an early stage in the tribal villages themselves, but it is in a relatively advanced stage outside those settlements, with tribal members mostly playing a passive role in the contrived attractions created and managed by others.

The Touristic Transition at the National Level

The process of touristic transition at the national level is manifested primarily in the gradual transformation of the remaining natural attractions in the course of the expansion of tourism into previously unexploited areas, and in the proliferation of new contrived attractions primarily in more mature tourist areas. The transition has mitigated Thailand's "exoticism," forcing a subtle reorientation of the image by which Thailand is promoted from "exotic" to "amazing" as the leading epithet for the country in recent promotional campaigns.

I shall briefly illustrate the transformation of natural attractions at the national level and the creation of some major contrived attractions in four domains: the national parks, archaeological sites, festivals, and theme and amusement parks.

National Parks

Although the establishment of tourist facilities in national parks is nominally prohibited, uncontrolled and often illegal, foreigner-oriented tourism development has in recent decades affected beyond repair the natural environment of Samet and Phi Phi islands (*Bangkok Post* 26 March 1989, 17 March 1994; *The Nation* 6 August 1991). Some other national parks have been penetrated by resort developers for domestic tourism on a smaller scale. The Thai Forestry Department and the Forest Industry Organisation recently proposed to regularise the exploitation of the national parks under the guise of eco-tourism (*Bangkok Post* 1 August 1998, 30 September 1998; *The Nation* 14 September 1998). Their proposal also seeks to legitimise the already irreversible tourism development of Samet and Phi Phi islands (*Bangkok Post* 24 April 1998), but it may also eventually lead to the transformation of some of the last niches of "untouched" nature in the country.

Archaeological Sites

The restoration of archaeological sites by the national authorities is officially intended to preserve the national heritage. However, this endeavour is also influenced by various political and economic considerations accompanying, and sometimes overriding, the purely historical, scientific ones. The political considerations are aimed primarily at domestic tourists and derive from the endeavour to reaffirm, in the selection of sites and the manner of their restoration, the hegemony of the official historical narrative that has been challenged by revisionist historians (Peleggi 1996:433). Moreover, this endeavour is accompanied by other more practical considerations deriving from the tourism potential of restored sites. In some instances, tourism potential overrides scientific considerations in the interest of making a site more accessible or attractive to tourism. Hence, one critic of the TAT conservation policy pointed out: "[s]ince the 1980s, 'conservation' has been clearly stated in the policy of TAT . . . However, this is only a euphemism because it has been done for economic benefits. The conservation of tradition by TAT, for example [and by implication of archaeological and historical sites], are carried out to please tourists primarily" (Chantarotron 1992:18). Another author points out that, according to critics, "a tourism-oriented policy prevails, archaeological sites are preserved to serve tourists rather than to help locals recognise their historical value. . ." (*Bangkok Post* 7 January 1995). As a consequence, a Thai journalist complained that "our historic monuments [are turned] into tourism venues that [may] easily be mistaken for amusement parks" (*Bangkok Post* 20 November 1996).

The desire to attract tourists led, according to one author, to the tendency for "reconstruction [of ancient sites], by adding and adapting to build up a complete structure according to ideas those in charge think are right, [which] is thought to give a better impression to tourists than a ruined one" (*Muang Boran Journal* 1987:11). Thus, for example, in "Sukhothai [Park] Buddha images were sculpted to replace all the missing ones. . ." (*Muang Boran Journal* 1987:11). The author concludes that "such renovation for commercial benefit is not based on reality and may even lead to self-indulgence" (*Muang Boran Journal* 1987:11). The invention of "ancient traditions" to accompany the restoration of Sukhothai has led, in the blunt words of another critic, to its "Disneyfication" (*Bangkok Post* 20 November 1996).

The context and ambience of restored archaeological sites is further transformed by their inclusion in historical parks or even by the more prosaic construction of roads, car parks, toilets, accommodation and other facilities (*Bangkok Post* 18 March 1993) to serve the needs and convenience of tourists. Furthermore, in some extreme cases, the fanciful restoration of sites is not just a mere transformation of attractions to adapt them to tourist visits; in the case of some of the more important restored archaeological sites, such as the old capital of Sukhothai, the alterations imposed upon the site and its surroundings in fact amount to the creation of a partially contrived attraction.

Festivals

Festivals are integral to Thai folk religion and constitute the high point of communal religious activities. Temple festivals and fairs are commonly held at Buddhist temples at least once a year throughout rural Thailand, while major Buddhist, Chinese and other popular festivals are celebrated in urban centres (Gerson 1996). Such festivals attract large numbers of visitors, and owing to their colourful rituals and accompanying events, constitute major tourist attractions. From a relatively early stage in the development of tourism in Thailand, some festivals became oriented to, and influenced by, tourism. Thus, Plion-Bernier (1973:55), after describing what he claims to have been the last traditional elephant round-up, in 1938, claims that, "the present time round-ups are organised each year for tourists . . . ." The elephant round-up in Surin, the principal staged representation of the traditional elephant hunt, was revived already in 1960 (Gerson 1996:53), and soon became a tourist attraction (*Holiday Time in Thailand* 1969). It features such events as soccer matches between elephants and the "re-enactment of an ancient battle when several 'warriors' charge on elephant back, handling long-handled weapons . . ." (Gerson 1996:53). The popular Songkran festival (the Thai New Year) was already in 1980 said to have become "more colourful, more riotous and more uproarious" than it used to be 30 years earlier (*Sawasdee* 1980); it has become even more so since then — attracting growing numbers of foreign tourists, not only as spectators but also as participants. A similar transformation has occurred in some other major established festivals, such as the Candle Festival in Ubon (*Kinnaree* 1988) and the Chinese Vegetarian Festival in Phuket (*Bangkok Post* 10 October 1999; *Phuket, Phi Phi and Krabi* circa 1990; *The Nation* 23 October 1998), at least partially under the impact of the sheer presence of growing numbers of domestic and foreign tourists, and of the desire of locals to attract and impress them (Cohen 2001a). The scope of participants has increased, the principal traditional events were elaborated and spectacularized, and in some instances, various new events, unrelated to the major theme of the festival, were introduced.

Even more significant in the present context is the creation of new festivals, intended to enhance the attractiveness of an established destination, or to place a new one on the tourist map. The Flower Festival of Chiang Mai, initiated in 1977 (*Kinnaree* 1993; *Trip Info* 1997) exemplifies the former; the Egg Banana Festival of Kamphaeng Phet (*Kinnaree* 1998; *Thailand Traveller* 1992), the Lamyai (longan) Festival of Lamphun (*Bangkok Post* 5 August 1993), the Straw Bird Festival of Chainat (*Kinnaree* 1987) and the recently started Fish Festival of Singhburi, illustrate the latter. Such invented festivals, the number of which continues to grow, illustrate well the dynamics of the tourist sphere. They are initially set up as contrived attractions but are soon "naturalised" and incorporated into the local culture, becoming an emergent "tradition." It appears that such incorporation is easier in the domain of festivals than in most other domains discussed here, since most festivals are not just implanted, but can be anchored in some aspects of the local environment, history or culture. They also serve to bolster local identity and pride, and are cherished by the local public even as they attract domestic and foreign tourists.

Theme Parks and Amusement Parks

The most prominent contrived attractions are the various theme parks and amusement parks which emerged in growing numbers and at an ever bigger scale in the boom years preceding the economic crisis of 1997. Their location indicates their intended public. According to a TAT publication devoted to these types of attraction, "most of Thailand's largest and most sophisticated parks are located within easy travelling distance of Bangkok, in the city outskirts. Others are located in popular tourist spots like Pattaya or Chiang Mai" (*Exotic Thailand: Theme Parks, Special Events, Amusement Parks and Water Parks* brochure, circa 1997:n.p.). Those around Bangkok are primarily oriented to the local population as centers of mass leisure activities, even though they also seek to attract domestic and foreign tourists; those around the major tourist centers are primarily oriented to foreign tourism but are also patronized by substantial numbers of domestic tourists.

All the theme and amusement parks are by definition contrived attractions. However, they differ in the extent to which they relate to, or reproduce, elements of the local or national environment, culture and history, or are completely unrelated, implanted affairs. Just as in the case of Pattaya, so at the national level, the more recently established a park, the greater the chance that it will be implanted. Some of the earliest parks, such as the Rose Garden (*Bangkok Pos* 29 July 1993), and the Ancient City (*Saen Sanuk* 1988; *Sawaddi* 1972), both established around 1970 in the vicinity of Bangkok, seek to reproduce some major aspects of Thai culture. The Ancient City, for example, is intended to represent Thailand in miniature and to enable visitors to "learn about many aspects of Thai culture without having to travel the length and breadth of the country" (*Bangkok Post* 25 December 1997). The Rose Garden is said to have become "a driving force in the promotion of Thai culture and tradition throughout the four corners of the globe" (*Bangkok Post* 29 July 1993). But some of the newer parks, like the Disney-inspired Fantasyland (*Exotic Thailand: Theme Parks, Special Events, Amusement Parks and Water Parks* brochure circa 1997) and Siam Park City, are completely alien to local themes and, as such, purely implanted establishments. Many of the latter have been conceived on a massive scale: "the most expansive of these amusement complexes, such as Siam Park City, Dream World and Safari World in the north of Bangkok, are entire cities unto themselves, combining world-class water parks, amusement parks, and cultural attractions on sprawling premises of several hundred thousand square meters" (*Exotic Thailand: Theme Parks, Special Events, Amusement Parks and Water Parks* brochure circa 1997:n.p.). Similarly, the new Phuket FantaSea park, constructed on 270 *rai* (67.5 ha) of land on Kamala beach (*Bangkok Post* 27 April 1998) at a total investment of about 3.3 billion baht (about US$90 million; *The Nation* 5 September 1998) is the largest establishment of its kind on the island. It is expected to attract 2.4 million of the 3.5 million tourists annually visiting the island (*Bangkok Post* 27 April 1998). Joining a plethora of other contrived attractions, the size of this new project and its expected attractiveness indicates the growing significance of contrived attractions on an island whose depleting natural attractions have initially been the sole basis of its touristic attractiveness.

The Touristic Transition at the Regional Level

The late Thai Prime Minister Chatichai Choonhavan's call to transform the Southeast Asia region "from battleground to marketplace" (*Bangkok Post* 7 December 1998) signified a re-orientation of Thailand towards its neighbours. The concrete expression of this re-orientation was the emergence of schemes of regional cooperation between Thailand and its northern and southern neighbours. In the north of Thailand, these schemes have been variously called the Economic Quadrangle (*Bangkok Post* 6 December 1994), the Golden Quadrangle (*Bangkok Post* 28 March 1994; *The Nation* 31 March 1994), or the Greater Mekong Sub-region (*The Nation* 29 July 1994, 8 August 1994) and involve up to six countries: Thailand, Laos, Burma, Vietnam, Cambodia and Southern China (*Bangkok Post* 30 January 1997; *The Nation* 29 July 1994). In the south of Thailand, such schemes are mostly related to a Southern Growth Triangle, involving Thailand, Malaysia and Indonesia (*Bangkok Post* 25 March 1995). Since tourism plays a major role in the northern schemes, I shall restrict my comments to that region.

It should be noted, however, that the optimistic plans of the mid 1990s for an integrated northern regional tourism development have encountered some serious obstacles, and that therefore the extent of the regionalization of tourism is still fairly limited (*Bangkok Post* 4 October 1998). Hence I have to speculate on future developments because established facts are fairly scarce.

Thailand is considered as the centre or "hub" (*The Nation* 7 April 1995) of regional tourism development (*Bangkok Post* 3 April 1995) and the "gateway" to the other mainland Southeast Asian countries (*Bangkok Post* 30 January 1997; TAT n.d.) due to its geographical position in the region, and its relatively well developed infrastructure. Its strategic position within the region can be expected to facilitate investments by Thai entrepreneurs in the development of tourist facilities and touring services in the capital-starved countries of the region.

The Thai tourist authorities are the primary promoters of regionalization, and consider it as one of the strategies for tourism development in the country itself. The representation of Thailand as the "Amazing Gateways" (to other continental Southeast Asian countries) has been chosen as one of the eight principal themes of the "Amazing Thailand" campaign (*Amazing Thailand* 1998–1999 brochure n.d.:19). According to one Thai tourism official, "Thailand, having reached the peak of its tourism boom in the early 1990s, risks losing its appeal unless it can be marketed as part of a more diverse region" (*Bangkok Post* 30 January 1997). This loss of appeal of Thailand is probably a consequence of the over-exploitation of its major mature "natural" attractions, as well as of the rapid development of the country, which affected its general attractiveness. In contrast to Thailand, according to the same official, the other "Mekong countries are considered the last frontiers of Southeast Asian tourism." These countries are said to possess great potential as tourist destinations owing to their fresh and, as yet, untouched environmental and cultural attractions.

I submit that the regional integration of tourism will have two principal consequences for the touristic transition of Thailand. On the one hand, on the national level, it will create a growing division of labour between Thailand, as the center of regional tourism, and the rest of the mainland Southeast Asian region. Thailand will become the staging area for regional tourism, offering its developed tourism facilities and contrived attractions to foreign tourists visiting the region (cf. *Bangkok Post* 15 December 1997). The process of touristic transition will thereby be reinforced and, in a sense, legitimized. In comparison with its neighbours, Thailand as a country will probably lose much of the exotic appeal it still possesses, and become increasingly a shopping, entertainment and vacationing destination, while the region will offer the tourists its "abundant historical and cultural heritage and unspoiled natural beauty" (*Bangkok Post* 19 December 1994).

On the other hand, however, at the local level, regionalization will help to expand the tourist sphere into some of the remaining remote, unexploited parts of the country. The gateway areas for overland tourism, which provide access to the neighbouring countries in the far north and deep south, will be opened up to passing foreign tourism. Hence the north-to-south tourist axis of the country will be extended right to the international boundaries. The natural attractions of these remote areas will thus be visited by growing numbers of tourists. Even more significantly, the huge northeastern region of the country (Isan), lying outside the north-to-south axis, and presently underdeveloped, can be expected to become the gateway to Indochina (cf. *The Nation* 11 April 1997), its diverse attractions becoming part of regional itineraries which will include Isan, Laos, Cambodia and Vietnam.

Regionalization can thus be expected to reinforce the growing importance of facilities and contrived attractions in the more mature tourist locations of Thailand and contribute to the gradual transformation of attractions in the more remote, as yet unexploited areas, thus intensifying the process of touristic transition of the country.

Conclusion

Thailand is an ambiguous example of success in tourism development. Enjoying a very positive tourist image, it succeeded in attracting rapidly growing numbers of foreign tourists. Tourism is a leading earner of foreign currency, and an important branch of the national economy. But this success was achieved at a high price: tourism contributed significantly to the often reckless destruction of natural resources, characteristic of the process of Thailand's rapid economic development as a whole, even as those resources constituted the basis of its success. Tourism has also been an important contributing factor to the process of commodification of art, culture, and sex in Thailand. It should be noted, though, that, in the domain of art and culture, tourism has contributed to the preservation of crafts and customs which would otherwise have disappeared, as well as to the emergence of new artistic styles (Cohen 2000) and cultural performances, however their aesthetic value may be judged.

The rapid environmental and cultural changes which the country experienced in the last two decades, and the self-defeating practices in the sphere of tourism, created a growing gap between the image of the country and its reality. The impact of this gap on foreign tourism was partly mitigated by the change in the composition of the tourism flow. The expansion of mass vacationing relative to sight-seeing, and the declining interest among contemporary tourists in "authenticity" probably ameliorated the impact which the degradation and transformation of the principal natural attractions could otherwise have had on tourist arrivals and satisfaction. The emergent development of eco-tourism, and other forms of soft tourism in as yet less exploited areas (*Bangkok Post* 20 December 1997) may also have siphoned off some of the remaining authenticity-seeking tourists from the mature tourism locations. The rapid growth in the number and scope of contrived attractions in these locations can thus be seen partly as a compensation for the depletion of natural attractions, and partly as a response to the tastes and preferences of the enjoyment-seeking vacationers who became their principal customers. The contrived attractions thus served both as a remedy as well as an incentive to vacationing tourism.

However, as we have seen, the touristic transition, the main characteristic of which is the increase in the relative number, size and significance of contrived attractions, is a nation-wide and not just a localized process. Many of the often gigantic entertainment complexes erected in the vicinity of the major cities, and especially Bangkok, were intended to serve primarily the leisure needs of the local population and of domestic, rather than foreign, tourism, although they also seek to attract foreign tourists. Such attractions are one of many expressions of the growing commercialization and westernization of Thai culture and, as such, provide familiar entertainment opportunities to foreign visitors.

The regionalization of mainland Southeast Asian tourism, as was pointed out above, may well reinforce the process of Thailand's touristic transition, with Thailand as a country specializing in the provision of facilities and contrived attractions while the newly opened countries and the remote border regions of Thailand provide fresh natural environmental and cultural attractions.

The problems at the bottom of Thailand's touristic transition, and the self-defeating practices which provoked them, have not escaped the attention of the planners of the regionalization of mainland Southeast Asian tourism. The need for "preservation" and "sustainability" of tourism in the areas to be newly opened up, and the emphasis upon eco-tourism and other forms of soft tourism, are common themes in the planners' "greenspeak" (Dann 1996:238–249; *The Nation* 2 February 1999).

It is highly questionable, however, to what extent the promoters and entrepreneurs of the regionalization of tourism will actually be willing or able to maintain the high principles of sustainability and soft tourism, especially under the pressure of the need of governments for foreign exchange and the desire of entrepreneurs for rapid profits. It should be noted that in all the countries surrounding Thailand, transportation infrastructure and tourist facilities are hardly existent outside the major urban centers (*Bangkok Post* 15 February 1996). However, their very establishment, accompanied by the arrival of great numbers of relatively wealthy foreigners into poor and isolated ethnic communities, may constitute a serious environmental and cultural threat, however well behaved the tourists and however "soft" their accommodation and means of transportation (*The Nation* 2 February 1999). Moreover, from the dire experience of other destinations, we learn that sustainability and eco-tourism tend to become mere slogans used to promote the image of travel and tour companies, who in fact pay them mere lip-service. Under the circumstances, a successful regionalization of tourism, measured in terms of numbers of tourists, length of stay and expenditures, will almost inevitably bring about the same phenomenon of transformation of natural attractions and their eventual destruction as has occurred in Thailand. It should also be noted that some of the surrounding countries are already eager to develop large-scale contrived attractions, though their natural ones have hardly been tapped. Thus both Cambodia and Vietnam have made deals with foreign companies to open casinos in various locations (*Bangkok Post* 2 May 1995; *Business Day* 17 January 1995) and Cambodia planned "to organize a major Ramayana festival at Angkor in 2000" (*Bangkok Post* 7 December 1998).

The basic question regarding regionalization is, will international promoters and entrepreneurs become convinced that the region is sufficiently attractive to large numbers of prospective visitors to be worth the risk to initiate and construct the needed infrastructure for large-scale tourism (*The Nation* 1 September 1998)? Or whether they will find it preferable, at least for the time being, to keep tourism in the remote areas of mainland Southeast Asia on a small scale, restricted to adventure and elite tourism, thereby saving these areas from the kind of devastation which tourism has wrought in similar areas elsewhere. Though such forms of tourism are not without detrimental environmental and cultural effects, these effects are "softer" and considerably easier to control than the "harder" effects of massive tourism penetration. Furthermore, they do not encourage the creation of contrived attractions, and the acceleration of the process of touristic transition, of the kind Thailand is presently undergoing.

Thailand's touristic transition represents perhaps an extreme case of a widespread type of interconnectedness between natural and contrived attractions, the latter complementing, and to an extent, substituting for, the former. Some developed urban destinations, such as Singapore, may constitute instances of a contrasting type of interconnectedness: initially based on contrived attractions, Singapore is presently opening up and promoting some complementary natural ones (Chang 1998). How widespread this type of interconnectedness is or will become remains to be determined by further comparative research.

Chapter 19

Conclusion: The Way Ahead

A profound paradox marks the prognoses on the future of tourism: while some observers, basing themselves on projections from current trends in tourism, enthuse about its robust future, others, observing that the diversity of the world is progressively diminishing, implicitly presage its future decline. Both positions can be found in the recently published third edition of the well-known compendium "Hosts and Guests," now subtitled "Tourism Issues of the 21st Century" (Smith and Brent (co-eds.) 2001). In that volume Valene Smith quotes WTO's *Vision 2020* to the effect that, by the year 2020, tourism will increase by about 241 percent over the year 2000, and reach 1.6 billion international arrivals (2001:381–382). However, in a section of his chapter in the book, significantly entitled "Why leave home," Dean MacCannell, sounding rather like a latter-day Boorstin, complains that, while tourism is predicated on the "quest for *otherness*" (2001:381; his emphasis), "the experiences one has going between any two points on the face of the Earth are increasingly similar. They do not resemble earlier travel as much as they reproduce the experience of sitting in hospital waiting rooms" (ibid.:382). In MacCannell's view, "the key characteristic of the [postmodern] culture of tourism is that ... every tourist destination begins to resemble any other destination and that tourist 'destination' increasingly resembles *home* (his emphasis) ... A question that emerges ... is whether tourism itself, in its drive to homogenize the travel experience and the destination, will eventually destroy the reason to travel" (ibid.:380). It turns out that, combining the two views, the more people will travel, the fewer incentives they will allegedly have to undertake their trip. I shall use this paradox as a point of departure for a glimpse on the road ahead for tourism.

My own position, most fully stated in Chapter 9, was in the past to a considerable extent congruent with MacCannell's as quoted above: I claimed there that the loss of "placeness" of destinations, the nivellation of experiences deriving from different "finite provinces of meaning" in postmodernity, and the ascent of simulation technology — culminating in Virtual Reality — pose the threat of the "end of tourism" as a distinct type of activity. Although I qualified that expectation, I have desisted from an attempt to augur the emerging features of future tourism. This will be briefly attempted here.

My principal claim is that two contrary trends can be discerned in contemporary tourism, each of which will become more extreme in the future. These contrary trends help to resolve the above paradox — so that, although MacCannell may be partially right, Smith's prediction regarding the future growth of tourism does not appear unreasonable.

The first trend is marked by a progressive decline of the "quest for otherness" as the principal tourist motivation in postmodern tourism — leading to a loss of extraordinariness of the tourist experience and the asymptotic merger of tourism and ordinary leisure. The contrary trend is towards a quest for ever-growing otherness culminating in the totally Other, and leading asymptotically to a merger of tourism and exploration. Both trends raise MacCannell's query "why travel?" but in different senses: the first, why take the trouble to travel in face of the allegedly growing sameness of the world? The second, why travel in quest of otherness, if otherness has allegedly vanished from the contemporary world? I shall first critically examine the concepts of sameness and otherness and then turn to the rationale underlying each of these contrasting trends in tourism.

I argue that the concepts of "sameness" and of "otherness," just like "authenticity" (Chapter 7) are not absolute concepts, but are context-dependent and socially constructed. Moreover, contrary to the impression one may get from MacCannell's (2001) article, these are not dichotomous concepts, but rather the end-points of a continuum. Points on this continuum represent various degrees of perceived difference between "home" and various destinations.

Some post-modernists claim that the "post-tourists" tend to travel in quest for the familiar, rather than of otherness (Ritzer and Liska 1997:99). However, one should not confuse the quest for the familiar, with a quest for sameness. This observation is particularly relevant in view of the emphasis in contemporary sociology on "taste" and "distinction" as a mark of class (Bourdieu 1984). Sophisticated "post-tourists" may appreciate slight but significant differences within the domain of the familiar, which make objects, sites, sights or events distinctive, and hence make the effort and expense of travel worth-while, even though their distinctiveness may not be perceived or appreciated by less sophisticated others, to whom they may appear all the same. The quest for such distinctions within the familiar is a significant factor in the increasingly important field of urban tourism, with major cities vying with each other to provide distinctive cultural opportunities in the form of museums, theatrical performances, music, exhibitions, and cuisine to attract contemporary tourists and revive thereby their declining central areas. The point to note is that these cultural offerings do not particularly stress the "otherness" of some local ethnic or cultural traditions, but belong predominately to an "un-marked" world culture. Cultural festivals, like the Edinburgh Festival (Prentice and Andersen 2003), or novel, impressive cultural edifices, like the new Guggenheim Museum in Bilbao (Lacy and Douglass 2002:15–16) strikingly illustrate this tendency. The apparent "sameness" of the contemporary world thus harbors socially significant differences and distinctions, which may attract visitors, even though "otherness" may have vanished from the face of the Earth — a claim which I shall seek to qualify below.

A further observation reinforces the preceding point from a different angle: the process of globalization is frequently seen as the source of an increased homogenization of the world, leading to complaints about its growing "sameness." This is popularly expressed in such catch-words as Cocacolization or McDonaldization (Ritzer 1993). But such a simplistic argument misses an important point: namely that globalization is not a unidirectional process, but interacts with local cultures, engendering often creative processes of "glocalization." A novel, post-modern aesthetics leads to the emergence of strikingly mixed, fused and otherwise innovative cultural phenomena, which introduce variety into the apparent sameness of the contemporary world, in the fields of popular culture, art, music, cuisine and even religion. As such processes mature, they tend to re-heterogenize the world, engendering a new kind of "otherness" of potential touristic attractiveness. In contrast to the otherness of the pre-modern world, the quest for which was assumedly a major motive of modern tourism (MacCannell 1976:5), this post-modern "otherness" is not locally rooted, and not marginal to post-modernity, but rather one of its distinguishing marks. It is not the "otherness" of the disappearing traces of the past, but the "otherness" of the unexpectedly novel. While in the modern "ecology of otherness" the degree of otherness encountered by the traveler tends to increase in direct relation to his distance from home, the post-modern "ecology of otherness" resembles a patchwork, in which the familiar and the strange, sameness and otherness, often co-exist in the same location. The foci of this interpenetration of the global and the local are the world's cities, especially the larger ones, which experience most intensely the effects of the movement of people, goods and cultures across national boundaries and between continents brought about by globalization. In many of the world's cities, contrasting social, cultural and religious groups can be found in close proximity, interacting with one another and engendering new glocalized cultural forms.

However, while such novel cultural forms may strike the visitor as startling and attractive, they are not, or not yet, perceived an "authentic" — although, authenticity being an emergent property (Chapter 7), they may be so perceived in the future, just as early jazz, a forerunner of glocalization, is presently perceived. Rather, many of the glocalized new cultural products, in art, music and cuisine,[85] appear to be tentative and playful, perhaps inadvertently reflecting a ludic strain in post-modernism.

It is not yet clear to what extent the novel, glocalized cultural products, constituting a new kind of otherness, tend to become significant tourist attractions. Would people travel to Africa to see, not just wild animals in their natural setting, but also a performance of "Shakespeare in the Bush" (Bohanan 1977) or to Thailand to see, in addition to the temples and nightlife, a Thai musical version of Goethe's "Faust" (Pravattiyagul 2002)? Will the sites of African Pentecostal churches in Amsterdam or Tel Aviv become as attractive as the tourist-oriented performances of "traditional" rituals in their countries of origin? If they will, the products of glocalization may have a profound impact on travel patterns: the new "ecology of otherness" may attract tourists to experience strange new attractions in locations close to home, while foregoing to travel to remote locations which, through modernization, ever more resemble "home," as MacCannell (2001) has argued.

One consequence of the glocalized cultural products becoming tourist attractions will thus be the further erasure of the boundary between tourism and leisure — since the experience of the new "otherness" may become incorporated into everyday leisure activities — just as dining in a variety of "ethnic restaurants" of foreign and often remote provenience, has already become (van den Berghe 1983).

But perhaps the principal factor leading to the erasure of the boundary between tourism and ordinary leisure is another rapidly growing contemporary phenomenon: the proliferation of large-scale theme parks and entertainment complexes, with the dual appeal to fantasy and consumerism. These centers are viable only if they have a catchment area incomparably bigger than that of the older local entertainment venues. The viability of such complexes as Las Vegas, the various Disneylands, or of the West Edmonton Mall is dependent on their attractiveness to whole countries or even continents. The growing ease and increasingly affordable cost of travel make such centers accessible to the contemporary consumers, who are thus able to expand the boundaries of the "action space" of their leisure activities far beyond the boundaries of their home environment to which they were until recently mostly limited.

One principal trend in contemporary tourism, which can be projected into the future, whether expressed in the quest for differences in the familiar, the novel and often ludic "otherness" of glocalization, or in the fantasy and consumerism of giant entertainment centers, thus leads to the gradual fusion of tourism and ordinary leisure, the former losing its special, extra-ordinary (Graburn 1977) character, and becoming ever more a routine leisure activity. This trend may well be a particular instance of a more general trend to de-differentiation between diverse social or cultural domains, said to be one of the distinguishing marks of post-modernity. But this possibly dominant trend in future tourism is not the sole one: it is contested by a perhaps numerically much smaller, but still significant contrary trend consisting of a tenacious search for authenticity and culminating in a quest for an encounter with the totally Other.

This trend constitutes a continuation of the modern quest for otherness, as well as a contestation of the alleged disappearance of "originals" (and hence of authenticity), of the supposed sameness of the contemporary world, and of the post-modern nivellation of experiences of all "finite provinces of meaning."

Tourists with a persevering modern inclination will persist in challenging the "post-tourist's" (Ritzer and Liska 1997) resignation to a world of increasing sameness in which travel tends to be reduced to "mere" leisure, enjoyment and fun. They will stubbornly engage in an intensified quest for authenticity and otherness — whether in the remaining traces of the past, in the challenges posed by the extreme, often inhospitable margins of the Earth, and, especially, beyond the Earth, in space. I shall briefly discuss these modalities of this contrary trend.

The principal expression of the concern with the traces of an "authentic" past is what could be called the "conservation movement," which operates in two principal domains: on the one hand, the preservation and restoration of the material heritage, archeological sites, such as old cities, urban quarters or buildings, and the salvation and museumization of arts and crafts; and on the other hand, the conservation or rehabilitation of some of the remaining natural environments, mostly in the form of nature preserves and national parks. Conservation is believed to render the seeker of authenticity a glimpse into the authentic past of human culture and terrestrial nature, even though the traces of that past are often heavily staged for economic, political, cultural or religious reasons, which may disqualify them as genuine originals in the eyes of post-modernists.

The aim to preserve the traces of the past while making them accessible to visitors in its turn encourages the concern for sustainability in tourism, which became a growing preoccupation of tourism planners and practitioners, as well as of tourism social scientists, in the last two decades.[86] This in turn, encouraged the emergence of various forms of "soft tourism," the most popular of which at present is "eco-tourism." Ironically, the very success of this form of tourism among concerned and reflective contemporary tourists has turned into a catchword used by the tourist industry for the promotion of destinations, facilities and amenities, which may threaten the very survival of the sites which "eco-tourism" is supposed to preserve. The sustainability of some of the most precious sites is in some instances dependent upon a restriction on the number of visitors; insofar as such sites are commercially managed, access to them may become prohibitively expensive for all but the most wealthy tourists, thus engendering problems of equity (Cohen 2002).

Owing to the process of increasing homogenization of the world, its surviving margins, which as yet have not been affected by modernity or penetrated by mass tourism, gain increasing significance for the contrary trend in tourism. These margins remain unpenetrated owing to their inaccessibility, inclement climate or harsh physical characteristics: the principal examples of such marginal areas are desolate deserts, high mountain ranges, polar regions and the deep seas. Moderns seeking to escape the growing homogenization of the world tend to go to great expenses, invest much effort and expose themselves to considerable dangers to take adventurous excursions to these regions: desert-crossing trips, high mountain climbing, polar excursions or deep-sea diving are the principal examples of the quest for extreme authentic otherness among contemporary nature tourists, which in some cases may straggle the boundary between tourism and exploration.

While such tourism to the remaining margins of the world tends to make use of all technical gadgets available or affordable to minimize risk and increase the travellers' comfort, a variant of this kind of tourism seeks to increase the excitement of danger and risk, by reducing the use of gadgetry to a minimum: unassisted crossing of polar regions, or solo trekking trips through deserts exemplify this tendency. Such danger-seeking tourism may in some instances be combined with novel kinds of "extreme sports," as for example in free rock climbing, para-gliding or heli-skiing.

I suggest that in the more extreme forms of adventure tourism, a sense of "flow" (Csikszentmihalyi *et al.* 1988) is often engendered in the traveler as he or she master the strains and risks of the trip in strange but fascinating surroundings. In such situations, a fusion may take place between two kinds of authenticity discussed by Wang (2000), the experience of the "objective" authenticity of the surroundings with the "existential" authenticity engendered by total involvement in the tasks of the trip and the awe-inspiring sublimity of the surroundings.

This brings us to a theoretical consideration which may have significant implications for future tourism: Tom Selwyn (1996:7, 21–28) has proposed an important distinction between authenticity as "knowledge" and authenticity as "feeling," or "cold" and "hot" authenticity, which led Wang to his distinction between "objective" (or "constructed") and "existential" authenticity, the former an amplification of "cold" authenticity, the latter of "hot" authenticity (Wang 2000:46–71). In their effort to disengage the experience of "hot" or "existential" authenticity from the authenticity of the tourist's surroundings, both authors paid insufficient attention to the conditions fostering the former experience. While I do not deny that "a good time" and a "hightened sense of living," can be attained in surroundings which are not perceived as particularly authentic, I still believe that the most exalted instances of the experience of existential authenticity are engendered in the presence of "authentic" natural sites which strike the tourist as majestic or sublime: the "mystique" of the deep forest, the view from a high mountain top, the loneliness of a desert night; and it is this fusion of "objective" and "existential" authenticity which is especially sought after by the tourists in quest of extreme otherness.

These considerations are of particular relevance for what to me appears to be the principal direction of expansion of otherness and authenticity-seeking tourism in the course of the new century and even the new millennium: space travel.

Space tourism is as yet in its very early stages, even though various kinds of virtual space experiences are already commercially available (Brent 2001). Real space travel, however, has at the time of writing been the privilege of only two super-rich tourists each of whom spent about twenty million U.S. dollars for his trip. But the number of space tourists will probably increase at an accelerating rate in the foreseeable future, as the costs of space travel gradually decline.

Space tourism, in its earliest stages, will in some respects resemble extreme adventure tourism on Earth; but it will also differ from it in some other important respects. The crucial difference lies in the nature of adventure in space. This resembles extreme adventure tourism on Earth in its quest for risk-taking and exhilaration and for elating sights, all of which may lead to profound existential experiences. Indeed, considering the alleged growing scarcity of opportunities for experiences of "real" otherness on Earth, space, appears to promise in the foreseeable future inexhaustible opportunities to encounter the radical Other.[87]

However, while in terms of motivation and desired experiences space tourism may resemble adventure tourism, in some other respects it is almost the opposite of it — and, paradoxically, may even feature some traits of mass tourism. The distinguishing mark of the adventurer is that, though he may be skilled and trained, his survival ultimately depends on his individual obduracy, determination and decisiveness when confronting menacing or dangerous situations. In space travel, though — at least at present — the prospective space tourist has to undergo extensive training, on the trip he is a passive guest, who is permitted to perform only minimal, if any, chores on the space-ship. In sharp contrast to the adventurer, the space tourist's conduct is severely circumscribed; he is powerless regarding any decisions of practical impact, and precluded from participation in emergency activities. Moreover, like the mass tourist, the space traveler is ensconced in an "environmental bubble" reproducing crucial features of the terrestrial environment, which — owing to the inclement conditions of space, he is precluded from leaving. Hence, like that of many mass tourists, his experience of *space* is exclusively visual, direct contact being absolutely out of the question — even though the conditions of *travel* in space lead to dramatic bodily experiences, such as of the increased force of gravity during ascent and descent and of weightlessness in the course of the trip.

The relative insulation and passivity of the space tourist thus contrasts sharply with the exposure and alacrity of the adventurer on Earth. Whether future developments in space technology, and especially the colonization of space and of the planets, will eventually alleviate some of the present constraints on space tourists and endow them with a greater opportunity for autonomous action is at present not yet predictable.

I have outlined two contrasting trends which to my mind will characterize future tourism. I have not, however, dealt with the important question of their interaction, whether on the individual or the historical level. Will individuals, after they playfully experienced the virtual otherness of space in some theme park, be inspired to seek the "real thing" in outer space? Will space travel become a popular form of entertainment? Will it become a routinized version of mass tourism in the course of the new millennium? As my own long journey in the exploration of tourism gradually approaches its conclusion, it is left to others to explore these, as well as many other, open questions regarding the future of tourism on Earth as well as in space.

Endnotes

1. If consequentially followed to its ultimate implications, the idea of "constructed" authenticity may in fact be used to relativise the concept of "objective" authenticity — its "objectivity" resting merely on the criteria of judgment of "authorized" professionals — such as curators, anthropologists, archeologists and historians. Insofar as their judgments are congruent, there is consensus in the professional community — and "objectivity" appears as a social fact; but this is destabilized if there are differences of judgment between professionals — thus revealing the constructed nature of "objective authenticity," making it in principle undistinguishable from the "constructed authenticity" of tourists — though the divergent professional judgments will be more explicitly grounded in the professionals' theoretical, methodological or philosophical assumptions.

2. Much of my empirical work on tourism in Thailand has been published in two collections of articles (Cohen 1996a, 2000) and in a recent monograph (Cohen 2001a).

3. Some of the ideas developed in this general article have later been applied to the analysis of "Thai Tourism in Transition" (Chapter 18).

4. The very term "tourism" was originally used in a deprecatory vein (Oxford 1933, Vol. XI:190). Ogilvie (1934:66) however, claims that "The term tourist became current early in the 19th century as a somewhat contemptuous synonym for traveller, but it is now used in the social sciences, without color."

5. A most outstanding example of such an acceptance of the stereotype are some of the generalizations in the otherwise brilliant essay by D. Boorstin: "From Traveller to Tourist: The Lost Art of Travel" in Boorstin (1962:77–117).

6. Thus, e.g. Dumazedier (1967) in a chapter devoted to "Vacation Leisure and Tourist Leisure," foregoes completely any attempt at a definition. Neither has Anderson (1961a) found it necessary to define the term. In the older German sociological literature, however, considerable care has been devoted to the definition of the somewhat broader term *Fremdenverkehr*. Knebel (1960:1–3) quotes several such definitions. Definitions of "tourism" constructed for purposes of (international) travel statistics also aim to capture this broader connotation of the term.

7. Cohen (1956:80–96) calls such indefinite boundaries of concepts "twilight zones."

8. Unfortunately, no adequate analytical framework has yet been proposed for the classification of the different types of migratory or travelling roles. Petersen's (1958) typological effort is largely irrelevant for present purposes. Kunz (1973) has recently attempted an analytical typology of refugees, as a sub-type of migrants. To my knowledge, no attempt has yet been made to provide a typology of non-migrant travelling roles. Tourism would obviously represent one type of such roles; other examples would be the (scientific) explorer, the wanderer, the adventurer, the (modern) nomad, the pilgrim, etc.

9. Zadeh's (1965) idea of "fuzzy sets" came to my attention through an unpublished paper by J. E. Pierce, who uses this tool in a different context.

10. Boorstin contrasts the term travel (derived from French "travail," to work) with tourist (derived from "tour") to provide an etymological underpinning for his argument that "travelling" is essentially active while tourism is essentially passive (Boorstin 1962:85).

11. Our definitional strategy is essentially one which Johnson (1972:23–31), in the context of the definition of the concept "profession" calls a "trait" approach. Johnson shows the inadequacies of such an approach and urges the formulation of a "functional" definition of the term (ibid.:32–37). In this he agrees with modern logicians, who consider transformational concepts preferable to mere classificatory concepts, emphasizing genus and species (Cohen 1956:82–83). Considering the underdeveloped state of a sociology of travel and travellers, it seems to me that nothing but a "trait" approach is as yet feasible; we shall refine this approach by introducing some order between the traits of the tourist role, and by taking account of partial tourist roles located on the fuzzy boundaries of the concept.

12. Kunz (1973), in a review of the literature on refugees, also distinguishes two aspects in the study of refugee movements: the study of "flight" (corresponding to our "travelling" component) and the study of "settlement" (corresponding to our "visitor" component). Kunz makes a point to emphasize that these two aspects should be studied in conjunction (ibid.:127).

13. The type of travellers who received considerable attention in the literature are the various types of wanderers and adventurers, e.g. hoboes (Allsop 1967; Anderson 1961a; Barth 1969) and urban nomads (Spradley 1970). Pilgrims and pilgrimages have recently been given some systematic attention (Turner 1973).

14. The extent of exposure to "real" novelty and change may vary considerably as between different types of tourists; this, in fact, was the basis of my typology of tourist roles (Chapter 3).

15. "One-day visitors" constitute in some countries a high percentage of the total number of international travellers; thus, the total number of people entering Canada in 1969 was well over 36 millions; but nearly 24 million of these were "one day excursionists," leaving the number of "real" tourists at 12.8 million (Commonwealth Secretariat 1969:24).

16. The combination of external exigencies and individual choices which leads a person to a wandering way of life comes through forcefully from the many descriptions of the life of hoboes in Allsop (1967).

17. Kunz (1973:130) quotes the definition of "refugee" of the Revised 1951 U.N. Convention Relating to the Status of Refugees: ". . . an individual who owing to well-founded fear of being persecuted for reasons of race, religion, nationality, membership of a particular social group or political opinion, is outside the country of his nationality, and is unable, or owing to such fear, unwilling to avail himself or the protection of that country; or, who, not having a nationality or being outside the country of his former habitual residence as a result of such events, is unable or owing to such fear, is unwilling to return to it." Kunz develops a typology of refugee movements, in which the variable "Form of displacement" implicitly distinguishes degrees of voluntariness in the emergence of such movements (ibid.:143).

18. Thus, Becker (1969:516) reports that the grandfather of the Deputy Governor of Hawaii came as a tourist in 1898 and stayed on, and Kaiser, one of the main tourist entrepreneurs in Hawaii, came originally on a five week vacation in 1950 (Fuchs 1961:352).

19. A study in France in 1957, for example, has shown that ruralites do not take vacations at all (Anderson 1961b:110). The traditional form of peasant travel, however, was the pilgrimage, combining elements of tourism with religious devotion.

20. Wall (1972:52), summarizing Bonsey (1968).

21. "... so keen is the demand for lunar holidays that across the world airlines report bookings in excess of half a million would-be moon vacationers" (Gibbins 1972).

22. Summer houses and week-end houses are a form of second-home ownership of rapidly growing importance, particularly in modem Western countries, but increasingly also in other parts of the world. There already exists an extensive literature on this subject: see e.g. on Germany, Dickmann (1963); on France, Clout (1971), Laborde (1969); on Britain, Patmore (1970:153–155); on Canada, Wolfe (1967:161); on Australia, Marsden (1969). For the growing importance of second homes in an East European country, see Neubauer (1973). For a general theoretical approach, see Wolfe (1970).

23. For further details on the development of spa towns, see e.g. Patmore (1968) and Bell and Bell (1972).

24. "Working holidays" are an increasingly popular form of travel for the adventurous but impecunious youth from developing countries in the developed ones, see e.g. Kwee (1973).

25. Williams and Zelinsky (1970:565) examining geographical trends in modern tourism suggest the existence of a "... certain 'heliotropic' factor ... namely a strong south-ward surge of sun-seeking, cold-shunning tourists among our Northern Hemisphere specimens."

26. Knebel (1960:137) speaks, following von Uexküll, of a "touristische Eigenwelt," from which the modern tourist can no longer escape.

27. For a similar approach to modern tourism, see Boorstin (1962:79–80).

28. "Not only in Mexico City and Montreal, but also in the remote Guatemalan tourist Mecca of Chichecastenango, out in far-off villages of Japan, earnest honest natives embellish their ancient rites, change, enlarge and spectacularize their festivals, so that tourists will not be disappointed" (Boorstin 1962:103).

29. Boorstin (1962:98-99), talking of the Hilton chain of hotels, states: "Even the mea-sured admixture of carefully filtered local atmosphere [in these hotels] proves that you are still in the U.S."

30. The tendency of the mass tourist to abide by the guidebook was noticed a hundred years ago by "A Cynic" who wrote in 1869: "The ordinary tourist has no judgment; he admires what the infallible Murray orders him to admire ... The tourist never diverges one hair breadth from the beaten track of his predecessors, and within a few miles of the best known routes in Europe leaves nooks and corners as unsophisticated at they were fifty years ago; which proves that he has not sufficient interest in his route to exert his own freedom of will." Quoted in Larrabee and Meyersohn (1952:285).

31. See e.g. the cover story of *Time Magazine*, entitled "Bargain in the Air: the Cut-Rate Travellers," and K. Allsop's humorous but quite insightful: "Across Europe and Out of Sight, Man" (1972).

32. I am not aware of any published full-scale study on the "tinkers"; G. and Sh. Gmelch of the University of Southern California have conducted a study of the topic in Ireland; see: Blumenthal (1972).

33. On gradations in involvement in the drug-culture, see: Keniston (1968).

34. At the time of writing (early 1970s).

35. Both of these are reprinted, as appendices to Neville (1970).

36. The description of the drifter community of Eilat is based on a paper prepared by my student, Miss Ruth Glaser, for a research seminar on "Small Minorities in Israel" at the Dept. of Sociology, Hebrew University, Jerusalem, in the academic year 1969/70. I am obliged to

Miss Glaser for the valuable information which she supplied. For a general description of drifters in Israel see: David (1970).

37. The intrusion of criminal elements into hippie communities seems to be quite common; see: Smith *et al.* (1979).

38. A Cornell teaching assistant described this type aptly: "You can go on the bum for a summer and still be back in time for classes'. You can live a counter-cultural life-style and not really mean it at all. It's like they say: 'scratch a hippie and you'll find a Porsche' " *Time Magazine* 1971:57 (box).

39. For example, a policeman claimed that the restrictions which the police were imposing upon local Arab youth so they would not associate with the drifters, were in fact intended to protect them from the latters' harmful influences (Chapter 15).

40. This was particularly the case in Singapore, where excessive Westernisation was often identified, in the pronouncements of national leaders, with "hippyism."

41. For a recent article dealing with the principal issues raised in this chapter in the contemporary world, see Cohen (forthcoming a).

42. Definitions of the concept "tourist" abound in the literature. "Travelling for pleasure" is the most commonly evoked dimension of the phenomenon; for additional dimensions necessary for a systematic definition of the tourist as a traveller role, see Chapter 2. The present chapter departs on a different track — it does not deal with the tourist's role, but with the precise nature of his supposedly "pleasurable" experience.

43. Cf. e.g. Gross, 1961: "In the area of tension management, the cathartic and restorative functions of leisure are pre-eminent . . ."

44. If the experience were available within the life-space, there would be no need to take the trouble to travel; cf. Stouffer 1940.

45. "Paradisiac cults" are predicated on the belief that paradise, i.e. the center, is a place which can be approached by an actual voyage, though that voyage may include miraculous elements (e.g. men flying over the sea, Eliade 1969c:101–104); if it is believed that the center is located on a wholly different sphere, it will be approachable by a "spiritual journey," such as that of the shaman (Rasmussen 1972), in which a man is miraculously transported to other spheres without actual physical movement through empirical space.

46. This is evidenced by the recurrent use of paradisiac imagery in modern mass tourism (see e.g. Turner and Ash 1975:149 ff). But the "paradise" these tourists seek is of a stereotyped, commercialized kind — it is an idyllic place equipped with all modern amenities. For a discussion of "paradise" as a "type of touristic community," see MacCannell (1976:183). For an example of the process of debasement of the paradisiac image, see Chapter 16.

47. An excellent example, in which the game of make-believe has been brought almost to the level of a fine art is mass tourism in Hawaii. Thus Crampon describes a three-stage game through which the "royal visitor to the Islands" (i.e. the tourist) becomes a Hawaiian; at the end of this process, the tourist comes to like Hawaii, since the Hawaiian *kama'aina* likes Hawaii. Crampon claims that "Probabl . . . this visitor is not 'acting.' He does like Hawaii. He is convinced that Hawaii is a Paradise" (Crampon m.d.:54). The game has terminated in successful self-delusion, with the full cooperation of the tourist.

48. For MacCannell's definition of "experience" in the sense here used, see MacCannell (1976:23); for some concrete examples of touristic "experiences," see ibid.:97.

49. This point is admirably illustrated in an anecdote told by Eliade of the famous German historian Th. Mommsen. After a lecture in which Mommsen gave by heart a detailed account of the topography of ancient Athens, a valet had to take him home, since ". . . the famous

historian did not know how to go home alone. The greatest living authority on fifth-century Athens was completely lost in his own city of Wilhelminian Berlin" (Eliade 1976:19). Eliade continues: "Mommsen admirably illustrates the existential meaning of 'living in one's own world.' His real world, the only one which was relevant and meaningful, was the classical Greco-Roman world. For Mommsen, the world of the Greeks and Romans was not simple *history* . . .; it was *his* world — that place where he could move, think and enjoy the beatitude of being alive and creative. . . . Like most creative scholars, he probably lived in two worlds: the universe of forms and values, to the understanding of which he dedicated his life and which corresponds somehow to the 'cosmicized' and therefore 'sacred' world of the primitives, and the everyday 'profane' world into which he was 'thrown' as Heidegger would say. Mommsen obviously felt detached from the profane, non-essential, and for him meaningless and ultimately chaotic space of modern Berlin" (ibid.:19). While the historian Mommsen's "real" world was remote in time, the existential tourist's real world is remote in space; but the cognitive structure of their respective worlds is otherwise identical.

50. This idea has been mostly fully developed in the work of the philosopher E. Bloch; most pertinent for our purposes is his discussion of "geographical utopias" (Bloch 1959:873–929). 1 am grateful to Dr. Paul Mendes-Flohr who introduced me to Bloch's ideas.

51. Reported to me by Paul Mendes-Flohr.

52. An excellent example is the Bhagwan Shree Rajneesh Ashram in Poona, visited primarily by Westerners. Rajneesh, who ". . . speeds up the usually slow Hindu attainment of meditation and bliss with a sort of pop-Hinduism. . .," argues that "Westerners want things quickly, so we give it to them right away" (*Bangkok Post* 1978:7).

53. I am obliged for the information on the U.J.A. to Dr. Janet O'Dea.

54. This theme is further elaborated in a paper on the "radical secularization" in late modernity (Cohen 1988); see also Ferrarotti 1979.

55. MacCannell, following Durkheim, means human Society in general, not any particular socio-culture. This is obviously a transcendent concept, which is, according to Durkheim (1954:206) symbolized by the divine. MacCannell therefore does not distinguish between pilgrimage to the socio-culture's own Center (or multiple centers), and tourism to the Centers of others, which, in my view, is a most important analytical distinction (Cohen 1992b).

56. The problem of Arab youth in Israel has been dealt with by several authors: see, particularly, Schwarz (1959:109–118), Peres and Yuval-Davis (1969). On Arabs in Israel, in general, see Landau (1969, part. Chapters 1–4). On the development of Arab-Jewish relations, see Stock (1968).

57. The Israeli Arabs became aware of this attitude when they met West Bank and Gaza Strip Arabs after the Six Days War in 1967. The former discovered to their amazement that the latter were rather hostile and reproachful, resenting the acquiescence of the Israeli Arabs to live in a Jewish state for almost twenty years. As a result of this encounter the Israeli Arabs became more hostile towards Israel than they were before the war. See Peres and Yuval-Davis (1969).

58. On the problems of Arab identity, see Peres and Yuval-Davis (1969).

59. See my complementary article on mixed marriages in the town (Cohen 1969).

60. This attitude is rather similar to the white redneck's attitude to blacks in the Southern U.S. See particularly Dollard (1949). However, some differences between the Israeli and the Southern U.S. situation ought to be noted: there is no idealization of the Jewish women by

the Jews and no sexual exploitation of Arab women by Jewish men, in the sense in which, according to Dollard, the black women were exploited by white males. The Arab woman, in fact, is much less approachable to a Jew than a Jewish woman is to an Arab.

61. For a general discussion of the problems involved in the "circumscription" of the system, for purposes of anthropological inquiry, see Devons and Gluckman (1964:185ff).

62. Cf. his "Nostalgia for Paradise in the Primitive Traditions," in Eliade 1968:57–71.

63. Cf. Manuel and Manuel (1972:113): "In its Christian form the paradise fantasy is a significant component of . . . the voyages of discovery." Thus, even for Columbus the discovery of the Earthly Paradise seems to have become the ultimate, paramount goal of his voyages (ibid.:118–119; see also Columbus 1969:220–222).

64. This interpretation of the symbol of paradise was developed from a suggestion by N.H.H. Graburn in a personal communication. The ideas of Center and Other are more fully developed in Cohen (1992b).

65. Strictly speaking, the seeker of Paradise is a Pilgrim-Traveller. The seeker of the Center in its socio-moral aspects alone, is the Pilgrim — e.g. pilgrims to a holy city, such as Jerusalem, which, though it may be located at the site of Paradise, is devoid of the organic aspect of paradise; conversely, the seeker of the Other in its dangerous but fascinating aspect, is the Traveller, cf. Cohen (1992b).

66. MacCannell (1976:3) has pointed out an interesting relationship between revolution and tourism: ". . . tourism and revolution . . . name the two poles of modern consciousness: a willingness to accept, even venerate, things as they are on the one hand, a desire to transform things on the other." But insofar as a person venerates "things as they are" (or were) elsewhere, outside the boundaries of his society and culture, he in fact relates to an alternative center in space (or time), in a sense which is analogous to the revolutionary's desire to establish an alternative center in the future in his own society.

67. For the difference between natural and contrived touristic attractions, see Chapter 9.

68. "A God comprehended is no God" (Tersteegen, quoted in Otto 1959:39).

69. I am obliged to Paul Mendes-Flohr for introducing me to E. Bloch's work.

70. Cf. e.g. Frankland (1966:148): ". . . he [Khrushchev] coined the phrase that might be taken as his political motto — 'And what sort of communist society is it that has no sausage?' "; such a crude interpretation of the communist utopia makes it look practically achievable.

71. For a detailed discussion of the image of the touristic paradise in the vacation literature, see Lewis and Brissett (1981).

72. On the attractiveness of islands for tourism, see Becker (1969) and Friedel (1978).

73. On the historical development of the paradisiac vision of the Pacific islands in the Western imagination, see Wettlaufer (1973). On the myth of the "Noble Savage," see Eliade (1968:39–56).

74. The publication of a tourist guide for Hawaii in 1893, significantly entitled "Pertinent Points for Pilgrims to the Paradise of the Pacific" (Godfrey 1893) attests to the early popularity of these islands.

75. The list of authors of various nationalities at the end of the 19th and the early 20th century, whose works are set in the Pacific is extensive; among the most popular have been the Australian L. Becker, the two American expatriates who lived in Tahiti, J.N. Hall and Ch. Nordhoff, and another American, R.D. Frisbie.

76. Distant, primitive, as yet uncivilized places lend themselves equally well to extreme idealized, or to horrifying representations, terminating, respectively, in the images

of paradise and hell. This is well illustrated in the title of Friedel's (1978) book. For an illustration of the controversy surrounding the actual conditions of life in primitive society, see Beaucage (1976). The dualism of a paradisiac image countered by an image of wilderness is also exemplified in the imagery of early America (Bellah 1975:8–12).

77. Eventually, the relics of World War II themselves became a touristic attraction; thus, an article in the Pacific Islands Monthly concerning the Solomon Islands claims that ". . . one of their selling points is the colourful war history of the group" (PIM 1967:61).

78. The desire of "existential" tourists to preserve the paradisiac pristinity of the islands against commercialized tourism may occasionally lead to open conflict, as e.g., in the case reported by Blakeway (1980), who claims to have helped the natives of remote Malalai island in the Carolines to frustrate the attempt of an outside entrepreneur to develop a tourist resort.

79. Studied primitiveness of physical plant, dress and interaction is one of the attractions of the Club Méditerranée (Turner and Ash 1975:108), which operates a resort on Bora Bora (Thompson and Adloff 1971:141), while the Mediterranean Club Japan planned to open resorts in Hawaii and later in the Caroline and Mariana islands (Turner and Ash 1975:109).

80. Cf. Huetz de Lemps' statement: "The Polynesian race in a pure state has practically disappeared from the archipelago, and besides, the only Polynesians which are not half-bred are found above all in those parts of the archipelago which are untouched by tourism" (Huetz de Lemps 1966:23, my translation).

81. For a biting criticism of Hawaiian tourism see Kent (1975).

82. The importance of images for the promotion of products is an old truism in marketing and advertising; see e.g. the paragraph entitled "Consumers Buy Images" in Littlefield and Kirkpatrick (1970:55–58).

83. Note, for example, the series of advertisements for Thailand in the 1980s in which the greyness of (Western) "everydayland" was contrasted with the colourful "Thailand."

84. The dynamics of change in the character of contrived attractions resembles the process of "heterogeneisation" of cornmercialised arts and crafts (Cohen 1993a).

85. For example, at a recent food festival in Bangkok, a Thai nutritionist offered bug sandwiches, in an attempt to promote insect food (Suwanpantakul 2002).

86. One of the principal expressions of the concern for sustainability in the social sciences of tourism is the launching in 1993 of a specialized periodical devoted to the topic, *The Journal of Sustainable Tourism.*

87. The transformative impact of space travel on astronauts was noted as early as in 1972 in an article in *Time Magazine* (1972).

References

Adams, J.
  1972   Why the American Tourist Abroad is Cheated: A Price-theoretical Analysis. Journal of Political Economy 80(1): 203–207.
Adams, K.M.
  1984   Come to Tana Toraja, 'Land of the Heavenly Kings'. Annals of Tourism Research 11(3): 469–485.
Adler, C.
  1980   Achtung Touristen. Frankfurt am-Main: Umschau.
Air New Zealand
  1968   Tourist Development Rarotonga (Cook Islands). Report, Air New Zealand, New Zealand Tourist Publicity Department.
Allcock, J.B.
  1988   Tourism as a Sacred Journey. Loisir et Société 11(1): 33–48.
Allsop, K.
  1967   Hard Travelin': The Hobo and His History. London: Hodder and Stoughton.
Allsop, K.
  1972   Across Europe and Out of Sight. Man. Punch 2(August): 130–132.
Almagor, U.V.
  1985   A Tourist 'Vision Quest' in an African Game Reserve. Annals of Tourism Research 12(1): 31–47.
Alneng, V.
  2002   The Modern Does Not Cater for Natives: Travel Ethnography and the Conventions of Form. Tourist Studies 2(2): 119–158.
Amazing Thailand
  1998–1999   (brochure).
Amoa, B.D.
  1986   Tourism in Africa: Report on Regional Consultation in Mombasa on December 16–20, 1985. Nairobi: All Africa Conference of Churches.
Anderson, N.
  1961a   The Hobo: The Sociology of the Homeless Man. Chicago: University of Chicago Press.
Anderson, N.
  1961b   Work and Leisure. London: Routledge & Kegan Paul.

Andronicou, A.
  1979   Tourism in Cyprus. *In* Tourism: Passport to Development? E. deKadt, ed.,
         pp. 237–264. New York: Oxford University Press.
Angell, R.C.
  1967   Growth of Transnational Participation. Journal of Social Issues 23: 108–129.
Animation
  1975   Animation im Urlaub. Starnberg: Studienkreis für Tourismus.
Appadurai, A.
  1986   Introduction: Commodities and the Politics of Value. *In* The Social Life of Things
         – Commodities in Cultural Perspective. A. Appadurai, ed., pp. 3–63. Cambridge:
         Cambridge University Press.
Appolonius of Rhodes
  1959   The Voyage of Argo. E. V. Rien, ed. Harmondsworth: Penguin Books.
Armanski, G.
  1978   Die kostbarsten Tage des Jahres. Berlin: Rotbuch.
Armin, L.A. and Brentano, C., comp.
  1921   Des Knaben Wunderhorn. Munich: Deutsch Meister Verlag.
Asia Magazine
  1988   "Soft City: Just How Great is Pattaya?", 20 March, pp. 8–13.
Aspelin, P.L.
  1977   The Anthropological Analysis of Tourism: Indirect Tourism and the Physical
         Economy of the Mamainde of Mato Grosso, Brazil. Annals of Tourism Research
         4(3): 134–160.
Atkinson, K.
  1973   More Jobs for the Thais. Business Review (February): 248–251.
Babcock, B.A., ed.
  1978   The Reversible World. Ithaca: Cornell University Press.
Bach, S.A.
  1996   Tourist-Related Crime and the Hotel Industry: A Review of the Literature and
         Related Materials. *In* Tourism, Crime and International Security Issues. A. Pizam and
         Y. Mansfeld, eds, pp. 281–296. Chichester, NY: Wiley.
Bales, R.F. and Slater, Ph.E.
  1955   Role Differentiation in Small Decision Making Groups. *In* Family, Socialization
         and Interaction Process. R.F. Bales and T. Parsons, eds, pp. 259–306. Glencoe, IL:
         Free Press.
Ball, D.A.
  1971   Permanent Tourism: A New Expert Diversification for Less Developed Countries.
         International Development Review 13(4): 20–23.
Bangkok Post
  1978   "Sex Guru Challenges Desai", 23 August, p. 7.
Bangkok Post
  1978   "Pollution Threat Clouds Pattaya's Future", 4 July.

Bangkok Post
 1989 "Loved to Death by Tourists", 26 March.
Bangkok Post
 1989 "Sakai to be Featured in Souvenirs", 13 May.
Bangkok Post
 1989 "Pattaya City's Growth Getting Out of Hand", 25 July.
Bangkok Post
 1990 "Festival Attracts 30,000", 21 April.
Bangkok Post
 1992 "Legalized Murder (ad) 2", 22 May.
Bangkok Post
 1993 "To Cut or to Keep", 18 March.
Bangkok Post
 1993 "Driving Force in the Promotion of Thai Culture and Tradition", 29 July.
Bangkok Post
 1993 "Lamphun Lamyai Festival", 5 August.
Bangkok Post
 1993 " 'Revive Pattaya' Project Aims to Boost Beach Resort", 26 November.
Bangkok Post
 1994 "Jet Scooters, Towed Floats, Destroying Koh Samet", 17 March.
Bangkok Post
 1994 "Golden Quadrangle United by Decision to Make Money", 28 March.
Bangkok Post
 1994 "A Week of Fun and Frolics in Pattaya", 17 April.
Bangkok Post
 1994 "Paintball 'War' Games More Fun Than Fury", 19 May.
Bangkok Post
 1994 "Cooperation in Quadrangle has Benefits for Thai North", 6 December.
Bangkok Post
 1994 "TAT to Host Mekong Forum", 19 December.
Bangkok Post
 1995 "Treasures Hanging in the Balance", 7 January.
Bangkok Post
 1995 "Paradise for Lovers of the Weird and the Wacky", 13 January.
Bangkok Post
 1995 "Council to Review Growth Triangle Projects", 25 March.
Bangkok Post
 1995 "TAT Plans to Promote Tourism in 'Greater Mekong' ", 3 April.
Bangkok Post
 1995 "Controversial Floating Casino Opens its Doors", 2 May.
Bangkok Post
 1996 "Quadrangle Tourism Needs Another Kick-Start", 15 February.

Bangkok Post
  1996   "Tourism vs. Historical Accuracy", 20 November.
Bangkok Post
  1997   " 'Resort City' Status a New Selling Point", 9 January.
Bangkok Post
  1997   "Thailand Needs Mekong Links", 30 January.
Bangkok Post
  1997   "Park Owner Aims for Regional Amusement Centre in Decade", 15 December.
Bangkok Post
  1997   "A New Approach to Eco-Tourism", 20 December.
Bangkok Post
  1997   "Thailand's Rocky Road", 24 December.
Bangkok Post
  1997   "Rediscovering the Ancient City", 25 December.
Bangkok Post
  1998   "Critics Decry 'Human Zoo' of Tribeswomen", 6 April.
Bangkok Post
  1998   " 'Parks for Tourism' Proposed", 24 April.
Bangkok Post
  1998   "Phuket FantaSea on Target for Opening in October", 27 April.
Bangkok Post
  1998   "Big-Spending Market Shows no Sign of Slowing", 21 May.
Bangkok Post
  1998   "State Forestry Firm Eyeing Eco-Tourism", 1 August.
Bangkok Post
  1998   "Isan Offers Phenomenal Tourism Opportunities", 10 August.
Bangkok Post
  1998   "Tide of Tourism Threatens Thailand's Natural Beauty", 30 September.
Bangkok Post
  1998   "Quadrangle Schemes Held Up", 4 October.
Bangkok Post
  1998   "Questions Cloud Bid to Revive Cambodian Tourism", 7 December.
Bangkok Post
  1999   "A Piece of the Action", 10 October.
Barker, S.
  1970   On Remote Islands in Forest Villages — Tourists Can Meet the Friendly Fijians.
          Pacific Travel News 14(12): 30–34.
Baroja, E.J.C.
  1965   El Carnaval. Madrid: Tarus.
Barth, Ch.P.
  1969   Hobo Trail to Nowhere. Philadelphia: Whitmore.
Baudrillard, J.
  1988   Simulacra and Simulations. *In* Selected Writings. J. Baudrillard, ed., pp. 166–184.
          Stanford: Stanford University Press.

Baumgartner, F. et al.
1978   Trekking Tourismus in Nepal. Zürich: E. T. H. INDEL, Arbeitsberichte, No. 2.
Beaglehole, J.C.
1966   The Exploration of the Pacific. 3rd ed. London: Adam and Charles Black.
Beaglehole, J.C.
1974   The Life of Captain James Cook. London: Adam and Charles Black.
Beaucage, P.
1976   Enfer ou Paradis Perdu: Les Sociétés Chasseurs-Cueilleurs. Canadian Review of Sociology and Anthropology 13(4): 397–412.
Beck, B. and Brian, F.
1971   This Other Eden: A Survey of Tourism in Britain. The Economist No. 6683, 25 September.
Becker, Ch.
1969   Die Anziehungskraft kleiner Inseln auf den Urlaubsverkehr. Zeitschrift für Wirtschaftsgeographie 13(4): 121–124.
Becker, J.
1969   Look What Happened to Honolulu! National Geographic 136(4): 500–531.
Beckerleg, S.
1995   'Brown Sugar' or Friday Prayers: Youth Choices and Community Building in Coastal Kenya. African Affairs 94(374): 23–28.
Bell, C. and Bell, R.
1972   City Fathers: The Early History of Town Planning in Britain. Harmondsworth: Penguin.
Bell, D.
1977   The Return of the Sacred? The Argument on the Future of Religion. British Journal of Sociology 28(4): 419–449.
Bellah, R.N.
1967   Civil Religion in America. Daedalus (Winter): 1–21.
Bellah, R.N.
1975   The Broken Covenant: American Civil Religion in Time of Trial. New York: Seabury Press.
Bellman, R.P. and Zadeh, L.A.
1970   Decision Making in a Fuzzy Environment. Managerial Science 17(4): B-146–B-164.
Berger, P.L.
1973   'Sincerity' and 'Authenticity' in Modern Society. Public Interest (Spring): 81–90.
Berger, P.L., Berger, B. and Kellner, H.
1973   The Homeless Mind. Harmondsworth: Penguin.
Berger, P.L. and Luckmann, Th.
1966   The Social Construction of Reality. Harmondsworth: Penguin.
Bernard, P. and Huteau, M.
1968   Karennis, les combattants de le Spirale d'Or. [n.l.]: Ed. L'Hartman.
Bernatzik, H.A.
1951   [1938] The Spirits of the Yellow Leaves. London: Robert Hale.

Berreman, G.D.
1991   The Incredible 'Tasaday': Destructuring the Myth of a 'Stone Age' People. Cultural Survival Quarterly 15(1): 2–44.
Bierbeck, C. and LaFree, G.
1993   The Situational Analysis of Crime and Deviance. Annual Review of Sociology 19: 113–137.
Bird-David, N.H.
1988   Hunter-Gatherers and Other People: A Re-Examination. *In* Hunters and Gatherers 1: History, Evolution and Social Change. T. Ingold, D. Riches and J. Woodburn, eds, pp. 17–30. New York: Berg.
Blakeway, M.
1980   The Dilemmas of Paradise. PHP (September): 73–84.
Blau, P.
1967   Exchange and Power in Social Life. New York: Wiley.
Bloch, E.
1959   Das Prinzip Hoffnung. Frankfurt a/M: Suhrkamp Verlag, Vol. II.
Blumenthal, R.
1972   The Irish 'Travelling People.' International Herald Tribune (19 September).
Boeles, J.J.
1963   Second Expedition to the Mrabri ('Khon Pa') of North Thailand. Journal of the Siam Society 51(2): 133–160.
Bohannan, L.
1977   Shakespeare in the Bush. *In* Conformity and Conflict. J.P. Spradley and D.W. McCurdy, eds, pp. 13–23. Boston: Little, Brown and Company.
Boisevain, J.
1977   Tourism and Development in Malta. Development and Change 8: 523–538.
Bonsey, C.
1968   The Rising Tide of Outdoor Recreation. City and Country Gazette 6(1): 306–309.
Boonthanom, S.
1988   The Jungle Life of the Sakai Tribesman. Bangkok Post (16 June): 8.
Boorstin, D.J.
1964   The Image: A Guide to Pseudo-Events in America. New York: Harper & Row.
Bourdieu, P.
1984   Distinction: A Social Critique of the Judgement of Taste. London: Routledge.
Bradley, D.
1983   Identity: The Persistence of Minority Groups. *In* Highlanders of Thailand. J.M. McKinnon and W. Bhruksasri, eds, pp. 46–55. Kuala Lumpur: Oxford University Press.
Brandt, J.H.
1961   The Negrito of Peninsular Thailand. Journal of the Siam Society 49(2): 123–158.
Brent, M.
2001   From Kitty Hawk to the ISS Hilton. *In* Hosts and Guests Revisited. V.L. Smith and M. Brent, co-eds, pp. 354–366. New York: Cognizant Communication Corporation.

Brewer, J.D.
  1978   Tourism, Business, and Ethnic Categories in a Mexican Town. *In* Tourism and Behavior. Studies in Third World Societies. No. 5. V.L. Smith, ed. Williamsburg, Virginia: College of William and Mary, Department of Anthropology.
Brodie, F.M.
  1971   The Devil Drives. Harmondsworth: Penguin.
Brodsky-Porges, E.
  1981   The Grand Tour: Travel as an Educational Device: 1600–1800. Annals of Tourism Research 8(2): 171–186.
Brookfield, H.C. and Hart, D.
  1971   Melanesia: A Geographical Interpretation of an Island World. London: Methuen.
Brown, A.
  1985   Where Pitfalls and Pleasures Await the Tourist. Bangkok Post (26 August).
Brown, P.
  1996   Catskill Culture: The Rise and Fall of a Jewish Resort Area Seen Through Personal Narrative and Ethnography. Journal of Contemporary Ethnography 25(1): 83–119.
Bruner, E.
  1989   Of Cannibals, Tourists and Ethnographers. Cultural Anthropology 4(4): 438–445.
Buck, R.C.
  1977   The Ubiquitous Tourist Brochure. Annals of Tourism Research 4(4): 195–207.
Buck, R.C.
  1978a   Boundary Maintenance Revisited: Tourist Experience in an Old Order Amish Community. Rural Sociology 43(2): 221–234.
Buck, R.C.
  1978b   From Work to Play: Some Observations on a Popular Nostalgic Theme. Journal of American Culture 1(3): 543–553.
Burns, F.A.
  1991   'Ecotourists' aren't All Good. The Nation (26 August): B4.
Burton, T.L.
  1965   Holiday Movement in Britain. Town and Country Planning 33(3): 118–123.
Burton, T.L.
  1971   Experiments in Recreational Research. London: Allen and Unwin.
Business Day
  1995   "Cambodia Plays Its Casino Cards Close to Its Chest", 17 January.
Business Review
  1986   "Getting ready for 'Visit Thailand Year 1987' ", July, pp. 51–60.
Butler, R.W.
  1980   The Concept of a Tourism Area Cycle of Evolution: Implications for the Management of Resources. Canadian Geographer 24: 5–12.
Butler, R.W.
  1989   Tourism and Tourism Research. *In* Understanding Leisure and Recreation: Mapping the Past, Charting the Future. T.L. Burton and E.L. Jackson, eds, pp. 567–595. State College, PA: Venture Publishing.

Butler, R.W.
  1992   Alternative Tourism: The Thin End of the Wedge. *In* Tourism Alternatives. V.L. Smith and W.R. Eadington, eds, pp. 31–46. Philadelphia: University of Pennsylvania Press.
Cappock, R.
  1978   The Influence of Himalayan Tourism on Sherpa Culture and Habitat. Zeitschrift für Kulturaustausch 28(3): 61–68.
Carter, J.
  1971   Do Fence Them In! Pacific Islands Monthly 42(6): 49–53.
Carter, J.
  1974   Cook Islands Open Cautious Arms to the Tourist. Pacific Islands Monthly 45(5): 117–118.
Casson, L.
  1974   Travel in the Ancient World. London: Allen and Unwin.
Cazes, G.H.
  1989   Alternative Tourism: Reflections on an Ambiguous Concept. *In* Towards Appropriate Tourism. T.V. Singh, H.I. Theuns and F.M. Go, eds, pp. 117–126. Frankfurt a/M: Peter Lang.
Chang, T.C.
  1988   Regionalism and Tourism: Exploring Integral Links in Singapore. Asia Pacific Viewpoint 39(1): 73–94.
Chantarotron, M.
  1992   Art and Culture Conservation in Thai Society. Muang Boran Journal (in Thai and English) 18(3–4): 6–19.
Charernwat, K.
  1980   Unique Sakai Society: Aborigines of Thailand? The Nation Review (29 June): 10.
Chen, P.
  1972   Social Pollution – With Special Reference to Singapore. NYLTI Journal (May): 117–125.
Clout, H.D.
  1971   Second Homes in the Auvergne. Geographical Review 61: 530–553.
Clyne, M.G., ed.
  1981   Foreigner Talk. International Journal of Sociology 28 [Special issue].
Cohen, E.
  1969   Mixed Marriages in an Israeli Town. Jewish Journal of Sociology 11(1): 41–50.
Cohen, E.
  1977   Expatriate Communities. Current Sociology 24(3): 5–133.
Cohen, E.
  1978   The Impact of Tourism on the Physical Environment. Annals of Tourism Research 5(2): 215–237.
Cohen, E.
  1979a   The Impact of Tourism on the Hill Tribes of Northern Thailand. Internationales Asienforum 10(1–2): 5–38.

Cohen, E.
    1979b   Rethinking the Sociology of Tourism. Annals of Tourism Research 6(1):
    18–35.
Cohen, E.
    1982a   Jungle Guides in Northern Thailand – The Dynamics of a Marginal
    Occupational Role. Sociological Review 30(2): 234–266.
Cohen, E.
    1982b   Marginal Paradises – Bungalow Tourism on the Islands of Southern Thailand.
    Annals of Tourism Research 9(2): 189–228.
Cohen, E.
    1982c   Refugee Art in Thailand. Cultural Survival Quarterly 6(4): 40–42.
Cohen, E.
    1982d   Thai Girls and *Farang* Men: The Edge of Ambiguity. Annals of Tourism
    Research 9(3): 403–428.
Cohen, E.
    1983a   The Dynamics of Commercialized Arts: The Meo and Yao of Northern
    Thailand. Journal of the National Research Council of Thailand 15(1, Part II): 1–34.
Cohen, E.
    1983   Hill Tribe Tourism. *In* Highlanders of Thailand. J. McKinnon and W. Bhruksasri,
    eds, pp. 307–325. Kuala Lumpur: Oxford University Press.
Cohen, E.
    1984a   The Dropout Expatriates: A Study of Marginal *Farangs* in Bangkok. Urban
    Anthropology 13(1): 91–114.
Cohen, E.
    1984b   The Sociology of Tourism: Approaches, Problems and Findings. Annual
    Review of Sociology 10: 373–392.
Cohen, E.
    1985   A *Soi* in Bangkok: The Dynamics of Lateral Urban Expansion. Journal of the
    Siam Society 73(1–2): 1–22.
Cohen, E.
    1987a   'Alternative Tourism' – a Critique. Tourism Recreation Research 12(2): 13–18.
Cohen, E.
    1987b   'Phut Thai Dai!' Acquisition of Hosts' Language among Expatriates in
    Bangkok. International Journal of the Sociology of Language No. 63: 5–19.
Cohen, E.
    1988   Radical Secularisation and the Destructuration of the Universe of Knowledge
    in Late Modernity. *In* Cultural Traditions and Worlds of Knowledge: Explorations in
    the Sociology of Knowledge. S.N. Eisenstadt and I.F. Silber, eds. *In* Knowledge and
    Society: Studies in the Sociology of Culture Past and Present. H. Kuklick, series ed.,
    Vol. 7, pp. 202–223. Greenwich: JAI Press.
Cohen, E.
    1989   'Primitive and Remote:' Hill Tribe Trekking in Thailand. Annals of Tourism
    Research 16(1): 30–61.

Cohen, E.
1990   Hmong (Meo) Commercialized Refugee Art: From Ornament to Picture. *In* Art as a Means of Communication in Pre-Literate Societies. D. Eban, E. Cohen and B. Danet, eds, pp. 51–95. Jerusalem: Israel Museum.

Cohen, E.
1992a   The Growing Gap: Hill Tribe Image and Reality. Pacific Viewpoint 33(2): 165–169.

Cohen, E.
1992b   Pilgrimage and Tourism: Convergence and Divergence. *In* Journeys to Sacred Places. E.A. Morinis, ed., pp. 47–61. Westport, CT: Greenwood Press.

Cohen, E.
1992c   Tourist Arts. Progress in Tourism, Recreation and Hospitality Management 4: 3–32.

Cohen, E.
1992d   Who Are the *Chao Khao*? 'Hill Tribe' Postcards from Northern Thailand. International Journal of the Sociology of Language No. 98: 101–125.

Cohen, E.
1993a   The Heterogeneization of a Tourist Art. Annals of Tourism Research 20(1): 138–163.

Cohen, E.
1993b   Open-ended Prostitution as a Skilful Game of Luck: Opportunity, Risk and Security Among Tourist-oriented Prostitutes in a Bangkok *Soi*. *In* Tourism in Southeast Asia. M. Hitchcock, V.T. King and M.J.G. Parnwell, eds, pp. 155–178. London: Routledge.

Cohen, E.
1996a   Thai Tourism: Hilltribes, Islands and Open-ended Prostitution. Bangkok: White Lotus.

Cohen, E.
1996b   Touting Tourists in Thailand: Tourist Oriented Crime and Social Structure. *In* Tourism, Crime and International Security Issues. A. Pizam and Y. Mansfeld, eds, pp. 77–90. New York: John Wiley.

Cohen, E.
1998   From Buddha Images to Mickey Mouse Figures: The Transformation of Ban Thawai Carvings. *In* Traditional Thai Arts in Comparative Perspective. M.C. Howard, W. Wattanapun and A. Gordon, eds, pp. 149–174. Bangkok: White Lotus.

Cohen, E.
2000   The Commercialized Crafts of Thailand: Hill Tribes and Lowland Villages. London: Curzon Press and Honolulu: University of Hawaii Press.

Cohen, E.
2001a   The Chinese Vegetarian Festival in Phuket: Religion, Ethnicity and Tourism on a Southern Thai Island. Bangkok: White Lotus.

Cohen, E.
2001b   Ethnic Tourism in Southeast Asia. *In* Tourism, Anthropology and China. Ch.-B. Tan, S.C.H. Cheung and H. Yang, eds, pp. 27–52. Bangkok: White Lotus.

Cohen, E.
2002   Authenticity, Equity and Sustainability. Journal of Sustainable Tourism 10(4): 267–276.

Cohen, E.
forthcoming-a   Backpacking: Diversity and Change. *In* The Global Nomad: Theory and Praxis in Backpacker Travel. G. Richards and J. Wilson, eds. Clevedon: Channel View.

Cohen, E.
forthcoming-b   Youth Tourists in Acre − from Disturbance to Initiation into a Life-long Preoccupation. *In* Towards a Tourism Social Science: Anthropological and Sociological Beginnings. D. Nash, ed. Kidlington Oxon: Pergamon.

Cohen, E. ed.
1985   Tourist Guides: Pathfinders, Mediators and Animators. Annals of Tourism Research 12(1): 1–149 (Special issue).

Cohen, E. ed.
1993   Tourist Arts. Annals of Tourism Research 20(1): 1–215 (Special issue).

Cohen, E., Ben-Yehuda, N. and Aviad, J.
1987   Recentering the World: The Quest for 'Elective Centers' in a Secularized Universe. Sociological Review 35(2): 320–346.

Cohen, L.E., Kluegel, J.R. and Land, K.C.
1981   Social Inequality and Predatory Criminal Victimization: An Exposition and Test of a Formal Theory. American Sociological Review 46: 505–524.

Cohen, M.R.
1956   A Preface to Logic. New York: Meridian.

Collins, R.
1984   Statistics vs. Words. *In* Sociological Theory. R. Collins, ed. San Francisco: Jossey-Bass.

Columbus, C.
1969   The Four Voyages of Christopher Columbus. J.M. Cohen, ed. Harmondsworth: Penguin Books.

Commonwealth Secretariat
1970   Organization in the Tourist Industry in Commonwealth Countries as at December 1969. London: H. M. S. O.

Cooper, R.L.
1982   A Framework for the Description of Language Spread. *In* Language Spread: Studies in Diffusion and Social Change. R.L. Cooper, ed., pp. 5–36. Bloomington: Indiana University Press.

Cooper, R.L. and Carpenter, S.
1969   Linguistic Diversity in the Ethiopian Market. Journal of African Languages 8(3): 160–168.

Cooper, R.L. and Horvath, R.J.
1973   Language, Migration, and Urbanization in Ethiopia. Anthropological Linguistics 15: 221–243.

Corben, R.
1990   How Card Swindlers are Robbing Tourists. Bangkok Post (17 May): 3.

Corder, S.P. and Roulet, E., eds
  1977   The Notions of Simplification, Interlanguage and Pidgins and their Relation to Second Language Pedagogy. Geneva: Droz.
Cornell, J.
  1980   A Brief Memorable Love Affair with Abemama. Pacific Islands Monthly 51(9): 47–50.
Cornet, J.
  1975   African Art and Authenticity. African Art 9(1): 52–55.
Cosgrove, L. and Jackson, R.
  1972   The Geography of Recreation and Leisure. London: Hutchinson University Library.
Coulter, J.W.
  1946   Impact of War on South Sea Islands. Geographical Review 36(3): 409–419.
Court, C.
  1971   A Fleeting Encounter with the Moken (the Sea Gypsies) in Southern Thailand: Some Linguistic and General Notes. Journal of the Siam Society 59(1): 83–95.
Coven, I.
  1971   'In Search of, in Search of . . ..' Lilit (7): 22–23.
Crampon, L.J.
  n.d.   The Impact of Aloha. *In* Tourism Development Notes. L.J. Crampon, ed., Vol. III, pp. 51–60. Boulder, CO: University of Colorado, Graduate School of Business Administration, Business Research Division.
Crampon, L.J. et al.
  1972   South Pacific Regional Tourism Study. Honolulu: University of Hawaii.
Cressey, D.R. et al.
  1968   Crime. *In* International Encyclopedia of the Social Sciences. D.L. Sills, ed., pp. 471–494. New York, NY: Macmillan.
Crocombe, R.G.
  1973   The New South Pacific. Wellington: Reed Education.
Csikszentmihalyi, M. and Csikszentmihalyi, I.S.
  1988   Optimal Experience: Psychological Studies of Flow in Consciousness. Cambridge: Cambridge University Press.
'A Cynic'
  1869   Vacations. Cornhill Magazine.
Dann, G.M.S.
  1996   The Language of Tourism – a Sociolinguistic Perspective. Wallingford, Oxon: CAB International.
Dann, G. and Cohen, E.
  1991   Sociology and Tourism. Annals of Tourism Research 18(1): 155–169.
Dark Society
  1984   The Dark Society: What the Law Says and How it is Used. Bangkok Post (8 October): 6.

Darling, F.
1970   The Evolution of Law in Thailand. Review of Politics 32: 197–218.
David, D.
1970   The Hippies Come to Israel. Israel Magazine 3(1): 69–78.
Day, A.G.
1965   Introduction. *In* Stories of Hawaii. J. London, ed., pp. 2–20. New York: Appleton, Century.
Day, A.G.
1966   Explorers of the Pacific. New-York: Duell, Sloan and Pearce.
deKadt, E. ed.
1979   Tourism – Passport to Development? New York: Oxford University Press.
Dearden, Ph.
1991   Tourism and Sustainable Development in Northern Thailand. Geographical Review 81(4): 400–413.
Dearden, Ph. and Harron, S.
1994   Alternative Tourism and Adaptive Change. Annals of Tourism Research 21(1): 81–102.
Desai, A.V.
1974   Tourism – Economic Possibilities and Policies. *In* Tourism in Fiji. pp. 1–12. Suva: University of the South Pacific.
Devons, E. and Gluckman, M.
1964   Conclusion. *In* Closed Systems and Open Minds. M. Gluckman, ed. Edinburgh and London: Oliver Boyd.
Die Zeitung
1995   Visit Myanmar 1996. mit Sklavenarbeit und Unterdrückung (39): 41–43.
Dickmann, S.
1963   Die Feriensiedlungen Schleswig-Holsteins. Schriften des geographischen Instituts der Universität Köln 21(3).
Din, K.H.
1989   Islam and Tourism: Patterns, Issues, and Options. Annals of Tourism Research 16(4): 542–563.
Din, K.H.
1993   Religious Tourism. *In* VNR's Encyclopedia of Hospitality and Tourism. M.A. Khan et al., eds, pp. 822–829. New York: Van Nostrand Reinhold.
Diran, R.K.
1997   The Vanishing Tribes of Myanmar. London: Weidenfeld and Nicolson.
Dollard, J.
1949   Caste and Class in a Southern Town. 2nd ed. New York: Harper & Brothers.
Donehower, E.J.
1969   The Impact of Dispersed Tourism in French Polynesia. M. A. Thesis, Honolulu, University of Hawaii.
Doumenge, F.
1966   L'Homme dans le Pacifique Sud. Paris: Musée de l'Homme.

Doxey, G.V.
  1975   A Causation Theory of Visitor-Resident Irritants: Methodology and Research Inferences. *In* The Impact of Tourism: The Travel Research Association 6th Annual Conference Proceedings. pp. 195–198. San Diego, CA.
Dumazdier, J.
  1967   Toward a Society of Leisure. New York: Free Press.
Dumont, J.P.
  1984   A Matter of Touristic 'Indifference'. American Ethnologist 11(1): 139–151.
Dupont, G.
  1973   Lourdes: Pilgrims or Tourists? Manchester Guardian Weekly 108(20, 10 May): 16.
Durkheim, F.
  1954   The Elementary Forms of the Religious Life. Glencoe, IL: Free Press.
Econ. Dev. Plan for Micronesia
  1966   Economic Development Plan for Micronesia: A Proposed Long-Range Plan for Developing the Trust Territory of the Pacific Islands. Washington, DC: Nathan Assoc. Inc.
Eisen, G.
  1991   The Concept of Time, Play, and Leisure in Early Protestant Religious Ethics. Play and Culture 4(3): 223–236.
Eisenstadt, S.N.
  1968   Transformation of Social, Political and Cultural Orders in Modernisation. *In* Comparative Perspectives on Social Change. S.N. Eisenstadt, ed., pp. 256–279. Boston: Little, Brown and Co.
Eisenstadt, S.N.
  1982   The Axial Age. European Journal of Sociology 23: 294–314.
Ekachai, S.
  1991   Sea Gypsies and Their Broken Way of Life. Bangkok Post 30(January 23): 40.
Eliade, M.
  1963   Myth and Reality. New York: Harper & Row.
Eliade, M.
  1968   Myths, Dreams and Mysteries. London: Fontana.
Eliade, M.
  1969a   Images and Symbols. New York: Sheed and Ward.
Eliade, M.
  1969b   Paradise and Utopia: Mythical Geography and Eschatology. *In* The Quest. M. Eliade, ed., pp. 88–111. Chicago and London: Chicago University Press.
Eliade, M.
  1969c   The Quest, History and Meaning in Religion. Chicago and London: University of Chicago Press.
Eliade, M.
  1971   The Myth of Eternal Return. Princeton, NJ: Princeton University Press.

Eliade, M.
1976   Occultism, Witchcraft and Cultural Fashions. Chicago: University of Chicago Press.

Eliade, M., ed.
1987   The Encyclopedia of Religion. New York: Collier McMillian.

Engel, D.M.
1975   Law and Kingship in Thailand During the Reign of King Chulalongkorn. Ann Arbor: University of Michigan, Center for South and Southeast Asian Studies.

Engel, D.M.
1978   Code and Custom in a Thai Provincial Court. Tuscon, AZ: University of Arizona Press.

EPCOT Center
1987   EPCOT Center Guide Book. Walt Disney World (brochure).

Ernsberger, R.
1990   Through the Looking Glass. Newsweek (7 May): 44–46.

Evans-Pritchard, D.
1993   Ancient Art in a Modern Context: Tourist Arts and the Commoditization of the Past. Annals of Tourism Research 20(1): 9–31.

Exotic Thailand: Theme Parks, Special Events, Amusement Parks and Water Parks circa
1997   (brochure).

Explore Pattaya
1993   Khao Khiew. 10(7): 12–14.

Fang, S.
1992   The Auspicious *Prahu* Ceremony of the Sea Gypsies. Phuket Magazine 3(3): 16–20, 44.

Far Eastern Economic Review
1991   "Wish You were Here", 28 November, p. 54.

Farrell, B.H.
1982   Hawaii, the Legend That Sells. Honolulu: University of Hawaii Press.

Faux, R.
1981   Getting to Know British Guides in the Alps. The Times (1 April): 14.

Fedler, A.J.
1987   Are Leisure, Recreation and Tourism Interrelated? Annals of Tourism Research 14(2): 311–313.

Feifer, N.
1985   Going Places. London: Macmillan.

Feleppa, R.
1986   Emics, Etics and Social Objectivity. Current Anthropology 27(3): 243–255.

Ferguson, C.A.
1971   Absence of Copula and the Notion of Simplicity: A Study of Normal Speech, Baby Talk, Foreigner Talk and Pidgins. *In* Pidginization and Creolization of Languages. D. Hymes, ed., pp. 141–150. Cambridge: Cambridge University Press.

Ferguson, C.A.
  1975   Towards a Characterization of English Foreigner Talk. Anthropological Linguistics 17: 1–14.
Ferguson, C.A.
  1981   'Foreigner Talk' as the Name of a Simplified Register. International Journal of the Sociology of Language 28: 9–18.
Ferrarotti, F.
  1979   The Destiny of Reason and the Paradox of the Sacred. Social Research 46(4): 648–681.
Fine, E.C. and Speer, J.H.
  1985   Tour Guide Performances as Sight Sacralization. Annals of Tourism Research 12(1): 73–95.
Finger, K. and Gayler, B.
  1975   Bereich und Ziele der Animation. *In* Animation im Urlaub. pp. 19–36. Starnberg: Studienkreis für Tourismus.
Fishman, J.A. et al.
  1986   Language Loyalty in the United States: The Maintenance and Perpetuation of Non-English Mother Tongues by American Ethnic and Religious Groups. The Hague: Mouton.
Fishman, J.A., Cooper, R.L. and Ma, R.
  1975   Billingualism in the Barrio. 2nd ed. Bloomington: Indiana University, Research Center for the Language Sciences.
Fong, A.
  1973   Tourism: A Case Study. *In* Fiji, a Developing Australian Colony. pp. 26–28. North Fitzroy, Vic. Aust.: I. D. A.
Forster, J.
  1964   The Sociological Consequences of Tourism. International Journal of Comparative Sociology 5: 216–227.
Frankland, M.
  1986   Khrushchev. Harmondworth: Penguin Books.
Friedel, M.
  1978   Inseln Zwischen Paradies und Hölle. Munich: Meyster Verlag.
Frow, J.
  1991   Tourism and the Semiotics of Nostalgia. October 57: 123–151.
Fuchs, L.H.
  1961   Hawaii Pono: A Social History. New York, NY: Harcourt, Brace.
Fujii, E.T., Mak, J. and Nishimura, E.
  1978   Tourism and Crime. Honolulu: University of Hawaii, Tourism Research Project, Occasional Paper No. 2.
Fussell, P.
  1979   Stationary Tourist. Harper's Magazine 258(1547): 31–38.
Gal, S.
  1978   Peasant Men Can't Get Wives: Language Change and Sex Roles in a Billingual Community. Language in Society 7: 1–16.

Garcia-Landa, M.
1981 –1982 La Traducción oral simultanea o interpretatión de conferencia. Yelmo 51/52: 22–24.

Geertz, C.
1973 Deep Play: Notes on the Balinese Cockfight. *In* The Interpretation of Cultures. C. Geertz, ed. New York: Basic Books.

Geographical Magazine
1971 Nomadic Tourists in Search of Adventure. 43(3): 242.

Gerson, R.
1996 Traditional Festivals in Thailand. Kuala Lumpur: Oxford University Press.

Giamatti, A.B.
1966 The Earthly Paradise and the Renaissance Epic. Princeton, NJ: Princeton University Press.

Gibbins, S.
1973 Trip in the Future You Can Moon About. Straits Times (15 October).

Giddens, A.
1976 Functionalism: *Aprés la Lutte*. Social Research 43(2): 325–366.

Giesz, L.
1968 Kitch-man as Tourist. *In* Kitch: The World of Bad Taste. G. Dorfles, ed., pp. 156–174. New York: Bell Publishers.

Gilmore, P.
1979 A Children's Pidgin: The Case of a Spontaneous Pidgin for Two. Sociolinguistic Working paper, No. 64. Austin: Southwest Educational Development Laboratory.

Glasser, R.
1975 Life Force or Tranquilizer. Society and Leisure 7(3): 17–26.

Godfrey, F.
1893 Pertinent Points for Pilgrims to the Paradise of the Pacific. Honolulu: F. Godfrey.

Goffman, E.
1959 The Presentation of Self in Everyday life. Garden City, NY: Doubleday.

Goffman, E.
1974 Frame Analysis: An Essay on the Organization of Experience. New York: Harper & Row.

Goldberg, A.
1983 Identity and Experience in Haitian Voodoo Shows. Annals of Tourism Research 10(4): 479–495.

Gorman, B.
1979 Seven Days, Four Countries: The Making of a Group. Urban Life 7(4): 469–492.

Gottdiener, M.
1982 Disneyland: A Utopian Urban Space. Urban Life 11(2): 139–162.

Gottlieb, A.
1982 Americans' Vacations. Annals of Tourism Research 9: 165–187.

Graburn, N.H.H.
1967 The Eskimos and Airport Art. Trans-Action 4(10): 28–33.

Graburn, N.H.H.
   1976a   Introduction: The Arts of the Fourth World. *In* Ethnic and Tourist Arts. N.H.H. Graburn, ed., pp. 1–32. Berkeley: University of California Press.
Graburn, N.H.H.
   1976b   Eskimo Art: The Eastern Canadian Arctic. *In* Ethnic and Tourist Arts. N.H.H. Graburn, ed., pp. 39–55. Berkeley: University of California Press.
Graburn, N.H.H.
   1977   Tourism: The sacred journey. *In* Hosts and Guests. V.L. Smith, ed., pp. 17–31. Philadelphia: University of Pennsylvania Press.
Graburn, N.H.H.
   1980   Teaching the Anthropology of Tourism. International Social Science Journal 32(1): 56–68.
Graburn, N.H.H.
   1983a   The Anthropology of Tourism. Annals of Tourism Research 10(1): 9–33.
Graburn, N.H.H.
   1983b   To Pray, Pay and Play: The Cultural Structure of Japanese Domestic Tourism. Cahiers du Tourisme, Série B 26: 1–89.
Graburn, N.H.H., ed.
   1976   Ethnic and Tourist Arts. Berkeley: University of California Press.
Graña, C.
   1979   Fact and Symbol. New York: Oxford University Press.
Greenwood, D.J.
   1977   Culture by the Pound: An Anthropological Perspective on Tourism as Cultural Commoditization. *In* Hosts and Guests. V.L. Smith, ed., pp. 129–139. Philadelphia: University of Pennsylvania Press.
Greenwood, D.J.
   1982   Cultural 'Authenticity'. Cultural Survival Quarterly 6(3): 27–28.
Greifer, L.
   1945   Attitude to the Stranger. American Sociological Review 10(6): 739–745.
Gross, E.
   1961   A Functional Approach to Leisure Analysis. Social Problems 9(1): 2–8.
Gumperz, J.J.
   1964   Linguistic and Social Interaction in Two Communities. American Anthropologist 66(6, Part 2): 137–153.
Hall, C.M. and O'Sullivan, V.
   1996   Tourism, Political Stability and Violence. *In* Tourism, Crime, and International Security Issues. A. Pizam and Y. Mansfield, eds, pp. 106–121. Chichester, NY: Wiley.
Hall, R.A., Jr.
   1962   The Life Cycle of Pidgin Languages. Lingua 11: 151–156.
Halliday, M.A.K., Macintosh, A. and Stevens, P.
   1964   The Users and Uses of Language. *In* The Linguistic Sciences and Language Teaching. pp. 75–110. London: Longman.

Halpern, L.
1986   A Meditation Retreat for Westerners at Wat Suan Mok. Bangkok Post (22 May).

Harris et al.
1970   Un Programme pour le Développement Touristique en Polynésie Francaise; Program of Tourist Development for Polynesia, Los Angeles.

Hassan, R.
1974   International Tourism and Intercultural Communication: The Case of Japanese Tourists in Singapore. University of Singapore, Department of Sociology. Working Paper No. 37.

Hastings, J., ed.
1925   The Encyclopedia of Religion and Ethics. New York: T. & T. Clark.

Haugen, E.
1953   The Norwegian Language in America: A Study in Billingual Behavior (Two Volumes). Philadelphia: University of Pennsylvania Press.

Heller, E.
1961   The Disinherited Mind. Harmonsworth: Penguin Books.

Hewison, R.
1987   The Heritage Industry: Britain in a Climate of Decline. London: Methuen.

Hilbert, C.
1969   The Grand Tour. New York: Putnam.

Hobsbawm, E. and Ranger, T., eds
1983   The Invention of Tradition. Cambridge: Cambridge University Press.

Hocart, A.M.
1952   The Life-Giving Myth. London: Methuen.

Hoffer, E.
1952   The True Believer: Thoughts on the Nature of Mass Movements. London: Secker and Warburg.

Holden, P., ed.
1984   Alternative Tourism: With a Focus on Asia. Bangkok: Ecumenical Coalition on Third World Tourism.

Hogan, D.W.
1972   Men of the Sea: Coastal Tribes of South Thailand's West Coast. Journal of the Siam Society 60(1): 205–235.

Holiday Time in Thailand
1969   Elephants at Surin. 10(3): 12–19.

Holiday Time in Thailand
1988   Thailand Arts and Crafts Year '88–89'. 28(4): 38–41.

Hollander, P.
1981   Political Pilgrims. New York: Harper.

Holloway, J.C.
1981   The Guided Tour: A Sociological Approach. Annals of Tourism Research 8(3): 377–402.

Hotel Information News
1990   A Visit to Thailand in Brief … at Mini Siam. No. 16, B. E. 2533 [1990] 22–28.

Hoyt, G.C.
1954   The Life of the Retired in a Trailer Camp. American Journal of Sociology 59(4): 361–370.

Huetz de Lemps, Ch.
1964   Le Tourisme dans l'Archipel des Hawaii. Cahiers d'Outre-Mer 17(65): 9–57.

Huizinga, J.
1955   Homo Ludens. Boston: Beacon Press.

Hymes, D., ed.
1971   Pidginization and Creolization of Languages. Cambridge: Cambridge University Press.

Ichaporia, N.
1983   Tourism at Khajuraho: An Indian Enigma. Annals of Tourism Research 10(1): 75–92.

Ikkai, M.
1988   The *Senbetsu-Omiyage* Relationship: Traditional Reciprocity Among Japanese Tourists. Kroeber Anthropological Society Papers 67/68: 62–66.

International Herald Tribune
1998   Thais Get an Unexpected Shot in the Arm: Chinese Tourists (6 April).

Ivanoff, J.
1986   Les Moken: littérature orale et signes de reconnaissance culturelle. Journal of the Siam Society 60(1): 9–20.

Ivanoff, J.
1991   La voix Royale: Revelations Identitaire Chez les Moken. *In* Identités Sud, regard sur trois minorités de Thailand. P. Le Roux and J. Ivanoff, eds, pp. 65–94. Patani: Prince of Songkhla University.

Jafari, J.
2001   The Scientification of Tourism. *In* Hosts and Guests Revisited. V.L. Smith and M. Brent, co-eds, pp. 28–41. New York: Cognizant Communication Corporation.

Jasvinder, P.
1981   Tourists Fall Prey to the 'Kings of the Road.' Bangkok Post (7 September).

Jinakul, R.
1987   Sea Gypsies Face Winds of Change. Bangkok Post (25 April).

Jivananthapravat, B.
1990   Phi Phi Sea Gypsies Struggle for Survival. Bangkok Post (11 January): 13.

John Paul II.
1984   *Turismo*. Pontificia Commisione per la pastorale delle migrazioni del turismo. (40): 225–261.

Johnson, D.M.
1981   Disney World as Structure and Symbol: Recreation of the American Experience. Journal of Popular Culture 15(1): 157–166.

Johnson, T.J.
 1972   Professions and Power. London: Macmillan.
Jones, H.
 1972   Gozo – the Living Showpiece. Geographical Magazine 45(1): 53–57.
Jud, G.S.
 1975   Tourism and Crime in Mexico. Social Science Quarterly 56: 325–330.
Juiff, P., ed.
 1990   Le Tourism Religieux. Espaces 102: 3–37.
Kajanavanit, I.
 1992   Sea Gypsies Beached. Alternative Tourism Newsletter 7(3): 5–6.
Kaje, D.
 1991   The Arrowless Sakai. Holiday Dairy 1(1): 106–116.
Kanomi, T.
 1991   People of Myth: Textiles and Crafts of the Golden Triangle. Tokyo: Shikosha.
Kanwanich, S.
 1993   A Salient Job for Sea Gypsies. Bangkok Post (18 May): 29.
Kanwerayotin, S.
 1987   Chao Lay: Two Sides of Their Primitive Life by the Seashore. Bangkok Post
      (19 January): 29.
Karasek, H.
 1980   'School-pen, Rupies, Bonbons.' Der Spiegel 34(17): 236–243.
Karmen, A.
 1984   Crime Victims. Monterey, CA: Brooks/Cole Publication Company.
Katriel, T.
 1997   Re-making Place: Cultural Production in Israeli Pioneer Settlement Museums.
      In Grasping Land. E. Ben-Ari and Y. Bilu, eds. Albany NY: State University of New
      York Press.
Kaufmann, C.N.
 1976   Functional Aspects of Haida Argillite Carvings. *In* Ethnic and Tourist Arts.
      N.H.H. Graburn, ed., pp. 56–69. Berkeley: University of California Press.
Kaufmann, W.J.
 1983   Tourism in the Twenty-First Century. Science Digest 91(4): 52–64.
Kavolis, V.
 1970   Post-modern Man: Psychocultural Responses to Social Trends. Social Problems
      17(4): 435–448.
Kenniston, K.
 1968   Heads and Seekers. American Scholar 38: 97–112.
Kent, N.
 1975   A New Kind of Sugar. *In* A New Kind of Sugar, Tourism in the Pacific. B.R.
      Finney and K.A. Watson, eds, pp. 169–198. Honolulu: East-West Center, East-West
      Technology and Development Institute, East-West Culture Learning Institute.
Keyes, C.F. and van den Berghe, P.L., eds
 1984   Tourism and Ethnicity. Annals of Tourism Research 11(3): 343–501.

Kidd, R.F. and Chayet, E.F.
1984   Why do Victims Fail to Report? The Psychology of Criminal Victimization. Journal of Social Issues 40(1): 39–50.
King, M.J.
1981   Disneyland and Walt Disney World: Traditional Values in Futuristic Forms. Journal of Popular Culture 15(1): 116–140.
Knebel, H.J.
1960   Soziologische Strukturwandlungen im modernen Tourismus. Stuttgart: Enke.
Kinnaree
1987   The Straw Birds of Chainat. 4(3): 12–17.
Kinnaree
1988   Ubon's Buddhist Lent. 5(6): 33–35.
Kinnaree
1993   A Fitting Celebration for the Flower of the North. 10(2): 74–80.
Kinnaree
1998   Banana Festival in Kamphaeng Phet. 15(9): 40–42.
Knox, J.M.
1978   Resident-Visitor Interaction: A Review of the Literature and General Policy Alternatives. PEACESAT Conference, The Impact of Tourism Development in the Pacific. Session 4, 18 April, Suva: University of the South Pacific, Extension Service.
Kroch, A.S.
1978   Toward a Theory of Social Dialect Variation. Language in Society 7: 17–36.
Kunstadter, P. and Chapman, E.C.
1978   Problems of Shifting Cultivation and Economic Development in Northern Thailand. *In* Farmers in the Forest. P. Kunstadter, E.C. Chapman and S. Sabhasri, eds, pp. 3–23. Honolulu: University Press of Hawaii.
Kunz, E.F.
1973   The Refugee in Flight: Kinetic Models and Forms of Displacement. International Migration Review 7(22): 125–146.
Kwee, M.
1973   Working Holidays. The Straits Times (8 August).
Knightly, Ph. and Simpson, C.
1969   The Secret Lives of Lawrence of Arabia. London: Nelson.
Laborde, P.
1969   Propriété foraine et séjour touristique à Biaritz. Annals de Geographie 78: 529–542.
Lacy, J.A. and Douglass, W.A.
2002   Beyond Authenticity: The Meanings and Uses of Cultural Tourism. Tourist Studies 2(1): 5–21.
LaFlamme, A.
1979   The Impact of Tourism: A Case From the Bahama Islands. Annals of Tourism Research 6(2): 137–148.
Lambert, R.S., ed.
1935   Grand Tour: A Journey in the Tracks of the Age of Aristocracy. London: Faber and Faber.

Lambert, W.E. and Tucker, G.R.
1972   Billingual Education of Children: The St. Lambert Experiment. Rowley: Newbury House.

Landau, J.M.
1969   The Arabs in Israel. London: Oxford University Press.

Larrabee, E. and Meyersohn, K., eds
Mass Leisure. Glencoe, IL: Free Press.

LeBruto, S.M.
1966   Legal Aspects of Tourism and Violence. *In* Tourism, Crime and International Security Issues. A. Pizam and Y. Mansfield, eds, pp. 297–310. Chichester, NY: Wiley.

Lee, R.B. and Devore, I., eds
1968   Man the Hunter. Chicago.

Lett, J.W.
1983   Ludic and Liminoid Aspects of Charter Yacht Tourism in the Carribbean. Annals of Tourism Research 10(1): 35–36.

Lewis, L.S. and Brissett, D.
1981   Paradise on Demand. Society 18(5): 85–90.

Lewis, P. and Lewis, E.
1984   People of the Golden Triangle: Six Tribes of Thailand. London: Thames and Hudson.

Leymore, V.L.
1975   Hidden Myth. New York: Basic Books.

Lieberson, S.
1970   Language and Ethnic Relations in Canada. New York, NY: Wiley.

Lieberson, S.
1982   Forces Affecting Language Spread: Some Basic Propositions. *In* Language Spread: Studies in Diffusion and Social Change. R.L. Cooper, ed., pp. 37–62. Bloomington: Indiana University Press.

Lind, A.W.
1969   Hawaii, the Last of the Magic Isles. London: Oxford University Press.

Littlefield, J.E. and Kirkpatrick, C.A.
1970   Advertising: Mass Communication in Marketing. Boston: Houghton Mifflin.

Loeb, L.D.
1977   Creating Antiques for Fun and Profit: Encounters Between Iranian Jewish Merchants and Touring Co-religionists. *In* Hosts and Guests. V.L. Smith, ed., pp. 185–192. Philadelphia: University of Pennsylvania Press.

Loeb, P.D. and Lin, V.L.Y.
1981   The Economics of Tourism and Crime: A Specification Error Approach. Resource Management and Organization 1: 315–331.

London, J.
1967   The Road. London: Arco.

Lookeast
1993   Long-neck Women − Stretching for Attention. 24(5): 36–39.

Lowenthal, D.
1962   Tourists and Thermalists. Geographical Review 52(1): 124–127.

Lowenthal, D.
1972   West Indian Society. Oxford: Oxford University Press.
Lyman, A.
1955   The Judicial System of Thailand. Journal of the Bar Association of the District of Columbia 23: 85–92.
MacCannell, D.
1973   Staged Authenticity: Arrangements of Social Space in Tourist Settings. American Journal of Sociology 79(3): 589–603.
MacCannell, D.
1976   The Tourist: A New Theory of the Leisure Class. New York: Schocken.
MacCannell, D.
1989   Introduction. Special Issue, Semiotics of Tourism. Annals of Tourism Research 16(1): 1–6.
MacCannell, D.
1992   Cannibalism Today. *In* Empty Meeting Grounds: The Tourist Papers. D. MacCannell, ed., pp. 17–73. London: Routledge.
MacCannell, D.
2001   Remarks on the Commodification of Culture. *In* Hosts and Guests Revisited. V.L. Smith and M. Brent, co-eds, pp. 380–390. New York: Cognizant Communication Corporation.
Magic Kingdom
1987   Magic Kingdom Guide Book. Walt Disney World (brochure).
Manndorf, H.
1962   The Hill Tribe Program of the Public Welfare Department, Ministry of Interior, Thailand: Research and Socio-Economic Development. *In* Southeast Asian Tribes, Minorities, and Nations. P. Kunstadter, ed., pp. 525–552. Princeton, NJ: Princeton University Press.
Mansfeld, Y. and Ya'acoub, K.
1995   Patterns of Tourist Destination–Choice and Travel Behavior Among Members of the Urban and Rural Arab Community of Israel: A Comparative Study of Haifa and Iblin. Geojournal 35(4): 459–470.
Manuel, F.E. and Manuel, F.P.
1972   Sketch for a Natural History of Paradise. Daedalus (101): 83–128.
Marsden, B.S.
1969   Holiday Homescapes of Queensland. Australian Geographical Studies 7(1): 57–73.
Mathieson, A. and Wall, G.
1982   Tourism: Economic, Physical and Social Impacts. London and New York: Longman.
McKean, P.F.
1976a   An Anthropological Analysis of the Culture Brokers of Bali: Guides, Tourists and Balinese. Paper, Joint UNESCO/IBDR Seminar on the Social and Cultural Impact of Tourism, Washington, December 8–10.

McKean, P.F.
1976b   Tourism, Culture Change and Culture Conservation in Bali. *In* Changing Identities in Modern Southeast Asia. D.J. Banks, ed., pp. 237–247. The Hague: Mouton.

McLemore, S.D.
1970   Simmel's Stranger: A Critique of the Concept. Pacific Sociological Review 13(2): 86–94.

McLeod, M.D.
1976   Limitations of the Genuine. African Art 9(3): 31, 48–51.

Meintel, D.A.
1973   Strangers, Homecomers and Ordinary Men. Anthropological Quarterly 46(1): 47–58.

Mercer, D.C.
1970   The Geography of Leisure – a Contemporary Growth Point. Geography 55: 261–273.

Messner, S.F. and Blau, J.R.
1987   Routine Leisure Activities and Rates of Crime: A Macro-level Analysis. Social Forces 65(4): 1035–1052.

Meyer, W.
1988   Beyond the Mask. Saarbrücken: Breitenbach.

Michaud, J.
1993   Tourism as Catalyst of Economic and Political Change: The Case of Highland Minorities in Ladakh (India) and Northern Thailand. Internationales Asienforum 24(1/2): 21–43.

Miller, D.L.
1973   Gods and Games. New York: Harper.

Million Years Stone Park and Pattaya Crocodile Farm circa
1994   (brochure).

Mini Siam circa
1994   (brochure).

Mirante, E.T.
1990   Hostages to Tourism. Cultural Survival Quarterly 14(1): 35–38.

Mitford, N.
1959   The Tourist. Encounter 13(4): 3–7.

Montague, S.
1989   International Tourism in the Eastern Seaboard Region of Thailand. Crossroads 4(2): 9–17.

Moore, A.
1980   Walt Disney World: Bounded Ritual Space and the Playful Pilgrimage Center. Anthropological Quarterly 53: 207–218.

Moore, A.
1985   Rosanzerusu is Los Angeles: An Anthropological Inquiry of Japanese Tourists. Annals of Tourism Research 12(4): 619–643.

Moscardo, G.M. and Pearce, Ph.L.
  1986   Historic Theme Parks: An Australian Experience in Authenticity. Annals of Tourism Research 13(3): 467–479.
Muang Boran Journal
  1987   Visit Thailand Year: Are We Going in the Right Direction? 12(12): 8–11.
Muhlhausler, P.
  1974   Pidginization and Simplification of Language. Canberra: Pacific Linguistics, B-26.
Muhlhausler, P.
  1981   Foreigner Talk: Tok Masta in New Guinea. International Journal of the Sociology of Language 28: 93–113.
Munt, I.
  1994   The 'Other' Postmodern Tourism: Culture, Travel and the New Middle Class. Theory, Culture and Society 11: 101–123.
Murphy, L.
  2001   Exploring Social Interactions of Backpackers. Annals of Tourism Research 28(1): 50–67.
Murphy, P.E.
  1981   Tourism Course Proposal for a Social Science Curriculum. Annals of Tourism Research 8(1): 96–105.
Nance, J.
  1975   The Gentle Tasaday. New York: Harcourt Brace Jovanovich.
Nash, D.
  1963   The Ethnologist as Stranger: As Essay in the Sociology of Knowledge. Southwestern Journal of Anthropology 19: 149–167.
Nash, D.
  1981   Tourism as an Anthropological Subject. Current Anthropology 22(5): 461–481.
Nash, D.
  1984   The Ritualization of Tourism: Comment on Graburn's 'The Anthropology of Tourism.' Annals of Tourism Research 11(3): 503–507.
Nettekoven, L.
  1973   Touristen sind eben keine Völkerkundler. Auslandskurier (3): 28–29.
Nettekoven, L.
  1979   Mechanisms of Intercultural Interaction. *In* Tourism: Passport to Development? E. de Kadt, ed., pp. 133–145. New York: Oxford University Press.
Neubauer, T.
  1973   Probleme der Naherholung für die Prager Bevölkerung in Mittleren Moldautal. Erdkunde 27(1): 69–75.
Neville, R.
  1970   Playpower. London: Paladin.
Newman, O.
  1993   Defensible Space: Crime Prevention Through Urban Design. New York, NY: Collier Books.

Niederland, W.G.
1957   River Symbolism. Part II. Psychoanalytic Quarterly 26: 50–75.
Nieto Piñeroba, J.A.
1977   Turistas y nativos: el caso de Formentera. Revista Española de Opinion Publica
47: 147–167.
Nimmanhaemindra, K. and Hartland-Swan, J.
1962   Expedition to the 'Khon Pa' or 'Phi Tong Luang.' Journal of the Siam Society
50(2): 165–186.
Nong Nooch Orchid Wonderland circa
1993   (brochure).
'Normita'
1991   Phuket's Painful Experience. Bangkok Post (24 November): 38.
Noronha, R.
1977   Social and Cultural Dimensions of Tourism. A Review of the Literature in
English. Washington: World Bank (draft).
Noronha, R.
1979   Paradise Reviewed: Tourism in Bali. *In* Tourism: Passport to Development? E.
de Kadt, ed., pp. 177–204. New York: Oxford University Press.
Nuñez, T.
1963   Tourism, Tradition and Acculturation: *Weekendismo* in a Mexican Village.
Ethnology 2(3): 347–352.
Nuñez, T.
1977   Touristic Studies in Anthropological Perspective. *In* Hosts and Guests. V.L.
Smith, ed. Philadelphia: University of Pennsylvania Press.
Ogilvie, F.W.
1932   Tourist Traffic. *In* Encyclopeadia of the Social Sciences. New York: Macmillan.
Orbell, M.
1974   The Religious Significance of Maori Migration. *In* Perspectives on Religion:
New Zealand Viewpoints. pp. 5–8. Auckland: University of Auckland.
Otto, R.
1959   The Idea of the Holy. Harmondsworth: Penguin Press.
Oxford
1933   Oxford English Dictionary. Vol. IV. Oxford: Clarendon.
Panfilis, E. de
1986   La conservazione del patrimonio storico-artistico della Chiesa in Italia. Rassenga
di studi turistici 6: 131–136.
Panyacheewin, S.
1990   Phi Tong Luang: A Culture for Sale. Bangkok Post (31 August): 33.
Pape, R.H.
1965   Touristy: A Type of Occupational Mobility. Social Problems 11(4): 336–344.
Papson, S.
1981   Spuriousness and Tourism: Politics of Two Canadian Provincial Governments.
Annals of Tourism Research 8(2): 220–235.

Parezo, N.J.
   1983   Navaho Sandpainting, from Religious Act to Commercial Art. Tuscon: University of Arizona Press.
Passariello, P.
   1983   Never on Sunday? Mexican Tourists at the Beach. Annals of Tourism Research 10(1): 109–122.
Patmore, J.A.
   1968   The Spa Towns of Britain. *In* Urbanization and Its Problems. R.P. Beckingsdale and J.M. Houston, eds. Oxford: Blackwell.
Patmore, J.A.
   1970   Land and Leisure in England and Wales. Newton Abbot: David and Charles.
Pearce, P.L.
   1982   The Social Psychology of Tourist Behavior. New York: Pergamon.
Peleggi, M.
   1996   National Heritage and Global Tourism in Thailand. Annals of Tourism Research 23(2): 432–448.
Peres, Y. and Yuval-Davis, N.
   1969   Some Observations on the National Identity of Israeli Arabs. Human Relations 22(3): 219–233.
Petersen, W.
   1958   A General Typology of Migration. American Sociological Review 23: 256–266.
Pfaffenberger, B.
   1983   Serious Pilgrims and Frivolous Tourists: The Chimera of Tourism in the Pilgrimages of Sri Lanka. Annals of Tourism Research 10(1): 57–74.
Phanchan, Y.
   1992   Chivit dang fan thii theuak khao banthat [Life like a dream in the Banthat mountains]. Bangkok: Sinlapa Wannekan Press.
Phatkul, N.
   1992   Sea Gypsies: Cast up on a Hostile Shore. Bangkok Post (6 February): 23–24.
Photikij, Ch., Chandrapanya, K. and Fahn, J.
   1993   Trial and Conflict Down by the Sea. The Nation (18 July): A9.
Phuket, Phi Phi and Krabi circa
   1990   Phuket's amazing Vegetarian Festival. 1(9): 10–15.
Picard, M.
   1992   Bali; Tourisme culturel et culture touristique. Paris: Editions L'Harmattan.
PIM
   1967   Solomons Sell the War. Pacific Islands Monthly 38(12): 61.
Pi-Sunyer, O.
   1977   Through Native Eyes: Tourists and Tourism in a Catalan Maritime Community. *In* Hosts and Guests. V.L. Smith, ed., pp. 149–155. Philadelphia: University of Pennsylvania Press.
Pitt-Rivers, J.
   1968   The Stranger, the Guest and the Hostile Host. *In* Contributions to Mediterranean Sociology. J.G. Peristiany, ed., pp. 13–30. Paris and the Hague: Mouton.

Pizam, A.
1982 Tourism and Crime – Is There a Relationship? Journal of Travel Research 20(3): 7–10.
Pizam, A. and Mansfeld, Y., eds
1996 Tourism, Crime and International Security Issues. Chichester NY: Wiley.
Pleumarom, A.
1990 Alternative Tourism: A Viable Solution? Contours 4(8): 12–15.
Plion-Bernier, R.
1973 Festivals and Ceremonies of Thailand. [n.l.]: Ed. L'Hartman.
Poirier, R.A.
1995 Tourism and Development in Tunisia. Annals of Tourism Research 22(1): 157–171.
Poix, G.
1985 Le loisir; est-il une voie bien sérieuse pour l'Evangélisation. Haltes 38: 11–14.
Pookajorn, N.
1992 The Phi Tong Luang (Mlabri): A Hunter-Gatherer Group in Thailand. Bangkok: Odeon Store.
Prang-riew, Y.
1992 The Wonders of Surin Islands National Park. Kinnaree 9(2): 48–55.
Pravattiyagul, O.
2002 Doctored Faust. Bangkok Post, Outlook (18 September): 8.
Prentice, R. and Andersen, V.
2003 Festival as Creative Destination. Annals of Tourism Research 30(1): 7–30.
Privat, P. and Gleizes, F.
1992 Presto! Let the Magic Begin. Newsweek 119(15): 14–15.
Przeclawski, K.
1994 Tourism and the Contemporary World. Warsaw: University of Warsaw.
PTN
1974 Hemmeter Center – Biggest new Waikiki Development. Pacific Travel News 18(6): 44.
Rasmussen, K.
1972 A Shaman's Journey to the Sea Spirit. *In* Reader in Comparative Religion. W.A. Lessa and E.Z. Vogt, eds, pp. 388–391. New York, NY: Harper & Row.
Redfoot, D.L.
1984 Touristic Authenticity, Touristic Angst, and Modern Reality. Qualitative Sociology 7(4): 291–309.
Reisen in Thailand
1988 Unbekanntes Thailand (ad. No. 7, 10).
Relph, E.
1976 Place and Placelessness. London: Pion.
Richter, L.
1980 The Political Uses of Tourism: A Philippine Case Study. Journal of Developing Areas 14: 237–257.

Richter, L.K. and Richter, W.L.
  1985   Policy Choices in South Asian Tourism Development. Annals of Tourism Research 12(2): 201–217.
Riedel, U.
  1972   Entwicklung, Struktur und räumliche Differenzierung des Fremdenverkehrs der Balearen. Erdkunde 26(2): 138–152.
Riley, P.
  1988   Road Culture of International Long-term Budget Travellers. Annals of Tourism Research 15: 313–328.
Rinschede, G.
  1992   Forms of Religious Tourism. Annals of Tourism Research 19(1): 51–67.
Ritter, W.
  1975   Recreation and Tourism in the Islamic Countries. Ekistics 40(236): 149–152.
Ritzer, G.
  1993   The McDonaldization of Society. Newbury Park, CA: Pine Forge Press.
Ritzer, G. and Liska, A.
  1997   'McDisneyization' and 'Post-Tourism'. In Touring Cultures. Ch. Rojek and J. Urry, eds, pp. 96–109. London and New York: Routledge.
Roberts, R.I.
  1970   Introduction. In Africa and Its Explorers. R.I. Roberts, ed., pp. 1–11. Cambridge, MA: Harvard University Press.
Robinson, G.W.S.
  1972   The Recreational Geography of South Asia. Geographical Review 62(4): 561–572.
Roisarn, M.
  1973   Thailand's Aliens and Legislation. Bangkok Bank Monthly Review (February): 100–104.
Rojanaphruk, P.
  1993   The Last of the Moken. The Nation (13 May): C1–C2.
Rubin, J.
  1968   National Billingualism in Paraguay. The Hague: Mouton.
Ryan, Ch.
  1993   Tourism and Crime – An Intrinsic or Accidental Relationship? Tourism Management 14(3): 173–183.
Ryan, Ch. and Kinder, R.
  1996   The Deviant Tourist and the Crimogenic Place – The Case of the Tourist and the New Zealand Prostitute. In Tourism, Crime, and International Security Issues. A. Pizam and Y. Mansfeld, eds, pp. 23–36. Chichester, NY: Wiley.
Ryan, J.
  1969   The Hot Land: Focus on New Guinea. Melbourne: St. Martin's Press.
Sacherer, J.
  1981   The Recent Social and Economic Impact of Tourism on the Sherpa Community. In Asian Highland Societies. C. von Fürer-Haimendorf, ed., pp. 157–167. New Delhi: Sterling Publisher.

Saen Sanuk
  1988   For Time Travellers Only. 8(2): 33–39.
Saen Sanuk
  1989   Mae Sai. 9(1): 44–47.
Sanford, C.L.
  1961   The Quest for Paradise. Urbana: University of Illinois Press.
Sargent, J.R. et al.
  1967   Promoting Tourism in the East Carribean. Development Digest 5(2): 63–69.
Sawaddi
  1972   'Ancient Land': Thailand's Best Kept Secret. (January/February): 15–18.
Sawaddi
  1993   Women of Padaung. 39(2): 17–20.
Sawasdee
  1980   Chiang Mai's Songkran Festival. (July–August): 48–55.
Schebesta, P.
  1929   Bei den Urwaldzwergen in Malaya. Leipzig.
Scheyvens, R.
  2002   Backpacker Tourism and Third World Development. Annals of Tourism
      Research 29(1): 144–164.
Schiebler, S.A., Crotts, J.C. and Hollinger, R.C.
  1996   Florida Tourists' Vulnerability to Crime. *In* Tourism, Crime, and International
      Security Issues. A. Pizam and Y. Mansfeld, eds, pp. 37–50. Chichester, NY:
      Wiley.
Schmid, E., with the cooperation of Savona, E.U.
  1995   Migration and Crime: A Framework for Discussion. ISPAC, International
      Scientific and Professional Advisory Council of the United Nations Crime Prevention
      and Criminal Justice Program.
Schmidt, C.J.
  1979   The Guided Tour: Insulated Adventure. Urban Life 7(4): 441–467.
Schmitt, C.
  1982   Translating and Interpreting: Present and Future. The Incorporated Linguist
      21(3): 96–102.
Schneebaum, T.
  1970   Keep the River to Your Right. New York: Grove Press.
Schuchat, M.G.
  1983   Comforts of Group Tours. Annals of Tourism Research 10(4): 465–477.
Schudson, M.S.
  1979   Review Essay: On Tourism and Modern Culture. American Journal of Sociology
      85(5): 1249–1258.
Schuetz, A.
  1944   The Stranger: An Essay in Social Psychology. American Journal of Sociology
      49(6): 499–507.
Schuetz, A.
  1973   Collected Papers. The Hague: M. Nijhoff (3 vols.).

Schwartz, H. and Jacobs, J.
1979   Qualitative Sociology: A Method in the Madness. New York: Free Press.
Schwarz, W.
1959   The Arabs of Israel. London: Faber and Faber.
Seckbach, F. and Cooper, R.L.
1977   The Maintenance of English in Ramat Eshkol. *In* The Spread of English: The
        Sociology of English as an Additional Language. J.A. Fishman, R.L. Cooper and
        A.W. Conrad, eds, pp. 168–178. Rowley: Newbury House.
Seidenfaden, E.
1926   The Kha Tong Luang. Journal of the Siam Society 20(1): 41–48.
Selänniemi, S.
2001   Pale Skin on Playa del Anywhere: Finnish Tourists in the Liminoid South. *In*
        Hosts and Guests Revisited. V.L. Smith and M. Brent, co-eds, pp. 80–92. New York:
        Cognizant Communication Corporation.
Selwyn, T.
1966   Introduction. *In* The Tourist Image: Myth and Myth Making in Tourism. T.
        Selwin, ed., pp. 1–32. London: Wiley.
Sentosa
1992   Discover the Many Worlds of Sentosa. Singapore: Sentosa (brochure).
Shamir, B.
1978   Between Bureaucracy and Hospitality – Some Organizational Characteristics of
        Hotels. Journal of Management Studies 15(3): 285–307.
Shamir, B.
1980   Between Service and Servility: Conflict in Subordinate Service Roles. Human
        Relations 33(10): 741–756.
Shanklin, E.
1980   The Irish Go-between. Anthropological Quarterly 53(3): 162–172.
Sherman, L.W., Gartin, P.R. and Guerger, M.E.
1989   Hot Spots of Predatory Crime: Routine Activities and the Criminology of Place.
        Criminology 27(1): 27–56.
Shiloah, A. and Cohen, E.
1983   The Dynamics of Change in Jewish Oriental Ethnic Music in Israel. Ethnomu-
        sicology 27(2): 227–252.
Shils, E.
1975   Center and Periphery. *In* Center and Periphery: Essays in Macrosociology. E.
        Shils, ed., pp. 3–16. Chicago and London: University of Chicago Press.
Shils, E. and Young, M.
1953   The Meaning of the Coronation. Sociological Review 1(2): 63–82.
Sigaux, C.
1966   History of Tourism. London: Leisure Arts.
Silver, H.R.
1979   Beauty and the 'I' of the Beholder: Identity, Aesthetics and Social Change
        among the Ashanti. Journal of Anthropological Research 35(2): 191–207.

Simmel, G.
1950 The Stranger. *In* The Sociology of Georg Simmel. K. Wolff, ed., pp. 402–408. New York: Free Press.
Simon, M., Barral-Baron, A. and Barbier, M.
1985 Une lecture sociologique et theologique des realités du tourism a la campaigne et à la montaigne. Haltes 37: 22–35.
Simpich, F.
1971 Anatomy of Hawaii [n.l.]. Coward, McCann and Geoghegan (n.1).
Singh, V.T., Theuns, H.L. and Go, F.M., eds
1989 Towards Appropriate Tourism: The Case of Developing Countries. Frankfurt a/M: Peter Lang.
Smith, D.E., Luce, J. and Demburg, E.A.
1970 Love Needs Care: Haight-Ashbury Dies. New Society 16(407): 98–101.
Smith, M.E.
1982 The Process of Sociocultural Continuity. Current Anthropology 23(2): 127–142.
Smith, V.L.
1961 Needed: Geographically-trained Tourist Guides. Professional Geographer 13(6): 28–30.
Smith, V.L.
1977a Introduction. *In* Hosts and Guests: The Anthropology of Tourism. V.L. Smith, ed., pp. 1–14. Philadelphia: University of Pennsylvania Press.
Smith, V.L.
1977b Eskimo Tourism: Micro-Models and Marginal Man. *In* Hosts and Guests: The Anthropology of Tourism. V.L. Smith, ed. Philadelphia: University of Pennsylvania Press.
Smith, V.L.
1992 Introduction: The Quest in Guest. Annals of Tourism Research 19(1): 1–17.
Smith, V.L.
2001 Tourism Issues of the 21st Century. *In* Hosts and Guests Revisited. V.L. Smith and M. Brent, co-eds, pp. 333–353. New York: Cognizant Communication Corporation.
Smith, V.L., ed.
1977 Hosts and Guests: The Anthropology of Tourism. Philadelphia: University of Pennsylvania Press.
Smith, V.L., ed.
1992 Pilgrimage and Tourism. Annals of Tourism Research 19(11): 1–121.
Smith, V.L. and Brent, M., co-eds
2001 Hosts and Guests Revisited: Tourism Issues of the 21st Century. New York: Cognizant Communication Corporation.
Smith, V.L. and Eadington, W.R., eds
1992 Tourism Alternatives. Philadelphia: University of Pennsylvania Press.
Snow, C.E., Van Eeden, R. and Muysken, P.
1981 The International Origins of Foreigner Talk: Municipal Employees and Foreign Workers. International Journal of the Sociology of Language 28: 81–91.

Sopher, D.E.
   1967   Geography of Religion. Englewood Cliffs, NJ: Prentice-Hall.
Sopher, D.E.
   1977   The Sea Nomads. Singapore: National Museum.
Sørensen, A.
   2003   Backpacker Ethnography. Annals of Tourism Research 30(4): 847–867.
Soussa, D. de
   1988   Tourism as a Religious Issue: A Third World Perspective. Contours 3(5): 5–13.
Spencer, S.A.
   1991   Illegal Migration in Japan. International Migration Review 26(3–4): 754–786.
Spiegel
   1972   Abenteuer nach Katalog – Urlaub 1972. Der Spiegel 26(30): 30–44.
Spiegel
   1973   Enge Bindung. Der Spiegel 27(4): 111.
Spradley, J.P.
   1970   You Owe Yourself a Drunk: An Ethnography of Urban Nomads. Boston: Little,
      Brown.
Srinivasan, K.
   1972   The Hippies Are not Welcome in India. Ha'aretz (19 January) (In Hebrew).
Srisang, K.
   1985   Prologue to a Theology of Tourism. Contours 2(3): 6–12.
Stephen, H.
   1971   Malayan Safari. Tropic 4(3): 19–20, 40.
Stock, E.
   1968   From Conflict to Understanding. New York: Institute of Human Relations
      Press.
Storey, D.
   1988   Time Running Out for 'Yellow Leaf Spirits.' The Nation (13 January): 16.
Story, G.M.
   1980   Guides to Newfoundland. The Newfoundland Quarterly 75(4): 17–23.
Stouffer, S.A.
   1940   Intervening Opportunities: A Theory Relating Mobility and Distance. American
      Sociological Review 5(6): 845–867.
Sutton, W.A.
   1967   Travel and Understanding: Notes on the Social Structure of Touring. International
      Journal of Comparative Sociology 8(2): 218–223.
Suwanich, P.
   1988   The Changing Life of the Sakai. Bangkok Post (27 April): 31, 44.
Suwanpantakul, K.
   2002   Waiter! There's a Bug on My Sandwich. The Nation (18 December): 15A.
Swain, N.B., Brent, M. and Long, V.H.
   1998   Annals and Tourism Evolving. Annals of Tourism Research 25(Suppl.):
      991–1014.

Sykes, G.M. and Matza, D.
1957   Techniques of Neutralization: A Theory of Delinquency. American Sociological
Review 22: 664–670.
Tangwisuttijit, N.
1990   Disappearing Populations. The Nation (18 February): 11.
Tarlow, P. and Muehsam
1996   Theoretical Aspects of Crime as They Impact the Tourism Industry. *In* Tourism,
Crime, and International Security Issues. A. Pizam and Y. Mansfeld, eds, pp. 11–22.
Chichester, NY: Wiley.
ten Brummelhuis, H.
1984   Abundance and avoidance: an interpretation of Thai individualism. *In* Strategies
and Structures in Thai Society. H. ten Brummelhuis and J.H. Kemp, eds, pp. 39–54.
Universiteit van Amsterdam Publikatieserie, Vakgroep Zuid-en Zuidost Azië, No. 31.
Thailand Traveller
1992   "Banana, Buddhas and Beauties", September, pp. 10–16.
Thailand Traveller
1995   "Pattaya in Action", 5(39), pp. 24–29.
Thailand Traveller
1996   "Odyssey to the Northern Hill Tribes", 6(59), pp. 28–35.
Thaitawat, N.
1990a   Tiny Nomadic Forest Tribe that Faces Extinction. Bangkok Post (16 April): 7.
Thaitawat, N.
1990b   Spirits from a Different World. Bangkok Post (19 April): 27–28.
Thaitawat, N.
1990c   Tourists and Tribesmen. Bangkok Post (6 December): 29–30.
Thaitawat, N.
1993   Listening to the Call of the Spirits. Bangkok Post (24 January): 24, 34.
Thaitawat, N. and Thepthong, P.
1991   Settling Down after the Leaves Turn Yellow. Bangkok Post (2 October): 29, 46.
Thaiways
1997   Amazing Thailand 1998–1999. 14(10): 41–48.
The Nation
1991   "Another Paradise Lost?", 6 August.
The Nation
1992   "A Little Known Southern Paradise", 28 February, classified section, p. 22.
The Nation
1993   "Pattaya: Dead or Alive?", 12 September.
The Nation
1994   "The Golden Quadrangle, Opportunities and Dangers", 31 March.
The Nation
1994   "Dream of Mekong Subregion Nears Reality", 29 July.
The Nation
1994   "Thrills, Spills and Kills in Pattaya", 7 August.

The Nation
1994 "Partners in Mekong Scheme Striving for an Identity", 8 August.
The Nation
1995 "Make Thailand Indochina Tourism Hub", 7 April.
The Nation
1997 "Trade Bustles in Sleepy Mekong Zone", 11 April.
The Nation
1998 "ADB Steps up Push for Tourism Along Mekong", 1 September.
The Nation
1998 "Safari World Branches Out into 'Fantasy' ", 5 September.
The Nation
1998 "National Parks for Tourism", 14 September.
The Nation
1998 "Holiday Spirits", 23 October.
The Nation
1999 "Mekong Tourism Brings Disasters", 2 February.
The Nation Review
1978 "The Birth of Pattaya City", 31 December.
Thepthong, Ph.
1990 Among the Yellow Leaves. Bangkok Post (19 April): 28.
Thompson, V. and Adloff, R.
1971 The French Pacific Islands. Berkeley: University of California Press.
Tichy, H.
1978 Reisen, Bücher, Reisebücher. Zeitschrift für Kulturaustausch 28(3): 19–24.
Time Magazine
1971 "Bargain in the Air: The Cut-Rate Travellers", 19 July.
Time Magazine
1972 "The Greening of the Astronauts", 11 December, p. 23.
Time Magazine
1976a Review of S. Bellow *To Jerusalem and Back*. Time (8 November): 62.
Time Magazine
1976b The Private World of Marlon Brando. Time (24 May): 37–39.
Tourism Authority of Lao Peoples' Democratic Republic circa
1998 Visit Laos Year 1999. Vientiane: National Tourism Authority of Lao PDR.
Tourism Authority of Thailand (TAT)
n.d. Thailand – Gateway to the Mekong Sub-Region. Bangkok: TAT.
Trease, G
1967 The Grand Tour. London: Heinemann.
Trilling, L.
1972 Sincerity and Authenticity. London: Oxford University Press.
Trip Info
1997 The Flower Festival. 2(41): 8–10.

Tudor, J.
1966 The Trouble with New Guinea Tourism is that it isn't Necessary. Pacific Islands Monthly 37(8): 121–125.

Tudor, J.
1970 It's Tourism – Phase Two. Pacific Islands Monthly 41(3): 63.

Tudor, J., ed.
1966 The Handbook of Papua and New Guinea. 4th ed. Sydney: Pacific Publications.

Turner, L. and Ash, J.
1975 The Golden Hordes: International Tourism and the Pleasure Periphery. London: Constable.

Turner, V.
1969 The Ritual Process. Chicago: Aldine Publishing Company.

Turner, V.
1973 The Center Out There: Pilgrim's Goal. History of Religions 12: 191–230.

Turner, V.
1978 Comments and Conclusions. *In* The Reversible World. B.A. Babcock, ed., pp. 258–295. Ithaca, NY: Cornell University Press.

Turner, V. and Turner, E.
1978 Image and Pilgrimage in Christian Culture. New York: Columbia University Press.

Uriely, N., Yonay, Y. and Simchai, D.
2002 Backpacking Experiences: A Type and Form Analysis. Annals of Tourism Research 29(2): 520–538.

Urry, J.
1990 The Tourist Gaze. London: Sage.

Urry, J.
1992 The Tourist Gaze and the Environment. Theory, Culture and Society 9: 1–26.

Valdman, A.
1977 L'effet de modeles culturels sur l'élaboration du langage simplifié (foreigner talk). *In* The Notions of Simplification, Interlanguage and Pidgins and their Relation to Second Language Pedagogy. S.P. Corder and E. Routlet, eds, pp. 114–131. Geneva: Droz.

van den Abbeele, G.
1980 Sightseers: The Tourist as Theorist. Diacritics 10: 2–14.

van den Berg, M.E.
1985 Language Planning and Language Use in Taiwan. Dordrecht: ICG Printing.

van den Berghe, P.
1980 Tourism as Ethnic Relations: A Case Study of Cusco, Peru. Ethnic and Racial Studies 3(4): 375–392.

van den Berghe, P.
1984 Ethnic Cuisine: Culture in Nature. Ethnic and Racial Studies 7(3): 387–397.

van Gennep, A.
1960 [1908] The Rites of Passage. London: Routledge & Kegan Paul.

Vichaidist, S.
   1973   Thailand's Recent Legislation on Aliens. Bangkok Bank Monthly Review (February): 58–74.
Vielhaber, C.
   1984   Vom Fischerdorf zu einem Zentrum des Fernreisetourismus: Beispiel Pattaya, Thailand. Geographischer Jahresbericht aus Österreich 43: 31–76.
Viraphol, S.
   1975   Law in Traditional Siam and China: A Comprehensive Study. Law Journal of Marut Bunnag International Law Office 4(3): 16–24; 4(4): 1–30.
Vizjak, A.
   1993   Vjerski turizam kao novi oblik turizma [Religious Tourism as a New Form of Tourism]. Ekonomski Vjesnik 6(1): 141–148.
Wagner, U.
   1977   Out of Time and Place: Mass Tourism and Charter Trips. Ethnos 42(1–2): 38–52.
Wall, G.
   1972   Socio-economic Variations in Pleasure-Trip Patterns: The Case of Hull Car Owners. Transactions of the Institute of British Geographers 57: 45–58.
Wang, N.
   2000   Tourism and Modernity: A Sociological Analysis. Kidlington, Oxon: Pergamon.
Waters, S.K.
   1966   The American Tourist. The Annals of the American Academy of Political and Social Sciences 368: 109–118.
Weber, M.
   1958   [1904]. The Protestant Ethic and the Spirit of Capitalism. New York: Scribner's.
Webster
   1961   Third New International Dictionary. London: Bell & Sons.
Weisskopf, W.A.
   1983   Moral Responsibility for the Preservation of Humankind. Social Research 50(1): 98–125.
Wettlaufer, D.
   1973   A Vision of Paradise. *In* Dimensions of Polynesia. J. Teilhet, ed., pp. 1–12. San Diego: Fine Arts Gallery.
White, W.G.
   1922   Sea Gypsies of Malaya. London: Seeley, Service and Co.
Whiteley, W.H.
   1969   Swahili: The Rise of a National Language. London: Methuen.
Wilkins, M.
   1966   The Businessman Abroad. Annals of the American Academy of Political and Social Sciences 368: 83–94.
Willett, F.
   1976   True or False: The False Dichotomy. African Arts 9(3): 8–14.

Williams, A.V. and Zelinsky, W.
 1970   On Some Patterns in International Tourist Flows. Economic Geography 46(4): 549–567.
Wolfe, R.I.
 1967   Recreational Travel: The New Migration. Geographical Bulletin 9(4): 159–172.
Wolfe, R.I.
 1970   Vacation Homes and the Gravity Model. Ekistics 29(174): 352–353.
World of Dogs. circa
 1998   (brochure).
Yablonsky, L.
 1968   The Hippie Trip. New York: Pegasus.
Yancey, W.L., Erickson, P. and Juliani, R.N.
 1976   Emergent Ethnicity: A Review and Reformulation. American Sociological Review 41(3): 391–403.
Yoshida, T.
 1981   The Stranger as God: The Place of the Outsider in Japanese Folk Religion. Ethnology 30(2): 87–99.
Young, G.
 1974   The Hill Tribes of Northern Thailand. Bangkok: The Siam Society.
Zadeh, L.A.
 1965   Fuzzy Sets. Information and Control 8: 338–353.
Zajonc, R.B.
 1985   Emotion and Facial Efference: A Theory Reclaimed. Science 228: 15–21.
Zaw, M.Y.
 1996   In Search of the Long-Necked Women. Geo-Australasia 18(1): 88–96.
Zulaika, J.
 1981   Terranova. Philadelphia: ISHI.

Author Index

Subject Index